PRAISE FOR **BLUE**

"Domanick gets everything right. [His] dramatic account of the Los Angeles Police Department's recent fall and rise . . . is steeped in his city's rich history, its fraught racial and ethnic conflicts, and the complex demographics that befuddle so many outsiders."

—*The New York Times Book Review* (Editor's Choice pick)

"*Blue* weaves a compelling, fact-filled tale of a turbulent city in transition and a police department that often seems impervious to civilian control. . . . The narrative is bustling with telling anecdotes between political and law enforcement figures."

—*Los Angeles Times*

"Could not be more timely, coming at the height of a national conversation about public trust in policing . . . As Domanick makes strikingly clear, fixing [our nation's police departments] will take commitment, determination, innovation, and endurance. A good way to start would be adding a copy of *Blue* to the syllabus of every police academy in the country. No rookie should hit the streets without having read it—and it wouldn't hurt to buy some extra copies for the top brass."

—*Brooklyn Eagle*

"An incisive examination of American policing, using a tumultuous two decades in Los Angeles as a lens . . . Journalist Domanick, associate director of John Jay College's Center on Media, Crime, and Justice, argues that the philosophical conflicts within the LAPD convey the 'larger saga of big-city American policing.' . . . This is a well-executed, large-scale urban narrative. Sprawling, engrossing, and highly relevant to the ongoing controversies about policing post-Ferguson."

—*Kirkus Reviews* (starred review)

"Racial conflict, urban violence, and big-city politics tangle in this intricate, incisive study of reform in the Los Angeles Police Department. . . . Multifaceted, evenhanded, sharp-eyed, and plainspoken, this gripping narrative is one of the best investigations yet of the explosive issue of police relations with minority communities."

—*Publishers Weekly*

"Stupendously timely and written with a finely calibrated understanding of the city's history and its unique cultural interweave, *Blue*'s page-turning narrative is borne aloft by a string of vivid nonfiction characters, including, of course, the agency's most recent chiefs, Bill Bratton and Charlie Beck. But while the heart of the book is a grand tale of the multilayered struggle to reform the LAPD, Domanick also uses L.A.'s police department as a lens through which to examine the state of US policing in general, and the crossroads at which it has presently arrived."

—WitnessLA.com

"The Los Angeles Police Department's pursuit of redemption in the wake of Rodney King and other scandals is detailed with a care undeniably attributed to a seasoned investigative journalist in Joe Domanick's *Blue*. . . . Well worth the read."

—*The Charlotte (SC) Post and Courier*

"In a time when controversial police actions have virtually split America apart, it's impossible to imagine a more important book than Joe Domanick's *Blue*. His mesmerizing account of how the Los Angeles Police Department descended into fanatic racism and was healed by new leadership's combined commitment to fairness and common sense is a lesson that must be learned by all of us, law enforcement officials and community activists most of all."

—Jeff Guinn, author of the *New York Times* bestselling *Manson*

BLUE

THE LAPD AND THE BATTLE TO
REDEEM AMERICAN POLICING

JOE DOMANICK

SIMON & SCHUSTER PAPERBACKS

NEW YORK   LONDON   TORONTO   SYDNEY   NEW DELHI

Simon & Schuster Paperbacks
An Imprint of Simon & Schuster, Inc.
1230 Avenue of the Americas
New York, NY 10020

First Simon & Schuster trade paperback edition August 2016

SIMON & SCHUSTER PAPERBACKS and colophon are
registered trademarks of Simon & Schuster, Inc.

For information about special discounts for bulk purchases,
please contact Simon & Schuster Special Sales at
1-866-506-1949 or business@simonandschuster.com.

The Simon & Schuster Speakers Bureau can bring authors
to your live event. For more information or to book an event,
contact the Simon & Schuster Speakers Bureau at
1-866-248-3049 or visit our website at www.simonspeakers.com.

Manufactured in the United States of America

1 3 5 7 9 10 8 6 4 2

The Library of Congress has cataloged the hardcover edition as follows:

Domanick, Joe.
Blue : the ruin and redemption of the LAPD / Joe Domanick
    pages   cm
Includes bibliographical references and index.
1. Los Angeles (Calif.). Police Department.   2. Police—California—
Los Angeles—History.   3. Police misconduct—California—Los Angeles—
History.   4. Police administration—California—Los Angeles—History.
5. Criminal justice, Administration of—California—Los Angeles—History.
                    I. Title.
            HV8148.L7D657 2015
            363.209794'94—dc23
                2015018052

ISBN 978-1-4516-4107-3
ISBN 978-1-4516-4110-3 (pbk)
ISBN 978-1-4516-4111-0 (ebook)

For the wondrous Andrea Domanick
and Ashley Hendra

Out of the blue he mentions *Chinatown*, the noir classic of prewar Los Angeles political corruption, graft, and police repression.

"You know," he says, "everyone thinks the last line of *Chinatown* is 'Forget it, Jake, it's Chinatown.' But it isn't."

"What is it?"

" 'Get off the streets.' "

—William Bratton to a reporter,
   shortly after being named chief of the LAPD

CONTENTS

Key Players   *xv*

Author's Note   *xvii*

PART ONE   **SOMETHING OLD**   *1*

PART TWO   **SOMETHING BORROWED**   *89*

PART THREE   **SOMETHING BLUE**   *181*

PART FOUR   **SOMETHING NEW**   *221*

                  EPILOGUE: 2015   *327*

                  Acknowledgments   *345*

                  Notes   *349*

                  Bibliography   *425*

                  Index   *429*

BLUE

BLUE

KEY PLAYERS

Charlie Beck: An antigang cop and a sergeant during the '92 L.A. riots. Beck would rise to become chief of the LAPD in 2009.

Tom Bradley: Los Angeles's first black mayor, Bradley served in that capacity for twenty years, including during the '92 riots.

William Bratton: A renowned reform chief from Boston and New York, Bratton was hired to reform the LAPD in 2004, afterward returning to New York in 2014 to again lead the NYPD.

Andre Christian: A black native son of Watts and a gang-banging member of the notorious Grape Street Crips.

Daryl Gates: Chief of the LAPD for fourteen tumultuous years, Gates's policies precipitated the L.A. riots, during which his leadership proved disastrous.

Alfred Lomas: A Florencia 13 gangster and hired muscle for Florencia's drug dealers.

William H. Parker: Chief of the LAPD from 1950 to 1965. Parker started as a reformer and then built the LAPD culture that sparked both the '65 Watts riots and the '92 L.A. riots.

Bernard Parks: Chief of the LAPD from August 1997 to May 2002. Parks presided over the Rampart scandal.

Rafael "Ray" Perez: A drug-stealing, drug-dealing LAPD CRASH anti-gang officer, Perez's revelations of a nest of dirty, abusive cops broke open what would become known as the Rampart scandal.

Connie Rice: A civil-rights lawyer, activist, and critic turned supporter of the LAPD.

Willie Williams: A former police commissioner of Philadelphia and the first African-American chief of the LAPD, Williams was hired after the '92 riots to reform the department.

AUTHOR'S NOTE

first became interested in the LAPD when I moved from Manhattan to Los Angeles in the mid-1970s. I was then a public school teacher working in a junior high deep in the South Bronx, where the frenzied halls reflected both the chaos of the time and the wild discord of the streets outside. At dusk, on the subway back to Manhattan, the vibe turned edgy as my subway car ground through some of the city's most violent neighborhoods without a cop ever in sight.

Back then, NYPD officers and their counterparts in the Transit Police seemed never to be around when you wished they were, and when they were, you couldn't help but notice how the weary slump of their shoulders and their disheveled appearance announced their disillusionment with their jobs.

When I arrived in Los Angeles I was astounded by how different LAPD officers were. First, it was clear that *they* hadn't given up. The department's jackbooted, superbly tailored motorcycle officers had the look and bearing of the prototype models they actually were for the film *RoboCop*, and acted the part.

Like the rest of the LAPD, they'd been trained to aggressively seek out crime and to "confront and command" a "suspect" in an aloof, intimidating, and often arrogant manner, even if that "suspect" had committed only a minor infraction, or done nothing wrong at all.

That attitude alone seemed to start more trouble than it stopped. And if you were black, the experience was astonishingly worse, and exponentially more frequent.

Every politician in town, moreover, seemed to kowtow to the LAPD, afraid of getting into a public spat with a succession of chiefs who, paradoxically, were not afraid of offending anyone. I wanted to understand the source of the department's extraordinary power, and wrote my first LAPD book, a character-based, historic narrative of the department called *To Protect and To Serve*, as a way to find that understanding.

I discovered that for the first half of the twentieth century a small oligarchy of right-wing business interests, led by the *Los Angeles Times*, had used the LAPD not only to rigidly control the streets but also to serve as a private goon squad, unapologetically maintaining the status quo by breaking the heads of union organizers and left-wing dissidents.

That changed in 1950, when Chief William H. Parker—the godfather of the modern LAPD—wrestled supremacy over the department away from the oligarchs and gave it to himself and his successors. In the process he created a faceless paramilitary police force that would dominate the streets of Los Angeles virtually independent of elected civilian control for the next forty years.

During those years, L.A.'s population dramatically transformed from a white, Protestant, conservative majority to a liberal, increasingly black, Latino, Asian, and Jewish population demanding that the LAPD's repressive policing change along with the city and the times—a demand the department both scorned and fought every step of the way.

In 1991, the tension finally snapped when four white LAPD officers were caught on videotape beating a black motorist named Rodney King. The grainy footage then found its way to CNN and became a cause célèbre around the world. A year later the four officers were acquitted, sparking the bloody insurrection known as the L.A. Riots. In response, a new chief from outside the department was hired, and City Charter reforms, including limiting the power of LAPD chiefs, were overwhelmingly approved by voters. Nevertheless, for the next decade, little changed on the street.

Wanting to understand why reform was proving so hard to implement, and then how it finally got started, I decided to revisit the LAPD's history starting with the '92 riots and, ultimately, to write this book.

I knew from the start I had to tell the tale through the lives of the people who'd lived through the crack-filled, violence-laden nineties, and then through the reforms that finally began taking hold in the first decade of the twenty-first century. Four such people immediately came to mind. Each illuminated an essential piece of the story.

Two were cops—one a police reformer and stranger to L.A., the other a chief-in-training with LAPD roots stretching back half a century. The others were L.A. gangsters who embodied the fraught relations between the LAPD and the beleaguered communities they policed.

The stranger in town was William J. Bratton, who in 2002 was hired to spearhead the reformation of the LAPD, as he'd done in the early and mid-1990s with both the New York City Transit Police and the 35,000-strong New York City Police Department. Before his tenure in those departments, New Yorkers had been obsessed with a crime wave that saw 2,245 murders in the city in 1990 and 700,000 serious crimes committed in 1989. Bratton changed that trajectory while building the launchpad for New York's currently unbroken string of more than twenty years of continuous crime drops (although not without some of the policies he pioneered also setting the stage for the NYPD's present conflicts with a new generation of black and liberal New Yorkers, as we shall see).

As in New York, once Bratton became L.A.'s police chief, he did what no one else had been able to do: put the LAPD on the long, still unfinished road to transformation. Before leaving L.A., Bratton pushed hard and successfully for his replacement—Charlie Beck, a street-toughened former gang cop who, under Bratton, rapidly became one of the department's foremost reformers.

The experiences of Alfred Lomas and Andre "Low Down" Christian demonstrate the impact of L.A.'s gangs on the city. Lomas was once a hard-core member the massive Mexican-American gang Florencia 13; Christian belonged to the fearsome black, Watts-based Grape Street Crips. Both are now gang intervention workers. Their stories illustrate both what it was like to be at the mercy of the LAPD, and the extraordinary violence with which the LAPD had to contend.

Other players also take center stage in *Blue*. One is Daryl Gates, Chief Parker's protégé, who headed the LAPD from 1978 to 1992. During those years Gates was a racial lightning rod, a white man implacably condoning the violent, humiliating excesses of his troops, who roamed

L.A.'s poor black and brown neighborhoods as though they were an army of occupation, accountable to no one.

Gates's adversary should have been Tom Bradley. Elected in 1972 as the first black mayor of Los Angeles, Bradley was an early champion of the city's liberals and minorities. For the next twenty years he presided over Los Angeles as it matured into a major American metropolis. But Bradley also wanted to be California's first black governor, and consequently refused to alienate white voters by confronting Gates's LAPD in a high-crime era—a failure that directly contributed to the '92 riots and the tarnishing of his legacy.

Following Daryl Gates's resignation in 1992, Philadelphia police commissioner Willie Williams stepped in as L.A.'s first black police chief. The city had high hopes, but his tenure demonstrated the difficult reality of transforming a big-city police department, especially when the forces aligned against reform are so deeply entrenched and the determination and skills needed to overcome them are so immense and multidimensional. Williams possessed almost none of those skills, and was dismissed five years after being hired, having changed almost nothing.

Bernard Parks succeeded Williams. Tall and handsome, the African-American Parks was known within the department as a smart, knowledgeable, efficient technocrat. Like William Parker and Daryl Gates, however, he thought he could run the LAPD as his own private fiefdom. But by 1997, when he took office, times had changed, and so had the city. And Parks, like Gates, was the last to see it.

He fought bitterly with the mayor, the press, two LAPD inspector generals, the DA, and, most especially, his own troops, who were in open revolt when Parks was dismissed at the end of his five-year term.

There is one other character to mention: LAPD officer Ray Perez. Both con man and sometime truth teller, Perez was at the heart of the 1999 "Rampart scandal," which involved drug-dealing cops and regular police frame-ups, beatings, and shootings on the watch of both Williams and Parks. The actions of Perez and the accusations he made about his gang-suppression unit, Rampart CRASH, would launch investigations by the *Los Angeles Times*, the LAPD, and the FBI. As a result, the U.S. Justice Department sent a team of lawyers to L.A. and forced the city and the department into a federal consent decree for violating the civil rights of residents. It was Perez's accusations, ultimately, that made the sins of the LAPD once again a national concern; as a result, Parks was driven out of office, and Bratton was hired as the department's new chief.

The stories of these men led me to ask essential questions about what constitutes good and bad policing, and how best to prevent crime, control police abuse, ease tensions between the police and the powerless, and partner with communities of color to enhance public safety. In that respect, *Blue* tells the much larger saga of big-city American policing over the past quarter century, and identifies the challenges we still face today.

Blue begins on Wednesday, April 29, 1992, at 6:30 p.m., as Alfred Lomas is watching on TV as history unfolds in the South L.A. intersection of Florence and Normandie Avenues. Watching as his city goes up in flames.

—Joe Domanick
West Hollywood, California
May 2015

PART ONE

SOMETHING OLD

PART ONE

SOMETHING OLD

Alfred Lomas, Wednesday, April 29, 1992

It all started for Alfred Lomas as he was sitting in a Florencia 13 crack house and across the TV screen flashed an image. That of blond-haired, white-skinned Reginald Denny lying on his back, arms outstretched, on the black-tar South L.A. intersection of Florence and Normandie Avenues.

A big-rig truck driver, Denny had just been dragged from the red cab of his sand-hauling eighteen-wheeler and thrown to the street by a group of raging young black men. One had then placed a foot on the back of Denny's neck as others took turns slamming an oxygenator into his back, pounding his head in with a hammer, and smashing a concrete block into his face.

High above, TV news helicopters circled, broadcasting the real-time scenes into half a dozen local stations and on to CNN, announcing to the world just after 6:30 p.m. on April 29 that the 1992 Los Angeles Riots had begun.

Before that moment, the Wednesday afternoon air had been warm and sweet, L.A. bucolic. Then the "not guilty" verdicts hit Los Angeles's airways with all the kinetic energy of one of those old 1930s movies with *Extra!* editions rolling rapid-fire off the presses.

The events of the day had been set in motion fourteen months earlier, shortly after midnight on March 3, 1991, when four white Los Angeles police officers had beaten a black motorist named Rodney King fifty-six times in eighty-one seconds with their two-pound, twenty-four-inch, solid-aluminum Monadnock PR-24 batons.

By chance, that beating too had been caught live on a grainy, smoking-gun video that CNN had then likewise broadcast worldwide, making Rodney King a household name, and the LAPD the shame of a nation. Now those officers had been acquitted of all ten counts against them but one—which had been quickly dismissed by the judge.

The four officers had been zealous in their work, using their batons to break Rodney King's cheekbone and ankle and eleven bones at the base of his skull, damaging his facial nerves and knocking the fillings out of his teeth. Each blow, said Rodney King, felt like "when you get up in the middle of the night and jam your toe on a piece of metal."

But the four cops were nonetheless now walking free. Freed by a jury in Ventura County, about an hour's drive north of Florence and Normandie. Freed in Ventura's Simi Valley, a then semirural, overwhelmingly white community, with a black population of 2 percent. Known as Cop Heaven by the cops themselves, Simi Valley, along with its sister city Thousand Oaks, had a population of about 4,000 active police officers, many of whom were part of the LAPD's 7,900-member force.

The new trial venue had been selected by a genius of a judge named Stanley Weisberg to ensure, he declared, that the trial would be fair and impartial and not influenced by local press coverage. But the new Simi Valley trial location was just twenty-five miles from the scene of King's beating, and thus part of Los Angeles's vast media market. By changing the venue, Weisberg had placed the trial into exactly the kind of community where Rodney King's actions—not those of the four LAPD officers who'd assaulted him—would be scrutinized. And that's the way it had played out.

In the courtroom, the defense team for the four officers collectively totaled about one hundred years of expertise in representing officers accused of abuse of force. They were the A-Team. In comparison, the District Attorney's Office had sent in a team from its Class-C farm club. Before long the A-Team was using the video of King's beating to de-emphasize the vicious nature of the crime. They played the video over and over in slow-mo, frame by frame, making the cops' baton blows look like caresses and King look like he was resisting, when in fact his body was simply reacting to the blows that he was trying to ward off. Ultimately the jury not only acquitted the officers, it effectively *endorsed* their behavior.

The image that Alfred Lomas, his Florencia 13 *vato locos* and his crackhead customers were now watching on TV, however, was not that of Rodney King. They were watching Reginald Denny.

Meanwhile, other unlucky white, Asian, and Hispanic motorists, crossing the same intersection where Denny still lay, were busy ducking chunks of concrete, rocks, bottles, and baseball bats shattering their car windows. Clusters of young black men then surrounded their vehicles, pulled open doors, dragged out occupants, and robbed and mercilessly beat them.

Earlier, just after the not-guilty verdicts were announced, outraged local residents had run into the street screaming "Rodney King! Rodney King!" Soon a crowd began to form, quickly attracting LAPD patrol cars to the scene. When two officers tried to make an arrest, they were encircled by a crowd hurling rocks and bottles at their patrol car and chanting "Fuck the police." The lieutenant on the scene responded by ordering his cops to beat a hasty retreat, thereby leaving a void where hundreds of people were now either watching the corner show or were the show themselves. Dressed in L.A. spring garb—that is, thigh-length shorts, jeans, T-shirts, tank tops, hoodies, cheap nylon windbreakers, and baseball caps—they were busy gulping beers, sipping Cokes, and milling about the intersection like it was some kind of urban beach party. "Fuck y'all, we killin'," one snarled into the lens of a TV camera. "Cops gonna die," promised a second. "Tonight it's Uzi time," shouted a third.

"Uzi time" was just another way of saying payback time. That's what all those bats and beatings—and the looting and burning of Tom's Liquor and Deli on the intersection's corner—represented; that and the brutality of living life on the lowest economic rung of America's increasingly slippery ladder of opportunity. Payback time for Rodney King.

Alfred Lomas, a Chicano U.S. Marine Corps veteran and gun-totin' enforcer of Florencia 13's drug deals in the age of crack wars and easy money, had understood that rage. Understood it in the way that one underdog understands another. So he should have been primed to vicariously feel the thrill of the brothers who were acting out their hatred of the LAPD on the head of Reginald Denny.

But Lomas and the others now watching the scene on a crack-house TV were not *down* with what was happening to the bleeding and now unconscious Denny. Smashing a concrete block into some innocent guy's head and then dancing around in celebration while pointing and spitting on him solely because of his skin color—that was just *wrong*. Not to mention the guy who'd rolled Denny over and methodically rifled through his pockets, stealing his wallet and taking off. What kind of shit was that?

Nevertheless, what the twenty-six-year-old Lomas and every gang banger in the room *could* relate to was the farce that was the acquittal of the cops who'd beaten Rodney Glen King.

A semi-illiterate high school dropout who worked at Dodger Stadium, King had a Baby Huey image on the street and penny-ante criminal aspirations. Once a $200 robbery of a 99 Market—during which he was chased out of the store by its irate Korean owner, who beat him with a three-foot metal rod he'd yanked off a display case—had landed him in prison for a year.

They could feel for King, a guy still on parole who'd downed a forty-ounce Olde English 800 malt liquor and was speeding down the freeway in the outer reaches L.A.'s San Fernando Valley, lost in the music of the night, when his reverie was suddenly interrupted by two highway patrol officers ordering him to pull over.

Scared of being sent back to prison on a parole violation, the twenty-five-year-old King took the officers on a high-speed chase instead. Finally pulling over, he peacefully exited his white economy-sized Hyundai, only to be twice zapped with 50,000-volt Taser darts, brutally beaten, and then hog-tied by the four LAPD officers from the local Foothill Division who'd arrived on the scene and decided to take the collar.

Twenty-seven other responding cops, meanwhile, casually stood around and watched the show while rubbernecking passengers in cars and buses drifted by, and a plumber named George Holliday, wielding a handheld video camera, stood on his condo balcony and recorded it all.

The crack-house crew, in short, understood exactly what had happened to Rodney King. They weren't black, but they weren't white either. They were Mexican-Americans who'd grown up hard in a gang-infested dump of a neighborhood in Huntington Park, just across Alameda Boulevard from the vast, impoverished, 650,000-strong black and increasingly Latino area known as South Los Angeles—an area better known by the name of one of its sections: South Central L.A. They knew about L.A. cops, and they knew about ass-kicking, L.A. cop–style—which, as Alfred Lomas would later tell it, "basically consisted of three or four cops handcuffing a person, and just literally beating him, often until unconscious . . . punching, beating, kicking."

Several actions, if taken by anyone like Alfred Lomas, would essentially guarantee an ass-beating. One was talking back. Another, as Lomas put it, would be "if they had to get out of their patrol car, or if you crossed over into a white neighborhood—that was always a sure-fire ass-beating." In short, Lomas and the crew did not need some guy on TV droning on and explaining how what was happening now was related to what had happened to Rodney King fourteen months ago. They knew.

Stacey Koon, he knew too. The veteran LAPD sergeant, who'd directed the Rodney King show as the other indicted cops whacked away, had seen it as nothing particularly noteworthy, just a routine job, well done. Or as he later put it: "We take Rodney King into custody, he doesn't get seriously injured. We don't get injured. He goes to jail. That's the way the system's supposed to work."

And not coincidentally, that was just the way that Alfred Lomas understood both the beating and the system as he'd first watched George Holliday's video fourteen months earlier.

In fact, Lomas and his crew's first words as they watched the video were not "Wow! The cops are beating his ass so bad!" but "Wow! The cops are beating his ass just like they always beat ours, so why are all these people [on television] acting like this is something new, some big surprise?"

The reality was that the officers had done "a lot more than just whack Rodney with their batons," according to now retired LAPD assistant chief David Dotson, who'd been among the first to see the video and read the officers' reports. "The arresting officers at the scene did not fully report what happened—that they had dragged him across the street, hog-tied, and Tasered him.

"And once their report was handed in, nobody said, 'Wait a minute, King's injuries are not consistent with what was written in the report [which was falsified], because nobody thought that what happened shouldn't have happened. They knew what they were doing was wrong and against policy and regulation, but the officers went to trial and said, 'Well, that's the way we do things.' And, in fact, that *was* the way things were done then in divisions like Foothill"—in divisions with concentrations of poor blacks and Latinos who were moving, unwelcomed, into otherwise white areas and who needed to be taught the rules of the game.

The rules of that game had also been well taught inside the department, according to Dotson. "You told the story you thought would sell, and covered everything else up, knowing nobody would dig into it, because before the tape surfaced nobody thought that Rodney's beating was anything out of the ordinary, much less a huge scandal or a landmark incident."

Yet Alfred Lomas felt a twinge of excitement as he watched the King beating video. He realized that the misty clouds shielding the truth about how the LAPD *actually* dealt with people in L.A.'s ghettos and barrios were finally being lifted.

Now occupying his attention, however, was the scene of Reginald Denny's battered body still lying at the intersection, beaten, battered and unrescued. Earlier, LAPD patrol officers had been present at the location. But when things started heating up, they'd been ordered to flee the scene and report to a police command center thirty blocks away. As a result, viewers all around the nation started asking a variation of the question Alfred Lomas was now posing to no one in particular: "Where the fuck are the cops?"

Tom Bradley, Wednesday, April 29, 1992, First African Methodist Episcopal Church; Bill Parker, Present in the Ether

As dusk settled across the L.A. basin that Wednesday evening, two thousand people strode into the main chapel of South Central's First African Methodist Episcopal Church. "Brothers," a banner above the entrance proclaimed, "Come Help Us Stop the Madness."

The crush of the crowd had already spilled into the church's packed, sweltering anterooms, basement, and foyer, and out into its parking lot, where about one thousand African-Americans from across Los Angeles had gathered after the church doors were shut. Some were in suits and ties; others were young brothers in Jheri curls, Raiders gear, and do-rags, standing beside elderly church ladies and families with children. They'd come to participate in the evening's announced goal of developing a peaceful response to the Simi Valley acquittals—an endeavor already being mocked by the looting taking place just blocks away.

Inside the church, Los Angeles mayor Tom Bradley rose and walked toward the podium. The man who had once been hailed as L.A.'s black savior, the six-foot, four-inch man with the winsome smile, preternatural physical grace, and effortless charisma, appeared—for perhaps the first time in his remarkable nineteen-year tenure as the city's first African-American mayor—to be bent and weary, and not just from the weight of his seventy-four years. He was, after all, aware that while responsibility for the calamity building outside the church's Passion of the Christ stained-glass windows fell squarely on the shoulders of the LAPD, the fault was also partly his.

****

Raised a poor black boy in Depression-ravaged 1930s America, Tom Bradley was born the son of a humble, churchgoing housemaid, two generations removed from slavery, and a former Texas sharecropping cotton farmer who deserted the family in Los Angeles. Despite that, Bradley had managed to beat the long-shot odds in a nation still deeply in the thrall of Jim Crow, going to integrated Los Angeles public schools, becoming an All-City and All–Southern California high school track star, and attending UCLA for three years before leaving in 1940, at the age of twenty-two, to join the racially segregated LAPD.

Over the next two decades he graduated from law school, passed the bar, and made lieutenant—then the glass ceiling for black LAPD officers—before retiring after twenty-one years, with head held high, never agreeing to condone the department's deeply racist, brutal treatment of its black citizens or to play the role of token, showcase Negro apologist for its abuses.

In 1965 he'd become one of Los Angeles's first elected black city councilmen and, during a city council hearing on the causes of the Watts Riots, had electrified the black community by challenging the legendary architect of the modern-day LAPD, Chief William H. Parker.

Parker had testified that the riots had been caused by black radical conspirators inflaming the area's criminals against the police, while the good Negroes of South Central had stood by aghast. Bradley, working as watch commander in a tough black district, had heard the pre-riot rumble in the streets and knew that the community's rage against the LAPD was widespread, and not just the work of some malcontents. But he'd waited his turn to reply to Parker.

Raised in the hard Black Hills and bleak Badlands of South Dakota, Parker was a man in constant struggle to reconcile his notorious alcoholism with his deeply ingrained nineteenth-century Victorian morals—a struggle that resulted in a disposition so cold that former LAPD sergeant turned TV writer Gene Roddenberry was said to have based the *Star Trek* character of Spock on him.

Pale, thin, and ailing with a bad heart that would kill him within a year, Parker was also famously short-fused. And now Tom Bradley was questioning his veracity. It was unheard-of for a *white* city councilman to question him in such a manner, much less a newcomer, a black man, *and* a former LAPD officer.

He was, after all, *Bill Parker, El Jefe* of L.A.'s criminal justice establishment. On becoming chief in 1950, it was Parker who had conceived and set in motion the policies, events, and departmental culture that culminated not just in the '65 Watts Riots but also those that would explode twenty-seven years later when the Simi Valley acquittals were announced.

Parker had decreed that his new LAPD would be a small, mobile force of faceless officers in patrol cars and on motorcycles able to rapidly traverse Los Angeles's sprawling 465 square miles. The department he created would be a top-down paramilitary organization steeped in the precepts of the United States Marine Corps and trained to aggressively seek out and often jack up "potential" criminals—a wide-ranging category focused mainly on young black and Latino men who had happened to be out on the street or behind the wheel of a car at the wrong moment and come into a cop's view.

On the ground in L.A.'s black neighborhoods, the LAPD acted as if it were an army of occupation. L.A.'s black population had skyrocketed from 62,000 in 1940 to 170,000 by 1950. Just fifteen years later, as the Watts Riots shocked L.A., Bill Parker would make the case for his army on a local television show. "It is estimated that by 1970, 45 percent of Los Angeles will be Negro," said Parker. "If you want any protection for your home and family . . . you're going to have to support a strong police department. If you don't, God help you."

The subtext behind Tom Bradley's challenge to Bill Parker in the city council chambers that day in '65 was therefore all about who would control the historical narrative of the causes of the riot. The LAPD's role in precipitating the rebellion was at stake and Parker knew it in his gut.

Parker's theory of a small group of outside agitators propelling the riots was simply wrong, Bradley told him, causing an enraged Parker to fire back, "I think you are trying to pin this [uprising] on the police, [and] I'll go to my grave thinking this was your intention. . . . This is not any inquiry," he added. "It's an inquisition!"

That day Tom Bradley earned the undying enmity of the LAPD while ennobling himself to black and liberal Los Angeles for years to come, not just for his courage, but for speaking the truth: a UCLA study would later reveal that at least fifty thousand people had participated in the Watts Riots.

But all of that was back in 1965. Now, twenty-seven years later,

Bradley was addressing a throng of overwhelmingly black Angelenos at the First AME. Below the raised platform where Bradley was leaning his long body into the podium, small TV monitors were flashing shots of Reginald Denny still lying semiconscious at Florence and Normandie Avenues.

"I was shocked, I was stunned, I had my breath taken away by the verdict . . . ," he told them.

Soon, however, it became embarrassingly apparent that it didn't matter what he was saying; the fidgeting and whispering audience was utterly uninterested in what he had to say.

Once L.A.'s great symbol of racial harmony, Bradley was now watching his shining legacy becoming forever stained by a rapidly metastasizing racial insurrection.

"I don't know where they were," Bradley continued on, speaking of the Simi Valley jury while eliciting more catcalls and pointed indifference from the First AME audience. "They certainly weren't watching that videotape. . . ."

★★★★★★★★★★★★★★

Defeated in his first run for mayor in 1969, Bradley had endured a classic campaign of race- and red-baiting laughably linked to the Black Panthers and other "radicals," and had been labeled an enemy of the LAPD by his incumbent opponent, "Mayor Sam" Yorty. Mayor Sam was a small, wavy-haired native Nebraskan with a pleasing smile and the gauche salesman's sheen of a mid-century, small-town, middle-American rube. He represented the city's rapidly fading, frightened, pre-Watts old guard: white Protestant conservatives who constituted a middle and ruling class born of a transplanted, corn-fed Midwestern bourgeoisie and a blue-collar working class of Dust Bowl Okies.

Running against Yorty again in '73, Bradley emerged the victorious leader of a new liberal political majority of African-Americans, Jews, Chicanos, Asian-Americans, organized labor, and voters of all stripes inspired by the idealism of John and Robert Kennedy, the righteous passion of Martin Luther King, and the promise of a leader like Tom Bradley.

Despite the American Nazi Party picketing his inauguration in uniform and carrying signs reading "No Nigger Mayors," the voice of the city's wealthy elite, the *Los Angeles Times*, welcomed his victory. Under the new, moderately liberal leadership of the scion of the family-owned newspaper, Otis Chandler, the once ultraconservative *Times* happily got behind Tom Bradley, a politician with whom they could do business, and who made an excellent front man for their dollar-sign dreams of Los Angeles as a powerful international port city and Pacific Rim center of communications and finance.

Bill Parker would die in office in 1966, but his legacy, and the department's deeply reactionary paramilitary culture, would continue on unquestioned by his two long-term successors, Edward M. "Crazy Ed" Davis and Daryl Gates. Both simply refused to accept Bradley's—or anybody's—right to exercise civilian control over the LAPD or to dare criticize the department.

It was Parker, in fact, who'd been the first to use the city's new, iron-clad civil-service statutes—statutes that amounted to lifetime tenure—for Los Angeles police chiefs. It was Parker who'd acted as if the LAPD was an *operationally independent* city agency. And it was Parker who had declared that he and he alone would be the sole arbiter of his and his troops' actions. Soon that notion would become gospel within the LAPD and accepted as reality by Tom Bradley's predecessors, and then by Bradley himself once he became mayor.

The reason was simple. Fear was in the air. The '65 Watts Riots were still a searing memory in a still predominantly white Los Angeles now led by a liberal black mayor. In six days of rioting thirty-four people had been killed, over one thousand injured, almost four thousand arrested and over $40 million in damages done—a huge sum in 1965 dollars that would amount to several hundred million dollars today. Moreover, in 1967, just two years after Watts, racial riots had broken out in 150 American cities, followed in '68 by the assassination of Martin Luther King and rioting in over a hundred American cities.

Then the 1980s had brought the city the crack-fueled gang wars of the Bloods and the Crips, marking the beginning of another era when no politician wanted to engage in a fierce protracted battle with a combative LAPD chief—particularly a politician like Bradley with aspirations not just to lead California but to secure the honor of becoming America's first elected black governor.

It wasn't until he'd lost both his bids for governor in the 1980s, and the King beating had become a worldwide cause célèbre in early 1991, that Bradley had finally had enough and took action by impaneling a blue ribbon commission to investigate the LAPD's use of force and abuse of power.

It was chaired by Warren Christopher—President Bill Clinton's future secretary of state and then the chairman of L.A.'s most powerful and prestigious law firm, O'Melveny & Meyers. The Christopher Commission issued a unanimous 228-page report four months after King's beating, documenting a pervasive pattern of excessive use of force by LAPD officers.

Calling the results of its investigation "astonishing," the commission declared that there existed "a significant group of officers who repetitively misuse force" and that the top leadership of the department and the Police Commission "had failed to . . . monitor [or to] control the use of excessive force."

Stingingly, they also indicted Tom Bradley for failing to "exert leadership" or to use "the inherent powers of his office" to appoint police commissioners willing to challenge chiefs like Davis and Gates, and to insist that the department halt its brutality and abuse of the public—thus "contributing to the Police Commission's ineffectiveness."

Nor was that all. The commission also noted that while the LAPD's civilian complaint system was "unfairly skewed against complaints" from the public, the same officers who "repeatedly used excessive force were often [being] rewarded with positive evaluations and promotions," and "patrol officers [were being] rewarded for hard-nosed" policing. "It is apparent," the report summed up, "that too many LAPD patrol officers view citizens with resentment and hostility; [and] too many treat the public with rudeness and disrespect."

Tom Bradley had had a choice during his almost twenty years in office: tack to the right, refrain from engaging in battle with the LAPD, and run for governor—or become a truly transformational mayor and fight the battles that needed to be fought, especially with the LAPD. His decision was to twice run and lose bids for governor in the eighties—the very decade in which the animosity toward the LAPD was again building to a boiling point.

By appointing the Christopher Commission, Bradley had finally acted. But it was too late for him. And too little too late for the folks at the First AME. They didn't require some report to tell them that Bradley, the Police Commission, and the city council had failed to do their oversight of the LAPD for decades. Like Alfred Lomas and the crackhouse boys, they too had lived it.

"We have come," Bradley gamely continued, "to say tonight that we've had enough, and to encourage you to express your outrage verbally."

Meanwhile, the television cameras rolled on, showing live footage of an LAPD guard shack outside the department's Parker Center Downtown headquarters going up in flames.

Finally finished with his weary speech, Tom Bradley exited the stage, bent and almost shuffling. Huddling with his aides in an anteroom, he received word that the riot was spreading. Huge swatches of South Los Angeles were now up in flames. Darting past demonstrators, Bradley and his entourage were soon hustled into his limo. As his car was pulling out of the lot, protesters screamed at him as they pounded their fists on the vehicle's roof, hood, and fenders.

Charlie Beck, Wednesday, April 29, 1992, Parker Center

"Where are all your patrol units? Can't you call somebody to help this poor guy?" Cindy Beck asked her husband, LAPD sergeant Charlie Beck, as he walked through the door of their home early Wednesday evening. She was referring to Reginald Denny, whose terrible fate she'd been watching on television.

A street-hardened veteran gang cop, Charlie Beck too was appalled.

Hoping to get some cops down to Florence and Normandie, he quickly phoned the watch commander at the adjacent 77th Division, where he'd once worked. But he couldn't even get his call through.

So he sat with his wife to watch the cavalry arrive in the person of his fellow LAPD officers. But they never came. Not one. Finally, Beck had had enough and decided to drive back to the LAPD's downtown Parker Center headquarters, where he'd been working in Internal Affairs for the past several years.

The Internal Affairs detective who'd been assigned to investigate the King beating had been on Beck's squad. Back then Beck was a self-described "type-A personality whose attitude had been: 'Hey, give me the biggest piece of meat on the plate and I'll finish it.'" The King case was certainly the biggest chunk of beef thrown at any LAPD IA investigator for decades, and Beck wanted it badly.

But he hadn't gotten it—a random twist of fate for which he would later be eternally grateful. The case was so politically charged within and outside the department—and so fraught with career-damaging cognitive-dissonance possibilities—that Beck later realized how "it would have consumed and squeezed the life out of [him]."

★★★★★★★★★★★★★★

Tall and swarthy, with jet-black hair and a full mustache, Beck made his bones as a charter member of a group of LAPD gang-suppression units with a name and acronym that both advertised and preordained its tactics: Community Resources Against Street Hoodlums, or CRASH. That alone made him one of the department's cultural hotshots.

But he was also a member of a budding LAPD dynasty: His father was a retired LAPD deputy chief, his sister an LAPD officer on her way to becoming a detective, and his wife a Los Angeles County sheriff. In time his then young son and daughter would both also join the LAPD. But it wasn't in his nature to play that card.

Instead he was very much one of the troops, one of the boys bound together by that sardonic camaraderie so common among street cops experiencing terrible things while nothing appears to ever change. He also possessed the ability to think both strategically and analytically; a charismatic warmth that could put people at ease; and a self-discipline that enabled him to mask a tough-as-nails cop's competitive determination to never be played for a chump.

Beck had first set out to be a professional close-track, off-road moto-cross racer, wrestling crude, 250-pound machines over roads pock-marked with high moguls and deep, treacherous holes. That fact didn't tell you everything needed to know about him, but it did tell you a lot about the fire in his belly.

He'd spent much of the eighties being one of the cops that N.W.A so blisteringly rapped about in "Fuck Tha Police." In the harsh, un-forgiving confines of the Southeast Division, Beck had been part of a narcotics task force that roamed black South L.A., busting open crack houses, three or four a day, arresting thousands of sellers and custom-ers. Four sergeants and their squads—about forty cops in all—would burst through a door and capture some hapless fourteen-year-old who'd been given fifty or a hundred vials of crack to sell, some cash to make change, and a gun to defend the stash.

Once, responding to a raid on a drug house, Beck arrived to find that his fellow gang officers had handcuffed and sprawled out a group of children on the street. It caught Beck up short, like a new line was being crossed. "They weren't evil people," he'd later tell the *L.A. Times*, referring to his fellow officers, "they were just doing what they were taught. There was [just] no room for independent thought in the department."

Sometimes after a raid, when they were cleaning up, customers would knock on the door to buy dope, and the undercover guys would make the sale and then the arrest. Having recovered thousands of dol-lars in small bills, they'd then go back to the station house, book the money, the kid, and the customers, and go out again the next day to repeat the same drill. "That," says Beck "was the LAPD's crack-war strategy"—a reminder that while the official motto of the LAPD might be "To Protect and To Serve," the unofficial motto was always "Hook 'Em and Book 'Em."

****

As dusk was settling in, Charlie Beck drove his Ford Bronco west, back to Parker Center. Along the route, he could see plumes of smoke spiraling up from South Central as he listened to the staccato beat of riot news on his car radio. He couldn't understand why the LAPD wasn't flooding officers into the riot's hot zones to nip the violence in the bud. He could readily fathom the reality of the riot. What he'd *never* imagined was that his department would fail to respond. If anything, the LAPD had long and famously been guilty of *overreaction*, as they had shown, for example, during the infamous 1988 raid on two small, adjacent apartment buildings on South Central's Dalton Avenue.

There, eighty LAPD officers had stormed the buildings looking for drugs on a bullshit tip. After handcuffing the terrorized residents—including small children and their grandparents—they then spent the next several hours tearing all the toilets from the floors; smashing in walls, stairwells, bedroom sets, and televisions with sledgehammers; slashing open furniture; and then sending it all crashing through windows into the front yard and arresting anyone who happened by to watch. As they were leaving, the officers spray-painted a large board located down the street with some graffiti. "LAPD Rules," read one message; "Rolling 30s Die" read another. So completely uninhabitable were the apartments rendered that the Red Cross had to provide the occupants with temporary shelter, as if some kind of natural disaster had occurred. No gang members lived there, no charges were ever filed. In the end, the city paid $3.8 million to the victims of the destruction. A report later written by LAPD assistant chief Robert Vernon called it "a poorly planned and executed field operation [that] involved . . . an improperly focused and supervised aggressive attitude of police officers, supervisors and managers toward being 'at war' with gang members."

The attitude too had come right from the top. In 1986, two years before the Dalton Avenue raid, LAPD chief Daryl Gates was videotaped giving his end-of-year address, which was then broadcast to his officers at roll calls throughout the department. In it, Gates laid out the operational template, the black-and-white world—both literally and figuratively—in which his officers should operate. "It's like having the Marine Corps invade an area that is having little pockets of resistance," he told them. "We can't have it. . . . We've got to wipe [the gang members] out."

It was no wonder that, of the over eighty LAPD officers who took part in the Dalton Avenue raid, nobody ever stopped to ask, "Wait a minute, what the hell are we doing here? What's the end goal?"

Daryl Gates, Wednesday, April 29, 1992, LAPD Headquarters

When the "not guilty" verdicts were announced at 4 p.m., Charlie Beck had agreed with the general consensus at LAPD headquarters that despite the pounding in the press since King's beating, "the department still maintained enough community support to head off any significant protests, and it could now get back to business as usual."

It was an astounding misreading of the situation, a catastrophic failure of intelligence gathering at the most basic street level, coupled with the inability of the LAPD high command to grasp the pulse and mood of the city it policed.

Earlier in April, in anticipation of possible trouble following the verdicts, Daryl Gates had earmarked $1 million for police overtime and to make a contingency plan. But according to then Assistant Chief David Dotson, "There never was a riot contingency plan. The Police Commission was never able to get Gates to tell them what it was, because it was nonexistent."

In fact, on Tuesday, April 28—the day *before* the verdicts were announced and the riots began—the Los Angeles Police Commission had convened its weekly meeting in Parker Center. During a break, then police commissioner Anthony De Los Reyes privately asked Gates about the contingency plan. "The jury was still deliberating in Simi Valley, so I said to Gates, 'You know, I have been practicing law a long time, and you just can't predict what a jury is going to do. What if these officers are acquitted?' And he said to me in that drawl of his, 'Well, Commissioner, we have a plan to take care of this.' And I said, 'Okay. Well, that sounds good.' But we never saw it. . . . Later, just after the riots, he was interviewed by [CNN talk-show host] Larry King, and King asked him about not having a plan, and Daryl came out with this big sheaf of papers and said, 'There it is.' And I thought, 'No, that's not it.' "

"Nobody believed those officers were going to be acquitted," Reyes's fellow police commissioner Ann Reiss Lane would later recall, "so we never asked to see the plan he said he had in writing. . . . He assured us that everything was in hand, but it turned out it wasn't."

At a news conference early on April 30—the second day of the riots—Gates would nevertheless maintain that the department was "as ready as we ought to be" and that "we deployed all that we could have deployed at that particular time without going in[to] some mode that allowed us to build our resources."

Not having adequate resources at "that particular time"—just as the riots broke out—was precisely the problem. *Prior* to the riots, in fact, Gates had failed to even declare a tactical alert despite a court news release issued by 10 a.m. that morning announcing that the verdicts would be handed down that afternoon. Instead, the department's one thousand detectives, who worked from 6 a.m. to 2 p.m., were allowed, like Charlie Beck, to clock out and go home at the end of their shifts. Moreover, many of the department's field captains, the critical ground-level operational decision makers in any police department, weren't even in Los Angeles—they were forty miles away, attending a seminar.

In addition, Dotson, one of the LAPD's most experienced assistant chiefs, was then considered persona non grata and went unused during the riots as part of his punishment for being critical of the department's leadership when he testified before the Christopher Commission in June 1991.

Simultaneously, Assistant Chief Robert Vernon was on leave pending his retirement. Earlier, he had been excoriated by the city council for preaching strict Christian fundamentalist practices to department officers, including, among other things, the benefits of using strict corporal punishment to discipline children and adolescents—advice that cumulatively would end his career.

Vernon had been in charge of field operations long enough that Daryl Gates and his command staff had grown accustomed to him being their operational go-to guy. It was a big job—the overseeing of about 85 percent of the department's cops, including patrol officers and detectives. But after Vernon had gone on leave, no one seemed able to pick up his mantle. A lot of people may have disliked Bob Vernon, but nobody had ever accused him of being afraid to make a decision on the spot—a command characteristic that was sorely missing as the riots began exploding.

Along with the leadership vacuum was the problem of communication. There was little between Gates and the Police Commission, and none between Gates and Mayor Bradley, with whom he hadn't spoken for over a year.

Most astoundingly, there had also been no coordination with the Los Angeles Fire Department—a particularly grievous act of arrogance and ineptitude, given that Gates had personally watched Watts go up in flames during the '65 riots. Six hundred buildings had been burned, damaged, or destroyed by fires and looters in those riots.

"One of the things that overwhelmed us," Gates would say at that April 30, 1992, news conference, "was the number of fires that occurred and the attacks on the firefighters. It simply became impossible for the firefighters to go out and do their job without police protection. . . . Our resources were [consequently] engaged with the Fire Department and protecting the Fire Department."

But it soon became clear that Gates had been making it all up as he went along. In a postmortem following the '92 riots, the city's fire chief bitterly complained about the LAPD denying his fire department's initial requests for escort service into South Central to fight the fires because, as the firefighters were told, it was "not a top priority."

Rumors would later abound in the black community that Gates and the LAPD had simply let the initial rioting explode so that, as Bill Parker had suggested twenty-seven years earlier, the white public would later get out and "support a strong police department." But the truth was far more complex.

Morale in the department was at an all-time low. Its leadership was in disarray and feared being accused by critics of escalating the violence if it responded forcefully. As Gates put it the morning after the breakout of the riots, "I think there was a lot of discussion that we [the LAPD] were being provocative . . . and so we were very, very, careful not to show that provocativeness."

But above all, the failure lay with Gates's contempt for outside voices and his stubborn determination to continue policing and running the department the way Bill Parker had decreed. All these traits had become deeply embedded in the LAPD's culture as well. Officers in station houses across the city literally cheered as the "not guilty" verdicts were announced. At the department's Foothill Station, a young officer named Corina Smith pumped her fist in the air and told the *Los Angeles Times*, "I'm elated, absolutely elated. It's like this sick feeling is finally going away." Another officer offered a similar view: "I feel the truth came out," he said, "and that the verdicts are a reflection of the truth."

That was how a lot of LAPD officers, perhaps most, felt: that the officers had really done nothing wrong, and that Rodney King had gotten what he deserved. Of course, if you dwelt in a blue cocoon of cops in lily-white suburban enclaves like Simi Valley, how could you relate to the outrage others would feel at a "not guilty" verdict? Or as Police Commission president Stanley Sheinbaum put it, "I don't think [Daryl Gates] understood the ramifications of acquittals, because he was so sympathetic to acquittals."

But it also had to do with how Parker's legacy and Gates's beliefs filtered down, operationally, on the street and at Parker Center. "The people who get promoted [within the LAPD] don't have differing points of view," Thomas Windham, Daryl Gates's former chief of staff, once pointed out. "The department is very slow to change, and rank structure from top to bottom thinks along the same lines, no matter what the situation might be." Or as former Police Commission president Stephen Reinhardt summed it up: in the LAPD "you can't bring in new people and get a cross-fertilization. Everyone is trained by the last generation [and] a certain bunker mentality has resulted."

Charlie Beck, Wednesday, April 29, 1992, Parker Center

Charlie Beck finally arrived back at Parker Center sometime in the early evening. Stopping first at his locker, he changed into his LAPD blues and then went upstairs to try to figure out what to do next.

Much had happened since he'd left police headquarters that afternoon. A small crowd of demonstrators had morphed into a large enraged mob—many of them white, including contingents from the Progressive Labor and the Revolutionary Communist Parties. They'd massed in the heart of the city's downtown Civic Center, a four- or five-block expanse that was home to both the midcentury Bauhaus box that was Parker Center and the *Los Angeles Times*'s cement mausoleum of a headquarters. Across the street stood the majestic neoclassical city hall, and a short block away were Los Angeles's principal Superior Court and District Attorney's Office and various other criminal justice edifices.

Soon, about three hundred of the protesters peeled away and strode down the Civic Center's streets, chanting "No justice, no peace," throwing rocks, rolling over and setting fire to an LAPD patrol car, demolishing a Rolls-Royce, and torching small, cheap coffee shops and taco stands. Nearby, they smashed display windows, looted a bridal shop and a Radio Shack, and shattered every ground-floor window of the *Times*'s city-block-square building.

Others remained at Parker Center, facing off against a disciplined, stone-faced line of LAPD officers in riot gear, members of the department's fearsome Metro Division—known as "the shake and bake boys" for their attacks on protesters for the slightest provocation.

But not that evening. Demonstrators hurled eggs, bottles, and aluminum cans at the officers, who impassively held their positions as they were hit by the projectiles. Protesters screamed in their faces, and a kiosk in front of the entrance to Parker Center was set ablaze. One enraged young African-American mockingly denigrated a black cop in front of an *LA Weekly* reporter. "You should be out here with us throwing stones," he told the officer. "You can't hide your color behind that uniform. You take that off and you're just another nigger to the LAPD."

Then an American flag was stomped on and burned, and as dusk settled in, protesters began heaving rocks through the windows above Parker Center's entrance doors.

Meanwhile, police commissioners Anthony De Los Reyes and Ann Reiss-Lane were passing by in an unmarked police car just as the kiosk outside Parker Center was going up in smoke. Deciding to play it safe, they headed to the mayor's city hall office across the street. "It was," recalls De Los Reyes, "the most sobering, somber experience I can ever remember." Sitting there with Mayor Bradley, Lane, and a couple of other people, the silence was so complete, remembers De Los Reyes, that he could hear the air-conditioning system humming and smell the smoke from the burning kiosk outside.

Daryl Gates, Wednesday, April 29, 1992, Brentwood, California

Just as the downtown protest crowd was exploding, sixty-five-year-old LAPD chief Daryl Francis Gates, looking trim and tan, had slipped out of a rear basement door of Parker Center and emerged into the building's tumbledown parking lot. He was headed to a fund-raiser in Brentwood, a Beverly Hills–style west L.A. community of multimillion-dollar homes located far from the escalating riots.

The event was to help defeat a forthcoming city charter ballot amendment to limit an LAPD chief's lifetime tenure and make it easier to replace him—reforms that had specifically been recommended by the Christopher Commission the year before.

It would say an enormous amount about Daryl Gates, a forty-three-year veteran of the LAPD, that he chose to attend the gathering rather than stay at the helm and direct his department at such a fraught moment in the history of Los Angeles.

Nevertheless, his decision at least had the logic of self-preservation. Daryl Gates was in trouble. Following the King beating, the Christopher Commission had bluntly called on him to resign, as had Mayor Bradley, the *Los Angeles Times*, *La Opinion*, the *Los Angeles Daily News*, the local CBS television affiliate, then U.S. Senate Judiciary chair Joseph

Biden, three of L.A.'s most powerful U.S. congressmen, California sena-tor Diane Feinstein, the UCLA Law School faculty, and Gates's favorite columnist, George Will.

Meanwhile, the Congressional Black Caucus; California's African-American assembly speaker, Willie Brown; the NAACP; the Urban League; Jessie Jackson; and a coalition of black churches and ministries were all pressuring Mayor Bradley to encourage his police commission-ers to at least suspend Gates while figuring out a way to permanently get rid of him—an action that even two years earlier would have been unthinkable.

Ever since Bill Parker was named chief in 1950, L.A. mayors had come and gone, but its police chiefs had remained as long as they wished. "I don't want to be mayor of Los Angeles," Gates's predecessor as chief, the bombastic Ed "Crazy Ed" Davis had once famously said. "I *already have* more power than the mayor."

But now, with the fallout from the King beating and a riot gathering steam, Gates could sense that power slipping away. This Christopher Commission charter-amendment proposal was the first step in that pro-cess. Heading to Brentwood, Gates rightly understood that he was in the fight of his professional life.

****

Daryl Gates's tumultuous reign as chief had begun in 1978, when Los Angeles was still deep in the throes of a second remarkable demographic and generational shift that would utterly transform the social and politi-cal architecture of the city, along with its ethnic and racial composition, size, culture, and sophistication.

The first had begun with a trickle in the 1920s and '30s, before ex-ploding during and after World War II, when hundreds of thousands of migrating black, Jewish, and various other white Americans joined the relatively small numbers of Japanese, Chinese, and Mexican minorities already in Los Angeles. Together, they would form the backbone of the coalition that would elect Tom Bradley as L.A.'s Democratic mayor.

Unfortunately for L.A.'s African-Americans, just as they were seeing a black man in charge in city hall, their fortunes in other ways were fast declining as America's corporate titans began shutting down their unionized factories with their well-paying jobs in the 1960s. By the mid-eighties they'd completed their task, setting up their production facilities in the sweatshops of Mexico and South Asia, and sending black unemployment soaring as the Bloods and Crips were birthed and the city's crack wars ignited.

Meanwhile, a second extraordinary new wave of immigration was erupting. Starting in the early 1970s and running well through the 1990s, about eight hundred thousand immigrants from the developing world would pour into the city from Mexico and Central America above all, but from Thailand, Taiwan, Korea, Pakistan, Russia, Israel, and other parts of the Middle East as well. By 1990, 87 percent of Los Angeles City's public school students were Latinos and/or other minorities.

Desperately poor rural Mexicans moved into low-income and working class neighborhoods throughout the city, searching for jobs and scratching out a living doing L.A.'s service work. By the late eighties Latinos would comprise a rapidly accelerating 40 percent of the city's population.

Simultaneously, just west of downtown, the district known as Pico-Union began overflowing with tens of thousands of equally impoverished Salvadorans and Guatemalans crammed together in substandard pre–World War II apartment buildings. Farther west, in the historic Mid-Wilshire district, Koreans were also arriving in numbers so high that a large section of the area would later be officially christened "Koreatown."

Concurrently, a generational revolution was also hurtling forward, one that began in the mid-1960s. Initially it featured civil rights and antiwar marchers and skinny college students with radical hair throwing off the corseted social constraints imposed by aging white men with beer guts and buzz cuts. By the early 1990s those students were middle-aged and now part of a social revolution being spearheaded by a new generation of Latinos, blacks, women, gays, and political and social liberals demanding equal rights, opportunities, and the right to be free of police repression.

At the same time, older white, conservative supporters of the LAPD were continuing to beat a rapid retreat from the city that had begun soon after the Watts riots.

What emerged from the historic turmoil was a city where race and class tensions pervaded the atmosphere. The very rich were mostly walled off in hidden mansions, and much of the white middle class remained living in hyper-segregated neighborhoods. The brown, black, and immigrant working class and poor—who were becoming the bulk of the city's ordinary people—were rarely seen by well-off, white L.A. unless they were cleaning houses, weeding gardens, working nonunion construction, driving buses, parking cars, stocking shelves in big-box factory stores, or cooking food and mopping floors in every restaurant in town.

By the early nineties L.A. was still being billed, along with New York, as the capital of American style and glamour. But in reality, over the last two decades of the twentieth century, Los Angeles was a city awash in crisis, led by people without answers, and filled with residents suffering the consequences.

Disastrously, no organization was less prepared or less willing to adjust to this transformation than was the LAPD and its leader, Daryl Gates.

****

Named chief in 1978, Daryl Gates entered office with a choice: to buck the headwinds of America's social revolution, or to try to accommodate it. His decision was never in doubt.

The son of an alcoholic and absentee father, Gates was raised in abject poverty in Glendale—a small city adjacent to Los Angeles—during the 1930s and '40s. It was a time when L.A., sans Hollywood, was still Peoria with Palms, still a city that billed itself as America's pure "White Spot," still a place where a mainstream mayoral candidate would proudly declare Los Angeles "the last stand of native-born Protestant Americans."

Though shaped by the legacy of that time and place, Daryl Gates would be required to police a new Los Angeles whose residents were demanding dramatic change in its institutions.

First and foremost that included an LAPD that was so notoriously racist and homophobic that it would take a court-mandated federal consent decree to force the department to start hiring more than a token number of women, blacks, and Latinos.

Daryl Gates, in short, was not just opposed to any changes to his LAPD; he was *appalled* by the very idea. For decades the LAPD had been portrayed on network TV as America's quintessential police department—sharp, trailblazing, efficient, effective, and admired by law enforcement organizations around the world.

In large part that image had been a PR coup fueled by the department's own skillful self-promotion and crafted by movie industry and public relations veterans. But there was also reality to the myth. Initially, Bill Parker had been a much-needed reformer. Entering office in 1950, Parker had been among the first to eliminate the kind of systemic, on-the-take corruption that had been part of the DNA of the LAPD and many other big-city police departments since their inception. And he did so at least a decade or two before other police forces in cities like New York, Chicago, and Philadelphia. Curbside courts where traffic cops would shake down bribes from errant motorists quickly vanished. And so did the routine black-bag payoffs to vice-squad detectives so perfectly personified by the all those brass-knuckled police detectives played by Ward Bond in the *film noir* 1940s.

Under Parker, the LAPD also became independent from the big-business downtown oligarchy that for more than half a century had used the department like a private army to muzzle dissent.

Parker himself had a hand in the creation of the LAPD myth. Not deliberately—at least, not at first. But he wanted to protect and project the department's newfound reputation (in white L.A.) for upright professionalism. His chance came in the early fifties, when radio/TV producer/actor Jack Webb sought the department's cooperation in mounting a TV series based on a fictional LAPD detective. Parker's approval came with a price: the department would have to approve all scripts and monitor the filming on the set. He used his office's oversight not just to ensure that his organization was portrayed as he wished but to reshape Ward Bond into Webb's signature *Dragnet* LAPD detective, the righteous Joe Friday.

And when Webb needed the department's cooperation to introduce a new series about a couple of LAPD patrol officers, Parker again got what he wanted with *Adam-12*: actor Martin Milner playing a toothy, all-

American model cop—white, clean-cut, athletic, with a moral code far superior to the people he policed. In all these things Bill Parker seemed nothing if not the police reformer for whom the city had yearned.

But in real life his model patrolman would quickly fall victim to Parker's extremely bleak, conflicting view of human nature. The department's Martin Milners were required to view their jobs *not* as one of service to the community but as a "thin blue line" protecting a venal public against the evils of "man, the most predatory of all in the animal kingdom" while policing in an America that was "the most lawless nation on Earth." By intent, his officers would therefore be distant and divorced from the city's social fabric. People are nice to cops only when they want something, Parker believed, and having professional relationships with the public could only corrupt them.

No one bought into Parker's policing philosophy and worldview more than Daryl Gates. And as the LAPD's new chief, Gates would regard himself as nothing less than the guardian of that legacy, the perpetuator of that myth, the keeper of Bill Parker's revered flame.

Early in his career, Gates had been fast-tracked by the childless chief, who treated him like a surrogate son. As an awestruck, impressionable twenty-three-year-old rookie, Gates had served as Parker's daytime chauffeur and bodyguard, and later as his adjutant and executive officer. Frequently in ugly, hungover moods during which he'd viciously berate unlucky members of his command staff, Parker nevertheless would heap praise on his superbly conditioned, sharply tailored young driver during the speeches cum sermons he'd deliver almost daily to his large, 1950s-conservative political base. "Now, look at him," Parker would sometimes tell his audiences, pointing to Gates. "Stand up," he'd say to him, "I want you to stand up!" And when Gates stood up, he'd say: "Now, this is a *policeman* . . . look at him!"

Unfortunately for the LAPD and Los Angeles, Gates remained frozen in that moment, unable to put himself in the shoes of those outside his narrow background, learn from experience and failure, or grow with the times. Instead, he became an uncompromising defender of the status quo, emerging in the process as a tough-talking symbol of the counterrevolutionary forces fighting against the transformational sixties and seventies. In the process he became among the last incarnations of the audacious, angry, socially divisive white police chiefs who rose to power during the era's historic turmoil.

On the East Coast the breed was best exemplified by Francis "Blackjack Frank" Rizzo, the former police commissioner who became mayor of Philadelphia in the 1970s. Rizzo was beloved by the white working class, who hated and feared black Philly. They cheered when Rizzo proclaimed that the best way to treat those who broke the law was "*Spacco il capo*"—break their heads—and applauded his department's crime-reduction strategy, which was to "make Attila the Hun look like a faggot."

Gates too sent messages to his troops and conservative supporters. "Casual drug users," he said, "should be shot." Of the demand that the department hire openly gay cops, he replied disgustedly, "Who would want to work with one?" Of a man who was awarded $170,000 by a federal jury after LAPD officers had broken his nose during a search of his home, Gates countered that the victim was "lucky that was all he had broken," and then asked and answered his own question: "How much is a broken nose worth? I don't think it's worth anything." During a 1985 interview on CBS he lauded Philadelphia's first black mayor, W. Wilson Goode, as "an inspiration to the nation" after Goode had approved dropping a bomb from a helicopter onto a row house in a densely packed, black, residential Philadelphia neighborhood. The aerial bombing resulted in a massive wall of flames that caused the death of eleven residents, including five children, and the incineration of sixty-one surrounding homes. In response, a federal jury awarded over $12 million to the homeowners. Nevertheless, Gates told wide-eyed reporter Lesley Stahl that Wilson Goode had "jumped on [his] heroes list," and "by golly," he added, "that's not a long list."

That same year, as the crack cocaine epidemic began to sweep across L.A., Gates searched his arsenal for a weapon to knock down fortified crack-house doors. He found an armored military personnel carrier with a fourteen-foot protrusion that the department then christened the "Battering Ram." Acting on an unsubstantiated tip to narcotics officers, he decided to ride shotgun on its maiden voyage. The vehicle geared up and smashed a giant, gaping hole into the suspect house while the invited press looked on. As officers poured in, they found only two terrified black women, a couple of kids eating chocolate-swirl ice cream, and a small amount of grass for personal use.

Despite all this, Daryl Gates was nevertheless taken very seriously by supporters and critics alike. Crime was high and fear was rampant, and the city's politicians had no stomach for the fierce, polarizing battle it would take to get rid of a ready-to-rumble law-and-order chief with *no* legal limits on his tenure in office. Statutorily, the part-time civilian Police Commission, appointed by the mayor, had the power and duty to set department policy and hold the chief accountable for its implementation. But in reality, the commission was simply ignored by Parker and his successors, who ruled the department unchallenged. Gates had even bragged about his job security in his 1992 autobiography, *Chief:* "To fire a police chief," he wrote, "a public charge [is] required and must be proven at a hearing of the Board of Civil Service Commissioners. Even if the board can demonstrate 'good and sufficient cause' for removal, the chief may appeal to the California Courts."

And "good and sufficient cause," Gates failed to mention, would be extremely hard to come by in his case, thanks to a bizarre act of political obsequiousness on the part of Mayor Bradley's part-time civilian police commissioners. In an effort to buy peace with Gates, they had allowed him to write his own civil service performance evaluations—which unsurprisingly, were uniformly "excellent." So any move to fire him, even in wake of the King beating, would directly contradict the favorable civil service evaluations on which the commission had already signed off.

Consequently, while most police chiefs served at the pleasure of elected officials, Daryl Gates was, in effect, accountable to no one. He used his independent status to cater to the two constituencies he cared most about: Los Angeles's dwindling conservative white voters and, most especially, his own troops—whose brutality he fiercely defended. In return, his officers gave him what he seemed most to crave: their adoration.

For the city, however, the price of love was steep. Camaraderie and esprit de corps are the glue that binds together paramilitary organizations like police departments. But under Gates those concepts were carried to such an extreme that they distorted the department's core mission of public service by placing the desires of his cops and the dictums of their culture above the public good.

A competitive runner, Gates would tool off with the troops to police department competitions throughout California and the Southwest. Among those he ran with were many special-unit macho guys infamous for getting into trouble on and off duty. Gates instinctively protected these officers, subverting the disciplinary system in the process. "In a lot of cases . . . an officer will appeal to the Chief," David Dotson would later testify to the Christopher Commission in 1991, "and the Chief [would] mitigate whatever the situation may have been . . . based on the officer's appeal. And he frequently did that without informing the chain of command that had been involved in the [initial discipline] recommendation."

Most importantly, Gates's acts of dispensation were having a direct effect on officers' behavior on the streets of Los Angeles, particularly in the sprawling black areas that were part of South Bureau. There, the spirit of Gates's disciplinary actions had filtered down to the captains, who were recommending slap-on-the-wrist penalties for serious use-of-force violations.

When Jesse Brewer, the department's first black assistant chief, assumed command of South Bureau, he began overruling the captains and imposing stiffer penalties before sending them on to Daryl Gates for final sign-off. And "in every case—*every case*"—as Brewer would later emphasize, Gates overturned his recommendation and imposed the lighter penalty; and within a year the officer was again in trouble for a similar or identical use-of-force violation. Gates's disciplinary leniency, as Brewer would later point out, was not just indicative of the department's use-of-force problem but "the essence of the [LAPD's] excessive force problem."

****

Bill Parker had never liked brutality for brutality's sake. It was amateurish and unlawful, and did not fit the new LAPD image. But he recognized both its utility and perceived necessity when used in the department's number one mission—keeping order. For Parker, order was everything. He was a man with values and perceptions forged in nineteenth-century South Dakota, when South Dakota was still the Wild West, and law and order had been hard-won. Loosen the screws even a little bit and all hell could break lose.

So when Parker became chief, he'd added a new twist to the old unwritten LAPD credo, one that would henceforth govern an LAPD officer's conduct: If you beat, shoot, or otherwise abuse a suspect because you felt that's what it took, we may not always condone it, but publicly we'll always have your back. But if you steal even one penny, your ass is ours. And that's the way it also was under Ed Davis, who'd served as chief throughout most of the seventies.

Daryl Gates's contribution had been to take the first part of that credo and apply it in a wider, deeper, astoundingly audacious manner. By doing so, and by proudly thumbing his nose at elected civilian authority and departmental critics, "Gates made himself a martyr within the Los Angeles Police Department—the guy who'd stepped up and died for their sins," as Charlie Beck would later say. "He seemed to never realize he was already holding that suit of cards. In an organization with a huge belief in physical fitness, sharp appearance, and esprit de corps, he was an athlete with immense personal charm who could walk into a room and command it. They would have loved him anyway. But he thought he didn't need the other cards, the other constituencies. He didn't see that he could win a hand with that suit, but never the game."

White conservative voters in areas of the city such as the San Fernando Valley loved him too. About two months after the King beating, they'd held a boisterous luncheon rally for their beleaguered chief in a Valley ballroom. In attendance were blue-haired matrons from the mansions of Hancock Park, members of Encino Republican Women, Valley real estate brokers and salespeople, housewives and concrete-faced LAPD officers—essentially the same people who served on the Simi Valley jury that had acquitted Rodney King.

When Gates walked in, the place broke into an ear-shattering standing ovation. Women rushed up to kiss him and men to shake his hand. The intensity of their emotions went well beyond political support. It was visceral, tribal. He was the defender of a city that was once theirs—a city that was now fading as surely as were they themselves. If they had still constituted a viable, influential majority in Los Angeles, no political force could have gotten rid of Daryl Gates. But they didn't. Los Angeles politics were now was dominated by the white and black liberals who had put Tom Bradley in office, along with a rapidly growing base of Latino voters. Gates's cops and a conservative white base that was fast becoming irrelevant could no longer shield him.

For over a decade Gates had ignored, suppressed, and made enemies of his department's other constituencies. Together they comprised a virtual Who's Who of much of Los Angeles's civic establishment: Mayor Bradley and his police commissioners, city council members, the black establishment, the ACLU and Latino civil rights organizations, women's and gay organizations, social-service nonprofits and academics, civilian organizations trying to decrease gang violence, and the local press corps, led by the *Los Angeles Times*.

It had not always been that way with the press. From the start of Bill Parker's tenure through the early 1980s, in fact, the local media had been what former Police Commission president Stephen Reinhardt had famously described as a "patsy for the police." By the early seventies, however, the once deeply right-wing, fiercely anti-union *Times*—the paper of record—had liberalized most of its coverage. But it was still failing to do hard-eyed, investigative reporting of the LAPD. The *Times*, after all, had been the embodiment of the ruling Los Angeles oligarchy that had made astounding fortunes in land speculation and selling real estate to middle-class, Midwestern immigrants flocking west to invest their savings in the happy home of sunshine and palms. News of local corruption and scandal was therefore studiously ignored. Consequently, the *Times* never developed a tradition of doing big, systemic investigative journalism. Bad news was bad for business.

But reporters who'd come of age during the 1960s were now being hired at the *Times* and other local media outlets. Young and unwedded to local assumptions, they were filled with questions about why the LAPD was going uncriticized for actions that would get them lambasted in other cities.

In 1976, newly arrived KABC reporter Wayne Satz produced a Pea-body Award–winning series about the astounding number of unarmed people shot and killed by LAPD officers. The reports questioned not only the department's whitewash investigations but the lack of oversight by the DA, the coroner, the Police Commission and the city council.

Outraged, LAPD chief Ed Davis denounced Satz as "an enemy of law enforcement" over the LAPD's closed-circuit TV station. "Satz Sucks" bumper stickers began appearing on LAPD patrol cars, and Satz's picture popped up on targets at the police academy firing range. "Their arrogance was incredible," Satz would later say. "They didn't think they had *any* public accountability." And "they"—Ed Davis and the LAPD leadership—were right. Despite Satz's searing broadcasts, *nothing* changed.

In 1979, the now-defunct *Los Angeles Herald-Examiner* began cover-ing the LAPD with new intensity. By focusing on the police-shooting death of thirty-nine-year-old South Central housewife Eulia Love over a $22.09 unpaid gas bill—and on dozens of other shoot-first-and-ask-questions-later police killings and inexplicable choke-hold deaths—the *Herald-Examiner* embarrassed the *Times* into action, and the paper began reporting on similar incidents.

But they would still pull great investigative reporters like David Cay Johnston off stories that dug too deeply into the LAPD's clandestine inner workings. Working for the *Times*, Johnston had found out amaz-ing things. That, for example, undercover LAPD officers were having sexual affairs with peaceful political activists in order to gather politi-cal information; that an LAPD lieutenant had posed as a Communist and traveled to Moscow and Havana; that LAPD agent provocateurs had infiltrated black and Hispanic organizations and were constantly calling for violent action; and that Gates had over two hundred officers working for his spy division. Johnston's stories got printed, but usually in just one edition, without background or explanation. Eventually he was forced off the beat.

After his departure, however, the *Times* finally started covering officer-involved brutality and shootings, and stayed with the coverage year after year, breaking scores of investigative articles and holding the

LAPD's feet to the fire in ways that the city's politicians simply would not. It was the *Times*, in fact, that broke the Brentwood fund-raiser story, establishing how long Gates had stayed at the event. On *Face the Nation* the weekend after the riot, Gates said he remained at the fund-raiser for ten minutes. An audio of his Brentwood speech obtained by the *Times*, however, revealed that he had in fact stayed at the gathering for about *twenty* minutes. Factoring in his travel to and from the event, Daryl Gates left his post for *at least an hour and twenty minutes* at the very moment when the riots might have been limited with a disciplined, centrally directed show of force. He may have been monitoring radio calls as he traveled, but if he was making decisions, they certainly weren't being reflected on the street.

Reginald Denny and other motorists were being beaten at Florence and Normandie during that time. And nobody from the LAPD even ordered the blocking-off of feeder roads into that chaotic intersection. Leaving the fund-raiser that night, Gates was asked about Denny and the others caught without police protection. "There are going to be situations where people are without assistance," he replied. "That's just the facts of life."

Bill Bratton, New York City, Early 1990s

As L.A. continued to burn on Daryl Gates's watch, three thousand miles away another police chief was taking center stage in another renowned American city. His name was William J. Bratton. And unlike Gates, Bratton liked new, outside-the-box ideas. Studied them, invited them, championed them; recognized that new crime prevention strategies were desperately needed by police departments across an urban America seething with racial fear and animosity. Nowhere was this truer than the agency that Bratton had taken charge of in early 1990: the New City Transit Police Department (NYTPD).

The NYTPD was then independent of the New York Police Department, and its primary mission was to protect the three and a half million daily riders of New York's heavily traveled subway system—a mission in which it was failing. Transit crime had risen by 25 percent a year for the past three years—twice the rate of crime in New York City as a whole—and robberies were growing at two and a half times the rate of those in the city, which itself was experiencing record-high crime numbers. The department's 3,500 officers, moreover, were demoralized, and looked it.

They were also ill-equipped, as well as ill-used, by an old, tired leadership cadre whose policies focused on reacting to crimes after they occurred, as opposed to trying to systematically reduce or prevent them.

Meanwhile, thousands of homeless people were living in cardboard packing-box bedrooms on the far ends of subway platforms, and hundreds were becoming sick or dying after being bitten by rats, bitten by frost, or killed by speeding trains.

Simultaneously, subway riders were jumping over turnstyle subway entrances at the rate of about 170,000 a day. Often panhandlers and hustlers would cover turnstyle token-slots with gum or wet paper so tokens couldn't be inserted. Then they'd hold open the entry gate and demand tokens from the already harried riders.

Aboveground, New York and the NYPD were absorbed in their own ongoing crisis. The city's 1989 homicide rate of 1,905 had set a sorry record, one promptly broken the following year with an astounding 2,245 murders. Nor was that the whole story. In 1993, a year of 1,946 killings in the city, a total of more than 5,800 people had been shot.

Seven hundred thousand serious crimes had been committed in New York in 1989—one crime for about every ten residents. Increasingly, New Yorkers were feeling overwhelmed by muggers, street corner crack dealers, crackheads, and crack wars, a record number of auto break-ins, in-your-face street hookers, sometimes violent, often mentally ill homeless people urinating and defecating on the city's sidewalks, and menacing squeegee men demanding a buck at every red light for rubbing your windshield with a rag that was often dirtier than your windshield.

All of this was compounded by the city's geography. Unlike car-centric Angelenos, New Yorkers of all working and professional classes and races converged in the city's subway cars or on its crowded streets. Mostly black and brown young men living in impoverished areas of the

Bronx, Brooklyn, and Queens were hopping on subway trains and "going to work," as they called it, robbing and terrorizing their fellow riders. At the same time African-Americans entering white ethnic neighborhoods in Brooklyn and Queens were being viciously beaten by impromptu gangs of raging young white men.

Few of the city's residents had any faith in the city's police to effectively intervene. In many ways the NYPD had never recovered from the self-inflicted blow it suffered in the late 1960s and early 1970s when it was racked by a deeply rooted corruption scandal. Hundreds of thousands—perhaps millions—of dollars in graft was being paid by heroin and other drug dealers to street cops, but most especially and most systemically to narcotics detectives. It flowed up to captains and field commanders, a fact that then was ignored by high-ranking police and city officials wanting to avoid the kind of embarrassing, epoch-defining police scandal that eventually erupted despite their best efforts to contain it.

Afterward the police commissioner resigned and was followed by much of the department's top-ranking command staff. In the decades that followed, a chastened, gun-shy NYPD focused on eliminating police payoffs and keeping its officers away from drug crimes and racially charged situations that could explode into scandal. In 1972, for example, a police officer was shot and killed with his own gun inside a Black Muslim mosque in Harlem. The officer had responded to a bogus 911 call of a fellow police officer reportedly under duress within the mosque. When additional officers arrived on the scene, they rounded up and detained a group of suspects; but, fearing a confrontation with an angry crowd gathered outside, they left the mosque without the suspects. The killing of a cop in such a circumstance is the kind of crime pursued with fierce, unbridled determination by police departments, but in this case no one was ever charged in the officer's murder.

Richard Goldstein, in his *New York Times* obituary of Albert Seedman, the legendary cigar-chomping NYPD chief of detectives during the early 1970s, exactly caught the dizzying tumult of the era. In just one eleven-month period, he wrote, "three pairs of police officers were shot—four of the officers were killed and two grievously wounded—in ambushes by the Black Liberation Army. The underworld boss Joseph A.

Colombo Sr. was shot in the head by a gunman who was himself shot to death seconds later at Mr. Colombo's Italian-American Day rally in Columbus Circle. The mob leader Joey Gallo was fatally shot at a Little Italy restaurant [and] gunmen posing as guests looted 47 safe deposit boxes at the Hotel Pierre."

That was New York City in the seventies. The decades that followed would also have their own watershed racial and criminal events. One occurred in 1989 when a lone young woman jogging in Manhattan's Central Park was so savagely attacked that she was near death when found. Five teenage boys from Harlem who'd been in the park that night were soon arrested. It was a lurid, horrific, electrifying story, made more so by the fact that "the Central Park jogger," as she was dubbed by the tabloid press, was white, and the five arrested and then convicted teenagers were black. There were significant problems with the case from the start, but little was said about that in the ugly heat of the moment. In 2002, however, the defendants were declared innocent by a new Manhattan district attorney, who, after reviewing the evidence, successfully petitioned to have their convictions overturned. (A murderer and serial rapist later confessed to the attack.) But all that hadn't taken place until thirteen years later—thirteen years during which the case as earlier adjudicated had played a pivotal role in stoking racial fears among white New Yorkers.

A second incident that stunned the city occurred early in William Bratton's tenure as chief of the transit police. In late August of 1990, during the U.S. Open tennis tournament in Queens, a twenty-two-year-old tourist from Provo, Utah, named Brian Watkins was standing with his family in a subway station when they were attacked by a gang of eight muggers. When one punched his mother in the face and a second slit his father's pants pocket open to expose his wallet, Watkins tried to defend them and got stabbed to death with a four-inch butterfly knife for his courage.

That September, *New York* magazine ran a lead story entitled "All About Crime," with a shiny black .38-caliber revolver on the cover, along with some questions and promised information: "Is it worse than ever?" "Who kills whom?" "How safe is your neighborhood?" and "The most dangerous subway stations." That same month *Time* magazine also ran a New York cover story, this one entitled "The Rotting of the Big Apple," while the *New York Post* addressed then Mayor David Dinkins with a banner headline: "Dave," it demanded, "Do Something!"

Six years earlier, another case of subway violence had also become a cause célèbre. A thin, pale man named Bernhard Goetz, fearful of being mugged, as he had been previously, armed himself with a handgun. When four would-be muggers crowded around him on a subway car, demanding $5, he shot each of them once. Moments later, standing above one of the fallen, he asked, "Want another?" and shot him again. Tellingly, astoundingly, Goetz was hailed as a hero by a vast number of New Yorkers and found not guilty by a jury (although he later was sentenced to eight and a half months in prison for illegal gun possession). The public's reaction was a signal of the growing movement for stronger police protection.

Perhaps because he was an out-of-towner, Bill Bratton looked at the situation with fresh eyes and saw something others did not in Brian Watkins's murder. He saw opportunity. "The whole catalyst for the turnaround in New York City occurred right then," he'd later say. "Watkins's murder became a cause célèbre; his death the face of crime in New York City."

****

A twenty-year veteran of the Boston Police Department, Bill Bratton was not a man who would catch your eye as he entered a room. Slender and just a bit below average height, he wasn't big on laughing or smiling. But charm never was what Bratton had to sell. Nor was warmth or flattery. As he himself once pointed out: "Some people are great back-slappers, quick with an embrace, a peck on the cheek or a pat on the butt. I didn't grow up with that." Instead, Bratton's strength lay in his head-down, no-nonsense manner, exceptional problem-solving and conceptual skills, and keen intellectual curiosity. At times he'd hold his chin in an upward tilt, the tilt of the supremely confident—a confidence best reflected in his actively seeking out smart, existentially alive people to generate ideas and serve as his trusted eyes and ears.

When he spoke, there was no flare, no smugness in his delivery. Rather, his attitude said: "I have the facts, I know what I'm doing and what talking I'm about, and I have too much regard for myself to try to bullshit you."

Which was not to say that Bratton wasn't an extraordinarily ambitious and calculating self-promoter. In fact, among the reasons Bratton had taken the job as chief of the New York City Transit Police, as he himself would later point out, was because those subways cars were running under the *media capital of the world*, and success there would be noticed when the job of New York City police commissioner became available. And if that didn't pan out, well, the LAPD had an aging, controversial police chief, and that job paid $175,000 a year—then the highest in the country.

He saw and billed himself as a "change agent," and that was the criterion on which he desired to be judged. In just the ten-year span from 1983 to 1993 he would head the Massachusetts Bay Transportation Authority Police, the New York City Transit Police, the Boston Police Department, and the NYPD. "Did I not come in, do what I said I'd do, and get the long-term crime reduction job started?" he'd essentially ask when criticized for jumping from one police department to another. "Yes, I did" was his answer. "Look at the numbers—there's your proof."

Above all, Bratton was a realist wearing a visionary's clothes. Big-city policing circa 1990 was a world mired in corruption and racism, proudly scornful of social science and data-driven policy. He loved his profession more than most, but saw it for what it was while understanding just how essential, how vital good policing could be to a city's well-being.

He was, in short, a new guy to the old-time religion, ready to preach a new, more effective gospel. One that was desperately needed. And that would prove his greatest gift.

****

A working-class Bostonian from the all-white Irish district known as Dorchester, Bratton was the son of high school sweethearts who'd met growing up in the Charlestown housing projects. They were of Scottish,

Irish, and French-Canadian descent. His mother, June, was a housewife, and his father, "Big Bill," worked two full-time jobs, one in a chrome-plating factory and one as a mail sorter for the U.S. Postal Service. He was, by Bratton's account, deeply respected by all who knew him, and adored by his son. A lot of Bratton's exceptional self-confidence came from his father, whom Bratton later described as "slight of build but just tough as nails." "Somewhere along the line," Bratton wrote in his auto-biography, *Turnaround,* "my father developed the confidence that he could handle whatever came along. You could tell in the way he carried himself. When he felt that somebody was misusing authority, he didn't care who it was, and I picked up his temper to react to unjust treatment. Throughout my life I've never been shy about professing my point of view against authority. It's ironic that I went into policing because so often I took on authority figures—teachers and others."

As a boy Bratton had been smart enough to be accepted into Boston Latin, the city's most prestigious public school, but not smart enough to master foreign languages, especially the required Latin, and was consequently asked to leave.

In 1966, he entered the United States Army, was assigned to the military police, and wound up in a sentry dog unit in Vietnam. Discharged two years later, he joined the Boston PD in 1970 at the age of twenty-three. The department at the time was poorly paid, listlessly corrupt, intensely, proudly inbred, and reflexively provincial, with a leadership cadre, as Bratton later put it, "steeped in Boston Irish culture [and] Irish Alzheimer's: You forget everything except the grudges."

In short, the 2,800 cops on the Boston PD were rarely the best and the brightest, or the most diverse. In 1970 there were only fifty-five minority officers in the entire department, and not one woman. Given the lack of first-rate competition, it initially proved a good place for a smart, ambitious young cop to shine. Fewer than twenty-five officers had college degrees, and when part-time scholarships were offered to officers at Boston State University, Bratton leapt at the opportunity.

The sixties were not a decade that had excited Bratton. He didn't like their flavor—their hedonism, anarchy, and drugs—nor did he like the radical politics of the counterculture. "I always loved my country and loved our system of government," he would later say. "When it became fashionable to be anti, I never bought into that."

BSU, consequently, would prove a kind of saving-grace finishing school for a provincial young cop, providing him a wider intellectual experience that enabled him to think beyond the closed world of the Boston PD, where "all your friends are cops, all your talk is cop talk, and all you hear are cop ideas." Listening to liberal, antiwar classmates and professors allowed him to break out of what he'd later call the "Blue Cocoon."

By 1980, at the age of thirty-two, he'd risen through the ranks to become the department's second in command, its executive superintendent. Not only had he become the Boston PD's wonder boy, he also became its media man, its face, and its chief spokesman.

It wasn't long, however, before he ran into trouble. Profiled in *Boston Magazine*, he let it be known that his goal was to become Boston's police commissioner. The comment was immediately deemed unseemly and self-aggrandizing by the department's old guard, and as he was unceremoniously being transferred out of the chief's office, he began looking around for a new opportunity.

He found it in 1983 when a corruption scandal arose at the Massachusetts Bay Transportation Authority, and he replaced its police chief. The MBTAP was a small, underfunded department, haphazardly led and badly equipped, but the scandal brought attention, and with it significant money from the state to change the situation. And Bratton did. He was then invited to join a select group of police executives, public officials, and academics developing innovative community policing strategies at the Executive Session on Policing at Harvard University's Kennedy School of Government. Around the same time, he was honored with a prestigious award by a newly formed organization of law enforcement professionals and prominent social scientists known as the Police Executive Research Forum. The award got him noticed, and in 1990—one year before the Rodney King beating—he accepted the job of chief of the NYTP. By then, hundreds of thousands of New Yorkers had come to view their subways as a series of dark holes—each one submerged in air so dank and foul you felt the need to hold your breath when you entered; each desecrated by discordant Magic Marker graffiti and encrusted in a coat of grime that sapped your soul; and many so unsafe that you feared mugging or harassment every time you stepped into them. That was the feeling. And there was truth to all of it.

But it was not necessarily the whole story. As Bratton later wrote in *Turnaround*, by 1990 the Transit Authority "had virtually wiped out graffiti on the trains." In TA focus groups, women interviewed believed that 30 percent of the city's crimes were committed on subways, and 40 to 50 percent of its murders. In fact, only 3 percent of felonies occurred in subways and only between 1 and 2 percent of homicides. But people felt trapped in subways, where there was no place to run.

Other focus groups found that many transit officers were deeply demoralized and hated their jobs. Many were assigned to stand by a subway station's turnstyles and make sure nobody evaded paying a fare. It was security guard work, and essentially fruitless. There weren't enough subway cops on any work shift to cover all the subway entrances, so someone determined not to pay could just walk a few blocks down to the next station. What they wanted to do, the officers said, was to protect the public.

Bratton gave them their wish. He started out by reforming officer training, forcing the transit police brass out of their city-owned, take-home cars and into the subways to travel to work in uniform, just as he was doing. Then he replaced a broken-down communication system with one that actually worked both inside and outside the subways, and identified and rapidly promoted talented, smart, ambitious people.

He formed teams of officers to lie in wait and arrest fare-beaters. To avoid flooding the jails with fare-beaters for twenty-four to forty-eight hours as they waited to be arraigned, he ordered the immediate release of those who'd been unarmed and had no outstanding arrest warrants. Missing the subsequent court date, however, would trigger re-arrest at their homes. Decoy units were also formed to attract and arrest would-be muggers, and gangs of muggers were targeted and broken up. Many were repeat offenders, who started receiving far stiffer sentences than previously. Thirty months later, when Bratton resigned as chief, felony subway crimes had decreased by over 20 percent, robberies by 40 percent, and fare evasions by 50 percent.

During this time, Bratton also introduced and championed social scientists James Q. Wilson and George Kelling's contentious but highly influential "Broken Windows" theory of crime. Such crimes as public drunkenness, aggressive panhandling, street prostitution, and loitering, Wilson and Kelling argued in a 1982 *Atlantic Monthly* article entitled "Broken Windows: The Police and Neighborhood Safety," created an atmosphere of fear and permissiveness that led to more serious crimes. Therefore, cops needed to enforce laws prohibiting those actions as a way to modify behavioral norms in public spaces, in the same way that broken windows must be repaired or they'll lead to a neighborhood's gradual physical deterioration. Later, serious problems would emerge as a result of the rigid use of the tactic, and a powerful backlash would discredit the widespread, indiscriminate use of "stop-frisk" policing—another policy Bratton would implement in New York. But for the subways of New York in those pivotal initial years, those strategies were critical first steps in restoring a sense both of safety and of sanity in a crucial public space. At a time when crime was becoming America's number one domestic obsession, Bratton proved on a national stage that smart, data-based policing could actually play a pivotal role in stemming crime and violence in big-city America. And in New York City circa 1992, that was a revelation.

Charlie Beck and Mike Yamaki, Wednesday, April 29, 1992, LAPD Command Post, South Los Angeles

About forty minutes after leaving home, Charlie Beck pulled into the same crumbling Parker Center parking lot Daryl Gates had left an hour or so earlier. There, he mounted a bus with forty-nine other sergeants and headed to a makeshift command center in the heart of South Central.

Riding down Western Avenue, Beck looked out, stunned. On both

sides of the wide-laned thoroughfare, apartment buildings; beauty salons; mini-marts; liquor, discount, and clothing shops; and storefront
churches were going up in crackling fires. A major Los Angeles thoroughfare was being set ablaze while Beck's LAPD continued to be
locked in an incomprehensible paralysis. Buildings were burning and
stores were already trashed and looted along the other multi-mile bou-
levards and avenues that snaked and crisscrossed South Los Angeles.
"For 10 miles between Santa Monica Boulevard in Hollywood and Manchester Boulevard in south Los Angeles," as the *L.A. Times* reported, a
vast section of the city "had become a holocaust of fire-gutted buildings
and shattered glass."

The command post where Beck and his fellow sergeants arrived was
a commandeered Metropolitan Transit Authority bus yard, chaotically
overflowing with growing numbers of police and fire trucks and vehicles. Several motor homes had also arrived, presumably to serve as a
central dispatch station. But no cops had been dispatched.

Los Angeles police commissioner Mike Yamaki was greeted by the
same scene when he arrived. Command-level officers from both the police and the fire departments were present, but no one appeared to be
in charge. Moreover, the LAPD's communication system, as he would
soon discover, was unable to transmit to the fire department, the highway patrol, or any other agency.

A taut, streetwise forty-three-year-old Japanese-American, Yamaki
had recently become L.A.'s first Asian-American police commissioner.
His parents had spent the Second World War in an internment camp,
easy targets for rounding up and imprisonment because they were
members of just another unwelcome, politically powerless minority race subject to legal abuse in the white America of 1941. Yamaki's
father emerged from the camp determined to change what he could
by becoming integrated into the American mainstream both in his job
in the insurance industry and in his active participation in Los Angeles's Democratic Party politics. He passed on the lessons he took away
from the camp to his son, who, in turn, became a well-known, highly
respected defense attorney. For many years Yamaki had worked to get a

stubbornly resistant LAPD to hire more Asian-American officers to join the handful of ten already on the force. As Yamaki saw it, hiring more Asians was not only a matter of fairness, it was also a part of smart basic policing. A lot of Asian immigrants, especially in Chinatown, were being exploited by their own communities, and failed to report shake-downs and other crimes because they mistrusted the police.

For all of these reasons, Mike Yamaki took his job as one of just five civilian police commissioners very seriously. And as he stepped out of his police vehicle and onto the grounds of the makeshift command center, he, like Charlie Beck, was immediately struck by the chaos of shouting men and idling vehicle engines around him.

One conversation in particular caught his attention: a discussion among ranking LAPD officers about whether they should call the Los Angeles County sheriff for help. They wanted to ask the sheriff—who, in L.A. County, was the only law enforcement agent who could officially request outside assistance—to call in the California National Guard. In the end they decided not to. Because, as Yamaki later put it, "nobody in the LAPD wanted to have to kiss ass to anyone in the Sheriff's Department."

Finally, officers from other local police agencies *did* start arriving, but nobody knew what to do with them, and *they* didn't know where to go or even where they'd be housed. So, astoundingly, Yamaki—a defense attorney by trade, and a part-time, unpaid, civilian police commissioner working at Parker Center just one morning a week—agreed to make on-the-spot phone calls to local hotels requesting they house and feed the out-of-town cops.

Meanwhile, Charlie Beck and his fellow sergeants continued standing around, leaders without troops, while lieutenants without personnel lists were trying to get some names down on paper. Beck had expected to see four-man squad cars going out with designated missions. Instead, nobody appeared to have a clue about how to even get officers out on the streets. Beck, a second-generation son of the LAPD, had never thought he'd be ashamed of being a Los Angeles police officer. But that night he was.

Andre Christian, Wednesday, April 29, 1992, Riverside County; Jordan Downs Housing Project, Watts

Switching on his television, Andre "Low Down" Christian sat down to catch some news of the acquittals. But his phone began ringing so incessantly that he found it impossible to focus.

For Christian and his friends from back in Watts, the announcement of the acquittals was "the biggest let-down ever." A veteran member of the Grape Street Crips, Christian, like Alfred Lomas, had firsthand experience of how the cops operated in Los Angeles. He had seen police beatings—and not just from the LAPD. The Los Angeles County Sheriff's Department was bad too. Once he'd even gotten choked out just because he'd called a deputy "man" instead of "sir." But the Rodney King beating—he'd never seen any police beating as bad as that. So when he received calls asking him to come into the city to do something about the injustice of those cops going free, he agreed.

Hopping into his '82 rust-colored Cadillac Coupe de Ville, Andre Christian took just over an hour to drive from his Riverside County home east of Los Angeles straight into Watts and the Jordan Downs housing project where he'd grown up.

Christian had moved from Jordan Downs to Riverside County two years earlier, in 1990, when he was twenty-two. He'd always liked watching the local news, and one day he'd seen those big San Bernardino Mountains out east and thought them the perfect place to get away from the violence he'd been involved in since junior high school. His intent, Christian would later recall, was to get a job good enough to pay for rent, gas, food, and taking care of his baby-mama, who wasn't working. But that didn't happen, so he'd quickly fallen back on his second option.

By 1990, the drug market in Watts and Jordan Downs was oversaturated with small and midlevel dealers fighting over too little business. But outside Watts, as Andre Christian saw it, lay opportunity, "all that open land that *nobody* was fighting over," *and* the chance to expand the Grape Street Crips brand into new, virgin territory, "just like when America went to the moon and set down its flag."

Christian was more than up to that job. Tall, dark, and powerfully muscular at 265 pounds, he possessed the self-assurance of a young man who not only liked to fight but was very, very good at it. He'd never been a gun man—that wasn't for him. But being able to seriously hurt someone without compunction and never reveal himself to be a punk was the basis of his self-esteem, and a key determinant of his respect in the projects and the gang pecking order. He was also someone who'd learned the hard way to await opportunity. This was true whether he was dealing drugs, recruiting new members for the Grape, or quietly, strategically conducting the serious business of maintaining his street credibility. He was known for lying low and waiting for just the proper time to avenge an insult or violence committed against him or those close to him—hence the genesis of his "Low Down" street name.

In any case, the Grape Street Crips had a famous, fearsome reputation in their own right, and there were plenty of potential young black recruits in Moreno Valley, the area of Riverside County where Christian now lived. A large number of African-Americans had settled there in the past decade, seeking cheaper housing and refuge from the crime and violence of South Los Angeles. And many of their sons were eager to wear Grape Street's colors—to wear its purple rag around their necks like a cowboy, or wrap it around their foreheads like the Lone Ranger's faithful Indian companion, Tonto.

Christian had no problem "getting young cats to start playin' it on the Grape Street side" and getting them to work as low-level dealers, subcontracted to him as their supplier. It wasn't like he had to *actively* recruit. Within seconds, it seemed, people would click on something he'd said, or key in on his wardrobe, and ask, "Where you from?" It just happened. Exposure to wider experiences was limited out there in Moreno Valley, along with aspirations and options. And an identity like that of the Grape had enormous appeal for young black men in the hip-hop culture of Southern California in the eighties and nineties.

****

The Jordan Downs housing project had been a flashpoint of the Watts Riots twenty-seven years earlier. It was a tough, violent place in which to grow up. And Andre Christian, who lived about two minutes away, hung out there with his cousins until he finally moved in with them when he was twelve. Twenty-five hundred people resided in the projects' low-slung, seven-hundred-unit apartment buildings, which, almost fifty years after their construction as temporary worker-housing during World War II, had acquired the weary patina of an old, mothballed army barracks. In the early nineties, the residents were almost entirely African-American, mostly single mothers raising kids who often had little supervision outside their homes. It was a place not just of broken families but of broken people, where alcoholism and drug addiction were a lifestyle, stability was a pipe dream, and every situation had the potential for violence. It wasn't surprising that it was also the incubator of one of L.A.'s most violent gangs.

Out in the projects' playgrounds and streets, a kid was essentially on his own. If he went to play on the swings, he had to establish his right, through physical force, to play on the swings. If someone tried to take his bike, it was up to him to keep it. Reputations were defined in the sandbox that would follow boys into manhood. There was absolutely no going to the cops or any other authority figure for protection. And if a boy dared bring his mama into any situation, he would be labeled a punk, derided, challenged, and beaten by his peers. That was just the law, the culture of Jordan Downs. If you weren't tough, weren't ready to fight at a moment's notice, you'd either have to stay inside or your mama would have to move the family out.

The other law of Jordan Downs was that the Grape was the bottom line. If you lived there you were destined to be a Grape Street Crip, just like if you lived in Watts's other huge housing project, the 1,054-unit Nickerson Gardens, you were destined to be a Bounty Hunter Blood. Even if you didn't actually join the gang, you'd have to answer the questions "Where you from?" or "Where you stay at?" from gang members across the city. If you answered "Jordan Downs," you'd have to be prepared to take a beating if they had a beef with the Grape.

Christian was fourteen years old and still in junior high school when his cousins Anthony and DeShawn vouched for his acceptance into the Grape Street Crips. The criteria was simple. "You could show no inferiority, no fear, no backing down. If you ever did, you failed the test," says Christian. That same year, 1982, DeShawn was shot in the head and killed after a fight. He was sixteen. In 1983, Christian was shot three times in the back with a .22 over a dispute with a guy who owed his cousin, Gloria, $80. He was fifteen.

Then, in August of 1986, when he was eighteen, Christian got caught in a gang ambush and was shot ten times. He was in Bounty Hunter territory staying over with a lady. When he left that morning one of his car tires was flat. As he was changing it, a short, thin guy suddenly approached him. Calling out his street name, "Low Down," the stranger then pointed a .45 and started shooting. Someone else opened up with a .38 as the shooter with the .45 kept firing away.

The ambulance brought him to Martin Luther King Drew Medical Center in South Los Angeles. The complex was known as "Killer King" as much for its abysmal reputation as an emergency care facility as for the high number of gunshot and knife wounds it regularly treated. The doctors there were so astounded when Christian survived that they pronounced him a medical miracle.

****

From the perspective of young men like Andre Christian and Alfred Lomas, trapped and segregated in places like Watts, the fifteen or so years from the mid-eighties to the late nineties seemed like a potential gold mine, thanks to the easy money to be made from crack cocaine. The drug gave gangs an organizing principle, a financial raison d'être. If your résumé read "high school dropout," the length of your rap sheet far exceeded any work experience you may have accrued, and your only option was a fast-food-wage kind of job in a city teeming with immigrants desperate for work and willing to bust their asses for pocket change, it seemed that opportunity had at last come knocking.

And Grape Street, like other black gangs in Los Angeles, was quick to answer the door. Soon it seemed like all of Jordan Downs High School was wearing T-shirts with "Grape Street" written on the back as an accessory to their purple rags. Twenty or twenty-five kids would show up flashing wads of cash at movies, concerts, malls or sporting events, dominating the scene and doling out beatings. As gang members became flush with cash from distributing and dealing crack, gang-related killings in L.A. County rose from 205 in 1982 to more than 800 a year into the 1990s.

Similar turf-war crack killings were driving up homicide rates to unprecedented levels in cities throughout America, and nobody seemed to know how to stop it. Conservatives found it impossible to comprehend that four hundred years of unspeakable brutality, a closed economic system, and insidious psychological degradation would have the kind of long-lasting, pathological consequences that were now playing out on a subset of the African-American population. Or that a lot of people segregated into an impoverished, racial subculture that mirrored and amplified the state-sponsored violence that maintained it had been damaged in a way that was simply not going to disappear overnight.

So, embracing their righteousness, conservative politicians demonized an entire class of people. And they successfully demanded and got the only solution they were capable of understanding: crime and drug wars that featured deeply inhumane, inflexible, mass incarceration policies such as California's three-strikes law—a law under which hundreds of petty thieves, many from Los Angeles, were sentenced to twenty-five years to life in prison for stealing a steak, $10 worth of sunglasses, a bottle of vitamins, or less than $3 in AA batteries.

Such was the lay of the land when Andre Christian and Alfred Lomas went from hustling to dealing crack cocaine in the early eighties.

****

The introduction of crack into Los Angeles started in about 1982, when America's multibillion-dollar War on Drugs successfully shut down the huge supply of cocaine flowing into south Florida through Cuban distributors connected to Colombian drug cartels. Given the amount of money at stake, a new port of entry for Colombian cocaine quickly sprung up, funneled through already established Mexican marijuana and heroin distribution lines into Los Angeles and Southern California—thus changing the entire dynamic of drug distribution in America. Suddenly there were huge amounts of money bubbling up inside South Los Angeles. African-American dealers like the entrepreneurial "Freeway Ricky Ross" became local legends, and then the gangs found themselves awash in cash.

★★★★★★★★★★★★★★

Powder cocaine in the eighties was not meant for poor people, not at $100 a gram. But then, as the Southern California coke market started becoming saturated, somebody figured out that by mixing powder coke with baking soda and boiling the combination, you could create twice as much product to sell. And *then*, by cutting it up into small pieces before it dried, you could turn the mixture into a hard, solid, smokable substance—"rock," or crack cocaine. The altered form provided an immediate, powerful, euphoric rush far more intense than snorting powder cocaine, while in the process creating a whole new class of insatiable consumers of the drug.

A hit or two of snorted cocaine and you'd be up for hours; a pull or two on a crack pipe would last about twenty minutes, and then you'd want another hit—desperately. Customers would come back sooner and far more often. And because it was so inexpensive—$5, $10, $25, $50, depending on the size of the rock—anybody could scrape up the money to try to keep their high going—making it initially seem to be the perfect ghetto drug.

And Andre Christian, who was nothing if not a son of the ghetto, soon became one of those kids that LAPD sergeant Charlie Beck was trying to bust in crack houses all over South Los Angeles. When he was sixteen, a dealer had set Christian up in a street-level apartment with an opening in the door through which he'd push his $25 or $50 rocks. He began making $300 or more a night, three or four nights a week. To an outsider it might not seem worth the trouble, given the risk. But for a high school kid from the projects, it was a dream come true. He bought new clothes, got a nice car and a regular motel room out by Los Angeles International Airport at the Snooty Fox, one of those rooms with a heart-shaped bed. Suddenly he had so much money he didn't know how to spend it all, and there he was, still just a kid.

Andre Christian, Wednesday, April 29, 1992, Jordan Downs

By 1993, Andre Christian had grown into a businessman—a part-time criminal businessman, to be sure, but one who was trying otherwise to put the thug life behind him. When he arrived in Jordan Downs on that first evening of the riots with his girlfriend and her kids, he'd been anticipating a demonstration. Immediately, however, he saw how wrong he'd been. Everybody was out on the streets and sidewalks talking about revenge. Nobody was yet rioting. But it was clear they were all just waiting for someone to get angry enough or drunk enough to throw that first chunk of concrete and kick it off—something Christian wanted no part of. So he left with his family to check out what was going on farther west, toward Florence and Normandie, where things had already turned ugly. Sensing that they were about to get far worse, he got back on the freeway and headed straight back to Moreno Valley.

As it was with the '65 riots, Watts had become an epicenter of *these* riots as well. That first night, snipers in Nickerson Gardens engaged in deadly firefights with the LAPD, which fired off eighty-eight rounds in defense. "It was anarchy, total anarchy," LAPD lieutenant Michael Hillman told the *Times.* "You had people running in the streets, looting, shooting at and killing firefighters, shooting at the police."

****

By 9 p.m. that night the situation had had grown so critical that Mayor Bradley declared a state of emergency, and California governor Pete Wilson ordered two thousand National Guard troops into Los Angeles over the strident objections of Daryl Gates. By 8 a.m. that following Thursday morning they started arriving at local armories. But it would take until late afternoon before they finally hit the streets. The disastrous delay in deployment was the result of ammunition and other crucial Guard equipment having not arrived in L.A. staging areas until seventeen hours after Governor Wilson had activated the Guard; and because the LAPD and the Guard couldn't agree on where the new troops should be deployed. During that time all hell would break loose across much of Greater Los Angeles.

Alfred Lomas, Thursday, April 30, 1992, Huntington Park, One Block East of South Central L.A.

Like Andre Christian, Alfred Lomas didn't participate in the first night's rioting, staying glued to his crack-house TV instead, watching it all go down. But the next morning, looking to make a profit from the chaos, he hopped into a beat-up, off-white, throwaway Camry with some homeboys and drove down to Pacific Boulevard, Huntington Park's main shopping thoroughfare.

How could they not? There it was, right there on TV: people looting, people rioting, buildings going up in flames, and no cops in sight.

On the boulevard, they first looked for what gang members wanted more than anything else: guns. But it was too late. Others had already methodically looted pawnshops and stores selling firearms through-out South and South Central Los Angeles. "On south Western Avenue [alone]," as the *Los Angeles Times* reported, "suspected gang members broke into the Western Surplus store and carted off as many as 1,700 guns, plus ammunition."

All around Lomas, people were breaking into stores and taking what-ever they wanted. But with his right leg encased in a three-month-old cast—the result of a tibia and fibula broken while he was trying to col-lect on a drug debt—Alfred Lomas couldn't get out of the car and join in the looting. So he sat back and watched as a fat, middle-aged Latina suddenly came into view, laboriously hauling away a looted TV.

Similar scenes were playing out in L.A.'s barrios. In Pico-Union—a port-of-entry section of L.A. crammed with tens of thousands of des-perately poor Salvadoran and other Central American immigrants—stores were being picked clean. Throngs of looters spilled out of tenements and into nearby shopping strips and malls. "At four in the af-ternoon," the great Los Angeles poet Rubén Martínez of the *LA Weekly* reported from the scene, "flames and smoke exploded everywhere in Pico-Union. . . . We should have expected it. This barrio's been on the edge of chaos for years, and the enmity between police and youth is almost as strong as it is in South Central."

Looking at the fat lady, it suddenly dawned on Lomas that this was her moment, not just the moment for gang members like himself to loot gun stores, but the moment for all the looters—many of whom were ordinary, minimum-wage working stiffs stealing what they needed: baby food, diapers, household essentials—to answer with their actions the utter contempt with which they were daily treated. (Later, a Rand Corporation study reported that 51 percent of those arrested during the peak of rioting were Latinos.) Of course, for others, it was just a chance to gather free stuff.

Thursday, April 30, Across L.A.

That very morning in a shopping center north of South Central, at Western Avenue and 17th Street, two big-bellied Latino men joyfully exited a drugstore, one with his fingers around four gallons of burgundy wine, the pockets of his red shorts bulging with pints of whiskey; the other wheeling out a shopping cart entirely filled with AA batteries and Ramses condoms. Meanwhile, four black teenagers strolled out of the center's large Sav-on, each carrying suitcases.

"I got a calculator home," said one.

"I got some ice cream," said another.

A balding black man of about forty wearing a gray ski jacket and gold wire-rimmed glasses walked up and said to the tallest of them, "Man, all the shit you take, it's gonna come back on you. It's real stupid shit you're doin'. Leave it and *respect* yourself."

For a moment the kid looked uncertain, until his friend in a Miami Heat cap told him, "Man, if you feel like you need this, then take it." "Take it?" The man replied, "And give up your respect?" "Fuck respect," Miami Heat shot back as they ambled away. "They don't give us no respect."

Meanwhile, exploding out of their South L.A. epicenter, the riots snaked north and east into similar shopping centers and commercial streets along the Wilshire Boulevard Corridor, into Koreatown, up to Hollywood Boulevard, where sidewalks embedded with bronze stars honoring America's actors and entertainers were run over by looters ransacking the area's cheap tourist-souvenir shops and other stores—including the famed lingerie emporium Frederick's of Hollywood. Soon the South L.A. rioting climbed into Baldwin Hills, home to many of L.A.'s middle-class and wealthy African-Americans. There, a bank's doors were smashed open and thieves stole computers and everything else they could carry. Simultaneously, in the western and southern suburban communities of Culver City, Compton, San Pedro, and Long Beach, the commercial streets were being plundered, as were those inland to the east, in El Monte, Pacoima, and Pomona. "During the day," as the *Los Angeles Times* later reported, "the crush of looters trying to get into and out of store parking lots would create gridlock in many areas of the city."

Michael Yamaki, Thursday, April 30, 1992, Koreatown

Much of the looting throughout the riots was random and opportunistic. But many Korean-owned mom-and-pop convenience stores in South Central were deliberately targeted. Most were run by Korean immigrant families who'd worked 24-7 to establish their foothold in America. But over the years a profound crash of cultures had developed between them and their black customers. Their shops had been among those first set ablaze, and as the violence raged, one of the oft-repeated scenes would be that of Korean owners using weak-flowing garden hoses in futile attempts to douse the flames engulfing their shops.

Like many urban black ghettos, there were astoundingly few major chain supermarkets, large retail stores, or banks in South Los Angeles. Filling the vacuum in residents' daily, routine shopping life—in thrift stores and swap meets as well as liquor stores and minimarts—were Korean immigrants, whose presence had become ubiquitous. From the perspective of many black customers the Koreans were prejudiced, abrasive, condescending, and distrustful—overcharging them by as much as 30 percent more than large retail stores, often refusing to extend much-needed credit, and watching them like hawks. "We trusted them to come into our neighborhoods," said "Big Mike" Cummings, a former Grape Street Crip and now a minister. "But they disrespect us and our kids, won't ever give credit and time to work out paying our bills. You gonna set up a mom-and-pop store, you got to show respect for the community."

From the Korean immigrant shopkeeper's point of view, a significant number of their mostly impoverished customers were potential shoplifters with a sense of entitlement, always ready to rationalize their criminality with a sense of victimhood, always asking for something for nothing.

In the months preceding the riots, the animosity between L.A.'s blacks and its Korean residents had grown particularly poisonous. A year earlier, in 1991, a store security camera captured Latasha Harlins, a fifteen-year-old African-American girl, as she was shot in the back of the head by a Korean shopkeeper following a dispute over whether she was trying to steal a bottle of orange juice. Harlins had put down the juice and was walking out the door when the shopkeeper, Soon Ja Du, opened fire. For Harlins's murder, Du received a sentence from a white judge of five years' probation.

L.A.'s African-American community reacted with stunned outrage; white L.A. with a collective shrug of its shoulders. It was yet another insult black Angelenos were expected to swallow, yet another wound to be rubbed raw and left to fester. And fester it did. What was disagreeable, sometimes heated racial distrust in other cities like New York morphed into a race war in Los Angeles.

On the second day of the riots at least three waves of cars loaded with armed African-Americans targeted hundreds of stores in Koreatown. In the vacuum left by the LAPD, they were met by serious people: Korean men, some of them veterans of a Korean marine corps known for its toughness, armed with shotguns, automatic weapons, and steel pipes. An eighteen-year-old Korean man was killed and three others wounded during hours-long gun battles with hundreds of would-be looters.

Earlier that morning Mike Yamaki and his small, three-patrol-car police caravan had driven through Koreatown en route to Watts. He'd been there the night before, and near the corner of Western and Olympic Yamaki again spotted the very same eyeball he'd seen lying on the same bus bench the preceding evening. And the man it belonged to was still there, still dead and awaiting pickup of his body. The same telephone pole that had been on fire, moreover, was still smoldering. And the same police officers he'd been with the night before were still talking about what kind of protection their small observer group might give people. And Yamaki repeated the same thing he'd told them earlier: "We can't give anyone protection."

Michael Yamaki, Thursday, April 30, 1992, Watts

After leaving Koreatown, Yamaki and his small caravan headed to Watts, where the offices of the Watts Community Action Committee—a social service agency which focused on jobs and assistance for the poor—were being mobbed. The offices and the surrounding complex of stores had risen from the ashes of the Watts Riots of '65 in hopes of stemming the despair and rage that had caused that earlier insurrection. Today, however, about two hundred rioters were giving no thought to that fact. They looted and set the complex aflame, destroying not only the offices but also the commercial enterprises within the complex—whose earnings, as the *Times* pointed out, "helped pay for a homeless shelter, job training center, and a senior citizens' housing project."

What would stick in Yamaki's mind years later, however, was the turmoil emanating from a different source: Cops from departments outside the city were streaming into Watts by late Thursday afternoon, alongside the National Guard. They were ready and eager for some serious stick-time, but were running around without direction. "We [the LAPD] didn't have anything ready for them," says Yamaki. "All we could do was ask them to cover a particular area, but we couldn't *tell* officers we just met from other departments what to do."

Finally, Yamaki and his entourage headed to the Wilshire Division station house for a breather, arriving at about 4 p.m. The division captain quickly asked Yamaki to jump into his role of police commissioner and address the troops. Yamaki tried, but had nothing to say. Outside the station house, fires blazed. Nobody seemed to know how to bring some order to the situation. And Mike Yamaki was no exception.

****

Meanwhile, Andre Christian, having returned to Moreno Valley, remained sitting in his chair watching the riots live on TV, shaking his head in disbelief. "The cops, they'd waited just too long to respond," Christian thought as he watched the riots spread that initial Wednesday night and into Friday. "Too many people were engaged now, too many supporting it. The gangsters, yeah, they were there. But there were just a lot of regular, normal citizens too."

****

Historically, Los Angeles's black citizens had always gotten the worst of both worlds when it came to cops and crime. Living in hyper-segregated communities crippled by violence, gangs, crack, and poverty, they were desperate for protection from a police department whose chief seemed to have no idea how to intelligently address their concerns. Instead, Daryl Gates led an army of occupation that waged war on the residents of black South L.A., Mexican East L.A., and Central American Pico-Union in the name of crime suppression.

Yet those residents weren't feeling any safer. The streets, in fact, were even more dangerous, despite the fact that those very residents were daily seeing a cop, talking to a cop, or interacting with somebody who'd just encountered a cop. And therein lay not just a problem but the heart of the matter. In the 1970s, ex–LAPD officer turned novelist Joseph Wambaugh put a name to the LAPD's self-image and their perception of their job. "The New Centurions," he called them.

And ever since Bill Parker's reign in 1950, that's exactly how the LAPD had policed: aggressively confronting and commanding anyone with whom they came in contact, owning the streets, and stomping out the street lice. The definition of "lice" was extremely broad and zealously adhered to. As Gates later boasted: "If someone looked out of place in a neighborhood, we had a little chat with him. If a description of a thief could be obtained, we stopped everyone fitting that description, even if it meant angering dozens of innocent citizens. . . . Using these proactive tactics [the] LAPD . . . became the most aggressive police department in the country."

Aggressive policing was more than just an LAPD modus operandi, however; it was a career-advancement imperative. Reputations were made and promotions bestowed based on high arrest numbers and, as David Dotson once put it, by "pounding the fear of God into people." Making lots of arrests was the measure of the man, the gold standard of one's worth among peers and supervisors—not just *one way* to achieve a public safety goal, but the goal itself. Few, however, dared question if aggressive policing correlated to *effective* policing. Instead, stepping out of the LAPD's narrow tactical and philosophical box, and using one's experience to develop new crime prevention strategies, was cause to be branded an upstart, a malcontent, a subversive.

Patrol was consequently looked upon as a dead end, dominated—as Wambaugh once wrote—by "super-aggressive twenty-two-year-olds, full of testosterone . . . absolutely immortal, and unable to admit [or] verbalize fear, even to themselves." This was not exactly a revelation, and certainly not exclusive to the LAPD. Tens of thousands of white cops who grew up in segregated white neighborhoods and went on to work in black areas in the decades preceding the '92 riots knew that feeling described by Wambaugh. Seeped in the racism of white America, and usually no more than high school educated, they policed a historically abused people whose experience and worldview most couldn't begin to fathom—a people who were also continually subject to the criminal behavior of a small but significant number of their own neighbors. For most of those white cops, their initial reaction was bewilderment followed by disgust and contempt—emotions that justified their special task of keeping all those racially segregated have-nots away from the white-skinned haves by using the violent power of the state.

James Baldwin, that prophetic messenger of what it meant to be black in Jim Crow America, spelled out the experience in the sixties in his book *Nobody Knows My Name*: "He is facing, daily and nightly, people who would gladly see him dead, and he knows it. He moves . . . therefore, like an occupying soldier in a bitterly hostile country, which is precisely what, and where, he is."

By its "aggressive" policing philosophy the LAPD was exacerbating what was already a highly charged situation, and literally mandating that Wambaugh's twenty-two-year-olds initiate racially volatile encounters where they'd constantly be challenged. As David Dotson later told the Christopher Commission: "We expect [our officers] to go out and aggressively identify people and investigate people. And that . . . results in police officers bluffing their way into situations, and when they stop people on the street, frequently the guy knows, 'you don't have anything on me' . . . and time after time, we get into these conflict situations that end up frequently with uses of force, frequently with manufacturing . . . probable cause."

Rewarding high arrest numbers might initially have had some merit, had it been part of a wider, long-term crime-prevention strategy. But the LAPD had no such strategy. Instead, as Charlie Beck later pointed out, "it was all search and destroy and blunt-force military tactics and assaults." The philosophy had deadly consequences. "There was a period at the time when I entered the police department in the fifties until 1977 when there was no shooting policy," says Jack White, a former LAPD commander and Police Commission chief investigator. "And this was by design. It was felt that a shooting policy would limit an officer's activities in a department [with] a proactive morality of seek out the criminal and take action. [Consequently], we shot people running away from us for a long time." As a result, among the police departments of the six largest cities in the United States, the LAPD ranked number one in killing or wounding the largest number of civilians, when adjusted for the number of officers on the force.

What made it all so maddening was the same-old, same-old nature of the problem. In 1980, Gates had only been chief for two years when the American Jewish Committee, the Urban League, and the National Conference of Christians and Jews released a study of the LAPD's treatment of the black community fifteen years after the Watts Riots. It concluded that virtually nothing had changed in terms of the department's abusive treatment of African-Americans. A year later, in 1981, LAPD deputy chief Lou Reiter warned in a retirement speech that the police in South Central had become "a hard-charging street army" that had "developed the philosophy that everyone who is black is a bad guy."

During his tenure as chief, from 1978 to 1992, Daryl Gates not only failed to address the problem, he made it worse. In pursuit of his war, Gates expanded the LAPD's traditional deployment of techno-cop machines and military tactics. Eighteen Bell Jet Ranger or French Aerospatiale helicopters with state-of-the-art surveillance technology would regularly circle deafeningly low in the city's ghettos and barrios. Sixteen-round, 9mm, double-action, semiautomatic Berettas had become the department's standard-issue sidearm. Search-and-destroy missions like the infamous 1988 raid on South Central's Dalton Avenue became an integral part of the department's drug war. Fierce-looking, heavily armed officers from the department's special-unit Metro Division—the department's "elite" shock troops—were deployed at the first hint of trouble, or just to make a point. By tradition, Metro's officers were pulled from the toughest divisions. Their mission, as Daryl Gates once described it, was to "roust anything strange that moved on the streets." And they did, brutally, at demonstrations, marches, and rallies, or in areas like South Central when things looked hot. And in 1988, they had been sizzling indeed—a prelude to the pot that would boil over into the flames now engulfing Los Angeles.

****

Separated by great distances, and cursed with a slow, inefficient mass transit system, street crime in Los Angeles is more a local, neighborhood affair than in more densely packed cities. But in January of 1988, there occurred an exception to the rule. As twenty-three-year-old Karen Toshima was strolling through Westwood she got caught in the crossfire between two warring black gangs and was shot in the head and killed. Toshima was just one of ninety-six homicide victims killed by alleged gang members in the city of Los Angeles in the first five months of 1988. Ninety-five of them were just business as usual.

Toshima's, however, had taken place in Westwood, a once small college town abutting UCLA. Over the years, it had grown into a commercial hub of restaurants, movie theaters, shops, and high-rise office buildings surrounded by the homes of the wealthy inhabitants of residential Westwood, Brentwood, Holmby Hills, Bel Air, and a string of million-dollar condos known as the Gold Coast. Consequently, not only did the largely white upper middle class feel threatened by Toshima's killing, but *Entertainment Tonight*'s wealthy "Hollywood Royalty" did as well. So while Toshima's shooting was an anomaly notable only for occurring where it did, it set off a furor. If you weren't safe in Westwood, where *were* you safe? In response, Daryl Gates ordered "Operation Hammer."

Crudely conceived, Operation Hammer was a series of LAPD "gang sweeps" during which streets were barricaded, police poured into South L.A., and at least twenty-five thousand overwhelmingly black men of all ages were corralled and arrested. The arresting officers' orders, as once summed up by a department spokesman, were simultaneously extremely vague and startlingly clear: "Pick 'em up for anything and everything."

Posting those massive arrest numbers took diligence as well as brute force and imagination. Using techniques they'd employed for decades in black L.A., motorcycle and patrol officers multiplied their justification for initiating stops, issuing tickets, and making arrests. Cars parked twenty-three inches from the curb when the law said it should be eighteen were ticketed, as were those whose windshield wipers didn't work, or that had a missing floor mat. And if a driver or passenger had an outstanding parking, jaywalking, or traffic violation, it was off to jail. Alternately, officers would *find* a reason to deem a car "unsafe" and have it hauled off to an impoundment yard where it would sit, gathering daily fines so large that many owners couldn't pay them and consequently would lose their vehicles.

Retrospectively, it seems astounding that such a plan of concentrated, indiscriminate mass arrests would be executed in a major, liberal American city a quarter of a century into the post–civil rights era. But then, in Los Angeles the tactic had a predicate: The LAPD had pioneered the modern use of the big-city police "dragnet" way back in the 1920s, when its officers would regularly fan out across ten or twelve major boulevard intersections for no particular reason and stop to examine all passing vehicles in an effort to ferret out any "suspicious characters." The tactical deployment apparently left such an indelible imprint on Jack Webb's imagination that in the late 1940s he named history's most famous LAPD radio/TV show after those infamously indiscriminate fishing expeditions.

Daryl Gates's sweeps of 1988 cast an equally wide net. In one, tracked by the *Los Angeles Times*, the DA filed just 103 cases out of more than 1,400 arrests.

But the sweeps weren't only ineffectual and mindless. They were extraordinarily counterproductive as well. "What the LAPD was missing," as Charlie Beck would later point out, was that its strategy of declaring war on vast swaths of the city and arresting everybody it could was "completely eroding the department's moral authority. The city's gang members hadn't dropped from the sky into a vacuum. They all had fathers, mothers, classmates, neighbors. And on the street, everybody wanted to get along with them because they had a huge presence and physical authority. By becoming everybody's common enemy and building a collective animosity toward us [the police], it gave the gangsters a tremendous authority and strength—like 'the enemy of my enemy is my friend.'"

Beck was right. Flush with federal funds, the intensity of the LAPD's war on drugs and crime provided the rationalization for the criminalization of entire communities. Black and brown kids on the fringes of gangs were automatically labeled the enemy. The LAPD put a lot of serious thugs in prison. No doubt about it. But they were also arresting tens of thousands marginal drug dealers, users, petty criminals, and small-time hustlers, some of whom would then be sentenced to decades-long prison terms under California's three-strikes law.

And to what end? As crime rates continued to rise, California saw its annual corrections budget top $11 billion, as over a third of state's prisoners flowed in from Los Angeles County. Meanwhile, the collateral damage that not just the LAPD but the entire criminal justice system were inflicting on the city's poor black and brown communities was incalculable: kids traumatized and grandmothers terrorized during no-

toriously abusive raids and sweeps; records hung on marginal or innocent teenagers and young men that would kill their already slim chances
of getting a job; families broken up and made even more impoverished
by long mandatory prison terms. Most of it did nothing to get at the
root of the problem. But Daryl Gates and his LAPD would just keep
doing what they did, which was all they knew or, worse, wanted to
know.

****

The LAPD's New Centurion policing philosophy and California's mass
incarceration policies, in short, were only further destabilizing the city's
low-income neighborhoods while dooming its young. More than one in
three young black men in Los Angeles was either in jail or prison or on
probation or parole on any given day. It was an astounding figure, but
one nevertheless that was similar to many other big American cities.

As was an additional consequence: death by police officer. During
the seventies and eighties, hundreds of unarmed people were shot or
choked to death by LAPD officers with virtual impunity. Often they
were shot while holding nothing more than a typewriter, a sweatshirt,
a wallet, keys, sunglasses, a silver bracelet, a hairbrush, a flashlight, a
liquor decanter, a bathrobe in a shower, or, sometimes, nothing at all.
From 1980 to 1986, for example, there were 372 shootings by LAPD
officers. Many of those shot were unarmed, but no officer was ever indicted. Only one was fired.

The secretive LAPD stakeout unit known as the Special Investigation
Section, or the SIS, in fact, had been assigned to what amounted to a kill
mission. The unit's purpose was to follow repeat burglars, rapists, and
armed robbers and wait for them to commit a new crime. In the case
of the armed robbers, the SIS developed a tactical policy of watching
and waiting until *after* a robbery occurred before taking action. Most
big-city police departments didn't have full-time surveillance squads like
the SIS, and most would never have allowed an armed robbery to take
place before intervening. It was too dangerous. One in three people involved in armed robberies got hurt, according to U.S. Justice Department statistics at the time. Nevertheless, the SIS's goal became not to

protect the people being robbed but to surprise and shoot the robbers immediately after the robbery as a way of taking them permanently off the street. Between 1967 and 1990, the SIS would shoot and kill twenty-three people and wound at least twenty-three more as they exited banks and stores. In 1988, the *Los Angeles Times* examined thirty-two shootings by the SIS and found that in twenty-eight of them the suspects had not fired at the officers, and that "SIS detectives over the years had shot 13 unarmed people."

There were other costs as well. Gates's "aggressive enforcement" policy was costing the city a fortune in excessive-force lawsuit settlements—$11.1 million in 1990, over $14.5 million in 1991. Rodney King was award $3.8 million in a civil suit against the city, and Hall of Fame baseball star and broadcaster Joe Morgan won $540,000 in another federal lawsuit after he'd been thrown to the ground and handcuffed by an LAPD officer for the sin of looking like the prosperous black man he was at the city's airport, and therefore a suspected drug courier.

The Christopher Commission Report detailed additional cases, far worse. A suspect in handcuffs and leg restraints was placed on an open driveshaft of a police vehicle and, with a police officer sitting atop him on a seat, driven to the station house. On the way he received "large third-degree burns requiring skin grafts" and was awarded a $28,500 settlement. There was no LAPD investigation, and no officer was disciplined. In another case, a "white male" who was in custody for outstanding traffic warrants "lost two teeth and suffered multiple concussions resulting in permanent brain damage" when officers punched him "over 15 times in the face, kicked him in the groin, and slammed his head against the floor." The city attorney recommended settling the case for $300,000. The LAPD suspended two of the officers involved for five and ten days, respectively. One of them "received seven [more] complaints between January 1886 and December, 1990. The other had 12 complaints . . . during the same period."

To Daryl Gates the suits were nonsense—people without legitimate complaint were suing because they were eager to get big settlements from "sympathetic juries." The same was true of those suing the department's canine units. Gates would explain away the extraordinarily high number of LAPD dog bites by blaming the victims, pointing out that the department's dogs were "the sweetest, gentlest things you'll ever find, who only bite if attacked."

The lawsuits provided compensation and a measure of vindication to the victims. But they didn't change how the department operated. Like William Bratton in New York, Daryl Gates had attended the Harvard Kennedy School of Government sessions that were then developing community policing strategies as alternatives to paramilitary policing. But Gates's obsession with brute-force suppression nevertheless continued unabated, despite the fact that it wasn't working.

Violent crime had risen dramatically from 1960 to 1989 across America. But in Los Angeles crimes reported per person grew at twice the national average. At the same time, the number of unsolved murders was piling up. By 2000, Los Angeles would have eight thousand unsolved murders, about 75 percent of which were gang-related killings. And, after hundreds of thousands of arrests, L.A.'s gangs were not simply growing but metastasizing.

Charlie Beck, Late Eighties to Early Nineties, Watts

For the vast majority of LAPD officers working areas like South Central and housing projects like Jordan Downs, their experience in the years leading up to the riots was searing, "wild and chaotic," as Charlie Beck once described it, "on both the community and police sides."

Once Beck was on a robbery stakeout in Watts. The task was to stop purse snatchers from the Nickerson Gardens Projects from sprinting across a major intersection, smashing the car windows of female drivers, and grabbing their purses as they sat backed up at long red lights.

Suddenly a smash-and-grab occurred. Beck, sitting in a backup response vehicle, followed the lead response car as it zoomed out to catch the perpetrator. As they sped out of the projects and onto the main street, the lead car smashed into a speeding Cadillac, killing one of the officers almost instantly. The wheels of the car seemed to still be spinning as Beck pulled his fellow officer from the vehicle and started administering CPR. A large crowd quickly gathered. Their hatred was palpable. "Why you workin' on him? Why not the brother? Go work on the brother [in the Cadillac]." Meanwhile, Beck's partner was dying before his eyes because he'd been trying to protect innocent women driving through *their* neighborhood.

It was then that Charlie Beck began to develop the white-cop-in-the-ghetto attitude so prevalent during the era. To develop that combination of hatred, fear, and utter incomprehension at the crazed, hopped-up violence he was seeing. And to begin to transfer his disgust at "the actions of the 5 percent" doing the crimes to the entire population of the area. He saw himself "becoming very affected by the drama [of his] everyday existence," and by seeing how jaded the older cops he was working with—"the Vietnam vets, the very old-school LAPD—had grown." Feeling himself slipping into the insane logic of it all, he asked for a transfer out of the Southeast Division, and got it.

****

The LAPD wasn't the only institution in the city bereft of ideas other than the big stick. Ira Reiner, the white, Democratic district attorney, offered up his own solution, declaring that his office would stop plea-bargaining and "use each occasion that a gang member was arrested for a crime, no matter how minor, to remove him from the streets for as long as possible."

Reiner was understandably frustrated at being unable to stem gang violence. But there were over seventy thousand young men in Los Angeles identified as gang members. "Well under five percent [of gang members]," however, were "engaged in serious criminal violence," according to a 1989 study done by UCLA. Many more were only loosely affiliated with their neighborhood gangs, and some were not involved in crime at all. But all a police officer had to do was conduct a "field interview" and fill out a card identifying a kid as a gang member, and he became one, no crime or proof required.

No matter. Reiner would take his lock-them-all-up approach one step further and suggest that an entire generation of L.A.'s marginal young, nonwhite males needed not simply to be locked up but "written off" as beyond hope.

But Gates's sweeps and Reiner's casually racist remarks barely registered with most white Angelenos. The truth—the hard, ugly, tribal truth—was that the city's power brokers and its politically liberal middle-class electorate simply did not care about L.A.'s poor black and brown population, or at least did not care *enough* to demand meaningful, comprehensive action to stem the violent deaths of over ten thousand of L.A.'s young men from 1970 to 1990. It was too hard, politically risky, and expensive. Too difficult to figure out how to do. It was far easier for their hearts to bleed over human rights abuses in then totalitarian regimes in South Africa, Central America, and the Soviet Union. At home, keeping the violence of the city's ghettos and barrios from spilling over into their neighborhood, and threatening their families and property values, was the real bottom line.

Curtis Woodle, Thursday, April 30, 1992, Los Angeles Police Academy, Elysian Park

Early Thursday morning LAPD sergeant Curtis Woodle drove through the lush, secluded confines of Elysian Park to the Los Angeles Police Academy, where he was working as a training officer. At thirty, Woodle stood six feet, seven inches tall, weighed 270 pounds, and had shoulders so wide, and a physique so massively muscled, that he appeared ready to burst through his tailored LAPD blues at any moment.

A veteran LAPD officer, he'd known all about the LAPD and its tactics long before he'd joined the department. He had grown up in South Central in the Blood gang territory of the Six Deuce Brims, but had stayed away from them. His mother was a no-nonsense woman who raised him and his two brothers and three sisters in a two-bedroom home while she cleaned other people's houses. She made sure that when Woodle left their house, it was only to go to school, attend football practice, make deliveries on his paper route, or do yard work for the neighbors.

Consequently, Woodle never got into trouble. Nevertheless, the

LAPD treated him as if he were a gang member, subjecting him to the same treatment generations of African-American males in Los Angeles had experienced as a pervasive rite of passage: routine vehicle stops and car tosses for no discernible reason, equally regular walking-down-the-street stop-and-frisks enhanced by curbside prone-outs and handcuffs.

Over the decades, what was once a peculiar, unique LAPD ritual had permeated the national police mentality. David Dotson observed it developing. "Watch any episode of [the TV reality show] *Cops*," he'd once pointed out. "Everything is overkill. Look at the tactics and techniques—most of which were pioneered by us and rippled out all over the country. Everything is 'down-on-the-ground' high volume. That's what we [the LAPD] taught in the name of officer safety."

On at least a dozen occasions, Woodle had been stopped and put through some variation of the routine: lean over and support your weight on your hands atop the hot hood of an idling patrol car; or get down on your knees with hands clasped behind your neck, and closely and immediately follow barked order after barked order. Be prepared for their constant mind games, for them to try to lay something on you, to make you feel like a chump, or "to find a reason," says Woodle, "to kick your ass."

When he was seventeen, an LAPD patrol car slowly cruised by Curtis Woodle's house as he and his younger brother were fixing Woodle's car in the driveway. The vehicle's rear end was slightly extended out to the sidewalk, and when the white cop asked if he wanted a ticket, Woodle replied, "No, do you?" Jumping out of his black-and-white, the officer responded immediately by beating Woodle's much smaller younger brother—who had said not one word—with his billy club and chasing him into the house, where he'd fled to escape, knocking down the boys' mother in the process. Meanwhile the cop's partner shoved the barrel of his gun into Woodle's face and ordered him not to move.

The incident left a deep impression on Curtis Woodle. He would vow to join the LAPD one day and work from within to change a department that was producing officers who would terrorize a law-abiding family over a three-word comment, without any fear of being held accountable.

Which didn't mean that Curtis Woodle, once in the department, hadn't sipped from the cup of the LAPD's special Kool-Aid. There was a difference, as he saw it, between the cop who'd billy-clubbed his brother and those who'd assaulted Rodney King. His brother had done nothing wrong. There was a right way, a courteous way to deal with people you stopped to "interview" on the street or who had committed minor infractions. Rodney King, on the other hand, "had just led officers on a high-speed chase, had been breaking laws, not truly following orders, probably had alcohol in his system, wouldn't go down, and was on his knees, which meant he still had some control of the situation." It was the *tactics* that the officers used, Woodle felt, that were wrong. What he would have done instead was "choke him out and try to stop the situation quickly."

But in 1982 LAPD officers, never trained for doing things halfway, had essentially been banned from using their baton or forearm in a choke hold technique that cut off oxygen to a suspect's carotid artery until he passed out. Departments in New York, Chicago, San Francisco, and Dallas had also been using the hold in dangerous and violent situations, and had recorded one choke hold death each during the period from 1975 to 1982. The LAPD, whose policy was to routinely use the hold, had racked up fifteen such deaths in the same time frame, causing such an uproar that the Police Commission finally forbade the choke hold's use. The ban, as Curtis Woodle saw it, left officers with little option but to use their batons in other ways, a bad alternative, because a baton beating "looked so terrible, so crazy." The King beating being a prime example. "Yet even that, years ago, would have been okay, because it was done all the time," thought Woodle. Now, however "people just weren't willing to put up with that kind of stuff anymore."

The cadet class Curtis Woodle had been teaching had just graduated that past Friday, and many had already been deployed into the riot zones. But not Woodle.

The afternoon before, after finishing work at about 3 p.m., Woodle was driving home in his burgundy four-door Coupe de Ville, when he tuned in to a local black talk-radio show. Blaring forth was an astounding, unbroken string of callers responding to the Simi Valley "not guilty" verdicts. They were ferocious in their reaction and sometimes tongue-tied in their indignation. Woodle immediately understood that, unlike previous LAPD scandals, this one wasn't simply going to blow over. In fact, the more he listened to the outrage of his fellow black Angelenos on his long drive home to the secluded, overwhelmingly white suburb of Walnut, the more he became convinced that the ramifications were going to be far worse than he'd ever imagined.

Back at his house, he'd waited for instructions from the department about what to do, where to report. But nobody called. Finally he fell asleep on his living room sofa, watching the scene at Florence and Normandie. At about 9 p.m. he awoke to the streets of L.A. going up in flames, shut off the TV, and went to bed.

Now, arriving back at the academy for his morning shift, he quickly realized neither he nor the rest of the training staff was on anybody's radar screen, let alone detail roster, and that they weren't going to be ordered to report anywhere. So they simply sat around for the rest of the day talking about the chaos that was exploding live on television while doing nothing about it. Periodically they'd break from their bull sessions to pass out shotguns and ammo to patrol cars coming in. That was their workday. At about two-thirty in the afternoon, Woodle clocked out and drove home, disgusted.

That Thursday evening, as the second day of the riots drew to a close, Woodle watched on his TV screen as an L.A. County Sheriff's Department bus pulled up to a grocery store that was being looted. About twenty deputies piled out and ordered fifty or sixty looters on the ground and then handcuffed them, arrested them, and loaded them onto the bus. The LAPD wasn't doing that. The LAPD, as Woodle saw it, was sitting on its hands, and he—like the rest of the department—wasn't doing any policing. That, he decided, at least for him, was going to change.

Alfred Lomas, Thursday, April 30, 1992, Florencia 13 Crack House

Thursday night, back at the dope house, Alfred Lomas felt like he was at a swap meet, what with all the addicts bringing in their Payless shoes, televisions, appliances, and every other kind of stolen good to trade or to sell for crack.

Lomas himself was a self-described "fearsome dope fiend," addicted not only to crack but also to alcohol and pills, so much so that blacking out had become a standard part of getting wasted. He'd begun smoking joints with his cousins when he was nine, and drinking not long afterward. He started getting arrested and serving time for shoplifting, commercial burglaries, assaults, and petty thefts. Nevertheless, in between stints in jail and prison, he still managed to function as a valued gang member. Born into a family of alcoholics and criminals, Lomas was a fourth-generation Mexican-American from San Antonio, Texas, who'd moved with his family into the Maravilla housing project in East Los Angeles in 1965, when he was one year old.

The Maravilla Projects were to impoverished Mexicans what Jordan Downs was to blacks: a vast expanse of about five hundred apartment units ruled by some of L.A.'s most notorious gangs—Lopez Maravilla, Lota Maravilla, Arroyo Maravilla. Lomas's mother found employment cleaning houses and supported the family, while his father, a serious alcoholic who came from a long line of hard drinkers, stayed drunk and didn't work—which, says Lomas, "was considered just normal Maravilla behavior back then."

Lomas, it turned out, also came from what would become a long line of murderers. One of his father's brothers, as Lomas tells it, was convicted of murder in a fight in downtown L.A. in the late sixties; one of his cousins committed an execution-style murder at the age of fifteen; and three others ambushed and killed one of his uncles over a drug dispute.

In 1969, his family moved from the Maravilla Projects to the seedy, run-down sliver of Huntington Park where Mexicans were permitted to live. Located just one block away from South Central's black ghetto, it too was saturated with gangs. No more than twenty feet from Lomas's new Huntington Park home was a deadly gang clique—kids fifteen or sixteen who would grow first into gang heavy-hitters and then into California prison lifers, or corpses.

Lomas's story from that point on was as standard as a slice of American apple pie—an uncanny echo of the Irish gangs of New York in the nineteenth century and the Italian and Jewish gangs that followed in the early twentieth century and grew into the powerful organized-crime syndicates that flourished during and after Prohibition.

By the early 1980s, when Alfred Lomas was coming of age, Los Angeles's Mexican street gangs were primed to move on from warring over territory, insults, and heroin distribution to dealing crack cocaine. They'd been part of the city's landscape since at least the 1920s, and for young kids like Lomas their violent machismo culture offered status in a world in which they otherwise felt frightened, marginalized, and powerless. It was therefore nearly preordained that when some older gangsters in an apartment building next door invited him to join Florencia 13 at the age of thirteen, he jumped at the chance.

One of the largest and most notorious gangs in L.A., Florencia 13 had a reputation as a treacherous street-fighting organization dating back to the 1940s, and was far better organized than black gangs like the Grape Street Crips. Lomas thought then and still does now that it "was an honor just to be a member." Becoming part of some other, smaller local street gang, as Lomas later analogized it, would be like "getting an A in a class at a small community college," whereas being a Florencia gangster was akin to "earning a Harvard MBA with honors."

Florencia was later labeled a "super" or "regional" gang by the U.S. Justice Department. Its territory was huge, covering the entire east side of South Central Los Angeles and flowing into L.A. County. Its numbers would eventually grow to three or four thousand, but no one really knew the gang's exact population—not the feds, not the local cops, not the academics, not even the gang members themselves. Like Jordan Downs and Watts, much of Florencia's territory, unsurprisingly, was an epicenter of the riots.

Charlie Beck, Thursday, April 30, 1992, Los Angeles Coliseum

Thursday night Charlie Beck reported back to the operations center at the Los Angeles Coliseum for his second twelve-hour midnight shift.

That morning, LAPD patrol cars had begun escorting fire trucks into riot areas. Yet they were still ignoring the looting. At the shopping center at Western Avenue and 17th Street, looting was brazenly, festively under way as two hook-and-ladder fire engines guarded by four LAPD police cars—each packed with five officers in riot gear—pulled into the parking lot. The twenty officers never got out of their patrol cars. The firefighters quickly looked around, saw no fires had been set, and pulled back out as the looting continued unabated.

Tom Bradley, Thursday, April 30, 1992, Los Angeles

After conferring with Mayor Bradley overnight, California governor Pete Wilson requested that President George H. W. Bush send federal troops into Los Angeles. Soon three thousand soldiers and fifteen hundred U.S. Marines began arriving. They would join the two thousand National Guard soldiers already deployed and three thousand more recently activated by Wilson. Dressed in full combat gear and hard-plastic face shields, and armed with M16s and other weapons, they rolled out to riot hotspots in armored personnel carriers. Many were accompanied by law enforcement agents from throughout California, as well as one thousand FBI agents, U.S. Marshals, and border patrol agents from as far away as Texas.

Meanwhile, a nervous, almost trembling Rodney King was holding a press conference for about a hundred reporters outside his lawyer's office in Beverly Hills. It was painful to behold. There stood Rodney King, emotionally spent and naked before the world, forcing himself to speak, and managing nevertheless to deliver what the *Los Angeles Times* would later correctly describe as "a halting plea for peace that, in its rambling, elliptical, tragic quality, became one the most memorable moments in the Los Angeles Riots." "Can we get along?" King famously asked. "I mean, please, we can get along here. . . . We've just got to, just got to. We're all stuck here for a while. . . . Let's try to work it out. Let's [just] try to work it out."

In the end, it would take more than twenty thousand police and soldiers enforcing a stringent dusk-to-dawn curfew that night to get it, if only temporarily, worked out, and finally finished by Friday's end.

Andre Christian, Saturday, May 2, 1992, Jordan Downs

On Saturday morning, Andre Christian pulled his car into Jordan Downs. For much of the city it was cleanup time, an event recorded in the media with pictures of people sweeping up with brooms and shoveling debris into wheelbarrows, with a smiling Mayor Bradley looking on. But in Jordan Downs it was self-congratulation time, party time.

Everyone from Watts and the surrounding area was joining together with the Grape for a gigantic block party. Bloods, Crips, the 8 Treys, and the Rolling 60s were all mingling together, drinking, laughing, and getting high. To Christian it was a strange scene. People who a week before would have killed each other had they met were now celebrating the destruction of their own neighborhoods. They reveled in the afterglow of closed stores, shut-off phone lines and electricity, suspended mail delivery, and broken telephone poles and trees, which had been used as fuel for raging fires that incinerated their local strip malls. Throughout Los Angeles, in fact, rioters just like them had caused the shutting down of schools, libraries, banks, courthouses, shopping malls, and train and bus service—the very services on which they and the rest of the city relied.

But as many of the people of Jordan Downs and much of black L.A. saw it, it was more than worth the cost. They'd finally fought back against a racist, stacked-deck system brutally enforced by the LAPD. It was a great day, full of joy, full of satisfaction, full of promise. And now, thanks to the LAPD and that clueless Simi Valley jury that had inadvertently laid the groundwork, their gangs were in a position to become even more powerful.

Curtis Woodle, Saturday, May 2, 1992,
Florence and Normandie

The festivities in Jordan Downs were just heating up when Curtis Woodle wheeled his black-and-white through the intersection of Florence and Normandie—the very spot where it had all started—and came to an abrupt stop. With him in the patrol car were three California state prison guards, part of the contingent of sworn California peace officers brought in to help halt the riots.

Woodle hated what he saw at the intersection. The city may have been beginning its cleanup, but the corner of Florence and Normandie was still a quasi–hot spot. A homeless guy, clearly intoxicated, with wild hair and filthy, ragged clothing, was directing traffic in the center of the intersection, wielding a shovel, as Woodle later related, like a conductor's baton. On the corner, six or seven LAPD officers were standing around, watching.

"What's with this guy?" Woodle asked the sergeant in charge. "We're just letting it happen," he was told. "We don't want to make any waves." Meaning, as Woodle understood it, that they didn't want to rile up the crowd. People were still firing off celebratory bullets in the air; they could hear the shots. But Woodle wasn't having it. Florence and Normandie had been his beat, his *stomping ground*, when he had been a CRASH officer. He knew that the territory surrounding the intersection was controlled by the 8 Trey Gangster Crips, and that they were using this homeless guy as a patsy, like a character in some kind of weird, satirical performance, with him—LAPD sergeant Curtis Woodle and everything he stood for—as the butt of the joke.

But it was more than that. Woodle was a black man in a white department with a racist history he was trying to change. And the shovel-man was directing the traffic by race. If you were black or brown, you didn't have to stick around, you'd be waved on through. If you were white or Asian, you weren't going anywhere, not on that guy's watch. And there was one more thing: For three days, Woodle—a native son of South Central Los Angeles—had watched his old neighborhood become engulfed in flames, violence, and looting. And he had done *nothing*.

Even now, Woodle's hands were tied. He was outranked at the scene, so he headed back to the 77th Street station house and received permission from a deputy chief to take another patrol car filled with officers as backup to move the guy off the intersection. But when he called for volunteers among the cops hanging around the station, not a hand shot up. His only option was to return to Florence and Normandie with just the three state prison guards.

Woodle deployed them on three of the four sides of the intersection, where they provided cover with shotguns. Then, related Woodle, he adjusted his riot helmet and strode up to the homeless guy. "Hey, man," he said, "I appreciate what you've been doing, but I'll take over from here." They locked eyes, and the man suddenly gripped the shovel very hard. Woodle moved close enough so that only the shovel-man could hear. "If you raise that shovel," Woodle told him, "I will kill you." And with that, the shovel-man moved off his stage and onto the sidewalk as the city and its shell-shocked police department settled back into an uneasy, unresolved calm.

Charlie Beck, Saturday, May 2, 1992, Coliseum

Charlie Beck also stayed busy that Saturday, shutting down the Coliseum command post. The last year, as Beck and many of his fellow officers saw it, had been horrific. But it had also been inevitable.

After all, the same bleak economic conditions and spiraling violence that existed in Los Angeles's ghettos and barrios in 1992 had also existed, in varying degrees, in most big cities across America since the 1960s. Back then, over 125 cities, from New York, Philadelphia, and Washington, DC, to Chicago, Milwaukee, and Detroit and on to San Francisco *and* Los Angeles, had erupted in violent rebellion. But in the nineties, Los Angeles stood almost entirely alone. The only difference was the LAPD.

In the wake of the riots, President George H. W. Bush declared Los Angeles County a disaster area, making it eligible for federal relief, and flew out to L.A. on Air Force One to personally tour the riot area as if it had been hit by some kind of category 4 Gulf Coast hurricane.

Connie Rice, Saturday, May 2, 1992, Jordan Downs

Shortly after the riots a lawyer named Connie Rice drove to Jordan Downs to see how she might help. Rice was the codirector of the Los Angeles office of the NAACP Legal Defense and Educational Fund, a position she held since her arrival in Los Angeles in September of 1990. That day in 1992, Rice had come directly from court in downtown L.A., and was still dressed for the part—all decked out in a business suit, lawyerly blouse, and set of pearls, looking like a self-described "black Republican" matron. But it wasn't just her outfit that made her appear out of place in Jordan Downs.

Although Rice unequivocally identified as an African-American, her heritage on both sides of her family was white as well as black, which sometimes led to confusion. Once, as a twelve-year-old in an Arizona junior high school—a "coal black" classmate and migrant worker's son— had "marched right up" to her, "thrust his ashy frown into [her] chin and blurted out in exasperation, 'What *is* you?'"

As she walked across the grounds of Jordan Downs that day, Rice cut a striking, distinctive figure. At forty-six, she was slim, fine-featured, and youthful-looking, with light-brown skin and a wavy mane of black-brown hair worn long and always perfectly coiffed. Consciously or not, she carried herself like a diva—no-nonsense, self-aware, and straight-ahead—like the dreamy girl she once was, who was now the star in her own movie.

Over the next decade she would become among the most articulate, high-profile political commentators in Los Angeles, a smart, analytical, activist voice in the know about issues people wanted to understand, such as why L.A.'s public transportation and criminal justice systems were so bad. With her style, reputation, and sense of self, she could easily have made the Hollywood party scene. But Rice, it would turn out, had no aspirations and perhaps no ability in that direction. For one thing, she didn't suffer fools lightly. For another, there seemed something of the loner about her, not fond of, interested in, or particularly good at frivolity or congenial, personal small talk.

But on this day in Jordan Downs in April of 1992, Rice was little known in L.A. Born into the black bourgeoisie, she'd yet to earn a dime

of street cred. Her family, she says, was all about "hope and achievement." Her mother had been a high school biology teacher, and her
father, Phillip Leon Rice, Sr., was a career officer in the U.S. Air Force
who'd retired as a major. He'd graduated from Howard University,
having majored in Russian, as had her second cousin, future secretary
of state Condoleezza Rice. Rice herself had graduated from Harvard-
Radcliffe College in 1978 and then went to New York University School
of Law, where she attended on scholarship. There, in her third year of
law school, she'd work long hours each week keeping up with her studies and assisting in capital punishment law cases. Thurgood Marshall
was her hero. She went on to clerk for Judge Damon J. Keith of the
Sixth Circuit Court of Appeals, taking tough cases and getting top cre-
dentials, because, she says, "I wanted people to understand that I *wanted*
to be a civil rights lawyer" and that she "could have been a partner in a
white-shoe law firm making $1 million a year if [she'd] chosen to."

****

Easing her way around the projects, Rice finally found what she was
looking for: a trailer in which Bloods and Crips, their colors wrapped
around their heads, were sitting around at a table negotiating a gang
truce. She'd heard about the negotiations, she told them, and wanted
to help out.

It was the wrong play, trying to support gang truces, Rice would later
learn, because "when you sit down with the Bloods and Crips *as* Bloods
and Crips, you just reinforce the symbols and ethos and dynamics of
the gang. They needed to work and to be worked with, but as *individuals*, as leaders in the neighborhood, as men in their community, sitting
at the table as community leaders." But Rice knew nothing of all this at
the time. For now, she would do what she could to make peace in the
wake of the riots, working for the gang members, as she later put it, as
essentially "a research assistant."

****

Even before Rice reached out to the gang members, she'd become aware
of the LAPD's cavalier brutality through reading headline stories in the

local African-American newspaper, the *Los Angeles Sentinel*. Stories, in particular, about the dogs of the LAPD's sixteen-man K-9 unit running wild and viciously, triumphantly, mauling and badly biting cornered suspects, almost all of whom were black and brown men and boys.

In three years, from January 1989 to January 1992, the dogs had bitten nine hundred people. The Philadelphia PD had twice the number of dogs deployed as did the LAPD during the same period, but the number of suspects bitten totaled just twenty. The LAPD dogs sunk their teeth into 80 percent of the suspects they cornered. In the process they had put more people in the hospital than had their nine thousand human counterparts on the department combined. Forty-seven percent of the canine unit's arrested suspects had to be sent to a hospital. The rest of the force had a less than 1 percent hospital rate.

"None of us opposes safe and effective canine training that enhances the safety of officers, the dogs, and the public," Rice would tell the Los Angeles City Council during a hearing on the issue in January 1992. "We do, however, oppose a 'bite first and ask questions later' policy that results in unleashing the dog to search and automatically bite whomever it tracks: Suspects. Non-suspects. Suspects who are non-threatening. Children. Bystanders. Whomever the dog finds."

But the LAPD's dogs were *trained* to do just that. Biting was their reward for hunting down and cornering or flushing out a suspect. "Find and bite," it was called. Most other police departments used a "circle and bark" approach, where the dog is trained to circle once it's found its suspect—not to bite. And like so many special units under Daryl Gates, K-9 cops were permitted to operate pretty much as they wished, defended always by Gates.

In fact, just before the city council hearing in January 1992, as the *Los Angeles Times* would later report, Daryl Gates had "fiercely defended the K-9 unit and rejected charges that its dogs [were] allowed to bite suspects as reward for their work. 'We do not teach our dogs to bite as reward. Absolutely not,' Gates told reporters. 'These are good dogs . . . (and) if they are attacked themselves, they react to that. . . . You would too,' he said. . . . 'We keep very careful records . . . and, I think, 70% to 75% are nothing more than Band-Aid injuries.'"

That turned out to be precisely the story that juries had been buying. Lawyers representing victims were losing case after case, even though their clients' wounds were egregious and the use of such force overwhelmingly unwarranted. Many of the victims were no angels. And when the K-9 officer would come into the courtroom, his dog would sit in a chair and pant as the officer threw a ball up in the air for the dog to catch. As Rice would later describe it, "The dog, these beautiful German shepherds, would catch the ball and sit back in the chair looking adorable. And the jury—now in love with the dog—would essentially rule in favor of the dog."

Finally, the ACLU and the NAACP Legal Defense Fund banded together and filed a class-action civil suit through the Police Misconduct Guild—twenty-one lawyers dividing up enough dog-bite cases to keep many of them busy, including one law firm that had two full-time lawyers who did nothing but K-9 cases.

It took two years of court discovery orders for the attorneys to finally get a version of the LAPD's in-house use-of-force database. The statistician they then hired did scatter-plot graphs that told a story of massive use-of-force abuse. In addition to the extraordinary number of bites and the hospitalization rates, they showed that the dogs weren't just being deployed for canine crimes but were being used indiscriminately in South Los Angeles. They also discovered that the K-9 unit had a special code to alert its members that a cop and his dog had a suspect cornered and that they should quickly hustle over to watch. They called it "feeding time."

Sometimes the live action would be videotaped, such as one night in March 1989, when a jumpy video camera recorded a young black car-theft suspect hiding under an overturned couch in a darkened backyard. The clip shows at least four officers standing around, some high-fiving each other. A large German shepherd, meanwhile, is straining and growling at his prey under the couch. When one of the officers kicks it off the suspect, the dog instantly reacts by sinking his teeth into the man's leg, where they remain embedded as Sergeant Mark Mooring yanks the dog backward and the man is dragged across the backyard, howling in fright and pain. Mooring would later describe the encounter as "one of the

greatest experiences ever." The video, entitled "Why Be a Cop," aired on
CBS Evening News nationally. Taped by LAPD officers, it was credited as
being "produced by [the LAPD] and Chief Daryl F. Gates."

When the consolidated class-action suit came to trial, the judge
viewed the video, looked at the statistics the lawyers had shown him,
and told the deputy city attorney representing the LAPD that if she
tried the case she'd lose, and that the LAPD had better settle. And that's
what happened.

During the settlement negotiations, as Rice tells it, something remarkable occurred. Several ranking K-9 officers proposed that instead
of being forced to meet court-structured and court-mandated changes,
they—the K-9 unit—be permitted to make the changes themselves.
Eventually, the Misconduct Guild attorneys agreed. "If you get the
bite rate down from 80 percent to below 10 percent and do it quickly,"
they responded, "you can do it on your terms." The unit then instituted
psychological profiling of each of the sixteen handlers. Four of them,
recalls Rice, "tested off the scales for sadomasochistic behavior. They
were the guys doing the filming. And they got forced out of the unit.
Within seven months every single dog had been changed from "find and
bite" to "find, circle, and bark." The bite rate plummeted from 80 percent down to 5 percent."

Later, after the case was officially settled, Rice called one of the lawyers whose practice focused on dog-bite cases. "Give me the bad news.
How bad did [the K-9 unit] revert?" she asked, knowing that they had to
have reverted, because that was what the LAPD always did. "We don't
even do K-9 cases anymore," the attorney replied. "They not only kept
it down," Rice later summed up, "they kept it below 9 percent for fifteen
years." It was then Rice realized that when the LAPD *wanted* to change,
they could change quickly, and they could change permanently. That
was realization number one.

Her second epiphany would come out of the same case. During
the settlement negotiation, the attorneys would go through a litany
of facts aimed at establishing the monetary amount in damages that
would be awarded to the complainant. Usually the facts would not
be good for him: gang member, drug addict, no high school diploma,

no job history, no career, no prospects of higher education, no large punitive damages settlement. "There was no value set for the post-traumatic stress that these kids had suffered from a young age," says Rice. "It was the underclass discount. You are from the underclass, your lives not only do not really count, they are discounted." Together, these two insights would profoundly shape the course of Connie Rice's career.

Anthony De Los Reyes, May 1992, Los Angeles

Three weeks after the riots, police commissioner Anthony De Los Reyes had a quiet, private conversation with Daryl Gates during a break in a Police Commission meeting. De Los Reyes had always gotten along with Gates, taking him, he says, for what he was politically—a "very, very powerful" player "who had a lot of troops lined up behind him." So he proceeded gingerly.

" 'Tell me Daryl,' " he asked. " 'What exactly happened? Why weren't [the riots initially] contained?' 'Well, Commissioner,' Gates replied, 'we had a lieutenant down there [at Florence and Normandie] who just didn't seem to know what to do, and he let us down.' He said it with a straight face," De Los Reyes later recalled. "It was unbelievable."

And it *was* unbelievable—not the fact that a public official so central to causing a disaster would lie, but that a police leader so beloved by his troops would punch downward and blame a mere lieutenant for failing to contain such a cataclysmic event.

The facts were quite the opposite. And De Los Reyes's fellow police commissioner Mike Yamaki had witnessed them. He had stood right there in South Central when the decision was made to pull all the officers out of Florence and Normandie instead of reinforcing them and trying to quell the riot at its start. "I was there," Yamaki would later recount, "with a deputy chief, two commanders and a captain [on-site]. I was standing right there with them in the street when they were conferring about what to do. They could have made that decision. But they didn't."

Meanwhile, the riots' staggering costs began to be tabulated: over 45 dead—most the result of civilian gunfire, not beatings or burnings or at the hands of the police, soldiers, or the National Guard—and 2,300 injured. Insured losses totaled $1 billion, making the '92 Los Angeles riots the deadliest and costliest U.S. insurrection of the twentieth century. Now L.A. would have to rebuild not just its burned-out structures but its sense of self, its future, its sunny, glamorous image.

Those riots may have taken place in Los Angeles, but their impact was nationwide. During three days in April and May of 1992, crowds rioted in downtown San Francisco and demonstrators shut down the San Francisco–Oakland Bay Bridge. The city was placed under a state of emergency. In Las Vegas, Nevada, the National Guard was activated. In Madison, Wisconsin, the windows of police cars were smashed in. Large protest demonstrations occurred in Harlem. And in Atlanta, stores windows were shattered and whites were assaulted on the streets by roving bands of young African-Americans.

As a result of the beating of Rodney King, a new federal law was passed. It empowered the U.S. Justice Department to force local police agencies into a federal consent decree mandating fundamental reforms by threatening to sue them if they refused. The factor triggering such a decree would be a determination that a city's police had engaged in a "pattern and practice" of civil rights violations.

****

There was a lot of blame to go around for the '92 Los Angeles riots. And while Gates tried to pin it on the lieutenant at Florence and Normandie, the truth was he shared responsibility for the events that began at that intersection.

Ever since Bill Parker's advent as chief, the LAPD had been an organization amazingly responsive to its leadership. Gates's two long-term predecessors, Bill Parker and Ed Davis—as well Gates himself—had been extraordinarily successful at forging an identity for the LAPD as an independent, omnipresent city agency entitled to stand above and outside the normal political checks and balances of city government. So successful, in fact, that after fourteen years under Gates's embattled command, the LAPD had become just like him: blindly stubborn, narcissistic, and deeply resistant to change. Gates had taught the department that being a responsive public agency meant acting only as *it* saw fit, while never questioning the policing philosophy that made it simultaneously so hated *and* ineffective. Consequently, in the weeks leading up to the riots the LAPD's leadership had misread the situation and failed to grasp the pulse, tenor, and mood of the city it policed.

Sharing the blame was an indifferent white establishment and a Police Commission, city council, and black mayor who ignored the decades-long poverty and deterioration of South Los Angeles and Pico-Union and the bitter, metastasizing rage at the LAPD, and failed to *demand* a police department that would do a better, smarter job of reducing crime in consort with the people from neighborhoods that were suffering from that crime the most.

They had stood by as Daryl Gates led the city toward a calamitous reckoning. Los Angeles had become a place where a huge cross-section of the city's residents felt they had no way of stopping a police department whose modus operandi was to abuse and humiliate them. And as a result, a police force once the Hollywood exemplar of all that was smart, good, and effective in American law enforcement became instead the poster boys for all that was bad, bigoted, brutal, and ineffectual in American policing.

★★★★★★★★★★★★★★

It would turn out that Daryl Gates's self-serving dash to Brentwood on the eve of the riots was pointless. That June, by a two-thirds majority, L.A. voters approved the charter amendment Gates had campaigned against, just in time to coincide with his forced resignation.

By mid-1992 many of the city's reformers thought that with a new LAPD chief on the way, the problems within the department—and the animosity between the department and the citizens that it had sworn "to protect and to serve"—would leave with him. But of course they didn't go away. Gates's departure was just the opening salvo in a battle that had only just begun.

PART TWO

SOMETHING BORROWED

SOMETHING BORROWED

Daryl Gates and Willie Williams, June 1992, Los Angeles

For a brief time following the riots, it appeared that the bitter police politics that characterized Los Angeles during the dawn of the 1990s had eased. That month, Daryl Gates was forced to resign by the near total collapse of support from both the electorate and from L.A.'s corporate titans and their elite attorneys on the Christopher Commission. It was those attorneys who had written Charter Amendment F, and it was the city's voters who had then approved by an overwhelming 2–1 margin, thereby codifying and limiting the chief's tenure, independence, and power. That month Willie L. Williams, the first black police commissioner of the Philadelphia Police Department, also stepped forward to be sworn in as the first black police chief of Los Angeles, and to bask in his moment in the sun.

The city's liberal establishment, the media, and much of the population of Los Angeles greeted him not just as another cop, but as a hero who would simultaneously transform the culture of the LAPD, institute community policing and the Christopher Commission reforms, reduce crime, slash gang violence, and lower the temperature of the blistering racial tension permeating the city. Nobody at the time seemed to realize the enormity of such a mission. But as he traversed Los Angeles in those first days and months, listening intently to questions and making notes on a little pad he kept in his pocket, Willie Williams had such extraordinary headwinds behind him that no one seemed ready to raise a note of caution. Spotting him as he strolled into Campanile, a chic, upscale eatery adjacent to the mansions of Hancock Park, the restaurant's patrons rose spontaneously and greeted him with a standing ovation. At the popular Velvet Turtle restaurant he and his wife hosted a luncheon for a contingent of female LAPD officers. During the meal, he charmed the group while simultaneously signaling his support for their equal treatment in a department that under Daryl Gates had grown infamous for sexual harassment and discrimination.

Juggling over two hundred requests for meetings, Willie Williams went to Chinatown, had dinner in Koreatown, received two standing ovations at the Black Women's Forum, and met with the mayor, the press corps, city council members, the Police Protective League, cops at Parker Center, cops in the San Fernando Valley, and the ranking LAPD officers he'd beaten out for the job. At the First Methodist Episcopal Church in South Los Angeles, the crème de la crème of L.A.'s black leadership all laid hands on Williams's broad shoulders as the church's pastor said a prayer for the Lord's "servant and son." At the Hollenbeck Youth Center in Mexican East L.A. as well as at the First AME, his warmth toward the brown and black people who'd turned out to see him—and theirs toward him—was palpable. The media coverage reflected their enthusiasm, led by the *Los Angeles Times*, which seemed just as relieved, dazzled, and eager to believe as the general public.

At forty-eight, Williams's ample girth made him seem taller than his height of six-foot-one, and the grace with which he moved caused him to appear less a fat man than a big man who exuded confidence and solidity. "I want you, the citizens, to hold me accountable," he told the crowd of about one hundred community leaders, cops from the Hollenbeck station, and kids at the youth center. Then, cranking up his easy charm, he asked some girls sitting in a row of bleachers, "So who's gonna be the first female police chief in this city?"

Like Tom Bradley, he appealed to black people and was utterly nonthreatening to white people. But perhaps Willie Williams's biggest attraction was that he was not his predecessor. Instead, he came across as someone with nothing to prove, a man who held his place as a city department head in the right perspective—a characteristic that would normally be taken for granted in a high-ranking public servant. But

Williams was replacing Daryl Gates, who wore his chief's star like an imperial crown and had publicly compared himself to two of his World War II heroes: the mythopathic General Douglas MacArthur and the pearl-handled-pistol-packin' General George S. Patton.

Williams, on the other hand, favored double-breasted business suits and power ties, and spoke about the LAPD as a "service organization" and the public as his "customer base." There was no talk from him of "enemies," as there was from Gates, who loved to lash out at his critics. True to form, in fact, at a press conference on his last day in office on June 1, 1992, Daryl Gates had underscored that he forgave nothing. Mayor Bradley? A washed up has-been with "no future . . . [who] hasn't got a chance in the world of ever [again] being elected in this city to anything." Willie Williams? A weak "disciplinarian" without a college degree. Amnesty International, which had just issued a report critical of the LAPD? A "bunch of knuckleheaded liberals [with] a lousy record."

Williams's instincts, by comparison, were to rise above criticism and to welcome outside input. "If there was one thing that sold [the] Los Angeles [Police Commission] on Williams," said Ian H. Lennox, the president of the Citizens Crime Commission, a business-funded Philadelphia police oversight group, "it might have been his willingness to permit a private agency like ours to come in and help set policy and procedures. That is Williams' strength," Lennox told the *New York Times*, "his willingness to look at new ideas."

He seemed also to *say* all the things reformers like Lennox wanted to hear. He'd been "shocked" and "embarrassed as a police officer" by the beating of Rodney King, Williams told the *Philadelphia Inquirer*, adding that he'd never "seen pictures of Vietnam or Korea where I saw one human being try to kill another human being the same way some of those officers tried to do that man."

During his tour of the Hollenbeck Youth Center he turned to the reporters accompanying him and, referring to a young girl recently killed by gang bullets in the neighborhood, said: "Our whole existence is to make sure these kids don't get shot and killed like the young child yesterday. That's a terrible way to be introduced to your city—to see the [L.A. Roman Catholic] Cardinal talking at a 3-year-old's funeral."

And he had soothing words too for his new troops. "Too many members of [this] Police Department have been painted with the broad brush of accusation because of the actions of a very, very few," he said. "Our collective goal must be to take an already great Police Department and strive to shine even brighter." In a city built on illusion, Willie Williams had said and done all the right things, and proved himself a master of the art. Now all he had to do was make it happen.

****

On an evening later that month at the Regent Beverly Wilshire in Beverly Hills, deep in the heart of wealthy, powerful west Los Angeles, Willie Williams also spoke at the annual dinner of the American Jewish Committee. An international advocacy organization, the AJC's Western Regional Office was then concerned about police abuse and race issues in L.A.

So too were many in the audience, including the AJC's interracial, interfaith, and international partners in the city: civil rights and other leaders from L.A.'s African-American, Latino, and Asian-American communities, as well as a bevy of politicians and other local leaders. But perhaps most important of all in terms of power and influence were the moneyed, socially conscious liberals and Jewish community leaders in attendance. They were precisely the people among the city's white voters most strongly inclined to support a black, progressive, reform chief.

That night they would prove highly receptive to Williams's preacher-like exhortations to begin "to apply the salve of cooperation, the salve of unity, and the salve of accountability to our wounded souls and spirits" and to no longer "cast aside our brothers and sisters who have not yet met our particular standard of living . . . do not speak the particular language that we speak or [are] of another color of skin."

Two decades earlier, a black-Jewish coalition inspired by the civil rights movement had made history by electing Tom Bradley as mayor, an event that announced the power of two new players in Los Angeles politics. By the mid-1980s, however, that alliance was in tatters. Black L.A. soon found itself locked in an economic free fall following the deindustrialization of South Los Angeles, a crushing event that plunged many of its residents into unemployment as its young men turned to gangs, violence, and crack cocaine.

Jewish L.A., meanwhile, prospered. They became accepted in ways they never quite were before: a 500,000-strong group of residents of greater L.A. whose influence penetrated every significant sphere of civic life; a people who by 1990 had become not just part of L.A.'s political and moneyed establishment but in many ways were the establishment itself.

Simultaneously, growing conservatism among working- and middle-class Jews in areas like the suburban San Fernando Valley further tested the coalition. And so too did black L.A.'s growing political assertiveness and unwillingness to continue in an alliance in which they considered themselves treated as junior partners (which, in fact, they had become).

"There was a whole sense, a kind of a lament in the Jewish community that by the early nineties around the country the Black-Jewish alliance had frayed and didn't really exist as it once did," recalls Rabbi Gary Greenebaum, then the director of the AJC's Western Regional Office. "I personally believed in it. And the people that I was meeting, the people that I was beginning to work with, they really wanted to see the Jewish community engaged too."

In short, on this evening in 1992, with Mayor Bradley in attendance, Willie Williams was speaking to a liberal, Jewish crowd who appeared to want to rekindle their historic alliance with the African-American community and to be in love again, if only for a last hurrah. Williams, after all, had been introduced to them by one of the Westside's iconic leaders, Stanley K. Sheinbaum, who also happened to be the president of the Police Commission. As Rabbi Greenebaum later put it: "There was not another person in the country we would rather have honored [than Williams] because he was the harbinger of change. The whole city seemed convinced that he was going to change the department. In the midst of all that excitement—and given that the AJC was an organization working in the community, building partnerships with other ethnic groups—you tell me who we would rather have had speak at that dinner? I mean, do you want Willie Williams, the incoming police chief of the LAPD? Or you want the Dalai Lama? We wanted Willie Williams!"

****

The rapturous response to Willie Williams seemed as inevitable as his selection. The logic of reform demanded it. Demanded an outsider, demanded a dramatic break from Daryl Gates and anyone even remotely tainted by his failed, divisive legacy.

"We needed somebody from the outside to give the appearance that we were going to clean out whatever problems there were," police commissioner Ann Reiss Lane would later say, "a person with no ties, and no friendships that he had to honor." Anthony De Los Reyes felt much the same way: "There was definitely a preference for going outside. There were all these loyalties and cross-loyalties and these intrigues and the agendas among the [LAPD] command-level staff. We just wanted to cut away from that and start fresh."

And, although nobody explicitly said so, it was a big plus that Williams was black. The politics of race, not to mention righteous justice, demanded *that* as well. It was the city's African-Americans, after all, who'd suffered the most and fought the hardest for reform under Gates. They needed more than a sign—they needed a *guarantee* in the person of a progressive black chief that the LAPD's institutional racism would finally end. With Williams as chief, there now appeared to be at least a chance of achieving that goal.

In 1963, Daniel Patrick Moynihan and Nathan Glazer had defined the tribal nature of big-city ethnic politics in their seminal book, *Beyond the Melting Pot*. Almost thirty years later, a tribal divide was still alive and well, as had been made vividly clear in Los Angeles by the recent riots. Willie Williams's selection by a liberal Police Commission spoke to that reality.

****

That Police Commission's five members were all Democratic stalwarts handpicked by Mayor Bradley after the King beating. Together they constituted an ethnic stew of identity politics that reflected Bradley's diverse, liberal constituency. Unpaid and severely understaffed, the civilian commissioners officially met just one morning a week, and were expected to oversee and set policy for a police department overtly antagonistic to the commission's oversight function.

It was an absurd situation, a throwback to the progressive, early twentieth-century Teddy Roosevelt era of "good government," when the wealthy elite performed their noblesse oblige civic duty and were assumed to be pure, incorruptible, and above the dirty political fray. When Bill Parker was named chief in 1950, he'd combined the city charter protections virtually guaranteeing his lifetime tenure as chief with the cunning of a junior-league Machiavelli to make the commission a virtual rubber stamp for him and his successors. Then he laid out the rules of the game. "The Police Commission doesn't run this police department," he once famously announced, "*I* run the police department." In the 1970s, as was mentioned earlier, LAPD chief Ed Davis would do Parker one better, contemptuously dismissing rumors that he might run for mayor because he "already *had* more power than the mayor."

Now this commission, in the wake of the riots and Prop F, had to choose a new police chief as its first order of business at an extraordinarily crucial juncture in the city's history.

The two moving forces on the commission were its Jewish, Westside president, Stanley Sheinbaum, and its African-American vice president, Jesse Brewer. Both men had led extraordinary but very different lives yet had come to the same conclusion regarding the urgency of thoroughly reforming the LAPD.

At seventy-one, the gray-bearded Sheinbaum put one in mind of a prickly professor who carried in his pocket a growing list of people not living up to his ever more demanding expectations. Stooped and ailing, he looked at least a decade older than his age. His mind, however, remained as sharp as ever, and focused on the two passions that dominated his orbit of interest: liberal politics and policy. Among other things, he was a potent donor to the national Democratic Party, and was considered something of a kingmaker—so much so that the biggest of Democratic presidential hopefuls would fly three thousand miles across the country to dine with him, to honor him or one of his causes or, most especially, to have their campaign coffers stuffed during his fund-raisers in *their* honor. You name them, they came: Senator George McGovern, Vice President Walter Mondale, Senator Ted Kennedy, Senator Joe Biden, New York governor Mario Cuomo.

But Stanley Sheinbaum was more than just a Democratic moneyman. Far more. He had the courage of his democratic, civil liberty–loving convictions. A plutocrat whose politics were fiercely anti-plutocracy, he was a middle-class New York City Jewish boy turned dirt poor by the Depression, who'd then kicked around the country until he finally wound up in a graduate program at Stanford. In 1964 he'd married a Hollywood rich girl he met at a party in Beverly Hills named Betty Warner, and for the rest of his life he tried to do good and salve his restless political soul with her money. She was a would-be painter, a woman with formerly Communist friends who keenly remembered the Hollywood Blacklist, and the daughter of movie magnate and Warner Bros. cofounder Harry Warner.

Together they'd conduct exclusive political salons from their Brentwood estate as Sheinbaum became a political center around whom liberals in the entertainment industry and others influential in the Southern California Left orbited. A former decadelong chairman of the American Civil Liberties Foundation of Southern California, he began *serious* fundraising for the organization, making it an advocate for social change and helping to turn it into the largest ACLU branch in the country.

He also raised over $900,000 for Daniel Ellsberg's legal defense after Ellsberg leaked the Pentagon Papers to the *New York Times*; battled for California's divestment from apartheid South Africa while a regent of the University of California; and led a delegation of American Jews who'd clandestinely negotiated for Middle Eastern peace with Palestinian leader Yasser Arafat.

Stanley Sheinbaum, in short, was a player.

And as a major donor to Tom Bradley's campaigns, Sheinbaum's phone call to Bradley after Rodney King's beating requesting he be named to the Police Commission soon resulted in his appointment— and to Sheinbaum being named president of the commission—a shot across the bow aimed directly at Daryl Gates.

****

Like Stanley Sheinbaum, Jesse Brewer, the commission's vice president, had lived a storied life. A combat infantry captain wounded in the bloody invasion of Italy during World War II, he'd been a Chicago cop before moving to Los Angeles. There he'd joined the LAPD, been voted president of his LAPD recruit class, and become the department's first black motorcycle officer and the department's first African-American assistant chief. At seventy years of age, he was named to the Police Commission by his close, longtime personal friend Tom Bradley.

Brewer was one of those men everybody liked, not just Bradley. Daryl Gates liked him; he was popular within the department, among the white political establishment, and with the city's black leadership.

Educated at Tuskegee, he had earned a master's degree in public administration from USC, and was by nature and temperament a natural conciliator. He was light-complexioned, modest, soft-spoken, and hardworking; confrontation wasn't in his nature. He was, after all, a man who'd spend his entire adult life in uniform and was, by inclination, the consummate gentleman. Quietly, however, Jesse Brewer was seething—scarred by a lifetime of grinding, soul-sapping Jim Crow condescension and by being a constant, often impotent witness to his people being abused by his police department. Even now, as vice president of the Police Commission, old slights still stung.

In 1952 he'd left the Chicago PD after five years, sickened by its corruption, after taking and passing the written exam for the LAPD. But then he'd been notified that he'd failed his physical for inadequate muscle development and a case of athlete's foot. The test, it turned out, had been administered by a doctor notorious for regularly flunking black applicants for city jobs. Brewer found out that twelve years earlier Tom Bradley too had been flunked by the same doctor for having a heart murmur. Bradley had then appealed, passed an examination by another physician, and finally been accepted by the LAPD. In response to a suggestion by Bradley, whom Brewer had met through his uncle, he too appealed, got reexamined by a different doctor, and also passed.

In the years that followed, Brewer worked in a segregated LAPD that relegated black officers to South L.A., did not permit them to work in the then lily-white San Fernando Valley or to join many of the department's elite special units, and did not integrate its patrol units until 1961.

Yet Brewer kept pushing. Three times he'd scored high on his written exam for lieutenant (then the glass ceiling for black officers), and three times he'd been rejected by white oral boards who displayed either outright hostility or a refusal to take his candidacy seriously. Finally he made it on his fourth attempt, in 1967—*after* Bill Parker had died in office, after the Watts Riots, after the passage of the Civil Rights Acts of 1964 and 1965, and almost twenty years after the U.S. armed forces had been integrated.

In 1991, as he was nearing forty years on the LAPD, Jesse Brewer finally retired, just two days before the beating of Rodney King—his dream of becoming the LAPD's first black chief forever thwarted by Daryl Gates's lifetime tenure. But he left with a copy of a report he'd commissioned several years earlier, as the commander of the department's sprawling South Bureau. Brewer had detected an alarming pattern: Gates was overturning every one of Brewer's deterrent-driven punishments for excessive use of force by his officers and replacing them with slaps on the wrist. Each of the officers involved, the report found, was then in trouble *again* within a year for similar or identical use-of-force violations. Brewer was outraged. Not only was Gates undermining his efforts to curb brutality, he was allowing the officers to continue their conduct.

Jesse Brewer didn't release the study right away. He waited for the right opportunity, which came when he was invited to publicly testify before the Christopher Commission following the King beating. Brewer pulled no punches. While sharing the findings of his South Bureau report, he denounced Gates for his lax disciplinary standards, giving him a grade of D. Disrespect for the public among officers was "out of control," he told the commission, adding, "We know who the bad guys are, reputations [are] well known." When Tom Bradley then named Brewer to the Police Commission, Brewer called on Gates to resign. Daryl Gates never spoke to Jesse Brewer again.

Brewer became the commission's essential member—the old friend and confidant of the mayor, the guy with institutional knowledge who knew all the players, and where the bodies were buried.

De Los Reyes came to regard him as "a saint"; Lane was "scrupulously honest, a straight-arrow human being"; Mike Yamaki compared Brewer to the legendry UCLA basketball coach John Wooden, a man renowned as much for being an old-fashioned gentlemen who never swore as for being an extraordinary coach who led his teams to ten national championships.

But Brewer was also LAPD. He wanted to be called "Chief," not "Commissioner." And when Sheinbaum or any of the commissioners "started beating up on the LAPD *itself*," recalls Yamaki, "I could see the conflict in him. But he was too much of a gentleman to be confrontational about it."

****

The other members of the commission also reflected Bradley's rewarding political supporters and his desire for diversity. Ann Reiss Lane was his designated woman.

There had been a history of appointing people to the Police Commission who didn't know much about the LAPD, and Lane fit that description perfectly. She was a resident of the wealthy enclave of mansions west of downtown L.A. known as Hancock Park. At sixty-one, she still had the slim, wholesome good looks of the L.A. girl next door circa 1947, the year she graduated from Beverly Hills High School. After also graduating from UCLA, she joined the League of Women Voters, where she grew to admire then city councilman Tom Bradley, whom she decided to work for during his first campaign for mayor. She knocked on doors trolling for votes with the then unknown actor Leonard Nimoy and their respective spouses. When the news came in that Bradley had lost, she burst into tears. When he won on his second try, Bradley appointed Lane to the Los Angeles Fire Commission, where she served for thirteen years, focusing on hiring and promoting female firefighters—with little success, due to the rigorous physical requirements. Then, in 1991, Bradley appointed her to the Police Commission.

For the first three months Lane served on the commission, Daryl Gates would pass her in the hallway without speaking or looking at her. He made it clear he that he didn't like her, or more precisely—since he didn't *know* her—didn't like the very thought of her and what she represented: a liberal, Democratic, Jewish feminist.

But Lane's comment when named to the commission might also have contributed to Gates's attitude toward her. "I have read [the Christopher Commission Report] and believe all of its recommendations should be implemented," said Lane, "including a start in the transition of the chief of police."

It took Lane a year on the commission before she began to decipher how things worked. But like Stanley Sheinbaum, she had the courage of her convictions, and the need to act on them.

Just as Gates surely felt he had to act on *his*. Gates wasn't just philosophically and professionally opposed to the feminist and gay rights movements, he was personally opposed as well. In the early eighties he'd been forced by a federal court order to hire more women and minorities.

Gates considered the order a disaster. He liked women. But not in his police department. According to Anthony De Los Reyes, Gates once told him that "he'd gotten complaints from female officers about being [sexually] approached by other women in the locker room; and that he (Gates) thought that maybe '50 percent of the women being recruited were lesbians'"—a comment De Los Reyes found extraordinary, but one that Gates had also made to several command-level officers, according to De Los Reyes.

The forty-eight-year-old Anthony De Los Reyes held the commission's Latino seat. His father was a Mexican musician of the Latin big-band sound, and his mother was of Scottish descent. De Los Reyes had come of age in East L.A.'s Lincoln Heights, in the heart of Mexican Los Angeles.

A personal-injury plaintiffs' lawyer, De Los Reyes had supported Tom Bradley's failed run for governor of California in 1982, and a year later he was appointed to the city's Civil Service Commission. There, he gained almost nine years' experience helping oversee Los Angeles's personnel department. Soon after the King beating, Bradley personally asked him to join the Police Commission.

Short, rotund, and ebullient, De Los Reyes was a friendly, open man who nevertheless was innately cautious in what he said and did—traits highly valued in Los Angeles's political circles, where the general consensus for decades had been that there weren't more than a hundred people in the city who really understood how it worked.

De Los Reyes was one of those people.

While on the Civil Service Commission, De Los Reyes helped to extend affirmative action hiring and promotion examinations to all city departments—including the LAPD. "I had cops and others' records right in front of me . . . every week for eight and a half years. So I knew a lot, and also knew how hard it was to get information."

At Parker Center he quickly learned exactly how hard. Every ranking officer there had his own agenda, De Los Reyes discovered, and sorting through them was an exercise in Byzantine bureaucracy, particularly given that the commission met only one morning a week. In the 1970s former Police Commission president Stephen Reinhardt had called the LAPD command staff "masters of the half-truth" in dealing with the commission. In the early nineties De Los Reyes learned that little had changed. "I learned that I had to ask very specific, precise questions to get any kind of information," he says, "and if I made a recommendation and didn't write it down, it might not ever come up again."

De Los Reyes nevertheless maintained a cordial relationship with Daryl Gates until they finally clashed over placing an LAPD recruiting booth at the annual Sunset Junction Festival. "He was adamantly opposed to having uniformed officers in a recruiting booth at what was predominantly a gay festival," recalls De Los Reyes.

Gates vehemently opposed allowing gays to join the LAPD, and when one officer publicly came out, he was so viciously harassed that he left the department so fearful that he set up an answering machine specifically so he could monitor all incoming calls.

Gate's *stated* objection, however, was liability-insurance costs. That and he didn't want to pay two officers to sit in a recruitment booth for four hours. When De Los Reyes discovered that the department's *total* cost would be just $400, he told Gates "that given the present [antagonistic] relations between this department and the [gay] community, four hundred dollars was simply not too much too pay." "He was very upset," says De los Reyes, "when the commission voted to approve the money."

****

Interviewing all finalists for a new chief to replace Daryl Gates took the commission sixteen hours—six of which were exclusively devoted to Willie Williams. His public persona was his calling card. It earned him the highest grade among the initial civil service selection committees, and then from the Police Commission. Well prepared, he answered questions confidently, was current on the issues facing the LAPD, and spoke as if he'd been carefully reading back issues of the *L.A. Times*.

"We'd been having confrontations with every single LAPD person dealing with us," recalls Mike Yamaki. When the LAPD candidates came in, he explained "it was obvious they were bullshitting us." As both Yamaki and De Los Reyes would later tell it, they all did terrible jobs during their interviews, arriving unprepared to answer the questions they'd been asked to address or to propose innovative solutions to long-standing LAPD problems.

Underscoring Williams's charm and preparation was a report the commission received from Ann Reiss Lane and Jesse Brewer. Earlier, they'd flown to Philadelphia and, working off a list from L.A.'s personnel department, interviewed fourteen people. Lane was particularly impressed with Williams's community policing program, finding it somehow significant that a woman at one of the community policing stations had cried and said, "Please don't take my police chief away."

After vetting Williams in Philadelphia, Lane sat down at the commission's table and announced, "If I was looking for a job, I'd like to have fourteen people say the things about me they said about Willie."

The commission's first vote was three to two in favor of Williams, with Yamaki and De Los Reyes voting against Williams because they felt an insider who knew the LAPD and the city might be better prepared to lead the department. Once it was established that the three-vote majority was determined to vote for Williams, the commission voted unanimously to recommend him to the mayor. They had to present a united front and move on—that much was clear. And none of the other candidates were impressive enough to fight over in any case.

It wasn't, as they saw it, as if they had any other really viable choices. The candidate who'd come in second—the autocratic African-American LAPD assistant chief, Bernard Parks—was disliked by both Lane and Brewer. As Lane would later put it: "Remember, Bernie Parks was our second choice, and everybody knew what *he* was like."

But beyond the inevitability of Williams's selection, more pressing questions about this appointment seemed to either not have been asked or not fully answered by the Police Commission. What, for example, had Willie Williams accomplished in his nearly four years as Philadelphia's police commissioner that was *transformational*? How original, innovative, and *effective* had he been in changing the culture of brutality, racism, and unaccountability within the Philadelphia Police Department? And besides his charm, did Williams have the strength of character, physical energy, sense of urgency, and political and managerial skills to get the hard things done?

In 1990 the Philadelphia police union official Richard B. Costello remarked that Willie Williams had "the right temperament" to reform the Philadelphia PD. "He's not one of these sword-swingers that wants to change things tomorrow. He's made changes, but he's done so gradually." Costello's appraisal seemed an endorsement of a quality that did not fit the high expectations of the powerful reform coalition of politicians and civic, civil rights, and civil liberties organizations awaiting him in Los Angeles. They were expecting big things, a visible, dynamic change, a swift beginning to a reform process that in their eyes was decades overdue.

And there was this: Willie Williams was coming to L.A. as not just an outsider but an outsider from the East Coast—synonymous, in the minds of many LAPD cops, with dirty, on-the-take corruption.

And perhaps even worse in their eyes was that Williams was coming from *Philadelphia*—then a tired, regressive, extraordinarily dysfunctional second-tier city—and from a police department with a reputation *worse* than the LAPD's.

The top command staff of the LAPD, people like David Dotson, knew exactly what the PPD was, and considered the department a know-nothing *joke*. "You have to understand how the Philadelphia police operated in those days," says Dotson. "It was right after the MOVE row house bombing. And they came out here to get advice from the LAPD, asking us how to keep officers on the straight and narrow, how to conduct personnel investigations—really basic stuff—and when we told them how to do it, their reaction was like, 'Really? I didn't know that.' That was the kind of department Willie came from."

In addition, Williams was completely unfamiliar with Los Angeles and its intrigue-ridden, deeply xenophobic police department—a department, not incidentally, where he had absolutely no power base and no friends. A department that, although bruised, battered, and demoralized, nevertheless still considered itself the best police department in the world, *unneedful* of reform.

Most officers, moreover, still admired Daryl Gates, despite everything the department had been through. For them he was still the symbol of the glory days, the man who, as Charlie Beck once sardonically put it, "had died for our sins."

****

Soon Stanley Sheinbaum began intriguing daily with the mayor's chief of staff to get rid of Gates and assert the commission's power. Given Gates's performance as chief, a disapproval rating of 81 percent, and a distrust score of 85 percent, Sheinbaum certainly had a point. The guy had to go.

The problem with that approach, as Mike Yamaki saw it, was that while Sheinbaum was forcefully asserting his and the commission's power, in reality the commission didn't statutorily have the *legal* power to force him to leave—nobody could—because nobody in all of Gates's fourteen highly controversial years as chief had built a negative civil service case against him.

Yamaki's attitude, therefore, was "Okay, fine, let's celebrate him, give him a retirement party and all that stuff, and get rid of his ass, not try to humiliate him."

Yamaki was right in terms of calculated, strategic governance. But a lot of people in Los Angeles had long hated Daryl Gates and his department, not just for their cavalier brutality and officer-involved killings of the unarmed but for their hard, preening arrogance and their contemptuous dismissal of complaints voiced by an extraordinary host of reputable critics both in and out of the body politic.

Going-away party? No. What they wanted was revenge. And if all they could get was Stanley Sheinbaum pissing off Gates, they'd take it.

****

It would require a *Sunday*-morning emergency meeting of all five police commissioners to get Daryl Gates to finally leave his department and his troops behind. Not much earlier, Gates had told the head of the city's Civil Service Department that he wasn't going to leave. Hence the call for an emergency meeting, during which the commissioners made clear that they intended to get him ready, threatening "to explore ways in which he could be held to his earlier commitment to leave." "That's when he finally caved," says Anthony De Los Reyes. There was nothing on the books that said he had to go. It was just that his support outside the department had almost entirely collapsed.

****

As he exited his sixth-floor Parker Center office on June 1, the hallway outside was filled with cops and staff applauding, crying, and shouting, "We love you, Chief." And so they did, including the "phalanx of police motorcyclists" who, as the *Los Angeles Times* reported, "escorted [Gates] onto the southbound lanes of the Santa Ana Freeway"—sending him off to his beachside home-in-exile condo in beautiful San Clemente. From this haven he would leave for his new job as host of a talk-radio show on a popular right-wing station. The show quickly failed, and afterward he'd periodically emerge to appear at old-timers' retirement parties, always to ponderous applause, reminding the faithful of what once was, and had been lost.

Willie Williams, Late Eighties to
Early Nineties, Philadelphia, Pennsylvania

The oldest of seven children, Willie Williams had grown up in West Philadelphia as a spindly, asthmatic child so sickly, says Williams, that he was "in and out of hospitals four times as a youth" and had been administered last rites on three separate occasions.

His father labored in a meatpacking plant, and when Williams was eight years old he began working at a neighborhood grocery store and delivering newspapers. By fifteen, he too was packing meat part-time, once almost losing his arm in a meat grinder. Following his 1961 high school graduation, Williams got a job as a city messenger for $2,600 a year. Afterward, he took the tests for both the Philadelphia PD and the city's Park Police. When the latter responded first, he jumped at the opportunity to almost double his annual salary overnight to $5,000.

He was just twenty years old, a hometown boy living the modest, working-class, apparitional life of those not fated for—or without interest in—making the middle class leap into college. When the Park Police merged with the city police eight years later, he merged with them. After he married, he and his wife, Evelina—a clerk-typist for the Department of Licenses—raised three children in a modest three-bedroom row house filled with family photos and mementos in a modest neighborhood. There they acquired a dog named Frisky, who was already fifteen years old by the time Williams was named Philadelphia's police commissioner.

They would live together in the city for twenty-three years, moving only when Williams was hired as chief in Los Angeles and after he'd sold the house to their son, who was also a Philadelphia police officer.

Williams worked and studied hard for promotions, but rose only slowly through the ranks. He took both the sergeants' test and the detectives' test three times before passing, and the captains' test twice. Meanwhile, he continued attending the Philadelphia College of Textiles and Science part-time, graduating with a two-year associate degree in 1992, just as he was departing for L.A. Throughout his entire career, he would never fire his weapon.

In 1980 he was finally promoted to captain—where he might have remained, had not an event Williams himself would later refer to as "the Rodney King [incident] of Philadelphia" occurred: the 1985 dropping of a bomb from a Philadelphia PD helicopter onto the roof of the West Philly row-house headquarters of the radical black group MOVE.

The bombing—which set off a fire that killed eleven people and incinerated sixty homes—took place at the end of a daylong stalemate that started with the PPD attempting to serve some misdemeanor warrants. It then continued as the police fired from eight to ten thousand rounds into MOVE's headquarters, and ended in a literal firestorm that was allowed to burn by order of a master strategist of a police commissioner named Gregore J. Sambor. So astounding was the event that former NYPD lieutenant and John Jay College criminology professor James Fyfe would later claim that "police officials around the country [considered it] the single most stupid police action in this [the twentieth] century."

In response to the bombing—and to a police shakedown and extortion scandal that resulted in the federal convictions of Sambor's deputy commissioner and over thirty commanders and officers—the city's mortified black mayor, W. Wilson Goode, hired a former Secret Service agent named Kevin M. Tucker to reform the department.

The son of Irish immigrants, Tucker had grown up in working-class Brooklyn and Rahway, New Jersey. He joined the army after high school, and was working his way through college as a patrolman in Rahway when he single-handedly arrested three men breaking into a car dealership. One of the suspects was wanted by the U.S. Secret Service, and the agency, impressed, offered Tucker a job after he graduated. Tucker happily accepted. During his career as a Secret Service agent, his assignments included guarding Jacqueline Kennedy Onassis and her children. He was heading the agency's Philadelphia field office when Goode named him police commissioner.

The fourth-largest police department in the nation, the Philadelphia PD that Tucker inherited had a long history of "favoritism, corruption, and brutality"—an assessment delivered in 1987 by a blue-ribbon task force appointed by Goode. Their report would also describe the department as "unfocused, unmanaged, unaccountable, undertrained and underequipped."

In terms of corruption, brutality, and unaccountability, the report portrayed much the same department that Frank Rizzo led in the late 1960s as commissioner and nurtured in the seventies as the city's two-term mayor. A six-foot, two-inch South Philly high school dropout, infamous for his love of the blackjack as his weapon of choice, Rizzo personified all the hatred, ignorance, and fear that white ethnic Americans were feeling toward African-Americans. It was a time of rising street crime, enormous social change and upheaval, and a rapidly growing black population that by the 1980s would comprise about 40 percent of the city's residents.

For Rizzo and his overwhelmingly white department, they—the Italians, Irish, Jews, and Eastern Europeans of Philadelphia—were the public, and black Philly—with its high crime rates and growing population threatening its neighborhoods—was the enemy.

Rizzo was credited with keeping crime relatively low. But the price was high: large numbers of shootings of unarmed civilians by a police force that as late as 1980 had no shooting policy, and Saturday night raids, personally led by Rizzo, on gay bars and counterculture coffeehouses and cafes. His officers stripped Black Panthers naked in the street after raids, and Rizzo himself used a secret unit of the police department to spy on his political opponents. Overall, acts of police brutality were so "widespread and severe" that in the mid-1970s the Philadelphia PD became the first department ever sued by the U.S. Justice Department for engaging in systemic brutality.

It was understood that Kevin Tucker had only been named commissioner to address these issues, initiate reform, and leave. He wasn't, after all, even a cop. But with no one to court, appease, or pay back in a hidebound city, Tucker, known for being a particularly thoughtful strategic manager, could move ahead unimpeded by normal career-advancement constraints.

****

Unlike the LAPD, which had a tradition of college-educated senior officers, the PPD didn't bother to keep records of its officers' education levels or even require recruits to have high school diplomas. Tucker started
confronting the situation by sending fifty commanders and other officers to Harvard's John F. Kennedy School of Government to participate
in three-week management and supervisory training seminars. At the
time, the school was working with law enforcement officials and social
scientists to develop the idea of community policing. A then evolving
concept, community policing focused on officers in local neighborhoods closely working with community organizations and city and
private agencies to solve problems and systematically *prevent* crime—as
opposed to just responding to crime calls. Tucker liked community policing and began applying some of its precepts to the Philadelphia PD,
in particular by establishing small, local police substations in high-crime
neighborhoods.

He also began diversifying the department, rapidly promoting black
officers like Williams, whose rise under Tucker would be meteoric—a
jump of three ranks to deputy commissioner in just the two and a half
years.

When Tucker resigned in June 1988, he was replaced by Willie Williams as Philadelphia's new police commissioner. He handed off to Williams both the initial building blocks of reform and a 195-page blueprint
for the future with over one hundred recommendations for reforming
the department, written by a task force of prominent criminologists
and criminal justice and civic leaders. During the nineties someone in
the PPD looked for the task force report, and there was not a copy to be
found within the department.

****

A year and a half after Tucker's departure, in the winter of 1990, some
strange things were happening. For one, the chair of the city council's
Public Safety Committee was comparing police commissioner Willie
Williams's police department to "a Mutt and Jeff" comedy act; Williams
himself was depicting Philadelphians as "living in a climate of fear"; and

the city's district attorney was characterizing its criminal justice system as "on the verge of collapse." In the wake of all this, many of Kevin Tucker's reforms already seemed ephemeral, a brief respite in the Philadelphia PD's otherwise dismal history.

The heart of the problem wasn't just Williams or just the PPD. The city's entire criminal justice system was falling apart, caught between a city government in dire financial straits and Philadelphia's settlement of a 1988 jail-overcrowding federal lawsuit. The city's ruinous solution to the overcrowding was to severely limit pretrial detention—a resolution that resulted in thousands of criminals being repeatedly arrested and immediately released because of lack of jail space to legally detain them.

Consequently, Williams and his department quickly became overwhelmed. With just 5,900 officers in 1988, compared to 8,400 in 1977, the PPD was already understaffed. Immediately releasing criminal suspects who normally would have been jailed—but instead were now out on the street committing new crimes—drastically exacerbated the city's crime problem, causing response time for "low-priority" crimes (such as stolen cars, burglarized homes, snatched purses and drug dealing) to rise to as long as two hours.

Moreover, many police facilities were operating without heat in the winter or air-conditioning in the summer, and without even basic supplies like, incredibly enough, uniforms and hats. As for the department's 854 vehicles, about 165 were out of service at any one time. Forty of the department's 400 unmarked cars had broken sirens. And even though the department did its own maintenance repairs, a vehicle with a flat could be out of service for a week.

Willie Williams hadn't caused these troubles, but he wasn't exactly on top of them either. During the same 1990 Public Safety Committee hearing in which the PPD had been compared to a "Mutt and Jeff" act, Williams seemed at a loss to solve what amounted to some extraordinarily straightforward supply problems with vendors and dysfunctional city agencies. "Are there problems with the bidding on [police] hats?" Williams asked during his testimony. "Absolutely, and we're trying to address it. Are there problems with the delivery of equipment for vehicles? Absolutely. . . . We have screamed and hollered and burned up the telephone making sure we get the equipment. We're fighting for that."

The crack-war years of the late 1980s to mid-1990s were also exacerbating the situation in terrible ways, as black and brown kids with automatic weapons were warring over drug distribution and crack corners. As a result, scores of cities like New York, Boston, Milwaukee, and Los Angeles were all experiencing explosive increases in their homicide rates. In 1989—Willie Williams's first full year in office—murders in Philadelphia rose as well, by 21 percent to 489, and they rose again by 19 percent over the first six months of 1990.

Like most big-city police chiefs and commissioners at the time, Williams had no new, innovative answers to Philadelphia's soaring murder rate (although in New York City crimes and homicides would soon begin to dip dramatically in part as the direct result of specific police policies introduced by its new police commissioner, William J. Bratton). And like the LAPD, the PPD under Williams had no answers to the crack wars, though they were staging high-profile drug-suppression raids in targeted areas and pointing to increasing arrest numbers as a gauge of success, even though such strategies were clearly having little impact.

In March of 1992, at the very time Williams was being interviewed by the Los Angeles Police Commission, a highly critical report on the PPD was released by an independent investigative panel convened at Williams's request. The panel confirmed allegations that about fifty officers had brutally attacked nonviolent demonstrators protesting President George H. W. Bush's AIDS policies, calling them "faggots," clubbing them down, and then refusing their requests for medical assistance.

In an interview following the report's release, Williams acknowledged the stubborn persistence of brutality within the department. "I'm trying to change a mentality that's been in police departments for one hundred years," Williams said. "Officers who want to do wrong or who think about doing wrong are going to change when they see what happens to others. . . . [The department's discipline is] not quite as hit and miss as it used to be. What we're about is nothing less than trying to change the culture."

Yet despite Williams's efforts, few people in Philadelphia thought that change in the department's culture was being reflected on the streets by the rank and file. Changing police culture required more than just firing some low-ranking bad actors. "Williams has paid lip service to many of the right ideals," Stefan Presser, legal director of the Philadelphia chapter of the American Civil Liberties Union, told the *Philadelphia Inquirer* following the report's release. "Where he as an individual can have some influence, he has moved the department the right way. But there are so many endemic problems in the department. I don't think he has put sufficient energy into making those ideals a reality."

The problems *were* endemic, and systemic to the city's criminal justice system as a whole. In addition to the prisoner-release and uniform and equipment fiascos, there was no structure or policy in place to even notify the PPD when a police abuse lawsuit was filed against one of its officers, and no follow-up notification when a judgment was rendered against an officer. Officer-involved shootings also increased, including many off-duty shootings, and Williams's new shooting policy, critics charged, remained filled with loopholes.

"The crime rate is up," Joan L. Krajewski, the chair of the city council's Public Safety Committee told the *Inquirer* after Williams's first full year in office. "We're in a state of crisis. I'm not saying that [Williams is] not a nice guy, but being a nice guy doesn't solve the problem."

****

At the American Jewish Committee dinner Stanley Sheinbaum had precisely pinpointed what Willie Williams was good at. "Watching him [in Los Angeles] work through some of the problems he sees ahead, and move in different parts of this city's society, [among] different races, different layers of the society—he does so with a strength," Sheinbaum told the audience. "It will take you time to understand why I emphasize that part of him. I look upon Willie Williams as a man of hope."

He'd also pointed out that before choosing Williams, the Police Commission had "sent two teams of people to Philadelphia to make sure about what we heard, some very good things . . . very positive things about him, and those people came back substantiating [the reports.]"

And indeed, there *were* good things to be said. During Willie Williams's three and a half years as Philadelphia's police commissioner he'd expanded the number of Kevin Tucker's community-policing ministations, required district commanders to meet at least one a month with local community groups, and committed the PPD to gender and racial diversity. He also increased the number of officers fired or disciplined for brutality, and assigned more officers from desk jobs to patrol during peak crime hours. By 1990, he'd even managed to get three hundred new officers added to the department.

Moreover, for reformers not delving too deeply into the weeds, Willie Williams was viewed as a godsend simply because he was who he was: a nice, dignified, measured, noncombative guy without the dimwitted and/or brutal and divisive characteristics of his pre-Tucker predecessors.

These were not small things.

They made Williams a perfectly fine commissioner, dealing with crisis after crisis as they came up, sometimes adequately, sometimes not, while trying to implement the reforms he could. But was that enough?

Ultimately it might not have made a difference if L.A.'s police commissioners could have considered more than just one outside candidate. Willie Williams's surface sheen may well have sufficed. Nevertheless, the police commissioners would have had a far better understanding of just what they might be getting with Willie Williams had they back-read the Philadelphia newspapers instead of relying on two part-time, unpaid, elderly police commissioners to vet Williams by talking to fourteen people in two days. They would have found a far more mixed picture of Williams and might have questioned his ability to handle a job where so much was expected and on which so much was riding. But in this, as in so many aspects of *governance*, Los Angeles wasn't the City of Tomorrow that it always promoted itself as being, but the City of Yesterday.

★★★★★★★★★★★★★★

In 1992 Charlie Beck took the lieutenant's test, and for the first time in his career came in first. His reward was assignment as watch commander in Watts, back to the site of the Jordan Downs and Nickerson Gardens housing projects that he'd earlier deserted to save his soul and sanity; back to ground zero for the '65 and '92 riots, and now the home of the area's Truce Parties.

The Truce Parties were celebrations of the Bloods' and Crips' decision to "tie their rags together" in an act of peace that symbolized their promise to end their gang wars. The truces may have been something that the gangsters and liberals like Connie Rice then believed in. But for Beck the parties were simply a "sham—more about celebrating the riots than about the truce." The first stage of each party, recalls Beck, "was the gathering of Bloods and Crips in huge numbers from all over the city on Friday and Saturday nights at one of the big housing projects in Watts—where they'd come together and drink and smoke weed in huge excess."

Then, sufficiently lubricated, they'd proceed to stage two: "driving around in circles in large convoys as they rode or raced in the streets, cordoning off blocks and taking over the street, and shooting their guns in the air. It was total chaos," says Beck, "like mini riots. There was no looting or burning, but once in a while they'd mob some convenience store or intersection, just to show that they could do it. Just to show that they were free from the constraints of the Los Angeles Police Department."

Charlie Beck and Andre Christian, 1993, South Los Angeles

It was a bad, bloody time, not just for Beck and the LAPD but for black and brown Los Angeles. While 1992 had been calamitous, 1993 would actually prove *worse* in terms of homicides, which topped out at 1,100— more murders than Los Angeles had ever experienced before.

Crack wars and street dealing were in full swing: young guys on the corners and in the parks dealing drugs, carrying guns, and killing each other over dope-dealing territorial rights, just as the gangs of Chicago and New York fought over liquor distribution rights during Prohibition— except now it was on a far bloodier scale.

To Charlie Beck, the post-riot LAPD had become something the department had never been before—a "cowed organization." "We tried to stop illegal behavior," says Beck, "but the department was so politically battered and thinly staffed that stopping the parties in Watts [or the murders in much of black and brown L.A.] wasn't really an option. Mostly we just tried to keep things under control."

Gradually, indignation mixed with frustration had started to produce in Beck a strong sense that the department was letting him and his fellow street cops down. "It's like your family," Beck would later explain. "All of a sudden your parents are getting divorced, and people are coming and repossessing the family car. You don't really understand what's going on but it's making you feel hugely anxious about the future. That's how I started feeling about the organization—like, is this ever going to stop?"

****

It took getting shot thirteen times for Andre Christian to reevaluate his life, as he was doing when the Truce Parties started to bloom in the projects. He was still dealing, trying to make a living as he moved back and forth from Riverside County to Jordan Downs, where he'd check in, see friends, and keep himself updated. But he was no longer directly involved in the Grape. Thirteen bullets and being declared a medical miracle will do that to you. He was "glad that [he'd] got shot, glad that it changed [his] way of thinking." A lot of the gang stuff, the banging and the young man's thirst for glory, had left him. All he was trying to do now was get some money and a job that paid the bills so he could turn the page.

The Truce Parties continued for about six months, fading each week until they petered out as the novelty wore off. Nevertheless, Christian viewed the parties differently than Beck. For him and a lot of people he knew, the parties were "sighs of relief." No longer did he feel as if he was under arrest, with invisible lines delineating his hood as his jail bars, and surrounding Blood gangs as the jailers who'd ensure that if he stepped over the line, he would pay. Thanks to the Truce Parties, he no longer had to constantly look over his shoulder. Instead, "it was a relaxed situation where you could just sit back and put your feet up."

At the Truce Parties, he recalls, "you'd see Crips like the Bounty Hunters from Nickerson right there with the Grape, getting high, riding around together, going into a store together to stock up." "*And*," Christian emphasized, "they'd be *showin'* their rags, not hiding them—that was a good feeling."

But despite their different perspectives on the potential value of the Truce Parties, in many of the particulars there wasn't a lot of daylight between how Christian and Beck remembered them. "There just wasn't enough nurturing of the peace part of the parties," says Christian. "There was just too much partying. Between the liquor, the weed, the gambling, the girls, and the jealousy, the situation just basically sprang right back to the way it always was."

Even then, it was crazy to think that it could have ended any other way. Los Angeles would learn that the same was true of the LAPD.

Willie Williams, June 1992, Parker Center

No one expressed that truth better than LAPD officer Bryan Eynon when discussing his new chief from out of town. "My first impression of Willie Williams started at the [police] academy," Eynon would later point out. "I was standing at attention in formation, waiting for [him] to arrive. . . . Then all of a sudden I smelled the aroma of cologne . . . and out of nowhere comes this really big guy weighing about 320 pounds, dressed in a double-breasted suit and draped in gold. . . . He had a gold watch, rings, bracelet and huge gold cufflinks. . . . So my first impressions—along with a number of other officers—were that his cologne was loud, he was fat and out of shape . . . and there was no way he could fit into a uniform."

But his point wasn't really *that*—it was rather that Willie Williams was wasn't one of them, wasn't a real member of the *elite* LAPD, wasn't looking dapper in a Johnny Carson sport coat, and, most importantly, would look appalling in the department's world-famous, classically tailored LAPD blues. Physical fitness, strength, and athletic ability were, after all, among the department's most revered tenets; being overweight was a direct assault on the LAPD's image, as well as on many officers' personal sense of self.

Rabbi Gary Greenebaum—who would soon find occasion to be around Willie Williams and the LAPD with great frequency—certainly thought so. "People would say to me, 'Oh, the department hates Willie Williams because he is black,'" recalls Greenebaum. "And I would say, 'Well, they don't particularly like Willie Williams because he is black. But the main reason they don't like him is because he is fat, which doesn't comport with their vision of the LAPD. The LAPD is not the NYPD. Those guys in New York, with their big bellies, are not going to get over the six-foot wall that LAPD [trainees] have to get over.' And they really did hate him for that."

It was a measure of the LAPD's priorities that looking good superseded far more important attributes in a new police leader, such as the ability to develop new concepts and strategies to lower crime and reduce friction between the department and black and brown communities.

But it was still early in Williams's tenure, and the significance of him being labeled "His Corpulence" by the troops might have faded—if, in their eyes, that had been his only problem. But it wasn't.

On the job, for example, Willie Williams was always missing the one thing—other than the department's oversized badge—that said to an L.A. cop, "I am an LAPD officer": his gun. He was missing his fuckin' *gun*. Didn't wear one, never carried one—in fact, *couldn't* carry one—because of a California law that required all peace officers to first pass a test in order to pack a gun on duty. That extended to out-of-state police officers as well. To qualify, Williams chose to take the "Basic Course Waiver Exam"—which David Dotson describes as consisting of a "bunch of basic police-academy information." Reportedly, Williams took and failed the waiver three different times. (The state legislature later changed the test requirement to exempt police chiefs as a result of Williams's dilemma.) Daryl Gates, on the other hand, always had a gun strapped to his ankle in addition to his sidearm and the Uzis he kept in his staff cars.

Moreover, although scorners of social science and social workers, the LAPD paradoxically had a tradition of valuing higher education—particularly master's degrees from USC's School of Public Administration. And here too Williams fell short. When he decided to take some graduate courses at the school, he was denied entrance because he possessed only a two-year associate's degree from the Philadelphia College of Textiles and Science. Bill Parker, after all, had earned a *law degree.* Tom Bradley had been working toward his law degree when he was an LAPD *lieutenant.* And now here was Willie Williams with an associate's degree from an institution with a trade-school name.

Soon, the command staff at Parker Center began gleefully leaking reams of biting gossip to the *L.A. Times* and anybody else who was interested.

****

Willie Williams's failure to anticipate that level of resentment—and consequently prepare for it—was, as Charlie Beck later told it, a major misstep. "Willie made a big mistake when he came into the department," says Beck —who witnessed the drama up close after being appointed the Police Commission's new adjutant at Parker Center. "He didn't scare [the command staff or troops]. He didn't have a plan. He just kind of sidled in, sat down, and said, 'What do you do around here?' He didn't demote anybody, didn't demand résumés, didn't come in with a team of people [he was barred by civil service law from hiring any], didn't do any of that stuff, and then he relied on the wrong people because he didn't know any better."

Williams had also neglected a second cardinal rule for any newly appointed big-city reform chief: if you want to change the behavior of officers on the street, then you'd better make the new rules of the game absolutely clear to the people *really* in charge of them—division sergeants and most especially division captains. What Williams needed to brand on their brains was about as basic and obvious as could be, something like "Henceforth, your promotions are going to be directly tied to how well you emphasize and implement real, two-way community-involved policing; how seriously you rein in, appropriately discipline and never recommend for promotion your Clint Eastwoods playing "Dirty Harry"; and how significantly you lower crime without acting like Israeli paratroops during an intifada."

But Willie Williams never made such a pronouncement, or put out that memo, or made that speech.

Willie Williams, September 1992, Police Administration Building

Approaching Jesse Brewer—now the new president of the Police Commission—and Mike Yamaki—the new VP—Willie Williams stopped, greeted them, and then asked if he could take a vacation. Neither could believe what they were hearing. Willie Williams had been chief for just ninety days. How could he not understand that as a stranger leading an already hostile and skeptical LAPD he had to show he was working ten times harder than everybody else? But instead, Williams was complaining about the long hours he'd been working and how tired he was. And not without reason.

During those first three months Williams's schedule had been grueling. He'd attended scores, if not hundreds, of meetings, with everyone from neighborhood block associations and district leaders to business associations, church and synagogue congregations, and every kind of advocacy organization. And everyone had seemed enthralled by his affable charm, confidence, and promises. But following those successful meets-and-greets, high expectations started giving way to low performance.

"Jesse Brewer tried—desperately—to tell him to go out to roll calls [at all the department's eighteen divisions]," recalls Ann Reiss Lane, "and he'd agree. He always agreed to everything." But Willie Williams did not go. Did not talk and listen to sergeants and patrol officers and address their questions and anxieties face-to-face; did not tell them what he intended to do and why it would be helpful and more effective for them to police in a new, modified way. Instead he left a vacuum for others to fill.

It was a bad decision, not listening to Brewer, made at a particularly bad time. Williams's arrival had coincided with a moment when the rank and file was especially—historically—demoralized and defensive. They'd just experienced the yearlong pain of a thumping collective headache, one brought on by the unceasing, near-universal denunciation of the department following the beating of Rodney King and then the riots. For many of them, Williams's appointment was just another insult—and Williams himself just another convenient surrogate for their anger, to be pounced on as if they were piranhas and Willie Williams the first flesh they'd seen in days.

Bernard Parks, Fall 1992, Parker Center

On the wall of the office of then assistant LAPD chief Bernard Parks hung a picture of Daryl Gates, an ode to the Great Man himself that showed the world who Parks was to his very core: a disciple of The Chief—*a Daryl Gates cop.*

Parks, however, was a very impressive guy in his own right: a tall, trim, movie-star-handsome African-American straight out of central casting, who would later be named by *People* magazine as one of the world's "50 Most Beautiful People." The son of a thirty-eight-year veteran Los Angeles Port Police sergeant, Bernard Parks had grown up in Watts and was as shrewd and smart as he was headstrong—the kind of perfectionist utterly convinced that whatever he thought was *the final word.*

Not for him was the subtle, inch-by-inch working for racial justice and in-house change in the style of Tom Bradley or Jesse Brewer. Parks rose through the ranks as the kind of black man who'd come of age in a still overtly racist America and made it by hard work and determination, and he brooked no excuses for those who hadn't. Intellectually he well understood the causal effects of crime; that society wasn't dealing with them, and that it was using police departments like the LAPD to contain the fallout. But he also felt that one of the biggest culprits in this crime tragedy was the profit-driven, quick-take, sensationalistic press.

Not only was it failing to *support* the police but in its own twisted way it was laying the blame squarely on the police instead. "It's easy to point [at the police] and say they shot so many black people in [a] city," he once said. "What's hard [for the press to explain] is why all those black people have guns that are creating crime and why the police are confronting them daily."

Once at a conference at USC Parks was asked about a series of LAPD crises going back to the 1940s—"the Zoot Suit riots, the Watts riots, the Rodney King beating, the '92 riots." With all that history and controversy, asked the questioner, "how do you think policing has evolved in L.A.?" "I think we've evolved in a variety of ways," Parks replied. "What's unfortunate [is] when you mentioned those highlights [Rodney King, etc.], many of those are ten or twenty years apart. . . . [And the press] doesn't view them in context. In between, there have been the day-to-day activities . . . of providing a service that the public appreciates." It was an astoundingly ahistorical appraisal, given that from at least the Watts Riots through the '92 riots, the entire twenty-seven-year history of the LAPD had been nothing *but* context, as one abuse bled into another like an unbroken daisy chain.

★★★★★★★★★★★★★★

Bernard Parks's modus operandi during interviews was to parry even mildly critical questions about the department with a deluge of "facts" so intricate, jargon-filled, and complexly drawn that a reporter would leave Parks's office with nothing he could use or even understand.

Unless, of course, he liked you, and Bernard Parks liked very few reporters. But he did like Jim Newton, who was the *Los Angeles Times'* deputy bureau chief at the city-county bureau, and the man to whom Parks was dishing dirt on Willie Williams with unbridled enthusiasm. "Parks always thought Jim was a good guy," says Tim Rutten, a veteran *Los Angeles Times* editor and columnist. "It was the Willie Williams era when they bonded. Jim was on the beat. Bernie was his source. Willie Williams was Jim's story." And what Parks was telling Newton and others was bad news for Williams.

Early in his term, Williams had made Parks chief of operations. It was a plum job, a key position where, on a daily basis, Parks—who'd placed second to Williams in the runoff for chief—would be in charge of about 85 percent of the force and could really make things hum. Or not. It all depended on how competent he or she was or, in the case of Parks—who was working for Willie Williams, who knew nothing about the inner workings of the LAPD—how good a job he *wished* to do.

And Parks wished to do a *very* good job indeed. Just not in that position under Williams. He'd made no secret of his anger at not being chosen chief. In fact, recalls Anthony De Los Reyes, "Parks didn't talk to Jess [Brewer] for more than a year after the selection."

"Parks was livid with Jesse because Jess had assured him that he'd be the next chief," says David Dotson. "And I have no doubt that Parks was really pissed off when he wasn't chosen . . . and felt that [the commission] had done a disservice bringing in Willie—whom he considered an inferior person."

Had Parks *not* been so enraged, he could have been very, very helpful to Williams. "Bernard knew everything about the Los Angeles Police Department—*everything*," recalls Charlie Beck. "He knew the combination to every locker in Parker Center. He did know. We all believed he did. Willy wouldn't have known where the locker room *was*."

And Parks wasn't about to show him. Instead he used his powerful position against Williams, as Curtis Woodle later put it, "to teach the department how to undermine the chief, to make sure that Willie failed." As the driver and bodyguard to the mayor, Woodle was in a position to know. "And when that happens, when you have the number two guy talking bad about the top dog, everything else is going to go under. You have eighteen different [LAPD] divisions all over the place just kind of out there. . . . So even if Willie was giving directions to Parks, it wasn't getting down to them."

Williams, fed up with his disloyalty, would later demote Parks as a way of forcing him into retirement. But Bernard Parks had many strong supporters on the City Council, who, astoundingly, decided to intervene in what should have been strictly an internal department matter. In the LAPD, assistant chiefs—who serve directly under the chief of police— are by statute chosen by him and serve at his pleasure. So, unable to thus rescind the demotion, the council decided instead to show Willie Williams who they really loved by awarding Parks a $15,000 raise.

Alfred Lomas, Early to Mid-Eighties, Scotland, the Philippines, and L.A.

While Bernard Parks had been busy climbing the LAPD career ladder in the early 1980s, Alfred Lomas was serving in the United States Marine Corps. He'd joined the Corps in 1982 when he turned eighteen, figuring it would be a good way to stem his burgeoning alcoholism. But it didn't turn out that way. Instead, three years later, he'd found himself sipping on a fifth of whiskey as he bounced around on a Greyhound bus seat, peeping out bleary-eyed at the landscape as the bus made its way from North Carolina to Los Angeles. In his duffel bag was an "other than honorable" discharge and behind him a year he'd just done in the brig.

The marines hadn't changed him much. After boot camp and specialized training, he'd had too much time on his hands, and found himself in a Marine Corps where hard-man attitudes and serious drinking had been cornerstones of the culture for centuries—if you kept it within bounds. But there were always guys like Lomas who knew no boundaries.

For a while, however, he'd done quite well. He was bright and a habitual reader, which, along with a keen ability to retain information and a fascination with military machismo, enabled him to test well enough to be assigned to specialized infantry units.

Assigned to Scotland, he told a lieutenant commander to fuck off and physically threatened him. That got him busted from lance corporal to private. Reassigned to the Philippines, his alcoholism spiraled into full-blown blackout drinking and brawling. There, he refused a lieutenant's direct order and also threatened *him*. That second threat landed him in a high-security red-line brig in North Carolina, where, if you stepped over any red line on the floor, you'd be smacked in the head with a billy club. Of all the places he would ever be incarcerated, Lomas would always remember that federal brig in North Carolina as the hardest time he'd ever done.

****

Stepping off the Greyhound after four or five days on the road, Lomas headed straight to the old neighborhood, dropped off his stuff at his mother's apartment, and beelined it to the Tami Amis—a dive of a joint in the heart of a warren of bars in Huntington Park, frequented by hardcore Chicano ex-cons.

He was sitting on a stool at the bar, drinking hard, trying to get *right*, when a pretty Latina struck up a conversation with him. She looked just like a hundred other neighborhood girls he'd known, nothing special, but she didn't seem beat down by life, or by some pimp-like boyfriend either. Still, she was in the Tami Amis, which meant there had to be something off about her. After a while she suggested they go to the Toles Motel nearby to party. When they entered her room, she asked for $10, left for a moment, returned, pulled out a pipe, lit up, took a hit, and passed it to Lomas. An instant after inhaling, he felt an intense wave of euphoria and clarity, followed by something akin to "an orgasm magnified—one hundred times," and lasting for about half an hour. It was a fateful experience. Alfred Lomas was about to spend most of his next twenty years chasing that crack high.

****

About a week later, Lomas placed twenty bucks in his pocket and set out to score at the Toles. Like the Tami Amis bar, the motel was a sad place of drugs and desperation. Walking up the Toles's seedy stairs into a hallway, Lomas felt intensely out of place. He was dressed in clean clothes, with clean fingernails, brushed teeth, and freshly washed hair. The contrast between him and the chronic junkies and crackheads he was passing stunned him.

At that time in much of South Central and greater South Los Angeles, blacks dominated the crack trade. Some older black guys had crossed Alameda Boulevard, the traditional black/Chicano dividing line, and set up shop at the Toles and other motels in and around Huntington Park. They were mostly old men using their Social Security checks to deal, not part of the aggressive black crack-cocaine gangs of the nineties, who would kill you over territory or most anything else. It was still way too early for that. This was still the beginning time; the Colombians' cocaine mule lines weren't established as a business model yet.

Making his way down the hallway, he spotted men sitting in their rooms through their open doorways. As he passed each room the door slammed shut, and Lomas, understanding what was happening, started shouting that he wasn't a cop. But nobody was buying that, until a homeboy diffused the tension with four simple words: "Hey, what's up, dawg." "Once he said that," says Lomas, doors started creaking open as the occupants realized that he was a customer with money.

****

In the days and months that followed, Alfred Lomas's addiction to crack played out like an oft-told tale from a million AA meetings. A week later he went back to the Toles and scored some crack and a woman—the latter being a given. There was always a sensual, addicted woman around, looking to get high, doing what it took. And, of course, his tolerance level soon became higher and higher in tandem with his desire for more and more, just as his money supply became smaller and smaller. Lomas was left with two choices: start stealing or start dealing.

Stealing, he figured, was too high-risk. And he was smart enough to realize that by the nature of his then drunken, dope-addicted, violence-prone life he wouldn't make a good salesman—which is one of the prerequisites of being a successful drug dealer.

For many years, however, he'd been one of those "five percenters" that the LAPD talks about—the 5 percent of the gang population responsible for most of the gang violence. He'd been exposed to those guys growing up, and had been one of those guys, one of those *vato locos*. And he'd learned from that experience that talk was cheap and violence ruled, and that violence and the threat of it was exactly what he had to sell. So he decided that he'd become the guy who would protect a dope dealer. And he had one in mind: a guy from his neighborhood, a fellow Florencia 13 gangster named Billy [not his real name] who was, says Lomas, "one of the best crack dealers I had ever seen." It was no coincidence that Billy was a Florencia 13 gangster. Even in the Corps, Lomas was always in the gang, still tagging the walls of buildings and bar bathrooms in North Carolina, Okinawa, and the Philippines with "F13" like he was still in the hood, claiming territory.

Billy was a businessman whose business was the drug trade. What he lacked was what Lomas had: a propensity for violence. Teaming up in the mid-eighties, their timing was exactly right. The customer base of desperately addicted users was starting to form. And Billy had both close ties within the drug world and a salesman's get-along affability— which he used to great effect with the then exclusively black wholesale dealers who were the first into L.A.'s crack trade.

The wholesalers' area of trade was the Newton area of South Central, which turned out to be as good as Billy and Lomas's timing, conveniently located as it was just a block or two from their home turf of Huntington Park—a great advantage in picking up the product quickly and returning home just as fast. Newton, moreover, was located just a short, quick turn onto the 110 Freeway, a major traffic artery with connections to all of metropolitan L.A.

Newton, moreover, was also situated on the border policed by the Los Angeles County Sheriff's Department on one side and the LAPD on the other. Neither liked the other. And their close proximity had long ago degenerated into a grudging aversion to cooperate or even communicate. Consequently, neither was patrolling the area in a sharp manner or on regular basis, each agency leaving it to the other.

Within that void Lomas and Billy set up shop and began what would prove a long-term, mutually beneficial relationship. Billy got what he lacked and needed from Lomas. And Alfred Lomas got an endless supply of the rock cocaine that was now what gave meaning to his life.

Once they started dealing crack in earnest, their business developed with remarkable smoothness—Billy making the deals, and Lomas supplying muscle, plotting pickup and delivery routes, and then making the runs.

Paradoxically, the LAPD and the L.A. County Sheriff's Department's indiscriminate war on black and brown young men actually helped in Lomas's pickup and delivery. Their myopic approach was geared to stopping and arresting *vato locos*; it was what they knew.

Consequently Lomas always made sure to be clean shaven, to dress like an ordinary citizen or suit-wearing businessman, to make runs with women, not gang guys—particularly with white girls involved in the dope trade. As a result of his planning, he never got arrested for heavy-duty drug dealing.

****

By the late 1980s Alfred Lomas was also freelancing his services to three or four other dealers in addition to Billy. He knew most everyone involved in drug-trade security in his operational area, and tried to keep gun and muscle use to a minimum, negotiating with his counterparts to avoid conflict as they moved their dealers' drugs around.

"I liked the action on the streets," he'd later say, "and I'd learned at an early age that most guys that got involved at a higher level got killed. So I never worked directly for top guys, never knew the direct lines of distribution or how they operated." In any case that would always be Alfred Lomas's rap.

****

In 1988 Alfred Lomas was finally arrested. One night he was supposed to collect a large sum of money from a resident of a house in Palos Verdes, an ultra-affluent hillside community overlooking the Pacific Ocean. But he started drinking and hitting his crack pipe early that day with his cousin, who had brought the collection deal to him. Sloppy drunk and crack high, they hopped into a car that night and actually made it over to Palos Verdes, a long, circuitous ride from South Central. Then they parked and entered the wrong house. The elderly woman inside quickly called the cops. They were arrested and Lomas was sentenced to eighteen months in a California state prison in Susanville, one of the northernmost of California's thirty-plus penitentiaries.

The Golden Rule in prison is this: you do what everybody else does, or you face often brutal consequences from your fellow inmates. California's prisons have a further code: you stay with your own kind. In fact, the state's prisons are so racially charged that inmates are often officially segregated by race—blacks, whites, and Latinos all housed separately. Because northern and southern Chicano gangs are sworn enemies, they are further divided and separated by geography. Lomas had the misfortune to be a Southern Californian in a hyper-violent northern prison where southerners were outnumbered three to one by blacks and *Norteños*. The hood writ large had come, in short, to the biggest prison system in the county.

One of the greatest fears of any inmate in California is to have his own race turn on him. Then he's open to attack by anyone. But Lomas was Florencia 13, and *that*, along with knowing how to act, kept him protected.

After serving sixteen months, he was released, having earned a stripe and a lot of street cred for being outnumbered in a prison war zone and not just surviving but coming back unscathed.

Then, about a year after the '92 riots, Lomas became a father. His new son's mother was also a crack addict. Lomas was serving a six-month stint in county jail for battery when the baby was born, and as soon as he was released he made a beeline to visit his child. He was appalled by what he saw: his son was startlingly thin, with a filthy diaper, surrounded by guys smoking crack and getting drunk. It was too much even for Alfred Lomas, who'd witnessed a lot of depravity in his day. In response, he "threw a Rambo, and beat the shit out of everybody that was there." Then he left with the baby and moved out of the hood and in with his father, who had sobered up and remarried and was living in Pasadena.

Soon he was working hard to stay straight. He landed a salesman's job with Safety Clean—an environmental company that did solvent and oil recovery—and, using his energetic, street-hustler persona, made good money, acquired a new, smart, nonaddicted girlfriend, and moved in with her to start a new life and actively father his son.

David Mack and Rafael "Ray" Perez, Tuesday, October 26, 1993, Hollywood, California

While Alfred Lomas was living straight, twenty-nine-year-old Jesse Vicencio was leaning into the driver's-side window of a beat-up Datsun B210 parked on a dark Hollywood side street at about nine-fifteen on an October night in 1993. As he did so, he either placed a pistol to the left side of LAPD undercover officer David Mack's head, or he did not. Whatever the case, Mack shot him dead.

Mack and his partner, Rafael Perez, were then part of the department's West Bureau [drug] Buy Team—one of Daryl Gates's special units that had carte blanche to proceed as they wished, few questions asked, as long as the arrested meat kept rolling in.

The Buy Team was a small unit primarily dedicated to making small crack buys from street-corner dealers. The unit featured two-man teams of youthful-looking undercover cops wired to both a supervising detective and a couple of patrol cars with uniformed officers, who waited to barrel in and make the arrest once the deal went down.

Like Charlie Beck, who'd spend much of his time in CRASH units endlessly raiding crack houses, Mack and Perez's job was to endlessly arrest street dealers, of which there were so many—particularly in Hollywood—that they often doubled their nightly arrest quotas.

It was a dirty job that involved living a life of deadly deceit, which was bad for the soul as well as devastating for whatever moral compass a young man might possess as he operated under the Buy Team's laxly enforced rules.

But from 1991 to 1994 David Mack and Rafael Perez would do it, and love it. "Just by its nature, there's constant danger," Mack and Perez's supervisor, Detective Bobby Lutz, would later explain to the *Los Angeles Times*. "A constant go, go, go . . . Those guys were on the edge all the time. . . . Every time you make a buy, it's a rush. They['d] lap it up . . . relish it."

Unlike fortified crack houses, street dealing, by its open-air-market nature, was fraught with inter-gang rip-offs that were among the leading factors in driving L.A.'s homicide rate to a record 1,100 in 1993. Among the dead was Jesse Vicencio, who'd lost his life over that potential sale of a $20 rock of cocaine.

David Mack, however, was not only exonerated for Vicencio's death, he was awarded the department's second-highest medal for heroism. As Mack and Perez later told it, Vicencio walked up to their Datsun undercover car dangling a chrome handgun on his right leg and proceeded to place it on Mack's temple, whereupon Mack jerked his head away and fired off a round before Vicencio could, and then blasted off twelve more shots. Two eyewitnesses, however—one Vicencio's cousin, the other his friend—would swear to police investigators at the time, and to an *L.A. Times* reporter six years later, that Vicencio never pulled a gun on the two cops. In any case, the shooting was ruled "in policy," and undoubtedly the case would have remained closed had not serious concerns arisen about David Mack and particularly Rafael Perez in the years to come.

****

Rafael Perez was the kind of guy who could size you up and give you back what you wanted to hear as if he'd just thought of it. A tall, lithe, half-black, half-white, cocoa-colored Puerto Rican, he wore his hair and mustache close and neatly trimmed. Effortlessly charismatic, he projected a boyish eagerness to please and a personal warmth ("Call me Ray!") that he could turn on and off like a light switch. Articulate in English, fluent in Spanish, he was also a great storyteller with a sharp cop's eye for detail. Many young Latinas consequently found him irresistible, and although he was already on his second marriage he felt the same way about them, and never hesitated to show it. His first wife divorced him when she found him cheating on her. Nevertheless, she remained inordinately fond of Ray, as did his second wife, Denise, an LAPD dispatcher who would stand by her man, even as their lives came crashing down upon them.

Born in Puerto Rico in 1967, Ray's childhood was not a happy time. One of three children raised alone by his mother, he never saw as much as a picture of his father until he was over thirty years old. Arriving in the States when he was five, he and his family lived briefly in Brooklyn before moving to the weary factory town of Paterson, New Jersey. When he was in his early teens, his mother moved the family again, this time to a punishing black ghetto in northern Philadelphia. There, as Ray later told it, he watched his uncle run a drug ring out of the corner house down the street and his mother being beaten by her drunken, common-law husband as Ray stood hopelessly by.

After a three-year stint as a U.S. Marine Corps infantryman, Ray joined the LAPD in June of 1989, when he was just twenty-one years old. Assigned first to the relatively sleepy Harbor Division, he then worked patrol in Wilshire Division before volunteering for the West Bureau Buy Team.

His partner, David Mack, was an African-American raised on the cruel streets of Compton, a small, then overwhelmingly black city adjacent to South L.A. that was also home to the seminal gangsta rap group N.W.A and Death Row Records and its thug impresario, Marion "Suge" Knight.

If anything, Mack—who was about a decade older than Ray and was Ray's role model—was an even more singular character than his partner: a ghetto kid who attended the University of Oregon on a track scholarship, became an NCAA 800-meter champion, qualified for the Olympics before being sidelined with an injury, and was rumored to have dated the beautiful Olympic track star Florence Griffith Joyner. Later he'd marry another track star with whom he had two children. But like Ray he was hardly a *Modern Bride* ideal family man. He liked the ladies and the action in L.A. and Vegas far too much for that. Still, he was a hero cop who, as Ray would always swear, had saved his life that night in Hollywood.

In 1994, however, their partnership would end when Mack became a training officer in the West Los Angeles Division, and Ray joined a special unit with which his name would become synonymous, and which he'd later make infamous: Rampart CRASH. The two, however, would remain close friends as each become notorious in his own right. Their future actions would have a far more profound impact on the future of the LAPD than anything that Willie Williams would ever do as chief of the Los Angeles Police Department.

Bill Bratton and Rudolph Giuliani,
November 1993, New York City

Rudolph Giuliani was not a subtle man. A balding, hard-nosed, strong-willed former U.S. attorney, he'd grown up in Brooklyn and Long Island, had four uncles who were cops, and in 1993 ran for a second time for mayor of New York City, narrowly defeating incumbent David Dinkins, New York's first African-American mayor, that November.

A rare Republican in a Democratic city, Giuliani perfectly understood the rage and frustration of New York's white working and middle class over the city's inability to reduce crime, because he was them and they were him. For decades, as they saw it, New York had been corrupted by ivory-tower liberals and weak clubhouse politicians who'd been giving away control of their city to self-designated, endlessly demanding black leaders personified by the then intensely divisive young minister the Reverend Al Sharpton. Giuliani's electoral success lay in him having the temerity to unapologetically ride the razor's edge of their fear to victory.

The city's African-Americans, for their part, were only too aware of the crime being committed by a minority of their young men, being, after all, the major victims of that crime. But they were desperate not just for their physical security but for long-denied opportunity and decent jobs in the strikingly polarized racial divide of the 1990s. Too much heat had built up over the decades to allow progress along both those fronts to occur without a wrenching transformation of the kind that had exploded in Los Angeles after the 1991 beating of Rodney King and the '92 riots.

Rudolph Giuliani's election brought that transformation to New York. Giuliani would turn out to be a touchy, revengeful, and sometimes buffoonish man, nasty, narcissistic, egomaniacal, and combative to a fault, who, like Frank Sinatra, had within him something of a wounded little boy who never forgot a slight. As a former U.S. attorney, he had *liked* putting people in prison, had taken delight in perp-walking suspects and seeing them shamed. That was just the kind of guy he was.

But in campaigning and governing it was clear that Giuliani also believed in the rightness of his cause, had a good case to make, and was exceptionally smart and fiercely, boldly determined to accomplish what he saw as his mission of saving New York City from itself. He did what he believed needed to be done, further polarizing an already polarized New York in the process. But he also helped spark the revival of a despairing city.

****

About a month after his election, Giuliani stood with William Bratton and declared him New York City's thirty-eighth police commissioner. Some of Giuliani's key advisors had favored retaining Raymond Kelly, who had served as former Mayor David Dinkins's police commissioner. Kelly was then regarded as a tough but reasonable NYPD veteran who shunned the limelight and had yet to develop the smug imperiousness that would later characterize his long tenure as New York police commissioner under Mayor Michael Bloomberg.

Those same advisors regarded Bratton as an unseemly publicity seeker, a characterization with at least a modicum of truth to it. Bratton *had* become the very public face and voice of the New York Transit Authority during his tenure there as chief, and had even been prominently featured in a series of transit commercials with the theme "We're Taking the Subways Back—for You." Back then, Bratton had been "pleased and flattered" when morning drive-time talk-radio host Don Imus started parodying him and the TA commercials on his show. Imus had become the darling of the white, male, New York–Washington media/ political "elite," who daily gathered on Imus's show to, in good-ol'-boy fashion, speak their minds and be insulted by Imus doing his acerbic, world-weary, dry-drunk, ex-cokehead routine.

That Bratton was flattered to be playing that game in that league was exactly the thing that would later get him in trouble.

But to be fair to Bratton, the commercials and the recognition were really a win-win situation: an extremely important opportunity to tout his reforms and his determination to reduce crime while enabling him to build public support for his efforts and improve the morale of his subway officers. It also allowed him to send messages directly to his transit cops outlining what he valued and what he wanted done.

He used the *New York Post* and its reporters in the same way, and the *New York Times* when he wanted to communicate to policy makers. New York's media happily ate up all Bratton fed it, and not without reason. He was doing something newsworthy, something important, and he *had* been "taking back the subways." He told reporters and the public all this, moreover, with a Boston accent so colorfully filled with clipped cadences and long, nasal vowels that his diction caught their ear and attention and spoke of something new.

Nevertheless, there was no denying that Bill Bratton had also managed to make the story all about him. And that was what Giuliani's advisors feared would happen should the mayor choose him as police commissioner. But Giuliani chose to ignore his advisors' misgivings. With the appointment of his top cop, he wanted to announce Big Change, not continuity. And in Bill Bratton he'd found a powerful vessel to carry that message.

****

If Rudolph Giuliani appeared to have found his vessel, several months after being named New York's police commissioner Bratton found his in a chubby former transit cop named Jack Maple. One night they were sitting with a crime reporter named John Miller at Maple's favorite table in an Upper East Side Manhattan bar called Elaine's, when Maple began to scribble on a cocktail napkin.

A tall, dapper star for local TV station WNBC, Miller had been hired by Bratton as his deputy commissioner of public information—that is, his press guy. And in many ways Miller was a good choice: "Fun, smart as hell, and [with] the best Rolodex in America," as Bratton would later describe him. He was also a popular, distinctive television personality who loved the city's nightlife, loved being a bachelor, and loved covering and sparring with the "Dapper Don," Mafioso John Gotti, perhaps because he fancied himself as something of a dapper don as well.

In other ways, however, Miller might not have been Bratton's best choice. For one, he was too much like Bratton: too brash and independent, too much the happy partying companion, too used to being the star in his own movie to allow him to see the bigger picture and to warn and protect his boss against the ruthless machinations of Giuliani and his loyalists, who wanted what both Bratton and Miller were incapable of giving: absolute subservience. They were supposed to do their work, keep their mouths shut, and allow the credit to go to Giuliani—who had once banned ads for *New York* magazine from city buses because of the line "possibly the only good thing in New York Rudy hasn't taken credit for."

Jack Maple, the man scribbling on a napkin across from Miller and Bratton, was a character in his own right: a stocky, carnation-in-lapel, homburg hat– and bow tie–wearing former up-from-the ranks transit cop straight off the streets of Queens—and, as Bratton affectionately saw him, right off the stage of a Broadway revival of *Guys and Dolls*. While chief of the New York Transit Police, Bratton had quickly recognized Maple as a brilliant crime-prevention, police-deployment strategist and, once he became police commissioner, had astutely hired him as his deputy commissioner of operations.

It was no accident that the three were sitting at Elaine's. For decades the bar and restaurant had served as a kind of a see-and-be-seen hangout club for celebrity journalists, columnists, and writers, and Miller and Maple had long loved frequenting the place. And now so did Bratton, whose third wife had returned to Boston. Soon they would be divorced.

Meanwhile, Bratton and his entourage of advisors were "having," as Bratton later put it, "a very good time." And, in so doing, he was becoming not only the kind of outsized "Broadway Bill" tabloid personality New Yorkers love but the face of the city's dramatically declining crime rate—heretofore a signature Giuliani issue. Bratton, however, was not only getting the credit, and taking it, he was cutting Giuliani out of the script.

On this particular night, however, as Bratton would later tell it, Elaine's would become famous not just for celebrity gossip but for that cocktail napkin upon which Maple had been writing.

On it Maple had been mapping out a new crime-suppression strategy. The theory behind it was startlingly simple: If you want to reduce crime, you had to understand the data-based reality of crime in a city like New York. In the still-new mass-computer age of the early nineties, you could find that information by regularly gathering and inputting data onto computer-generated maps designed to then show exactly where and when specific types of crimes were occurring, and where they were clustering into "hot spots."

Once a police manager had monitored and analyzed the map, he or she could then deploy enough cops and resources to reduce crimes in "hot spot" areas in a logical, data-driven manner. It was not a one-shot deal but a continuously updated daily accounting of data keyed to localities that held supervisors up and down the chain of command accountable for solving problems and preventing them from reoccurring. Maple called it COMPSTAT, and its concentration on crime prevention and suppression, and on supervisorial accountability, would have a profound impact on increasing the effectiveness and efficiency of the big-city police departments that would soon employ it.

****

As it turned out, 1994 was an auspicious year for Bill Bratton to plunge into his new job as police commissioner. The public was hugely supportive; New York's economy was starting to boom; under President Bill Clinton federal money was flowing in for training, equipment, and hiring new police; and, most importantly, the ten thousand new NYPD cops that Giuliani's predecessor, Mayor David Dinkins, had found the money to hire were now trained and ready to hit the street. The nationwide crack epidemic that had fifteen-year-old street-corner dealers carrying Glocks and shooting each other in record numbers all over urban America, moreover, was finally winding down, and partly as a result, the decline in violent and property crime that had begun nationwide in 1991 was accelerating.

Bill Bratton's contribution would be to maximize that trend in New York City. By using COMPSTAT to track crimes and complaints and efficiently respond to them, and broken windows and stop-and-frisk policing to reorder the city, Bratton reenergized and refocused a previously adrift NYPD that was now thirty-eight thousand officers strong.

As if by magic, New York's homeless—a large number of whom were mentally ill and/or drug or alcohol addicted—also seemed to suddenly disappear. Bratton had ordered the formation of a special thirty-five-officer unit to push the homeless off the sidewalks of Manhattan. But that was just a quick cosmetic fix. What really began impacting the homeless problem was the success of David Dinkins and New York governor Mario Cuomo in raising funds for the building of 7,500 units of single-residency apartments for the homeless. One hundred million dollars, meanwhile, was also being provided by the Clinton administration for homeless housing, while large numbers of new public housing units commissioned by Mayor Ed Koch during the eighties were simultaneously coming on line. The disappearance of the homeless and of aggressive panhandlers—who were being arrested for any code violation the NYPD could come up with—would have an instant impact, as the city's residents realized that seemingly intractable, high-visibility problems could actually be made to go away.

Meanwhile, crime was plunging dramatically. The number of murders in New York City in 1995 dropped by almost 385 from 1994—an almost 25 percent decline in just one year. By the end of 1996 they would fall by almost 590, a decrease of over 37 percent. Total felonies in 1995, moreover, would also decrease by 27 percent, robberies by over 30 percent, and burglaries by 25 percent.

So remarkable was Bratton's impact on the city that in January 1996 his image, dressed in a 1940s tan raincoat, collar turned up Bogie-style, appeared on the cover of *Time* magazine. "Finally," read the story's cover line, "We're Winning the War Against Crime. Here's Why." By sheer force of will, William Bratton had become that rare thing not seen in America since the gangbuster days of the 1930s, when J. Edgar Hoover had become the face of not just the FBI but American law enforcement: a national celebrity cop, one who was being hailed as New York's savior.

Willie Williams, 1992–1993, Los Angeles

Meanwhile, back in L.A., Willie Williams, despite his troubles with departmental insiders, was also being hailed by the public, who continued to hold him in high esteem. In October of 1992, his job approval rating was 67 percent. By February of '93 it had jumped to 72 percent. And by the winter of 1993, a *Los Angeles Times* poll found Williams the most popular public figure in the city.

Unfortunately, exactly the opposite was growing even truer within and around the LAPD, where something akin to bewilderment had set in, and a pattern was starting to emerge. The commission would give Williams policy directives, and he would ignore them. His energy seemed to be flagging, and his organizational skills seemed weak or nonexistent when it came to planning for big policy changes. It was as if he'd run extremely hard to get the job of chief, continued to sprint toward the finish line as he attended those hundreds of confidence-building meet-and-greets, and then suddenly realized that he was only at the start of the marathon ahead.

Meanwhile, another realization was starting to set in: not only did Willie Williams have no idea how the political process and important LAPD-related bureaucracies of Los Angeles worked—which was understandable—but he had no desire to *learn*, about either the city or how the department's history informed its present.

Being incurious was a particularly grievous character trait for Williams, given that he was in many ways a one-city provincial. He knew only the Philadelphia PD, and was an utter stranger to Los Angeles and the Machiavellian machinations of the LAPD.

In Los Angeles, for example, the political control of the police department was multilayered, and many people needed to be courted as potential allies if Williams was to succeed at reform. (The Philadelphia police commissioner, on the other hand, was directly accountable only to a powerful mayor.) But instead of learning about and using L.A.'s elected officials to further his goals, Williams chose to ignore them as much as he could.

In fact, Williams would tell reporters as a point of pride that "in Philadelphia he had only one boss—the mayor," but in Los Angeles "he had 21 bosses" (the mayor, the Police Commission, and the city council) and "didn't want to be seen in the camp of any one of them."

Williams was also uninterested in building professional alliances, at least in Los Angeles. He quickly stopped attending L.A.'s Criminal Justice Group, for example. The group, which met regularly, comprised the city's and the county's top law enforcement officials and judges, and representatives of the state attorney general's and governor's offices. Throughout his five years in office, Williams would attend only two of the group's meetings, missing the opportunity to rub elbows with people who had an enormous amount of collective experience working in his strange, new city and county, and who could also have become highly influential allies.

But he wanted none of that. Not even when he was being courted. "He never talked to the commission about building partnerships or soliciting advice," says Anthony De Los Reyes. "Anytime I tried to broach the subject of creating a political power base or at least a network of people that could support him—because it was already clear he wasn't getting any support within the department—he wasn't interested."

So De Los Reyes, who believed that "a chief of police can't function without a constituency," organized a group of influential players from Los Angeles's business and political community to meet with Williams. "I got them together . . . and we all sat in a dining room waiting for Willie to show up for our breakfast meeting," De Los Reyes later recounted. "Then he called and said he couldn't make it. I asked if we could meet another time, and he said he'd get back to me. But he never did."

David Dotson had a similar experience. "He invited me into his office after I'd been in retirement for a while, and he presented me with this nice certificate of service," recalls Dotson. "And I asked him if there was anything I could help him with, or fill him in on. But he didn't want to know anything. And I never heard back from him. It wasn't that I had all this unique, wonderful information. But nobody else got in to tell him anything either."

It said a lot about Williams that he didn't pump Dotson dry for information. Dotson had been the chief of operations responsible for running the department on a day-to-day basis. Over the decades he'd served in just about every executive position in the department, and had publicly testified against Gates to the Christopher Commission. Dotson didn't just know a lot, he essentially knew *everything*.

Williams might have assumed that Dotson had a self-serving agenda.

And maybe he did. But Basic Police Work 101, like Basic Management 101, is that you take people's motives into account as you talk and listen, and then come to a conclusion based on multiple sources. But Willie Williams never did.

Richard Riordan and Willie Williams, June 1993, Los Angeles City Hall

Sitting in his office in June of 1993, Los Angeles's newly elected mayor, Richard Riordan, gave Willie Williams an order in the form of a request—just as he had been accustomed to giving orders for decades as a multimillion-dollar junk-bond speculator, attorney, and businessman.

"I want you to increase the size of the LAPD to 10,500 officers," he told Williams, "and to do so within five years." Although Riordan, according to the *Times*, had already had Williams and his wife for dinner at his home and had once even referred to him as the best police chief in America, they didn't really know each other. Nevertheless, they were about to embark on a mutual journey that was vital to the future of Los Angeles, so it was unfortunate to all concerned when Willie Williams replied with the wrong answer. "Sorry, Mr. Mayor," he said, "it can't be done." And with that, Willie Williams began his swift slide to persona-non-grata status in Richard Riordan's world.

A short, sixty-three-year-old Irishman with a weathered face and hair graying at the temples, Richard Riordan looked like he'd been born rough-and-tumble clad in a Wall Street three-piece suit. But there was more to him than that. An ex–New Yorker raised in Queens and suburban New Rochelle, he seemed torn between his desire to amass big money in the mean, cutthroat junk-bond industry and to do good by lavishly supporting L.A.'s Roman Catholic archdiocese.

Elected mayor on a slogan of "Tough Enough to Turn Los Angeles Around," Riordan had poured hundreds of thousands of dollars into his own campaign, and secured the strong support of both the LAPD's then reactionary union—the Police Protective League—and the city's white voters, who still made up two-thirds of the electorate. He'd run on a promise to add three thousand cops to the LAPD, and *that*—as he'd been making clear for months prior to his election—was his bottom-line consideration.

As a corporate CEO who headed two law firms—one of which specialized in business law—he'd been accustomed to picking up the phone and dictating unquestioned orders. And now, at his first official meeting with Williams, his major campaign promise was being unceremoniously dismissed by a new police chief whom he hardly knew and had had no input in selecting.

No matter that there were sound logistical reasons behind Williams's negative reply. "The whole idea of training and assimilating that many new officers in that amount of time," as David Dotson later pointed out, "was ridiculous. That kind of expansion has to be planned and done gradually. Otherwise you'll get a whole lot of people who have not been properly investigated and aren't well qualified. The mayor put Willie Williams in a terrible position."

So it wasn't that Williams was wrong in terms of practical policy, just that his answer was politically naïve. The passage into law of the Christopher Commission reforms limited an LAPD chief's tenure to two five-year terms. So Richard Riordan's Police Commission could simply refuse to rehire Williams when his first five-year term expired. But five years was a long time in politics. And in that interval, Richard Riordan would damn Willie Williams with little praise and even less support.

Richard Riordan, 1993

When he was running for mayor, Richard Riordan hadn't campaigned as an LAPD critic or police reformer. Nor was he one. He may have owed the police union a political debt, but he also loved cops. They were the good guys, the criminals the bad guys. For him it was about as simple as that.

What Richard Riordan was sure he wanted in his LAPD was a bigger, better-run, less controversial crime-fighting machine led by a tough, efficient police chief. One who would change the harsh fact that in 1993,

Riordan's inaugural year as mayor of Los Angeles, the city had the highest homicide rate in its history. One with whom he was philosophically in sync, with whom he could work, and whom he could back when the going got tough. He wasn't exactly *opposed* to the kind of reform the city's liberals were championing, he just believed it was secondary to law and order and didn't matter very much.

He had a sense of purpose and a few simple goals: strengthen the LAPD and reorganize city government so that it ran more efficiently and was more "business friendly."

He wasn't a wild-eyed, social-wedge-issue, law-and-order Republican of the type that had dominated California Republican politics into the early 1990s and that would lead the charge to pass the state's notorious 1994 three-strikes law. And he couldn't be if he hoped to be elected mayor. While many of the lunatic punishments for petty crimes under the law were coming out of Los Angeles courts filled with state-appointed judges, Los Angeles itself was a liberal, immigrant-friendly Democratic city. One that had the largest ACLU chapter in the country, and whose politicians waved from a Cadillac convertible every year in the West Hollywood Gay Pride Parade. In short, if Riordan had been a standard-model hard-right, slick-haired, white-male Inland California Republican of the nineties, he would never have been the first Republican in thirty years to be elected mayor of Los Angeles.

****

It was Richard Riordan's philanthropy that had first brought him to civic prominence. The Catholic Church had never been the political force in Los Angeles that it had become in cities like New York, Chicago, and Boston. Instead, during the first seventy years of the twentieth century, Los Angeles politics, culture, and economy had been almost entirely dominated by the conservative sons and daughters of white, native-born, middle-class Protestant emigrants from the Midwest. For most of those decades Los Angeles's Catholic establishment and its archdiocese had influence but never decisive power. (Bill Parker was Catholic, but never a Catholic chief in that sense.) Instead the archdiocese worked with a powerful layman from the Catholic community who served as its chief fund-raiser, consigliere to its archbishop, and a conduit to the world of the WASP power elite that then controlled L.A.

By the early 1990s, however, that had changed, and the archdiocese was thriving as the beneficiary of the hundreds of thousands of Latino immigrants flooding into its pews and Catholic schools. Meanwhile, the Church was holding $3 billion in assets and funding an annual budget of nearly $300 million, covering 284 parishes in L.A. and adjacent Orange County.

In the 1980s a dynamic young Los Angeles cardinal, Roger Mahony, found his consigliere in the person of Richard Riordan. Over the course of eight years, Riordan would raise over $84 million to create a permanent endowment that would grant scholarships to inner-city students and construction funds for Catholic schools.

Thanks also to Riordan, in 1989 Cardinal Mahony, despite his mission to the poor, also began soaring into the heavens in his new $395,000 blue-and-white Hughes 500D four-passenger helicopter—a gift from a very select group of donors who, like Riordan, had given the archdiocese at least a million dollars in the preceding year. (Mahony was later forced to step down in disgrace as archbishop after covering up for priests accused of sexually abusing children.)

It was this philanthropy, not politics, that first brought Richard Riordan to civic prominence. For his run for mayor he needed an architect to craft both his image and his message, and for that he chose William Wardlaw, a local master of realpolitik, who also knew how to count the votes you needed to get you where you wanted to go. It was he who came up with Riordan's campaign message: "Tough Enough to Turn Los Angeles Around."

A well-connected Democrat who began his political career working as a thirteen-year-old in John F. Kennedy's presidential campaign for president, Wardlaw had been active in both state and national politics ever since, working as a savvy consultant in Bill Clinton's crisis-filled first presidential campaign, as well as in almost every important statewide campaign for Democrats in California.

Bill Wardlaw was thus able to quickly build a campaign coalition for the Republican Riordan that included organized labor and the city's Latino leadership. Once Riordan was elected, Wardlaw would manage all the mayor's appointments, including to the Police Commission.

****

Working for Riordan at the law firm of Riordan and McKenzie, Wardlaw had been his protégé, lawyer, partner, and closest friend and associate.

Like Riordan, he was a key fund-raiser for the construction of Cardinal Mahony's new $35 million downtown cathedral, and was as well a member of the Regents Council at Mount St. Mary's College. In short, William Wardlaw was a very busy guy who rarely left fingerprints.

Although they were both practicing Catholics, neither he nor Riordan had a problem with gays. And at a homophobic time, when Bill Clinton was offering up "Don't Ask, Don't Tell" and signing the Defense of Marriage Act, Wardlaw chose openly gay officials, including a defense attorney and former head of the ACLU, as police commissioners.

Wardlaw was also a Bernard Parks guy. He liked Bernie Parks, and thought Willie Williams a disaster. It was he, in fact, who would coach Parks in his oral exams to replace Willie Williams as the next LAPD chief. He believed, like Riordan, that in a city plagued by crime, the LAPD needed to be tough.

For the previous decade Tom Bradley and Daryl Gates had detested each other so strongly that by the end they couldn't bear to speak with one another. Now Richard Riordan, as a new mayor, was joining a new police chief in the person of Willie Williams. And like Bradley and Gates, their chemistry was also bad. Their estrangement, however, would be a one-sided game of attrition in which Willie Williams wasn't playing and would always be on the defensive.

Gary Greenebaum, Summer 1993, Parker Center

Once elected mayor, Richard Riordan chose Rabbi Gary Greenebaum as his Police Commission president. At forty-seven, Greenebaum was tall, broad-shouldered, energetic, and witty—a man of casual, cosmopolitan demeanor soothingly offset by his attire of rumpled suits and ties (sans yarmulke). He was also proud, judgmental, and anxious to get things done.

In 1990 Greenebaum began working with leaders of the city's ethnic and religious communities—focusing most keenly on improving Jewish-black relations—which in Los Angeles had deteriorated sharply from the glory days of the civil rights movement and their work together in electing Tom Bradley as L.A.'s first black mayor. It quickly became obvious that a major issue for the city's African-Americans was trying to end the harsh treatment they were receiving at the hands of the LAPD.

After being part of the successful political campaign to codify into law the Christopher Commission reforms, he was now prepared, as a new police commissioner, to see them implemented by the department.

"I'm sure I was put on the commission partly because I was Jewish," says Greenebaum. "But I also think it was because Riordan or his advisors felt they needed someone who looked like reform. Later it became clearer and clearer that that's what I was there for—to represent the reform movement and help change the department."

During the transition from Jesse Brewer's outgoing Police Commission to Gary Greenebaum's new one, among the first things that Greenebaum did was to meet with Brewer for a working lunch. Sitting at a table in the summer of '93, Brewer handed Greenebaum a manila folder as he talked about the great job Willie Williams was doing—this despite the fact that he was privately growing increasingly disappointed with him.

Inside the folder was a self-evaluation that Williams had completed that past May. Greenebaum remembers being stunned. After the King beating, the Police Commission had found it nearly impossible to fire Daryl Gates because for over a decade a succession of Police Commissions had let him write his own always "outstanding" job performance evaluations. And here was a post-Gates commission making the same mistake instead of taking ownership of an essential task that was rightfully theirs. Brewer, however, told him that the self-evaluation was "no problem" and that the commission was merely following a "time-honored tradition."

Examining the performance report later, Greenebaum was even more shaken. "Not only was it a self-evaluation," recalls Greenebaum, "it was a multiple-choice, circle-the-box kind of questionnaire: outstanding, excellent, not so hot, could do better, etc. It didn't tell me anything about what the guy was capable of or what he was good at and not good at. And, of course, Willie Williams was outstanding in virtually every category." Williams had also added one concluding comment: "I believe that I have met all expectations placed upon me as the chief executive in the Police Department in areas such as: restoring community confidence; developing emergency plans; and refocusing department management to work as a team. I have, as an executive, exceeded the usual expected standards."

It certainly was accurate that he'd done a great deal to restore community confidence in the department, at least on a PR level, and had developed a plan to deal with another riot. The first was important and necessary, the second pro forma following the '92 disaster. But there was no mention of planning for—let alone implementing—high-priority tasks like community policing, the Christopher Commission reform recommendations (including changing the department's training and policing philosophy), or reforming the department's use-of-force policies and related discipline procedures.

Nevertheless, Willie Williams's success would be Gary Greenebaum's, would be the reform movement's, would be the city's. Consequently Greenebaum wanted desperately to put his doubts behind him and work hand in glove with Williams. So Greenebaum took it personally, took it hard, when, after six months, it became apparent "that Williams just didn't have the capacity to do the job; was never going to succeed; had no real contact with his department and no real interest in what was going on." The stakes were huge. Opportunity for reform had finally arrived. But instead, Gary Greenebaum found himself watching opportunity's door slowly slamming shut.

One of his first acts as Police Commission president was to visit Williams in his Parker Center office. "Chief," he told him, "this city and this department have a long history of racism. I want you to know that I am here to be your ally in making the necessary changes, and that this is my main agenda as president of the commission. He looked at me," recalls Greenebaum, "and then looked down at his papers, and changed the subject. He never responded to me then, and he never referenced it again."

Later, "at meetings," says Greenebaum, "he would stand up and say anything that popped into his head that would sort of answer a question and get him out of the room—basically making it up as he went along. In the morning he would say there's fifty thousand 'somethings' and at the next meeting he would say a different number [about the same subject], like twenty thousand. . . . In all the seventy-five meetings I attended in my two years as a police commissioner, he never spoke up when a [reform] issue was before us. He'd sit with us on the platform during commission meetings and take notes. But he never *did* anything."

If Jesse Brewer and his Police Commission had deliberately ignored those same deficiencies, Greenebaum's commission did not. And if 1992 and 1993 were good years for Williams in terms of his public popularity, that would begin to change dramatically in 1994.

****

The first attack on Willie Williams that drew public blood came in May of '94, when the Police Commission delivered its official evaluation of Williams following completion of his second year in office. "Consistently," the commission wrote, "you seem to lack focus and discernible purpose in managing the Department. It is often unclear throughout the ranks exactly who is in charge and who is making decisions affecting the operations and direction of the LAPD. Often, you seem unable to move the Department, to have your decisions understood and followed in a timely manner, if at all."

But the ineffectiveness of Williams and the turmoil within the LAPD would continue unabated and still largely unnoticed by the general public. Then one June night in 1994, the brutally butchered bodies of Nicole Brown Simpson and her friend Ron Goldman were discovered, and Los Angeles and the LAPD would again hold the world spellbound.

O. J. Simpson, June 1994, Brentwood, California

Besides the King beating and the '92 riots, nothing would demonstrate the depth of black mistrust of the LAPD more than the arrest and trial of African-American former USC Heisman Trophy winner and NFL football superstar O. J. Simpson, and the surreal media circus that followed.

It began with the famous low-speed car chase, a dozen or more LAPD patrol cars following Simpson, who was fleeing in Al Cowlings's Ford Bronco as a phalanx of media helicopters whirled overhead, beaming his flight into the TV sets of tens of millions of Americans across the nation.

As the chase continued, the LAPD showed remarkable restraint as a friend of Simpson's drove him around L.A., while Simpson sat beside him holding a handgun to his head and threatening to kill himself. In the end Simpson was peacefully arrested and charged with the stabbing death of his fair-skinned, blond-haired wife and her white friend as they strolled the streets of the wealthy Westside Brentwood section of Los Angeles.

It's difficult now for those who didn't live through it to grasp what an extraordinary, racially charged extravaganza the trial of the lithe, handsome O. J. Simpson was. The case had all the requisite elements of an over-the-top *telenovela* script: sexual fervor and crazed carnage, mixed together with what they used to call miscegenation, involving a black man white America had fully accepted as one of its own.

The early and mid-nineties were a nasty time characterized by sizzling racial tension in America, fueled by soaring crime rates, white fear and prejudice, and an astounding ratcheting up of America's already heavy "wars" on crime and drugs. In many cities like L.A., one in three black men were caught in the web of the criminal justice system at any one time, either in prison, in jail, on probation, or on parole. There was no black president, interracial marriage was not yet commonplace, there were still a relatively small number of African-Americans working in the professions and the media, and just a handful of black actors working in movies or commercials. O. J. Simpson was one of them.

So it would be ironic that Orenthal James Simpson would become a symbol of black mistrust of a justice system that was landing them in prisons in unprecedented numbers while police departments throughout the country were proving incapable of keeping them safe in their own neighborhoods. For Simpson surely had enjoyed the finest treatment from the LAPD of any black man in Los Angeles. Through his friend, former LAPD officer Ronald Shipp, Simpson had been introduced to about forty police officers, many of whom would swim in his pool, soothe their aches in his Jacuzzi, and play on his tennis court. Every year he would appear at a Christmas party thrown by the officers of the LAPD's West Los Angeles Division. Even the gun Simpson so tightly clasped as he threatened suicide during that low-speed chase was registered to an LAPD lieutenant.

There were, in addition, all those frantic calls from Nicole Brown Simpson to the LAPD that failed to result in an arrest until the department's *ninth* response in 1989. But even on that occasion, after Simpson was finally placed in custody after horribly beating Nicole, he had temporarily evaded arrest by fleeing in his Bentley—an act no police agency, particularly the LAPD, would normally tolerate, as Rodney King had brutally discovered.

Ironically, however, King's beating, along with the Simi Valley acquittals, would hover over the Simpson courtroom like the ghosts of bad deeds past.

O. J. Simpson and Johnnie Cochran, Superior Court, Downtown Los Angeles

Those ghosts did not make their appearance in the pretrial coverage. Based on the evidence, there appeared an extremely high probability Simpson would be found guilty, and that was what had been focused on. But guilt is in the eye of the beholder, and Simpson, with the rest of his life on the line, secured a "Dream Team" of high-priced, powerhouse defense attorneys to change that focus. On the team was sixty-year-old F. Lee Bailey, famed for representing, among others, Albert DeSalvo, the "Boston Strangler," and Patty Hearst, the wealthy kidnapping victim turned Symbionese Liberation Army brainwashed warrior-dupe. And so was forty-seven-year-old Barry Scheck, a forensic-evidence expert and professor at New York's Cardozo Law School who, with cocounsel Peter Neufeld, founded the legendary Innocence Project, reopening the cases and freeing over three dozen wrongly convicted men and giving them back their lives. But most crucially, Simpson had hired Johnnie Cochran, the brilliant African-American police-abuse trial attorney who had long been an icon in black Los Angeles. Short, wiry, and dark-skinned, Cochran was one of those people who had that special flash when he was onstage, and his stage was the courtroom.

Back in the seventies, he'd been one of the only people in Los Angeles who'd had the courage to stand up to the LAPD, speaking out publicly as he represented scores of victims of police abuse who'd been shot or choked to death under highly questionable circumstances. In the process, he became the most effective of the city's police-abuse attorneys—a subspecies of Los Angeles lawyer that, thanks to the abusive policing of the LAPD and the Los Angeles County Sheriff's Department, had become a thriving industry. His success, along with his audacity, gave him enormous authority in the black community and with black jurors.

So it wasn't coincidental that Johnnie Cochran understood, better than any of the other members of Simpson's "Dream Team," that while the prosecution was in possession of extremely strong evidence of Simpson's guilt, the best defense would be to put not Simpson but the LAPD and its history of abusing and framing the city's African-Americans on trial. Give me one black juror, Cochran had allegedly told his former mistress, and I'll get an acquittal. It was hardly a far-fetched idea. He knew what black jurors knew deep in their bones—that racism, planting evidence, shading the truth, and lying in court had been part of the Los Angeles Police Department's modus operandi throughout its history.

Simpson and his Dream Team's big break came when a judge ruled that the trial would take place *not* in the white, affluent Westside, where the murders had been committed, but in L.A.'s downtown Superior Court, where the jury pool was drawn from south of downtown, from the very African-American community that had exploded with rage at the LAPD just three years earlier. From that jury pool Johnnie Cochran did much better than getting just one black juror. He got eight African-American women and one black man. Los Angeles hadn't seen such a stacked deck since that predominantly white Simi Valley jury had acquitted those guilty-as-sin officers who'd beaten Rodney King.

Rafael "Ray" Perez, August 1995, Rampart Division

Meanwhile, Ray Perez had left the West Bureau [drug] Buy Team and transferred to Rampart CRASH (Community Resources Against Street Hoodlums). CRASH had been created in the 1970s in South Central and later expanded and decentralized into twelve units as gang violence proliferated during the eighties. CRASH's mission, as its acronym indicated, was to crush L.A. gangs by being tougher than they were. Period.

Rampart CRASH, however, as Ray would later tell it, had carried the mission to its logical extreme. On the right shoulders of their blue uniforms the Rampart officers wore their CRASH unit patch, which was identical to the image some had tattooed on their right arms: an elongated, wickedly grinning white skull with deep-set, demonic-looking eyes. Atop the skull sat a black cowboy hat with a large silver LAPD badge prominently displayed above the brim. Fanning out in the background were four playing cards—the dead man's hand of aces and eights.

Often Rampart CRASH officers wore street clothes, not uniforms. They worked by themselves, did all their arrests and searches by themselves, and, as Ray would later testify to investigators, rarely spoke to other Rampart Division cops while on patrol. They worked out of a small substation to which only they had the entrance code. Located about two miles from the Rampart Division's station house, the substation had only sergeants as supervisors, most of whom, according to Ray, were "in the loop." Being in the loop meant you were willing to lay a case on a suspect because you wanted him off the street, or simply to get your arrest numbers up, and would actively help cover up a bad shooting, or a brutal beating, or whatever else went down.

One of Rampart CRASH's unofficial rules was that to get into the unit, you had to be sponsored by someone who was in or had been in Rampart CRASH. Ray was sponsored by an LAPD officer named Sammy Martin. Sammy's and Ray's wives were good friends, and Sammy, like Ray, was a player, the type of guy, as Ray would later tell it, "who, when he'd come to work, had a girl to go visit."

The area that Rampart CRASH policed was known as Pico-Union, a poor, hard place of 7.8 square miles just west of L.A.'s downtown skyscrapers, with the unhappy distinction of being the most densely inhabited area west of the Mississippi.

An immigrant, first generation, port-of-entry community, Pico-Union's slum housing was overstuffed with 267,000 acutely impoverished, often illegal Central American immigrants. Many barely spoke English and had brought almost nothing with them when they'd fled the U.S.-backed right-wing death squads and vicious civil wars in El Salvador, Nicaragua, and Guatemala. Their new home was bloody too. The area policed by the Rampart Division was experiencing about 150 homicides a year back then, and violence was a rite of passage and way of life.

In rich-and-sunny L.A. they lived thirty-six thousand people per square mile and did the grunt and mule work that made Los Angeles run or, barring that, floated down to the lowest spot on the totem pole: *paletero* men. These were the guys who sold ice cream from a crate and struggled to make $5 or $10 a day so they could eat—while living, like the rest of Pico-Union, in fear of local gangs composed of their own sons.

Within this island of misery up to twenty-four Rampart CRASH officers raged war on some thirty to sixty local street gangs—Aztlan, Temple Street, 18th Street, the Crazy Riders. Many of the gangsters were too enmeshed in gang culture to contemplate any other future, and found both security and status in their *mi familia* gangs.

Most took their commitment to their adopted family with extraordinary seriousness, and viewed the world first and foremost through its prism and code of loyalty and behavior. Often that dictated warring with other gangs over the merest slight, or for control of a few blocks of turf where they could extort drug dealers or deal themselves. Every action was about the powerless having power over another group of young men that was also powerless outside of their neighborhood, and a cause for violent counteraction, refined over the decades into a special gang theology with its own adaptive, self-destructive logic.

****

One of the things about Ray Perez was that he was a good storyteller—so good, in fact, that he could weave a story with every detail you could want, and so convincingly that you'd think he was the nicest, most honest guy in the world. What follows is the tale that Ray Perez would tell DA and LAPD investigators in over three thousand pages of transcribed testimony. Some of it was fantastical; some was real. But it was also the story of a bungled investigation, an attempt to limit that investigation, and what it brought in its wake.

By 1996, Ray was so firmly in the loop that he was training new, wanna-be Rampart CRASH cops, and putting them to the Rampart Test. Once when he arrested a suspect for possession of rock cocaine, a new female officer named Raquel Argomaniz asked him how they could book the guy when he wasn't actually in possession of any rock cocaine. Don't worry about it, Ray told her. After that, Rampart CRASH cops deliberately made life so unpleasant for Argomaniz that she finally transferred out of the unit.

In their isolation, Ray would tell investigators, they were a law unto themselves, with their own set of rules and playbook. For example, it rarely, if ever, mattered if someone was innocent or guilty. If a Rampart CRASH officer wanted a guy in jail, he *would* go to jail. Drugs and guns would be planted. Misdemeanors would turn into felonies. "Throwdown" guns had their serial numbers shaved off so that the suspects could be charged with an additional felony. And if the planted gun was an automatic weapon, that would add another felony to the charges. According to Ray, he planted evidence or made up phony arrest scenarios in 40 percent of the arrests he made in his two and a half years in Rampart CRASH.

There was even a ten-sheet loose-leaf binder that was eventually given to all Rampart CRASH officers, according to Ray, a kind of proto-col on how to cover up problematic incidents written and printed up by a Rampart CRASH sergeant. Among the instructions most emphasized was how to make a bad officer-involved shooting or use of force look tactically correct and by the book.

A cardinal rule was to always quickly discuss the incident with the other Rampart CRASH officers on the scene, get your story down, and never change it. If a witness favored your story, you told him to stick around and talk to the investigators from the department's officer-involved shooting team; if a witness's account didn't jibe with your story, you told him to get lost. Or so Ray said.

Another rule was never do searches of buildings with non–Rampart CRASH patrol officers, but to wait instead for other Rampart CRASH officers to arrive on the scene before doing the search. Why? Because if something bad goes down, you don't want outside-the-unit cops with you who might tell the truth. It was all "plain and simple," as Ray would later explain. "If you were in a bad position, you're gonna be in a good position . . . if the guy [who was shot] didn't have a gun, we'll get him a gun . . . whatever we have to do to make it look like a justified shoot-ing." Collectively, these rules became known as "the Rampart Way." Gerald Chaleff, the president of the Police Commission during the mid-nineties, would later describe the Rampart Way thusly: "Whatever the way they did it, is the way they did it, and they didn't give a shit what anybody else said."

Pico-Union, with its powerless population, was the perfect place to make up the law and to be the law; and Rampart CRASH—with its separate unit, separate location, and near total independence—was in the ideal situation to never get caught. Enhancing that situation, said Ray, were two attorneys assigned to CRASH full-time: a deputy DA and a deputy city attorney. Both female. They were on-site to swiftly add alleged gangsters to a local gang injunction stripping them of many of their civil liberties—especially their right to freely assemble—and mak-ing them highly vulnerable to arrest for virtually any cause. According to Ray, the attorneys would sit in the CRASH office, listen as the cops joked about their cases, and later go out drinking and hanging out with the boys over at the cop bar known as the Shortstop, not far from Dodger Stadium. They were all part of one group, said Ray, the "Rampart CRASH group."

****

In 1996, Ray got a new partner. Nino Durden was a dark-complexioned twenty-two-year-old African-American straight out of South L.A., handsome, slim, well built and delicately featured. He also wore a pencil-thin mustache that, at least from his pictures in the media, gave him the look of a pretty-boy star on an early fifties R&B road show.

Sometimes Durden would wear his 77th Division CRASH bomberjacket to work. The 77th's station house was among the very toughest areas to police, and Durden had worked there as a probationary officer for about four months before transferring to Rampart CRASH. Like Rampart, 77's gang cops also wore a unit patch. It too featured a skull, but 77th's had crossed bones in the background and a king's crown sitting on the skull. Its motto read, "77th Street eats their dead." You could buy them up at the police academy in its small gift shop.

One day, said Ray, he and Durden seized a one-pound bag of cocaine and a beeper from a dealer. Not long afterward, the beeper went off. Ray did what most smart cops would do in such a situation: he called back the number. A native speaker of Spanish, Ray acted as if he worked with the dealer and ordered a quarter pound of coke. Then he and Durden hopped into their unmarked black Thunderbird and drove to meet the guy and bust him. But once they arrived, they made a snap decision and decided instead to steal the quarter pound of cocaine and sell the product. Then they hid the rest of the coke in a green ice cooler in the CRASH trailer. Thereafter, the cooler became their drug-storage container.

Ray and Durden soon began selling more seized coke they'd stolen or extorted from dealers, setting up shop outside of a Latino supermarket on Third Street, right across from the Nutel Motel, in the Ralph's market parking lot at Third and Vermont. Soon, continued Ray, they began partnering with a few other Latino CRASH officers who were also ripping off coke from dealers.

Ray also told investigators another story: One day a fellow CRASH officer received a call from one of his snitches—a dope dealer looking to get rid of some of his competitors. He told him about three midlevel dope dealers from Mexico who were cooking, cutting, and packaging about $20,000 worth of coke a day in an apartment nearby.

Ray and Durden immediately agreed to meet him there. The apartment's window was blocked with a mattress when they arrived, and, unable to see in, they decided to just go ahead kick in the door. It took a couple of tries, but down it went. Then they immediately grabbed a man breaking up a bunch of rock and trying frantically to flush it down the toilet. There was rock, powder cocaine, and cash lying everywhere they looked.

They seized it all and brought the suspect and everything else back to the Rampart trailer. On the arrest report they wrote that they'd knocked on the door and said they wanted to make a buy, and a guy came out holding a brown baggie, saw they were cops, dropped the baggie (which was filled with dope), ran back inside, and locked the door. Consequently, they kicked in the door.

When they booked the dealer, as Ray told it, they also booked some of his dope. But not the twenty-four ounces of already rocked-up cocaine and eight ounces of powder that they kept for themselves.

Willie Williams, October to December 1994, Las Vegas

Willie Williams liked Las Vegas—liked the atmosphere and liked the action. He once even considered leaving the Philadelphia PD to work security at an Atlantic City casino before discovering how badly the Donald Trumps of the world paid their employees. In October of 1994, when he was away in Las Vegas celebrating his twenty-eighth wedding anniversary with his wife, Evelina, a popular Metro officer was shot and killed in the line of duty on a Friday night in Hollywood.

After he heard the news, Williams took his time returning to Los Angeles, not arriving until sometime Sunday. For many officers Williams's leisurely arrival was an unforgivable breach of the professional ties that bind, especially since Williams had still not begun to build those ties. When a police officer is killed in the line of duty, goes the unwritten rule, the chief of police had better swiftly make an appearance unless he's on a hunting trip deep in the Siberian tundra, unable to be contacted by phone. Daryl Gates had always been there for his cops, and his downed cops in particular.

"Daryl's speeches always promoted the thin blue line—us against them—the fact that the officers of the LAPD were the only ones who really knew what was going on in the city of Los Angeles, and that nobody from the outside could possibly understand them," says David Dotson. "'They were the best,' he'd tell them, 'and any one of our captains could run any police department in the country. So how could anyone from the outside *possibly* do as well as any number of our people from the inside?'"

Undoubtedly the same LAPD complainers would have cut a new *insider* chief some slack, happy that at least their worst fears about a "reform" chief had not been realized. But they cut Willie Williams not one inch.

Charlie Beck got to see it in real time while working for the Police Commission. "The organization never gave Willie a fair chance to succeed," says Beck. "It stonewalled him, blindsided him. I am not disagreeing with the fact that he probably wasn't ready to be the chief of police of Los Angeles, but the organization just built a wall around him and just threw crap over the wall in order to run itself around the chief. There was a big disconnect between upper management and him. And the organization just ate him up because of that."

★★★★★★★★★★★★★★

Part of the crap that continued being thrown over wall at Willie Williams was the time he had been spending in Las Vegas. It all came to a head in December when the Police Commission questioned him about a letter they'd received written by a former LAPD deputy chief named Stephen Downing. It claimed that Williams and his wife had misused city cars and phones and were comped free rooms and service while gambling at Caesars Palace in Las Vegas.

Receiving something of value without paying for it was prohibited under LAPD policy, and Williams doing so just reinforced the West Coast perception that these East Coast cops always had their hands out. Nevertheless, the letter may well have amounted to nothing, been explained away as a mistake, resolved by offering to pay for the rooms and promising not to do it again.

Instead, Williams categorically and repeatedly denied the allegations and put his denial in writing to the commission. "I have never accepted without cost lodging, meals, and/or show tickets at any Las Vegas Hotel. Whenever I stayed in Las Vegas I paid all bills due from my personal expenses."

Thus, what started out as a petty vendetta and played as a big story by the *Los Angeles Times* was turned into a far bigger and more serious event by Williams's denial. The commission ordered an investigation, and when the results came back they were bad for Willie Williams. He and/or his family had indeed been comped rooms at Caesars Palace *five* different times. Ignoring the initial issue of the comped rooms, the Police Commission voted to unanimously reprimand Willie Williams for lying to the commission. Riordan's Police Commission had now twice correctly exercised its oversight responsibility and at long last was functioning as it was meant to function under the city charter.

Williams appealed to the City Council, and, usurping the power of the Police Commission, they overturned the reprimand. Making public his letter to the commission, however, had its intended effect of publicly embarrassing Williams, who had been caught in an official lie—just as the overturning of the reprimand had the unintended consequence of revealing how dysfunctional the government of the city of Los Angeles remained in its dealings with the LAPD.

O. J. Simpson, January 1995, Los Angeles Superior Court

From the opening arguments through the next 134 days of the "Trial of the Century," there would be two defendants in the docket: O. J. Simpson and the LAPD. No homicide investigation, of course, can ever be perfect. But with the whole world watching as the trial began in January 1995, *this* investigation had to be. Not only because of the Dream Team's LAPD frame-up strategy, but because the omnipresent gaggle of reporters camped out in the downtown superior court's shabby parking lot would be scrutinizing every aspect of the trial.

Inside the courtroom, Johnnie Cochran would argue that Simpson was the victim of an intricate LAPD conspiracy to pin the murders on him—going so far as to accuse one of the veteran investigating detectives, Mark Fuhrman, of being "a lying, perjuring, genocidal racist" in the tradition of "Adolf Hitler" who wanted to "take all black people and burn them or bomb them."

Cochran's cover-up theory would have been laughable even given the department's past history had it not been for the LAPD's startling incompetence and hubris during its investigation. The only cover-up attempted by the case detectives, in fact, would be to hide their own sloppy investigative work, and most especially their failure to follow standard operating procedures for homicide investigations. And that had nothing to do with O. J. Simpson. They neglected to follow the procedures because that was how many detectives in Robbery-Homicide operated. It was one of Daryl Gates's "elite" special units, a division with the latitude to operate as they wished. *That*, like so much else, had changed very little under Willie Williams.

Because of late notification by the detectives, for example, the coroner failed to arrive at the murder scene until almost ten hours after the two bodies were discovered. Consequently, the ability to take the temperature of the victims and better focus on the time of death was lost.

The Los Angeles County coroner's staff, moreover, had a long and justly deserved reputation for incompetence. As a result, LAPD detectives would frequently wait as long as possible before notifying them. Once the coroner arrived, he was in charge of the body. But in this case, lead detective Philip Vannatter—a twenty-five-year LAPD veteran who'd been involved in two hundred homicide investigations—had not only notified the coroner very late but had also then stalled him.

The failure to notify the coroner on time was a violation of both state law and department policy. It wasn't the first time. In 1992, the coroner's office had written two letters to Willie Williams urging him to ensure that his officers promptly notify them in murder cases. And again, Willie Williams had done nothing to effectively change the situation.

Four detectives, including Vannatter, then left an active murder scene and went to O. J. Simpson's house on the pretext of making a death notification. They also claimed that they hoped to ensure that Simpson and anyone else in his compound were safe. That would be their story, one they'd stick to because upon their arrival they failed to obtain a telephonic search warrant. Then Detective Mark Fuhrman jumped over a wall adjacent to the house looking for evidence and found a leather glove that would become a key piece of evidence—even though his actions constituted an illegal search. According to the trial judge, Lance Ito, Vannatter, in "reckless disregard for the truth," made it appear in the search warrant as if Simpson were running away.

And then there was the murder scene. "Contaminated, compromised, and corrupted," as the defense would describe it while showing the jury videos of investigators and criminologists traipsing through the evidence.

The defense also showed how some of that evidence was badly maintained and poorly tested. Former LAPD detective Bill Pavelic helped the defense compile loose-leaf notebooks filled with mistakes that had been in the LAPD's crime book, such as violations of procedures and breaks in the chain of custody of the evidence.

Detective Vannatter, after having Simpson's blood drawn at Parker Center, put the evidence vial in his pocket and went back out to O. J. Simpson's house. He then handed it to criminologist Dennis Fung, who didn't book it until the following day. Simpson's defense team used this delay to discredit the blood evidence. They then attacked the LAPD lab as "a cesspool of contamination," with bad equipment, underpaid and overworked staff, and frequent job turnover. They accused Dennis Fung of using a broken blood storage refrigerator in his van that stopped working "after [being on for] several hours." Barry Scheck so thoroughly decimated Fung on the stand that a new verb sprung up in legal circles to describe crushing a witness: he got "Schecked."

DNA expert and defense witness John Gerdes, moreover, would testify that the LAPD's DNA lab was "by far" the worst of the twenty-three he had inspected around the country.

There was also the failure to adequately secure O. J. Simpson's Bronco. It was left at an impound yard, where many unauthorized people had access to it. Here again was a break in the chain of custody. As a result, the defense was able to demonstrate that evidence in the Bronco, like that in the crime lab, might well have been contaminated or planted.

Finally, there was Detective Mark Fuhrman, that "genocidal racist," who, under oath in the courtroom, had sworn he hadn't used the "N" word over the past ten years, contradicting previous defense testimony and allegations that Fuhrman was an old-school, walking, talking LAPD bigot. After Fuhrman's denial, an audiotape was then played before the jury on which Fuhrman casually used the word "nigger" several times. Cochran, in the person of Mark Fuhrman, had thus found his racist cop. And in Phil Vannatter he had found his cop who was smart but not really smart, and used to doing things his own, casual way, unchallenged.

And in Willie Williams he had found a chief of police who seemed unable to respond, who had nothing to say as his police department was being ripped apart for past bad deeds and sloppy police work. His silence was deafening. But perhaps that was preferable to Daryl Gates's landing on the cover of some weekly news magazine, combatively defending *his* detectives and further embarrassing the department.

When Simpson's not-guilty verdicts were announced just before 10 a.m. on the morning of October 3, 1995, most of white America could not believe that Johnnie Cochran had done exactly what he said he was going to, and that O. J. Simpson was about to walk away scot-free.

But at black colleges like Howard University and from black students in university lounges at UCLA and all across America, the cheers couldn't have been louder. They weren't about O. J. He was no black hero. It was that *they*—black Americans—had finally won one, had finally beaten a criminal justice system that had been grossly stacked against them since African slaves had set foot in America. *That* was what their reaction was all about—an instinctually tribal sort of vindication, sort of like the '92 riots played out differently but with underlying emotions remaining the same.

White America, on the other hand, was stunned. Not just by the verdict, but by that inexplicable reaction of so many African-Americans. On talk-radio's KFI-AM—L.A.'s most popular English-language station—"John and Ken," the hosts of a highly rated conservative, white-male talk show, almost choked on their rage.

Meanwhile, on the blighted eastern end of Sunset Boulevard, Brien Chapman, a wild-eyed former detective and retired twenty-six-year veteran of the LAPD, was slipping into a bar seat at the Saratoga restaurant, ordering a Bloody Mary with a salted rim as soon as he was greeted by bartender Mike Lambert, who'd worked LAPD homicide for twenty years.

"Some shit," said Chapman.

"Everybody here is *so* pissed," replied Lambert. "But I'm not surprised with *that* jury. I've had less evidence than that and sent guys to the chair—all circumstantial evidence, and that was before DNA. It's just unbelievable . . . I wouldn't have called the coroner," he continued. "I mean, I'd have called him as a *courtesy*, but I wouldn't have wanted him messing around with *my* crime scene. Hell, we used to pick up our own stuff [evidence], throw it in a bag, and book it later."

"Yeah," replied Chapman, "and maybe stop and have a couple of pops along the way."

Katherine Mader and Willie Williams, May 1996, Parker Center

Meanwhile, back at Parker Center, Willie Williams's problems were continuing unabated, even as forty-nine-year-old Katherine Mader reported in to her new job as the first inspector general in the history of the LAPD. Like Gary Greenebaum she'd arrived expecting to be a Williams ally. After all, he was an LAPD outsider just like herself; someone who possessed the same progressive ideas as she. Together, she thought, they would work to reform the department.

Appointed IG in May of 1996, Mader was a smart, ambitious Jewish liberal who lived on Los Angeles's moneyed Westside. After graduating from UCLA and UC Davis Law School, she lost her most famous case in 1980 when she was appointed as co–defense counsel for Angelo Buono, the notorious Hillside Strangler, who was found guilty of pretending to be a cop and stopping young women under cover of law to rape and strangle them to death. It was a famous L.A. case, later made into a TV movie. But Mader considered it a win. Buono had killed nine women. It was a foregone conclusion that he was guilty. The win was that he wasn't sentenced to the death penalty.

After that she worked with the Los Angeles District Attorney's Office, and among other things became part of a unit investigating public officials and police officers.

The Office of Inspector General was another recommendation of the Christopher Commission, and had been approved by voters in 1995. Its mission was to be both an LAPD watchdog, to which the public could go with complaints, and the eyes and ears for a strengthened Police Commission that needed an IG reporting to them who could cut through the fog that for decades had shrouded the LAPD's inner workings from the commission.

Despite her initial assumptions, it wasn't long before Mader become one of Williams's most caustic critics. Armed with the moral indignation of a loyal subject who finds the emperor has no clothes, Mader began—both in public reports and to individual reporters—to set the record straight.

"The problem," said Mader at the time, "wasn't that any of the [negative] things that Williams was doing were new to the LAPD chief. The problem's that Williams is a reform chief. You expect a reform chief, a progressive chief, to be at the top of the spectrum in terms of integrity. . . . But he isn't. Not in his verbal pronouncements, not in his written reports—which don't have integrity, because he's not honestly dealing with issues and saying we have a problem."

Once, talking to a reporter, she let lose a string of complaints almost in a single breath: he'd say he was cracking down on sexual harassment and then transfer the complaining officer out of the unit and do nothing to the harasser. He'd testify under oath that the department was investigating and punishing code-of-silence-related offenses and Mader would find that code-of-silence investigations weren't going up but instead were plummeting.

"Have you seen any police officers prosecuted for a bad shooting?" she once asked the reporter. "There have been *bad* shootings. I know, I review the shootings every week. . . . But there's just no sense of what's permissible and what's not."

When Willie Williams's popularity was pointed out to her in response to her criticism, she said this: "Yes, you can pick out [positive] qualities like how well he relates to the black community. . . . But the momentary absence of the potential for a riot isn't reform, certainly not long-term structural, cultural or procedural reform."

Mader would land her strongest blow, however, in January of 1997 when Willie Williams declared he would be seeking reappointment to a second five-year term as chief while announcing that civilian complaints against the department had "declined by 43 percent" over the course of his first five-year tenure. Almost immediately Mader very publicly disputed Williams's claim by pointing out the various ways in which complaints were being hidden and how Williams's stats were, therefore, meaningless.

****

In fact, after two and a half years in office, Willie Williams had done little to alter the legacy that Daryl Gates had left behind. The unsupervised and non-rigorous robbery-homicide investigations revealed in the O. J. Simpson trial were one example. The highly controversial officer-involved-shooting team was another. It remained headed by Daryl Gates's handpicked man, whose mission upon arriving at the scene, so the joke went, was to announce what the unarmed civilian had done wrong to get himself shot.

Meanwhile, natural, reform-minded allies of Williams were becoming increasingly critical. "Glacial," said Joe Hicks of the Los Angeles chapter of the Southern Christian Leadership Conference of the pace of implementation of the Christopher Commission reforms. "Inexcusably slow," spokesman Alan Parachini of the ACLU told the *L.A. Times*. Meanwhile, in New York, Bill Bratton was dealing with his own escalating problem.

Bill Bratton and Rudolph Giuliani,
Monday, April 15, 1996, New York City

While William Bratton was being celebrated by *Time* magazine as New York's savior, Rudolph Giuliani and his administration were *seething* over the attention their police chief was receiving. Giuliani was obsessed with controlling information from city departments to the media, particularly major stories, such as the *Time* magazine article.

Early in his tenure, Bratton had been put on notice when he was quoted on the front page of the *New York Daily News* with a headline proclaiming: "Top Cop Bratton—'I'll End the Fear.'" He'd really gone off the reservation with that one. Everyone knew that in Giuliani World only *Rudy* would end the fear. As Giuliani once said, correcting a radio talk show host who'd referred to the NYPD as Bratton's police department, "It isn't his police department, it's the mayor's police department."

Soon, Bratton, John Miller, and others from Bratton's staff found themselves dressed down by Giuliani's enforcer, Deputy Mayor Peter Powers, for violating the talking-without-authorization media gag rule. The issue became so extraordinarily contentious that John Miller resigned, and the Mayor's Office let it be known that they were also willing to accept the resignations of Bratton and his top deputies if it came to that. And with the publication of the *Time* magazine cover story, it *had* come to that. *Time* was an extremely powerful and far-reaching national publication back in 1996, and Bratton had outshone Giuliani just one time too many.

Forced to resign after just two and a half years at the center of the

policing capital of the world, Bill Bratton was now on the outside looking in, trying to make the best of an inglorious situation by forming his
own security firm and advising police departments in South America
and elsewhere abroad. When the 9/11 planes hit, he sat watching the
biggest calamity in New York and modern American history unfold on
a television screen in his Manhattan apartment, helpless in the face of
what could have been—*should* have been—the defining moment of his
professional life.

****

Bill Bratton may not have been rebelling against anything as a young
cop in the sixties, but as journalist and author James Lardner would
later correctly point out, during his tenure in New York, he'd emerged
"as leader and archetype of a generation of police managers who, when
they got the chance, mounted a rebellion from within that mirrored the
intense criticism that the profession was getting from the outside."

But that was only part of the story. Major felonies were going down
throughout big-city America, with and without Bratton's innovations—
a point his detractors were quick to make. But nowhere did they drop as
quickly and last as long as they have New York City, and under an NYPD
utilizing the innovative policing strategies that Bratton pioneered.

By July of 1995, for example, crime had decreased nationally by 1 percent from the preceding year, but by 16 percent in New York City. And
over the next twenty years, crime in New York City would fall by over
75 percent—nearly twice the rate of the rest of the nation.

And there was this: in 1994, Bratton's first full year in office, there
were 1,561 homicides in New York City, 931 in Chicago, and 850 in Los
Angeles—the latter two cities with populations far less than half the size
of New York's. By 2002, a remarkable inversion had occurred. Chicago
recorded the highest number of murders of the three—656—Los Angeles had 647, and New York had just 587: almost one thousand fewer
homicides than eight years earlier.

Today, leading criminologists like Frank Zimring and Jerome Skolnick
point out that New York City had 75 percent fewer homicides, robberies,
and auto thefts in 2012 than it had in 1990, with basically, says Zimring,

"the same populations of schools, transportation, and economy." By institutionalizing efficient policing tactics such as COMPSTAT—which mapped, tracked, and swiftly and skillfully massed officers in areas where crimes were occurring—and holding captains accountable for crime in their precincts, Bratton proved that cops could actually play an important part in long-term crime reduction, as opposed to simply reacting to individual crimes after they occurred, as they'd done in the past.

And he introduced quality-of-life policing, a concept with long-term benefits as well. "In New York," as Bratton himself would tell it, "we changed the culture of permissiveness in that city that for 30 years had said don't bother people with the little things. You know, they're poor, they're black, they're brown. It was a failure not to recognize that they were just like everyone else, they wanted peace, tranquility, and a civil environment to bring their kids up in." And that was right.

Along with that success, however, was the potential for "broken-windows" policing to be seriously abused. The difference between promoting order and making communities livable and intrusive, invasive policing can be very small. Especially when beat cops are told it should be applied with "zero tolerance" or that consistently tight policing in poor black and brown neighborhoods was the key to keeping crime down. That potential was even greater with another Bratton innovation: stop-and-frisk—which would later allow for the tactic's routine and astronomically frequent use in the ghettos and barrios of America. Bratton would not only reinstitute this old policing practice, he would re-pioneer it, and declare it an essential component in the mix of strategies he'd used to dramatically lower New York's crime rate. In so doing, he *legitimized* the widespread use of stop-and-frisk, making the practice not just acceptable and routine but a *necessary* part of everyday policing. And that, as New York would discover, came with its own set of very real problems.

But at the time many New Yorkers viewed such tactics as necessary correctives to a deeply ineffective police department and saw Bratton as the miracle worker who was giving them back their sense of public safety, lifting the city's spirit and helping to reignite its prosperity. As a result there was relatively little resistance.

In a sense, however, it doesn't matter exactly how much of the extraordinary decline in crime that New York has experienced is attributable to Bratton's policies and policing strategies. His undeniable contribution was to introduce modern, data-driven managerial concepts, practices, and strategies to American big-city policing in a high-crime era when they were desperately needed.

Rafael "Ray" Perez and Nino Durden, Sunday, October 13, 1996, 18th Street Territory, Rampart Division

Arriving at a boarded-up apartment building for a surveillance stakeout sometime after 10 p.m., Ray Perez and Nino Durden parked their unmarked light-blue Taurus undercover car under a large, low-hanging tree. In uniform and armed with their 9mm Berettas, radios, flashlights, binoculars, and radio earpieces, they lifted a board covering a back entrance to the largely vacated apartments and began a cursory search, looking for gang members or others who might be crashing there or dealing drugs.

They'd been briefed at roll call about the murder of two 18th Street gangsters by a rival gang right in front of this building, and warned to be on the lookout for retaliation killings. Ray and Durden and another two-man unit had been ordered to set up observation posts in 18th Street territory and see what they could see.

After entering the building, they had begun walking to their stakeout spot in an empty apartment with a large corner window overlooking the streets below when they decided to check out some other apartment units. In one, they found a guy called "Nene" and a small, thin nineteen-year-old Honduran immigrant named Javier Ovando, a member of the notorious 18th Street Gang. Ovando had joined the gang when he was sixteen and homeless, and he was crashing in the abandoned unit. They had thrown him out of the building the night before and were unhappy to see that he'd returned.

Handcuffing the two men, Ray and Durden marched them into their stakeout apartment in unit 407. "I'm sending you out of here one at a time, beginning with you," Ray said, unshackling Nene, who left immediately.

★★★★★★★★★★★★★★

As Ray and Durden later described it, sometime after releasing Nene and Ovando, they heard a loud knock on the door of darkened apartment number 407. As it opened, there stood Ovando, backlit by the hallway light, pointing a semiautomatic rifle at them. Durden yelled, "Police officer, drop the gun!" and then pulled out his double-action Beretta and shot Javier Ovando—who was standing directly in front of him—dead center in the chest.

Ray instantly reacted, firing off three rounds so fast it felt like one, the blast of the muzzle lighting up the room in a weird orange glow. Ovando had been shot in the head, arm, chest, and back. Or at least that was Ray and Durden's fabricated first, official account of the incident.

Initially Ovando himself had no recollection of the event, having been shot in the head. But later he would recover his memory and tell a very different, very real story about that evening: Handcuffed, he was taken into 407, where Durden and Perez began interrogating him. When he didn't know or would not offer up any information, Perez suddenly pulled out his Beretta and shot him in the chest, quickly followed by Durden doing the same. Then, according to Ray himself, he reached down, pulled Ovando off the floor by the front of his shirt, and fired a round into the side of his head.

★★★★★★★★★★★★★★

Using what Ray described as Rampart CRASH's secret radio code for a dirty shooting, Durden and Perez sent out a call for assistance. Only those in the loop, said Ray, understood the code, which always went out first, giving CRASH officers a heads-up while keeping outside supervisors away from a crime scene until everything could be properly arranged and a suitable cover-up story agreed upon.

CRASH officers understood, explained Ray, that when they arrived at the scene of an officer-involved shooting, everybody had a role to play.

It could be discouraging potential witnesses who might have damning testimony to offer. It could be taking a door and guarding it, making sure to keep everybody—absolutely everybody—away from the crime scene until the CRASH officers involved inside got their story straight with a sergeant in the loop and made sure the crime scene reflected that story.

Once the story was decided on, said Ray, it never—ever—changed.

✶✶✶✶✶✶✶✶✶✶✶✶✶✶

The sergeant in charge that evening soon arrived in room 407 and huddled with Ray and Durden, tying together all the loose ends of the story.

The tale Ray later told investigators—and the story the DA would promote as gospel—was that a wild-eyed Javier Ovando had kicked in the apartment door, burst into the room, aimed the semiautomatic rifle at the two cops, and tried to ambush them. His motivation, as the DA would later explain, was to "eliminate the police from [18th Street] territory, to intimidate the police and force the police to reassess the use of observation posts in their policing activity."

Although Ray was the senior officer, Durden did all the explaining to the sergeant, improvising on the basic story he and Ray had agreed upon. He didn't tell the sergeant how he'd run down to their parked Taurus and returned holding a filthy red rag wrapped around a chopped-down Tech .22 semiautomatic with a loaded twelve-round banana clip protruding from its underside and a serial number Durden had previously scraped off. Or that Durden had then placed the weapon next to Javier Ovando's fallen body. The sergeant didn't need to know about the gun.

They then decided where Ray needed to be when he fired his rounds: a stuffed chair lying on its back, right next to where he actually *was* when he fired. That part of the story required no change; it was only to make sure, said Ray, that when he told his *official* story, the shooting position he said he was in was consistent with the rest of it.

✶✶✶✶✶✶✶✶✶✶✶✶✶✶

About three weeks after the shooting of Javier Ovando, Rampart CRASH held a big mug party for Ray and Durden to celebrate. The word that a gang member had tried to ambush two officers and had himself been critically wounded had spread, and past and present CRASH officers showed up to give Ray and Durden a hero's celebration.

The party, according to Ray, was held at "the benches," a secluded spot within the hills of the police academy containing picnic benches and a barbecue pit. There, as Ray would later describe it, the Jack Daniel's and cold beer flowed and steaks were grilled.

As usual, the party for Ray and Durden started early in the evening, right before sunset. Earlier, Ray's workday had consisted of picking up the beer, steaks, chips, and ice over at the Glendale Galleria and getting the award plaques from a sergeant who always made them.

CRASH parties were always boozy affairs. Sometimes there would be officers on duty and in uniform with drinks in their hands, which was no problem, according to Ray.

They'd bring a thirty-two-ounce mug, fill it up with beer, and throw in three or four shots of Jack Daniel's. It was always Jack, the hard-man's drink, nothing else. They'd drink casually for a while and then sit around a blazing bonfire while each of the guys gave the honorees their props. They'd toast them, tell a little war story about working together, or about the shootings they'd been involved in and how it happened—how it *actually* happened, said Ray, not the way it was written in some official report.

The honorees' plaques—their *awards*—consisted of two framed playing cards with red hearts and red bullets—if, that is, the wounded victim lived. If he *died*, the playing cards were black hearts—by far a more prestigious color.

The celebrations, the unit logos for sale at the police academy, and the attitude on the street were, after all, no secret. The warning flags were everywhere. There were also the doctored civilian complaint reports and tainted shooting scenes that were routinely accepted by the department's officer-involved-shooting teams and never questioned by the DA's Office.

****

Miraculously, Javier Ovando survived his shooting, although he was paralyzed and wheelchair-bound for the rest of his life. In February of 1997, he was brought into L.A. County Superior Court on a gurney. The prosecutors presented a choreographed dance to the judge, who might as well have been part of the prosecution's team.

No round was in the gun's chamber when Ovando arrived at the door of room 407, according to the prosecution's story. Nevertheless, according to the deputy DA, within a few seconds Ovando had burst through the apartment door, paused long enough for Ray to yell "Gun, gun, gun!" and for Durden to get his bearings and yell "Police officer, drop it," and then for Ovando to point the weapon directly at Durden. Durden, in turn, was able to reach into his holster and shoot him before Ovando could squeeze off a round from the unchambered weapon. Then as he was falling to the ground, as if in a slow-mo scene in an action movie, he continued to point the gun at Durden while *rotating* to then point it directly at Perez.

"The defendant," the DA told the jury, "[had] equipped himself with a weapon especially adapted for this crime, and tried to sneak up on the officers and murder them. This indicates planning, sophistication, and professionalism." When Ovando's deputy public defender, Tamar Toister, argued that the scenario was far-fetched, the prosecutor replied: "What would defense counsel have you believe? That they found this guy on the street, dragged him up there, and shot him for some obscure reasons of their own?" (Ovando may have been doing some small-time dealing on Ray and Durden's turf, although that was never officially established.)

Then, as his pregnant girlfriend watched from the courtroom, an emaciated, wasted-looking Javier Ovando was found guilty of two counts of assaulting a police officer with a semiautomatic rifle and one count of brandishing it in the presence of a police officer.

Although Ovando had that number "18" tattooed on the back of his neck, he had no felony arrests on his record and was, at best, a very, very minor member of a very large local gang. Moreover, LAPD detectives had never even bothered to interview him.

Nevertheless, the presiding judge, J. Stephen Czuleger, swallowed the story whole, in one long, greedy gulp. And why not? He was a former federal prosecutor appointed to the bench during the 1980s by the extraordinarily conservative law-and-order California governor George Deukmejian. Throughout the trial J. Stephen Czuleger ruled against Toister at almost every turn.

"What happened was dirty," Toister later told journalist Lou Cannon. "I did all I could, but I wasn't allowed to put on a defense." Czuleger then sentenced Javier Ovando to the maximum sentence—twenty-three years, four months in state prison—because, as he said, "the defendant has no remorse."

Richard Eide, Spring 1997, Los Angeles Police Academy

If further evidence was needed of Willie Williams's failure to begin transforming the LAPD, it came in on a sunny spring afternoon in 1997 as Captain Richard Eide stood on a roadway at the Los Angeles Police Academy, deep in conversation. Behind the stiff, tailored, sandy-haired Eide was one of the academy's slightly off-kilter brick buildings constructed by jail labor during the hard-luck 1930s.

In front of him was a reporter who'd just asked Eide a question about the LAPD's traditional emphasis on paramilitary policing and how the department's training had changed since Willie Williams had become chief almost five years earlier.

"We don't have paramilitaristic [sic] training, never have," answered Eide, not bothering to hide his annoyance. The captain responsible for in-service training for the entire LAPD, Eide had been involved in training at the academy for "eighteen months this tour." As he continued, his irritation seemed to accelerate. "The Police Department," he says, "has a job to do, sometimes that's finding lost kids, and sometimes that's removing a suspect who's barricaded himself in a building and who has weapons. . . . Militaristic training is kind of a loaded term."

"What about community-based policing?" the reporter asked.

"That," said Eide dismissively, "is a catchall term that started here [with the LAPD], rolled across the country and now has come back packaged up with a ribbon on it, but the LAPD has been at it for 25 years, there's been no difference. . . . The idea of problem solving, that's what team policing was about back in 1971, '72 and we've had senior lead officers ever since then, and have been and are today at the forefront of—quote-unquote—'community-based policing.' . . . This is new to writers and other people: it is not new to this Police Department."

It was astounding that Eide, five years into Williams's commitment to community policing, was still holding out the 1972 LAPD version of a community policing model that was all police and no community. Under that model, the LAPD defined *who* the community was and what organizations could be involved, maintaining the right of approval and refusal. It also dictated the agenda and refused to consider complaints about how officers in the community were doing their jobs or how they might do them better. Community policing circa the 1970s, in short, had never been implemented with a real level of grassroots involvement— as a meaningful partnership with a broad, representative spectrum of residents. It was owned and operated by the LAPD interacting with the same old cop groupies, even as police-community relations continued to deteriorate in vast segments of the city.

If Eide—as a captain in such a key position—didn't see any problem with that old model, it was no wonder that Willie Williams's version of community policing was being so roundly criticized four and a half years into his tenure. Community policing had been one of Williams's key selling points as a candidate for chief, and he had pointed to community policing in Philadelphia as a model. But he'd never really gotten it off the ground in Los Angeles. Instead it became more of a talking-point sales pitch than an activated reality.

"I helped put together a community policing plan for the LAPD under Williams," Ron Noblet, the highly respected veteran gang intervention worker would later say. "We spent a year on it, and it was fantastic. We had a big public meeting to announce it. And the report went up on some shelf and we never heard from the department again."

"The Police Commission Office started monitoring the Community Policing Advisory Board," says Gary Greenebaum. "A lot of City

Council members were having trouble with them, because all the decisions were being fiercely held on to by the department, so that nobody
else could make recommendations or put members on [the local community policing boards]. The civilian leadership was worried that the
boards would just become police booster organizations, and be seen
that way by the community."

****

As Captain Eide's interview continued, he then moved, unsolicited,
to another area he thought the media hadn't gotten right: the department's use of force. "The people who think the LAPD had problems
with excessive force 10 or 15 years ago are wrong," he said. "I can lay
out the numbers that show that the newspaper opinion and the media's
opinion is not borne out by the facts. The use of force was a big issue
with the Christopher Commission. . . . I can explain to you . . . why
that's all nonsense."

In short, while Richard Eide was fuming about some stats from a
decade earlier and declaring that nothing had been wrong in the first
place, Willie Williams had allowed Eide to be in charge of shaping the
attitudes and training of what was supposed to be a new reform generation of LAPD officers.

That same year the *L.A. Times* ran a story that profiled Sergeant
Nicholas Titiriga, an eighteen-year veteran of the department who
was also an instructor at the Police Academy. When he was in the field,
Titiriga had "compiled a total of eighteen misconduct complaints—all
unfounded or unresolved." "At times," wrote reporter Stephen Braun,
"when [Titiriga] talks about the changes taking place around him, his
voice tightens in fury. What reformers reject in the old department,
they reject in him." In other words, in what should have been the Holy
Temple of the new LAPD, in what should have been the Fountain of
Change, there stood an officer with *eighteen* complaints and a pissed-off
attitude teaching the department's new recruits. King's beating and the
riots brought new laws that increased oversight and limited the LAPD's
heretofore impenetrable political power. But because of the LAPD's resistance and Williams's weak and indifferent leadership, those statutory

changes were never reflected on the street. As Deirdre Hill, an African-American Police Commission president during Williams's tenure, would later point out, the LAPD had "no in-service training" to change the way officers operated.

That same pivotal year of 1997, Allan Parachini, an ex–*Los Angeles Times* reporter who was then handling the press for the ACLU, had a conversation with Commander Tim McBride, the LAPD's chief media spokesman. "McBride was talking about what he thought was wrong with Williams, and assassinating Williams behind his back," says Parachini. "And if Tim McBride would say these things to me as Williams's official spokesman, God knows what else he'd say to others. He went off on the chief about being uneducated—which you hear all over the top ranks of that department—about how Williams had come into the department not knowing anything, and about how his learning curve was too slow. . . . He used everything but the 'N' word. It was a hostile, ultimate slam job." And very soon, like Willie Williams's very real failures, it would have its effect.

Willie Williams, March 1997, Parker Center

In March of 1997, the Police Commission voted unanimously not to rehire Willie Williams, saying that "the department cannot continue without more effective management and . . . strengthening the department management will require a change at the top, a new chief." And it was true.

Midway through Williams's tenure as chief, thirty-three of the forty-four cops with records so bad that the Christopher Commission report had specifically dubbed them "problem officers" were still on the job—nineteen in frontline positions. In mid-1995, one of them, Michael Falvo, had been involved in a highly controversial shooting death of a fourteen-year-old boy in a Mexican section of L.A. The shooting was so highly charged it almost sparked a riot. Then Andrew Teague, another of the problem forty-four, who was in training to be a detective, admitted to falsifying evidence in a homicide case and lying about it under oath. It was amazing that those officers were not only still on the job but were working in the field.

"In the most basic way," Gary Greenebaum would say in 1997, "it is business as usual. And this is something that the commission cannot legislate; this is something that has to do with this chief's commitment to change—to real change."

When Willie Williams finally woke up to what was going on under and around him, it was late October of 1995 and it was too late to do anything about it. Calling an hourlong meeting of about a dozen of the LAPD's deputy and assistant chiefs, Williams shed his amiable persona and talked to them in blunt, tough language. He'd been receiving pressure from City Hall about the slow pace of reform, he said—particularly the implementation of community policing and new officers being hired to work on the street.

The department needed to be "kick-started," he emphasized, and he wanted to see action on community police and other matters—now. "Senior officers unwilling to back [him]," said Williams, according to the *Times'* then police-beat reporter, Jim Newton, were "not welcome in the department and should consider changing careers."

Later, Newton spoke with some of those attending the meeting. One of those was Assistant Chief Ronald Banks, the department's second-ranking officer. "The tenor [of the meeting]," Banks told Newton, was "[Williams] saying: 'I'd like to get more help from you when I ask for these things rather than being told that this is the way we've always done things.'" Others at the meeting told Newton that, in effect, it was the same old Willie Williams, criticizing the department and saying in general what he wanted but not offering specifics about *exactly* what he wanted or how to implement it.

Both interpretations of the fault line between Williams and his top staff were true. Williams didn't have the leadership skills or strategic ability to succeed at big reform. And his command staff and many at Parker Center conspired to ensure that whatever he asked for would be ignored.

But there was so much more to it than that. The Stanley Sheinbaum/ Jesse Brewer Police Commission had to select a candidate based on antiquated civil service laws that precluded their considering another outsider. Tom Bradley had been working toward Daryl Gates's ouster ever since the beating of Rodney King, yet he failed to change those civil service laws that so limited the competition, or to order his personnel department to thoroughly vet Williams.

Earlier that Commission had stepped far beyond the comatose, rubber-stamp Police Commissions prior to the King beating and worked hard to force Daryl Gates out of office and to choose what they believed was the best man to replace him among a limited group of candidates.

But then, remarkably, they had failed to set Williams straight when he ran out of steam after just ninety days in office, and didn't say strongly enough, if at all, "Hey, you're not reforming the department; this is not acceptable; get a grip." Instead they allowed Willie Williams to give himself an excellent evaluation.

Still, over Williams's next four years the Riordan Police Commissions, with people like Gary Greenebaum in leadership positions, did their job—or tried to—on this critical issue, writing tough, critical evaluations of Williams that were right on the money, publicly sanctioning Williams for lying to them, and then refusing to rehire him.

All the while Williams faced the passive and active resistance of a department that was determined to see him fail and that worked very hard to ensure that he would. He never understood, until too late, that L.A. was the kind of place that, when they stabbed you, they did it in the back and then told you to have a nice day.

But ultimately Williams was responsible for his own failure. His modus operandi was to deal with problems as they came up, be pleasant to everybody, let the department kind of run itself, and not waste too much time following up on promises and commitments that required any heavy lifting. With his selection his lucky number had come up, and his competition for the position had been either lackadaisical or barred as outsiders from being considered. So why wouldn't he have taken that big fat pay raise and moved to the L.A. of swimming pools and movie stars and gone to the Academy Awards as the *Chief of the Los Angeles Police Department* and occasionally weekend in Vegas? Who would say no? Unfortunately, he was the wrong guy, in the wrong place, at the right time.

PART THREE

SOMETHING BLUE

SOMETHING BLUE

Bernard Parks, August 1997, Los Angeles City Hall

"It was an absolute love-in," gushed Los Angeles city councilwoman Laura Chick, referring to the council's unanimous approval of Bernard Parks as the LAPD's fifty-second chief of police. Immediately afterward Parks received a spontaneous standing ovation in City Hall. He had not been asked a single question beforehand.

Just a week later, Parks's triumph was replicated in a ceremony on the grounds of the Police Academy before a crowd estimated at three thousand that included the mayor, the Police Commission, and various local, state, and national politicians and law enforcement leaders.

Many of the locals were breathing a collective sigh of relief that at last the LAPD was in the hands of a man they respected and trusted, a man whom—unlike his out-of-town predecessor—they knew and were sure they could work with.

As if to underscore that very point, during his speech Parks alluded to the fact that on this happy occasion he was wearing the same belt he'd worn on the day he was sworn in as a rookie police officer over thirty-two years earlier—a double-edged swipe at Willie Williams that Gary Greenebaum interpreted to mean: "I'm a man of Los Angeles and the LAPD, not an outsider, and I'm slim, not fat; I'm not Willie Williams."

For most of the locals in attendance it seemed that a new era of good feelings between the department and the city's political establishment had already commenced. As the fifty-six-year-old Parks said after his earlier swearing before the City Council: "I don't view conflict as something bad. I think it's [about] how it's played out and whether we can agree to disagree but not be disagreeable."

Unfortunately, that would emphatically not turn out to be the case.

****

That summer of '97, Richard Riordan was also fresh off a landslide reelection victory, and he too "beamed" after the council's official swearing-in ceremony for Parks. "I'm so thrilled," the mayor told *L.A. Times* reporter Matt Lait. "*Chief* Bernard Parks just sounds perfect."

It had taken Bernard Parks over thirty-two years of faithful service to be named chief—an honor, he felt, that he'd been unfairly deprived of five years earlier by Willie Williams, whose selection also destroyed Parks's other dream of becoming the department's first *black* chief. Both losses had stuck deeply and notoriously in his craw ever since.

Now, however, his moment had arrived. He was enthusiastically received by civic leaders and political friends—many of whom seemed not to know or care that he'd spent much of the last five years undercutting Willie Williams while successfully projecting himself as the only alternative.

Certainly Parks at least *appeared* to be a perfect fit: tall, handsome, ramrod-straight, and an LAPD man through and through. But it wasn't just that. He was also an African-American replacing a failed African-American, so no hint of racism could be attributed to Williams's forced departure. Within the department his reputation was that of a smart, knowledgeable, efficient technocrat. He had placed second to Willie Williams in the search to replace Daryl Gates. He was a son of Los Angeles, a favorite of the black bourgeoisie and, even more importantly, of the downtown political establishment—who really *liked* Parks. And that was no accident. He'd spent years cultivating them. He was very charming one-on-one, and had been astute and solicitous in delivering favors that helped cement their friendships.

As a result, he'd made an impressive circle of friends and supporters that had sprouted ever wider as he'd risen in the ranks. Many of those supporters, moreover, had unquestioningly assumed that Parks would

be the reformer they wished for. But that was the most interesting thing
about Bernard Parks. That he wasn't a *fundamental* reformer at all. Early
on he'd signaled precisely that, pointing out that he didn't so much want
to reform the department as fix it, but his more liberal backers either
missed the comment or were unaware of the significant difference between the two approaches.

It would therefore prove ironic that the seeds that would shatter his
upcoming administration had been planted by none other than his idol
Daryl Gates, and that they would bloom under the leadership of Willie
Williams, his hapless foil.

Sometimes trouble comes from places or people not even remotely
on one's radar screen. So it was for Bernard Parks: a couple of dogged
young reporters on the make, a couple of grizzled editors left to their
own devices, and, above all, one lowly crooked cop. That's all it finally
took to ignite a scandal so explosive it would force a police chief out of
office; the federal government to officially intervene in the running of
the LAPD; and the hiring of the most prominent reform cop in America
as the LAPD's new chief of police.

David Mack, Thursday, November 6, 1997, South Central Bank of America

Wearing a gray three-piece suit, a tweed beret, and dark sunglasses, Ray
Perez's old partner, David Mack, strode into a South Central Bank of
America branch just north of USC on a November morning in 1997,
filled out an entry form to view his safe deposit box, and was then twice
buzzed through security doors leading to the bank vault. Accompanying him was twenty-six-year-old customer service/assistant branch
manager, Errolyn Romero.

Just the day before, Romero had made a request that $722,000—more
than twice the amount usually delivered—be sent in twenty-, fifty-, and
one-hundred-dollar bills to the bank branch at 9 a.m.—about ten minutes before Mack would arrive that morning. Because Romero had ordered the money, she was personally responsible for securing it in the

vault directly upon delivery. But instead she'd left the three plastic bags of cash outside the vault on a cart. When a coworker asked her why, her reply was succinct and direct. "Don't bother me," she said. "I have a headache."

Once at the vault, Mack knocked Romero to the floor, glared at the two other bank employees present, and slung back his jacket to reveal a semiautomatic pistol hanging on a gun sling. Pointing the weapon directly at them, he ordered them to the floor, threatening to kill them if anyone pushed a buzzer or pager or in any way failed to comply. Absolutely convinced of Mack's seriousness, they remained in place and did exactly as they were told. As Mack exited the bank lobby, he was joined by a black accomplice who had been holding a handgun to the head of the bank's security guard. Once outside, they hopped into a waiting white getaway van driven by a third member of the robbery team and took off.

The following weekend David Mack went to Las Vegas. With him was Ray Perez, a fellow cop named Sammy Martin, and Ray's foxy part-time nightclub-singing Honduran girlfriend, Veronica Quesada. In addition to being Ray's lover, she also dealt cocaine for him and was one of his best informants. They checked in at the Rio, then the Vegas Strip's hottest casino, and spent thousands of dollars partying and gambling the nights away. In the weeks that followed Mack would also spend over $30,000 on a sport-utility van, new household furniture, and the payment of a personal loan to a fellow cop.

The robbery and Vegas weekend said a lot either about David Mack's sense of financial desperation, his sense of hubris, or both. Armed bank robbery is a federal crime taken *very* seriously by both the LAPD and the FBI. Yet he went ahead with his astoundingly audacious scheme anyway.

****

David Mack had first met Errolyn Romero, the nineteen-year-old daughter of Belizean immigrants, in 1990 when she was working as a ticket-taker at the Baldwin Theater in southwest L.A. Though Mack was married, they soon became lovers and engaged in a heated affair that lasted for the next seven years. Eventually Romero got a job as a teller for the Bank of America, and in August of 1997, at age twenty-six, was transferred to the South Central branch where the robbery took place.

When investigators brought Romero into Parker Center for questioning, she took a polygraph test that declared her "deceptive." Under intense questioning she began to fold, but was so unnerved she couldn't spit out David Mack's name. Finally, she reached into her purse and slid something across the table. It was David Mack's LAPD business card. With that, she gave them Mack. Mack, in turn, didn't give them anybody. Which might have been very good for Ray Perez, who both the LAPD and the FBI always suspected was the second man in the bank. But they could never prove it, in large part because Mack refused to reveal the name of that second robber or the driver of the getaway van.

When the LAPD arrested Mack he had $1,500 cash in his wallet and $2,600 more in his home, owed the IRS $20,000, and had $17,000 in credit-card bills.

On September 14, 1999, a federal judge sentenced him to fourteen years and three months in federal prison and Romero to two and a half years. The stolen money was never recovered. But credible allegations about David Mack live on to this day—most especially including those made by the principal LAPD detective investigating the criminal actions of Mack and Ray. The detective, Russell Poole, would claim that Mack was the hit man who killed the East Coast rapper Biggie Smalls when he was in L.A. That allegation and others about Mack have never been proven. But one, made by the same detective, sticks out: that Bernard Parks shut down the investigation and thereby limited its scope and presaged its outcome—an action that would become a Bernard Parks MO throughout what would soon come to be known as the Rampart scandal.

Bernard Parks, Autumn 1997, Parker Center

When Bernard Parks worked for David Dotson, Dotson had always liked him, liked his intelligence, his tenacity, and his work ethic. He'd first gotten to see Parks in action when Parks was a lieutenant and Dotson a captain in the beachfront area of L.A. known as Venice, which was then populated by down-and-out hippies and plagued by street gangs.

Dotson also liked the fact that, even then, they both agreed on the need to make changes in the LAPD—to make it smarter, more efficient, and to stop doing stupid, counterproductive things just because they'd always been done that way. Dotson was impressed even then with the fact that Parks was thinking and problem-solving.

But he was not blinded to Bernard Parks's flaws, to his obsessiveness, and particularly to his famous *minutiae flaw*. "Bernie always got enmeshed in minutiae," recalls Dotson. "He had to check everything officers did, not just by the *results* of what they did, but by the entire process of the task. And if he found one little glitch in the process, they had to do it over or get their asses chewed. So his people didn't want to tell him anything. They just pulled their hair out."

The other lieutenants consequently hated him. Particularly the detectives. But Parks was right: if any of the LAPD units were stuck in the inefficient and ineffective attitudes and procedures of thirty or forty years earlier, it was the detective units throughout the city. The problem was that Parks let them know that he didn't give a *goddamn* about how they had always done things. This, he told them, was the way it was going to be—starting now. But, as Dotson would later point out, "you can't get an organization moving in any direction except against you, if you act like that."

Later, up at the Police Academy, working with guys like Richard Eide, it was the same story. Many of the instructors were flying by the seat of their pants—teaching what they wanted. A ludicrous situation for an organization as large and important to the life of the city as was the LAPD. So Parks rightly demanded a syllabus from each instructor. The problem was that many had no idea how to even *write* a syllabus, and in response they became irritated and angry at Parks. "That was the kind of downward pressure he put on people even then," says Dotson. "He didn't say, 'Hey, guys, let's get together and talk about where we're going with the instruction program; or let's see what we can come up with to make it better' and then move into the syllabus phase. He had no understanding of preparing for change. He just didn't. 'This is the way I want it, and this is the way we're gonna do it—my way or the highway.'"

****

For decades the LAPD had been notorious for "yellow-sheeting" civilian complaints—that is, writing up a civilian's complaint of abuse at the local station house and, instead of sending it up the chain of command, hiding it in case someone on high needed it or a lawsuit was filed, but other than that leaving it in a drawer to be forgotten.

To his credit, once Bernard Parks sat down in the chief's chair, he decided to set in motion new procedures to ensure that civilian complaints would henceforth be taken seriously. The problem was, according to his critics, that *every* complaint would be taken seriously and receive the same weight during the investigative process. The result was that hundreds of officers were coming under investigation and waiting for a ruling at any one time. And hundreds of those officers began to seriously hate Bernard Parks. Not particularly because he was a tough disciplinarian, although they didn't like that, but because he lacked a sense of *proportionality*. The apocryphal story always told was that someone stealing a fellow officer's can of Coke from the station-house refrigerator would require the same level of investigation as a cop accused of grave misconduct. Although absurd in practice, the story was true enough in spirit to be routinely repeated as illustrative of Parks's need for control and the lengths to which he'd go to get it.

Brian Hewitt, February 1998, Rampart Division

Within Rampart CRASH, the grim-faced, fair-skinned Brian Hewitt was known as a blunt, hard-charging guy who loved action, intimidating anyone he thought was a gangster and making arrests—lots of arrests. Ray would later tell investigators how Hewitt enjoyed beating up people who were handcuffed. Once, in a CRASH interrogation room, Hewett was beating Ishmael Jimenez while screaming at the nineteen-year-old gang member to tell him about a gun—not a particular gun having to do with a particular case, just a gun, any gun. He continued in the same vein until he suddenly stopped, slammed the handcuffed Jimenez against the wall, grasped him by the throat, and began choking him so furiously that Jimenez nearly passed out. Before that could happen, however, Hewitt punched him so hard in the chest, neck, side, and solar plexus that Jimenez flipped backward onto the floor. When Hewitt then left the room to take a brief break, Jimenez threw up violently. Investigators would later find the outline of his blood-saturated vomit on the carpeted floor of the room. It matched Jimenez's DNA and measured slightly less than two feet across.

But it wasn't Ray who initially brought Hewitt to the attention of LAPD Internal Affairs investigators. After the beating Jimenez had been taken by a friend to a local hospital, where a doctor and a security guard reported his injuries to the LAPD, causing Internal Affairs to focus attention on Rampart CRASH just as investigators were looking at Ray.

It was right around this time that Ray decided to pull off a caper that was in its own way as desperate and audacious as David Mack's $722,000 armed bank robbery.

Rafael "Ray" Perez, Monday, March 2, 1998, LAPD Property Division

On a rainy L.A. day, Ray Perez tightly clutched his oversized jacket to his neck, stepped into the basement of the LAPD's downtown headquarters, and headed to the department's cavernous Property Division evidence room, which then held over two hundred thousand items.

As he entered, he tucked his black "NY" cap down low over his head. He'd disguised his face in five days of bearded stubble that blended into his mustache, above which he was wearing a pair of his wife, Denise's, Coke-bottle reading glasses. Although he had attached his badge-holder to his jacket, there was no badge inside.

Approaching a property officer, he slid a folder with a booking number across the counter to her. "I need this," he told her. Without asking for an ID, she took the folder, disappeared, and, after a few minutes, returned with a taped and sealed cardboard evidence box. Inside were three keys of coke—6.6 pounds of powder cocaine.

Signing a release form with a near-illegible scrawl, Ray jotted down a phony badge number and the name of a fellow LAPD CRASH officer, *Joel* Perez. Then he picked up the box, walked out the back door, snaked through Parker Center's ramshackle parking lot to his maroon deluxe-model Ford Expedition SUV, and drove off.

About twenty minutes later he pulled into a Home Depot parking lot. Checking to ensure he'd brought his role of gray duct tape, he then hustled over to a nearby strip mall and bought some bags of Bisquick flour. Back in his van, he unsealed the evidence box, pulled out the two plastic bags inside containing the cocaine, poured it into some bags he'd brought along, and replaced the drug with the Bisquick, exactly as he'd done the two previous times he'd checked out cocaine to sell. On those occasions he'd resealed the bags, now containing Bisquick, placed them back in the box, and then checked the substituted flour back into the property room as if it were the coke. Typically, the coke was never retested and, after the disposition of the case, was destroyed. Thus, although dangerous, it seemed a perfect deal for Ray.

This time, however, Ray decided on a different course of action—perhaps because his cop's instincts sensed his vulnerability and the risk of bringing the Bisquick back to the property room and getting caught in the process. Whatever the case, he picked up the two bags of flour along with the empty evidence box and shoved them down a nearby storm drain.

****

Ray hadn't been his usual charming self when he checked out that last 6.6 pounds of coke. But it was understandable. He was, after all, engaging in some high-risk stealing. Consequently, he'd been short and gruff; "rude" was the word that property officer Laura Castellanos used when later describing him to LAPD investigators. Rude enough that Castellanos was able to recall him. Rude wasn't the way officers normally acted in the property room, where the system was based on trust.

That attitude made Ray stand out. Castellanos remembered him and told detectives that Ray had "Negro" features and spoke Spanish effortlessly. That, along with a further narrowing down of the field of suspects to those who had knowledge of such a large amount of coke, and the fact that Ray had been temporarily lent to a narcotics unit before going back to Rampart CRASH, enabled the detectives to zero in on him as a suspect.

They quickly discovered that Ray and Mack—who'd been arrested for the bank robbery about three months earlier—were close friends and former partners. That made the detectives even more intrigued. They were investigating not only the Bank of America robbery but also Brian Hewitt's beating of the handcuffed Ishmael Jimenez; a strange, road-rage, LAPD cop-on-cop shootout that had left a black officer named Kevin Gaines dead; and now the theft of large amounts of cocaine from the department's evidence locker. All had occurred within a four-month period from early November 1997 to late February 1998, and all appeared in one way or another to be linked to Ray Perez.

Matt Lait and Scott Glover, August 1998, San Fernando Valley

Something big was afoot and *Los Angeles Times* police reporters Matt Lait and Scott Glover had received a tip about it. A briefing was being held at a church in the suburban San Fernando Valley, and about two hundred CRASH officers were expected to attend. The purpose was to inform them about an investigation swirling around some of their fellow officers. The two journalists wanted desperately to be there. They already knew that the department was investigating two bad Rampart CRASH shootings, and surmised that the story could be very hot. The fact that this meeting was occurring only confirmed that suspicion. Lait and Glover knew they had to somehow get into the room. When they arrived at the church there were no "LAPD only, check your guns at the door" signs, nothing that said stay out. So one of them blended in and sat down with the officers, and the other remained outside, close at hand, waiting to quickly jot down the insider's observations when he emerged during a break. The situation inside was not one in which a reporter wanted to call attention to himself by taking notes.

Soon enough, a guy in blue jeans got up and greeted the officers. And as he talked he didn't say that the department was looking at two bad shootings. Instead, he said, they were investigating *seven* shootings.

He also told the officers that there was a sergeant who'd been quarterbacking the cover-ups and that, recalled Scott Glover, Rampart CRASH "had a crash pad and that they were using it to bring in prostitutes and drugs." This admission confirmed something the two reporters had heard a couple of days before, when a woman they interviewed told them, "Well, yeah, I had sex in this CRASH pad all the time."

Meanwhile, the guy in the Hawaiian shirt kept spilling more secrets, which Lait and Glover memorized and called in to their editor. The next day they wrote the story. It was among the very first times that Matt Lait and Scott Glover knew they were onto something really big.

****

Earlier in that summer of '98, Matt Lait had gotten another tip: 6.6 pounds of cocaine was missing from the LAPD property room, and the department suspected it was an inside job. Lait quickly started writing stories about what he was learning. Meanwhile, Scott Glover, who was covering the LAPD out in the San Fernando Valley, checked with one of his sources and learned that not only was the department investigating the stolen coke but they were looking at Perez, Mack, Gaines, and other LAPD cops. The two reporters started "backgrounding" the officers, says Scott.

Gradually, Lait and Glover also began talking to some Rampart cops for background, off the record, and with prosecutors, defense attorneys, public defenders, and civil attorneys. They also filed several Freedom of Information Act requests to get access to the cops' shooting reports and discipline records.

The first story they wrote was about the relationship between Ray Perez and David Mack. By now they already knew a lot about Perez's officer-involved-shooting history and his disciplinary record. They were also hearing about Javier Francisco Ovando, whom they'd recognized from one of Ray's shooting reports that they'd already set aside "as sounding weird."

When Lait finally got ready to write the story, he met with the top LAPD brass, who asked him to hold off running it. Their concern was legitimate: Perez didn't know he was under surveillance, and if they wrote the story, they could foil the department's investigation.

Lait went back to his editor, who decided to make a deal with the LAPD: the *Times* would hold off running the story, and the LAPD would give the *Times* the exclusive prior to a news conference announcing the arrest of Perez.

****

Lait and Glover were not happy when they heard one morning that Bernard Parks was going to hold a press conference that night. And they were on the phone to their editor, Tim Rutten, to tell him so.

Then in his forties, Rutten was a brilliant, crusty, subversive old-school journalist with a working-class Irish Catholic's sense of right and wrong, a passion for the underdog, and a fierce commitment to good journalism. Short, heavy, bearded, and a little disheveled, he liked to drink and tell a good story. He seemed to have met everybody in L.A. and was married to the crusading firebrand defense attorney Leslie Abramson, who'd defended the Menendez brothers for murdering their parents as if, like them, her life was on the line.

Now he was listening intently as Lait and Glover told him of their suspicions. "I think they [Parks and the LAPD] may announce that they made an arrest in this Perez thing," they told Rutten. "Can we go with the story?"

"We gave our word," Rutten replied. "We can't break our word."

"Well, you know Tim, they are going to fuck us," they told him back.

"I can't believe they would do that," Rutten answered. "But beyond that we can't be the one to break our word. We can't operate unless we keep our word." And that was that.

Rutten remembers afterward feeling "a little prissy, a little self-righteous." But also sure that he'd done the right thing. Then, as he later told it, "I'll be damned if that evening they [the LAPD] didn't call that press conference and announce they'd arrested Perez. And they gave [the story] to everybody, including the TV stations [to air that night]." Just as Lait and Glover had feared, they had indeed been fucked.

****

"I want you to glue yourself to this guy Perez," Rutten told Laitt and Glover afterward. "I want to know everything there is to know about him. I want to know about his history in the department. You don't do anything else but this story. No breaking news. If there is breaking news on your beat, you tell me and I will send somebody over there to get it. But I want you full-time on this now, nothing else. This story is your life."

Curtis Woodle and Joel Perez,
April and May 1998, Las Vegas and Los Angeles

Like Ray Perez, Sergeant Curtis Woodle too was now a CRASH officer, working over at Operations Central Bureau CRASH. One evening Woodle was in a Las Vegas casino with his ex-wife when she excused herself to go to the restroom. Nonchalantly Woodle took a seat to wait for her, which coincidentally obstructed the view to the left of him. Sitting there waiting, he suddenly noticed a guy wearing a Hawaiian shirt with a frantic look on his face, craning his neck in every direction. Then the guy turned and spotted Woodle out of the corner of his eye, stopped, and stared long and hard directly at him. "What the fuck?" thought Woodle. Then he got it. Hawaiian shirt, a cop-looking white guy craning his next around like Linda Blair in *The Exorcist* and then locking his eyeballs on him: it was an LAPD undercover tail. But why?

Back in Los Angeles he quickly learned that LAPD Internal Affairs had been following not only him but everybody in the Operations Central Bureau CRASH unit that he supervised, especially one of his officers named Joel Perez.

Woodle had been getting kickback memos from Parker Center's evidence room about some cocaine Joel Perez had checked out but not returned. "After the third memo," says Woodle, "I really got on him about it." Joel Perez in turn left their meeting and headed to the Property Division evidence room, determined to straighten out the situation.

"When Joel returned he was carrying a piece of paper," recalls Woodle, "and looked like he had lost about two shades of color. He looked at and me and said, 'Sarge, I have never checked out anything like this amount of cocaine.' 'What?' I said. 'How much is it? Let me see that.'" Then Curtis Woodle looked at the paper and said, "What? This is crazy man, this is crazy!"

Bernard Parks, Summer 1998, Parker Center

Bernard Parks was not a big exchange-of-information guy. He could be very charming. But if you were a reporter he didn't like—and they were legion—or a subordinate within the department, you never felt as if you were actually having a conversation with him.

Charlie Beck found that out when he began working directly under the new chief. Beck, it turned out, really liked Bernard Parks. He found him "funny, cordial, and immensely personable." He'd gotten to know Parks in 1998, after leaving his liaison work for the Police Commission—which he'd found invaluable in understanding the inner workings between the department and the commission—to transfer into the Management Services Division. His new job required him to report to Parks about once week for about a year. One of his tasks was coordinating the department's grassroots community policing, which he found frustrating. How, after all, do you coordinate a grassroots community policing effort from inside a Parker Center tower? But centering the operation there was very much a part of Parks's hands-on leadership style.

He also helped Parks draw up the department's yearly work plan, which normally would have been an itemized page or two, but under Parks would grow to a forty-page strategic plan for the organization that was rewritten every year. The plan, says Beck, was "clear to Parks. But it just wasn't clear to the rest of us."

One of the first things he learned was that Bernard Parks was *very* demanding. A second was that Parks thought he was the smartest guy in the room—and "in a lot of ways," says Beck, "he was."

Lots of bosses can be like that. But there was this other thing: "Parks [would] demand a report and then grade it. He'd say something like 'I'm thinking about running a jail out of some location,' and then assign someone to look into it. Once the report was submitted, it was like getting back a homework assignment. He'd raise all these points and questions in the margins of the pages—and act like he already knew everything about the subject *before* you even looked into it." He would antagonize people in the department, as well as the press and Protective League officials, "because," says Beck, "his attitude was always 'I am teaching you and mentoring you. Don't bring me something I *don't* already know.'" Like Willie Williams's unwillingness to reach out and develop a network of allies, Bernard Parks's superiority complex would cost him when he most needed friends in high places.

Rafael "Ray" Perez, Summer 1998, Ladera Heights

That summer, Bernard Parks's Internal Affairs investigators were busy working Ray Perez's case hard, really hard. Every morning when Ray would leave his house for work, there'd be guys working up in one of those green high-wire telephone boxes. Then he started noticing that his phone was clicking during conversations and that a van was constantly parked right outside his garage.

In May of 1998 Bernard Parks and Internal Affairs had assembled a task force to investigate a handful of CRASH officers, most prominently Ray. Once on his case, the LAPD detectives became suspicious about the property room and other cocaine that had been checked out and returned in the last few years. When they tested those batches of coke, they discovered the Bisquick. Now Ray, like Curtis Woodle, was seeing that investigation in action, just as it was closing in on him.

Later, according to Ray, he would find out that investigators had recorded over four hundred of his telephone conversations and had put traces on his pager and cell phone. They knew every phone call he made, every phone call he'd received. They even knew exactly where he was standing each time he made a phone call, down to the square block.

Two of the phone calls Ray made caught the attention of LAPD detectives. Both were to his girlfriend, Veronica Quesada, who had accompanied him to Las Vegas after the bank robbery, with Sammy and Mack. One of the calls was made right before he'd checked out that batch of missing cocaine, the other right after the deed was done.

In a drawer inside Quesada's apartment, Detective Mike Hohan would later tell PBS's *Frontline*, they found a photograph of Ray dressed in a red running suit—the color of the Bloods—and making the hand signs of a Blood gang. In the course of their investigation, they also discovered that Ray and his wife had a new home in the high-end middle-class African-American neighborhood of Ladera Heights, in addition to his old home. They also learned that Ray was driving a deluxe Eddie Bauer–model Ford Explorer, and his wife a BMW. That was a big nut for a low-level cop to pay off every month.

Then one day in late August of '98, he was driving with a partner on patrol when a maroon-and-silver helicopter started following them. He was familiar with the type of helicopter used by the LAPD in surveillance, because he often coordinated with air support when he worked undercover narcotics. It would hover just above them, driving Ray crazy. He'd maneuver on one side of a building so the helicopter couldn't see him. But once he reappeared, there it was again, waiting for him on the other side. But it didn't matter. The discovery of that missing coke would get him arrested shortly thereafter for one count of possession of cocaine for sale.

Bernard Parks, August 1998, Parker Center

Ray wasn't the only Perez that Bernard Parks had on his mind that summer. There was also *Edith* Perez, the president of the Police Commission and a downtown corporate lawyer who had a habit of casting awestruck looks at Chief Bernard Parks every time they held a joint news conference. Short, broad, and quietly intense, she seemed to adore Parks even more than did Richard Riordan.

In August of 1998, she and Parks called a press conference with great fanfare to announce that 85 percent of the Christopher Commission reforms had been implemented and that it was now time to move on.

Yet while some reforms had indeed been put in place, the major Christopher Commission recommendations were never implemented. Among them, according to Merrick Bobb, a former deputy general counsel for the Christopher Commission, were several "that [bore] directly on the current [Rampart] scandal," including development of a tracking system to follow an officer's use of force, civilian complaints and lawsuits generated, and the number of times an officer had been disciplined. The idea, Bobb continued, was to use the computerized information to evaluate officers' performance and to select officers for specialized units such as CRASH.

At the very least, said Bobb, such a system would have engendered questions about exactly why so many officers were involved in "so many Rampart shootings, excessive-force complaints and other incidences."

****

The tracking system, however, was proving difficult to implement and Bernard Parks meanwhile was concentrating on something he seemed to regard as more pressing: ousting IG Katherine Mader from office. During Willie Williams's tenure as chief, Mader had held his feet to the fire, vigorously pursuing the many tips leaked to her from within the department. And although Richard Riordan's police commissioners were not, in general, interested in IG investigations that would embarrass the department, they and the mayor, according to Mader, were pleased that she was embarrassing Williams, whom they wanted to get rid of.

But what had gone around was now coming around for Parks, at least as far as Mader was concerned. Early in Parks's administration Mader had made it clear that there might be a new chief, but the Inspector General's Office remained on the job, ready to challenge the department by issuing critical reports and holding the department accountable to the commission and the public, just as she had done when Williams was chief. But she was dealing with an entirely different man in Bernard Parks than she had been in Willie Williams. Parks had no interest in playing the game of compromise and could not abide being challenged. And now Mayor Riordan had a police chief whom he *wanted* to succeed, as did the commission, and not to be underminded by IG reports.

So he, with the help of Edith Perez, began to vilify Mader, undermining her power and forcing her to resign. "There were comments made about Mader at staff meetings, chief-of-police meetings, bureau meetings," says former Internal Affairs officer Captain David Smith. "The atmosphere was that we did not need her. They treated her like they had treated Chief Williams. Nobody cooperated with him either." "Two directors of the Police Protective League," says Mader, told her "that the president of the Police Commission [Perez] had requested that they go after me, and if they did, they'd be supported by the Police Commission."

The strategy barely got off the ground, however, before the *Times* discovered the source of anonymous brown envelopes containing letters and press clippings sent to political leaders and the press condemning Mader and praising Perez and the Police Commission. It was none other than Edith Perez herself who had sent them marked with the postal meter of Perez's very own high-powered downtown law firm.

Nevertheless, the result was that Mader was effectively stripped of her power, particularly the right to initiate investigations. Later, Perez and Parks doubled down and tried to limit Mader's scope of work to examining only "adjudicated complaints"—that is, to those *already* investigated, ruled on, and disposed of by the department before coming to her desk. Eventually they backed away from imposing such a limitation, but only after the attempt was exposed in the *Los Angeles Times*.

Finally forced to resign, Mader was replaced by Jeff Eglash, a former federal prosecutor. He too promptly found himself battling with Parks, publicly complaining that the department was "unilaterally . . . putting restrictions on [him] and the Inspector General's Office."

Parks's resistance to the IG's office was an indication of his autocratic belief that he and *only he* ran the police department—a belief and attitude modeled for him by Bill Parker, Ed Davis, and Daryl Gates. This was time-warped thinking. It was now post–Rodney King, post–'92 riots, post–Christopher Commission, and also post–Willie Williams. And the city was still waiting for the LAPD to change. Parks, however, seemed incapable of accepting the hard truth that police chiefs throughout America were being forced to swallow: that you had to be a police chief for your time; recognize the political landscape and complement that landscape.

Bernard Parks, Summer 1998, Parker Center

Bernard Parks was in office for just a year when Police Protective League vice president Gary Fullerton told the following story to a reporter: "A woman walked into the Rampart Division Station recently and accused an officer of stealing her ovaries. Not that [the officer] had sex with her or anything like that, just that he'd taken her ovaries. Obviously she was crazy. But it was even crazier when the desk sergeant wrote it up and placed it in the officer's permanent file, where it will now be looked at every time he goes up for promotion or special assignment. That's how absurd the discipline system has gotten under Chief Parks."

Coming from a highly political official in a highly political union, the story sounded apocryphal—just what one might have expected in the bitter, constantly escalating war between the LAPD's rank-and-file union and Parks.

But strange things *were* indeed happening. Bernard Parks's laudable efforts to curb "yellow-sheeting" had resulted in a 25 percent increase in the number of civilian complaints against LAPD officers for using excessive force, and a 400 percent rise in civilian complaints against officers overall. As a result, there were close to two hundred Board of Rights disciplinary hearings pending—compared to eighty-one two years earlier—and thirty-five officers had been fired as opposed seventeen in Willie Williams's last year as chief.

For many LAPD observers, the change from the lax discipline of the Daryl Gates era to a chief finally holding his officers accountable was long, long overdue. The credit, moreover, belonged solely to Bernard Parks, who was making it all happen and taking intense union heat for doing so.

But there was a flip side. Because Bernard Parks was squeezing so tight, he was losing his moral authority to lead his troops.

****

By July of 2001 it had become apparent that Bernard Parks, like Willie Williams before him, was not going to achieve Mayor Richard Riordan's stated goal of adding thirty-five hundred new officers to the department. In fact, the situation was quite the opposite. The number of applications to join the LAPD had dropped from fourteen thousand in 1995 to under seven thousand in 1999, while the number of LAPD officers had declined by eight hundred during Parks's first two years in office.

Charlie Beck experienced the retention-rate problem after being promoted to captain and assigned back to Watts to run the Southeast Division. "I was having the best [young officers] come into my office," says Beck, "and tell me they were resigning to go work in freaking Manhattan Beach [and other small cities surrounding L.A.]—in places where I thought their talents would be wasted. And I mean I was losing a lot of them. Every week I would lose one. And I think [they] thought that the discipline system was completely skewed in disfavor to the officers."

What was primarily causing the problem, as Beck saw it, was "the ludicrous nature of the kind of prioritization that was taking place. We catch the guy who took the Coca-Cola can [that wasn't his], and in the meantime, freaking Rafael Perez is taking out dope by the kilo and we don't catch that. So what the F? You can't spend the same amount of resources on each case. That's insane." That kind of discipline system, Beck summed up, "is what I think drove the wedge between Parks and the rank and file."

Unquestionably the new emphasis on discipline and accountability was an honest, even courageous attempt by Bernard Parks to halt the LAPD's abuse of the public. But unfortunately for him and his officers,

Parks's rigidity had something in it of Captain Queeg in the book and movie *The Caine Mutiny*, who demands a full-scale investigation to discover who ate some missing portions of leftover strawberries in the officers' mess. People hate that in a boss. And Parks began to be really hated.

"Parks wasn't a popular chief," says LAPD deputy chief Patrick Gannon. "He really wasn't. He had the ability. He was the smartest guy I have ever met. He knew this police department left and right. . . . But he was arrogant to the degree that he was the only one who knew how to do things—there was nobody better. . . . [So] he lacked the leadership to take his institutional and encyclopedic knowledge of the department and transfer that into the leadership skills he needed to change the LAPD into a high-energy functioning police department."

Parks, however, never seemed to understand that his rank and file and middle management weren't up in arms because he was stupid or black or an incorrectly perceived liberal but because he was treating them really badly at a time, as Pat Gannon pointed out, when "we were begging for leadership as an organization, just begging for it."

The tragedy of Bernard Parks was that he truly believed that by imposing such rigid discipline on nine thousand strong-willed men and women, he was doing the right thing. The LAPD's top-down paramilitary managerial model was all he knew. But once that merged with his obsessive personality and operational style, the resulting brew became toxic, and he ended up with much of the department essentially despising him—and what made matters worse, the Police Protective League, in a frantic manner it had never displayed with other chiefs, was at his throat, trying to take a fatal bite out of it.

Rafael "Ray" Perez, Wednesday, September 8, 1999, Los Angeles District Attorney's Office

Ray Perez's first trial in December of '98 ended in a 8–4 hung jury, and about a year later, just as he was set to be retried with new evidence making for a stronger prosecutorial case, he decided to make a deal

with the Los Angeles District Attorney's Office: plead guilty to the cocaine theft and agree to a five-year sentence. In exchange he received
immunity from prosecution for all other crimes he'd committed except
murder.

But there was a second part to the plea deal. Ray would have to tell
the DA everything he did in Rampart and everything he knew about
Rampart CRASH. They did not, however, require him to tell them
anything about Mack and the bank robbery, about the killing of Biggie Smalls, or about any relationship he and the others might have had
with the Bloods—the part of the probe, according to Lieutenant Russell Poole, once the lead detective in the investigation, that Parks had
ordered shut down.

Nevethless, Ray Perez still had a lot to say.

****

It took nine months of his sworn testimony during secret interroga-
tions by a task force of LAPD detectives and prosecutors from the DA's
Office before Ray Perez was finished telling his tale. Meeting over fifty
times in two secret locations, beginning in early September 1999, Ray
gave them more than four thousand pages of answers to their questions, totaling almost five hundred thousand words. Investigators mar-
veled at his extraordinary memory and eye for detail, and one later
testified that "70 to 80 percent of Perez's allegations had already been
corroborated."

One of those leading the investigation was then LAPD captain Pat
Gannon, who described the questioning of Ray not only as him simply
answering investigators' questions but as something more: members of
a team of sixteen LAPD investigators and DA prosecutors would huddle
with Ray and some of the fifteen hundred pages of Rampart CRASH arrest reports culled from the DA and LAPD files. And they would say to
Ray, "What about this one?" And as Pat Gannon tells it, Ray would say,
"'Oh, that's a bad one, that's a good one . . . those were manufactured,
those were dirty cases. The gun was planted. The dope was planted.'

"In some cases," Gannon continued, "Rafael was credible, in other
cases he wasn't. And the stack [of files] kept growing tremendously.

"What complicated the matter was that Rafael Perez was a liar. So, in many respects, it was tough to get at the truth. Do I think that he was lying all the time? Not at all. But was there some stuff that was dishonest? Absolutely. That's what we found the most difficult. We were able to put together some pretty good cases that we were able to substantiate. And in others we absolved the officer of any misconduct." (Ray failed an LAPD polygraph test but subsequently passed two others administered by a defense expert and the DA's Office.)

Gannon ended his description of the interview process by adding that there was also a statute of limitations on all the cases looming over their shoulders, and consequently they had to move quickly. That fact alone was a key problem that would compromise the LAPD's investigation throughout the Rampart scandal. And there was also this, says Gannon: "We were limited only to Rampart CRASH and to what Rafael Perez said and brought to the attention of the investigators." And that was all.

Bill Boyarsky, December 1999, Downtown Los Angeles Minibus

Bill Boyarsky loved public transportation and riding buses. In Los Angeles nobody takes the bus unless they have to. But Boyarsky did. That was his quirk.

One afternoon in December of 1999, he stepped onto a downtown minibus, sat down, and continued a conversation with the man sitting next to him that they'd struck up while waiting for the bus to arrive.

"Are you a lawyer?" the man asked Boyarsky.

"No, just the opposite," replied Boyarsky. "I am a reporter." They introduced themselves and Boyarsky told the man he was currently city editor at the *Times*. He was also the immediate boss of Tim Rutten, and intensely involved with the *Times* Rampart coverage. Close friends with Rutten, Boyarsky was a working-class Jewish guy from the Bay Area, cut from the same cloth as Rutten. Both were decades-long veterans of the *Times*, loved journalism, bridled at injustice, and liked to drink. Boyar-

sky was also an unassuming scorner of pretense, at various times a star
at the newspaper, and always deeply respected by his fellow reporters.

While on the bus, Boyarsky listened as David Lewis [not his real
name] began talking about his job in law enforcement, and about the
Rampart scandal. It was a pleasant conversation, as Boyarsky later recalled it; they said good-bye, and he thought nothing further about it.

Afterward, however, Lewis phoned Boyarsky and told him he had
transcripts of the DA/LAPD Perez interviews and wanted to give them
to the *Times*.

They agreed to meet in front of a bank adjacent to the *Times* building. There they spoke briefly, and Boyarsky then brought Lewis to a
small room that served as his unused city editor office, where he introduced him to Rutten.

It soon became apparent that Lewis knew precisely what he was talking about. "Hold on for a minute," Lewis then said, reaching into his
briefcase and pulling out parts of the Perez transcripts.

Rutten quickly sent for a messenger to start copying the transcripts
and to find his Rampart reporters, Lait and Glover. When the two arrived, they immediately began chatting up Lewis.

A few minutes later, they told Rutten, "You know something? This
guy has everything. The whole set of the transcripts."

****

Once all of the transcripts were delivered to Rutten and copied, he met
with his two reporters at his house. He told them not to go home but to
check into a hotel and work overnight. Rutten knew they had to protect
the transcripts from subpoenas. So a workplace was arranged for them
at the printing plant away from the main *Times* building.

Even before the *Times* received the Perez transcripts, Boyarsky and
Rutten had decided to play the Rampart story big and, just as importantly, to run each story as they got it, day after day, rather than to wait
and run a two- or three-part series all at once—the usual manner in
which investigative stories win Pulitzers.

Pulitzers, however, weren't what they were after. They wanted *impact*. And they understood that if a newspaper wanted to have that kind

of impact on a powerful institution like the LAPD, they'd have to slam it home every day. And that's what they did. The result was everything they could have wished for. "One simply had to look at the *L.A. Times,*" L.A. County district attorney Gil Garcetti later told *Frontline*. "They set the agenda for the electronic media every morning, and they'd go with it. . . . They had big stories almost constantly. There was that drumbeat. And of course the pressure was on all of us . . . on the chief, [and] on me from the chief . . . the mayor and others . . . [to] just bring the case."

The first big story the *Times* ran was about the Ovando shooting. Then, for the next five or six days, Rampart articles were the lead stories. Soon the word "Rampart" became generic for police corruption, and the number one item on the City Council's agenda. Richard Riordan became so angry, he demanded a meeting with the then *Times* editor, Michael Parks, who essentially shrugged and said, "We're running the stories. That's what we do."

One of the reasons Boyarsky and Rutten say they were able to feature the stories with the frequency and prominence that they did was because Kathryn Downing, the *Times'* publisher, and Michael Parks, the editor, had no connections to Los Angeles's power elite. The Pulitzer Prize–winning Parks, a short, oval-shaped man with a fifties crew cut, had been with the *Times* for decades, but for most of those years he had worked as a foreign correspondent in South Africa, China, and Moscow. And Downing was never a journalist. She came from the corporate business side of the paper and thought the stories were good for the *Times*. So as long as Parks and Downing were happy—and they were—Boyarsky and Rutten pretty much had carte blanche to run Lait and Glover's pieces.

"In the old days before Michael Parks was editor, that never would have happened," says Rutten. "The mayor or police chief would have come across the street [to the *Times*] one Friday afternoon, gone up the elevator to the editor's office, closed the door, and they all would have had a drink. Everyone would have then agreed that what we didn't need was yet another crusade. Everybody would have been reasonable, trying to get along, and agreeing they all had the best interest of the city at heart.

"And then somebody would have come to me and said, 'You know what, let's tone it down, wrap this thing up, do a story, be done with it, and then let's move on to other things. Let's not be obsessional.'" But that didn't happen with the Rampart scandal, and the fact that it didn't can't be overemphasized. Without the game-changing nature of the scandal coverage, much of what was about to happen almost surely wouldn't have occurred.

Rafael "Ray" Perez, Friday, February 25, 2000, Downtown Los Angeles Superior Court

"Whoever chases monsters," says Ray Perez, dressed in shackles and blue jail garb, *"should see to it that in the process he does not become a monster himself."*

Nervously clutching her handbag as she sat in the first row of a packed courtroom in downtown Los Angeles, Denise Perez leaned forward and listened intently to her husband. A former LAPD dispatcher and devout Jehovah's Witness, she was still finding it hard to believe the litany of unconscionable crimes her thirty-two-year-old husband had just admitted to committing, and the number of lives he'd left shattered in his wake.

Certainly the disgraced LAPD officer now standing before Los Angeles Superior Court judge Robert Perry, reading a statement of contrition before being sentenced, bore no resemblance to the husband she knew, to the police officer she'd always believed him to be.

She'd met a lot of cops as a civilian LAPD employee, and had worked with them daily. But Ray had been special—as fearless and gung-ho a police officer, she'd always thought, as he'd been a gung-ho marine. But that Ray Perez was nowhere on display on this February day in 2000. Instead, her husband's powerful arms and wrists, visible through his short-sleeved blue prison jumpsuit, were handcuffed.

And he was referring to himself as a monster.

"For many years," Ray Perez continues, *"I proudly wore a badge of honor and integrity. . . . Determined to make a difference . . ."*

Both Denise and Ray's first wife had steadfastly supported him throughout his entire ordeal. But that was no real surprise. Ray, like Mack, was a player, a charmer, who appealed to women. According to what LAPD detective Brian Tyndall told *Frontline*, during Ray's first trial—and before his current plea deal—Ray had "made a lot of eye contact with the female jurors" during the jury selection process. Subsequently, when the judge asked if anyone in the jury pool had problems continuing with the case, a woman had stood up and said that Ray "was too good-looking [for her] to be involved in the jury," because she would never be able to find him guilty. The jury had later deadlocked 8–4 and a hung jury was declared. All four female jurors voted to acquit. Nevertheless, the other jurors had voted guilty, and the judge seemed to believe he was as well. Ray had to serve another year in county jail before a new trial could be convened. Those facts convinced him to take the deal the DA was offering.

For the past five months Ray's life had been a media circus, and today was no exception. The beat reporters, the journalists from the networks and national newspapers and magazines, were all there, packed so tightly together that any reporter with bad breath would nauseate the four people nearest to him or her. Ray's defense attorney, Winston Kevin McKesson, had been approached, he said, to arrange interviews with Perez by all the press corps' then national stars: *60 Minutes'* Lesley Stahl, *Dateline's* Maria Shriver, NBC's Geraldo Rivera, producers from *Nightline* and *Frontline*, and reporters from a score of magazines and newspapers, including *Time, Newsweek, Esquire,* and the *New York Times*.

"The atrocities committed by myself and those who stand accused are unforgivable acts," continues Ray, his voice now growing stronger. *"It didn't occur to me that I was destroying lives, the lives of those we victimized, and the families who loved them . . . Time after time I stepped over the line."*

Well, yeah. But nobody had cared, nobody had questioned Ray's stories or his sworn testimony in earlier courtrooms. It wasn't important as long as he produced the numbers that they'd total up every month; the numbers that told them how many bodies he'd hauled into the station house. Arrest numbers, that's what counted.

"What I most want at this time is to remind the greenest of rookie cops

*that we have [all] this power. If used wrongly, at the most they could plant a
defendant's feet on the path to the death house. At the least they will leave a
landscape of broken lives in their wake."*

God knows, Ray certainly had. Just ask Javier Ovando.

"I was living two unmistakable lives," says Ray Perez as he winds down
his statement. *"Each day the bad would consume a little of the good. You were
right, I was wrong. I pray that one day I can demonstrate my worthiness of
being forgiven."*

With that, Ray Perez was finished, and Judge Perry handed down
Ray's plea-bargained five-year sentence in prison.

Ray's act of contrition was pure Ray. Ray at his eloquent, believable,
likable best. Ray blaming circumstances for his sins. Even knowing that
he'd beaten and/or framed and terrorized hundreds of people and shot
the unarmed Javier Ovando for *no good reason*. But then, you never knew
if what Ray was saying was true or part of the con.

Bernard Parks, March 2000, Parker Center

Just moments after being flanked by fifteen starched and pressed members of his command staff, Bernard Parks would give his department's
official version of Ray Perez's sins and Rampart CRASH's transgressions.
Stepping forward on the Parker Center auditorium stage, he announced
to the seventy-five or so journalists and twenty-five TV cameras that
he was releasing what Mayor Riordan would later describe as the most
detailed and candid document "in the history of mankind."

Riordan's reference was to the LAPD's voluminous *Board of Inquiry
into the Rampart Area Corruption Incident*. People were already skeptical
about Parks's LAPD investigating itself. And their skepticism proved
more than warranted. The 362-page inquiry was one of those mammoth
documents so big it seemed designed *not* to be read. But it was far more
notable for what it failed to cover than what it did. A few bad players
and "mediocre" midlevel management, according to the report, had
been responsible for Rampart CRASH operating without the necessary
accountability, hence the resulting scandal, which had now been taken

care of. After dismissing every pointed question from the journalists, Parks then left the stage.

Nothing in the report pointed to why Parks, having led Internal Affairs and then the entire department during years of Rampart CRASH's crime rampage, had not sought a wider investigation. Nothing in the report touched on the LAPD's other CRASH units and what might have been occurring in those units, even though Nino Durden, for one, had told Ray Perez that similar crimes and abuses where taking place in 77th Street CRASH. Nor did the inquiry ask or answer how deep and wide the abuse had gone on throughout the department's other seventeen divisions and special units, or how high up the chain of command knowledge of the abuse had gone.

Bernard Parks's inquiry, in short, had been focused on telling reporters and the public what they already knew, and nothing more.

Connie Rice, 2003, NAACP's
Advancement Project Offices, Los Angeles

Even in 2010, a decade after the event, civil rights attorney and police reform activist Connie Rice was still irate as she talked about the questions investigators put to Ray Perez during his nine-month interrogation by the LAPD and the DA's Office. In 2003, Rice, who heads the Los Angeles branch of the Advancement Project, was asked by a new LAPD chief to chair a "Blue Ribbon Rampart Review Panel" to revisit lessons learned from the Rampart scandal, and how those lessons could be applied in the future.

As part of her investigation and report, recalls Rice, she and her office went through all seventy volumes of Rafael Perez's testimony transcripts. An associate attorney named Kathleen Salvaty was helping her. One day Salvaty walked into Rice's office and said, "Connie, am I crazy or are there pages missing?"

Rice was finding not only missing pages but also transcripts rife with problems: seemingly dozens of people had been asking Ray Perez questions, but often they'd failed to identify themselves. "Perez is answering willy-nilly all these questions coming at him from what seemed like twelve different interrogators," remembers Rice, "when one of them says: 'But you don't have any direct, firsthand knowledge that other CRASH units were involved in the same thing [as Rampart CRASH], you are not saying that. . . .' And Perez interrupts, and essentially says: 'Oh, but I am. I was loaned out to other CRASH units . . . and they were doing the same thing.' This is at the end of the page. The next page goes on to a separate topic. No follow-up. No nothing! Nothing! They made a mistake in asking a critical question that they did not intend to ask, got an answer they really never wanted, changed the subject, and shut it down."

"*That* question was one of the things that frustrated me very much about Rampart," Bill Boyarsky would later say. "I remember Perez's answer, and I believe he was right. It had to be happening in other divisions. Maybe not in [the white, wealthy] Pacific Division but certainly in Newton, 77th Street, and all those other [similar] divisions. You had the same dynamic. The same kind of guys."

"Were the same kinds of things done in other divisions?" Deputy Chief Patrick Gannon would later ask and answer. "Absolutely. Absolutely. Do I think for a minute that it was widespread throughout the department and that there was this underlying theme of guys out there stealing drugs and selling them and beating the crap out of everybody they came in contact with? I don't think so. But there was some of that."

****

While all this was happening, Gerald Chaleff, then the president of the Police Commission, was having deep concerns about the limits placed on the Rampart investigation—particularly a procedural one that Bernard Parks insisted on applying.

According to LAPD regulations, an officer can be punished not only for what he does but also for witnessing a fellow officer break a law and not reporting it. Chaleff, who had had a long career as a defense attorney, wanted to open up the investigation, to enable LAPD officers to corroborate Perez's allegations.

So he asked Bernard Parks to grant departmental immunity to Rampart CRASH officers who hadn't reported unlawful conduct to their commanding officers, as they were required to do. Period. Only that. Not immunity for misconduct an officer himself might have committed, as Chaleff would later explain, but for witnessing a fellow officer violating the law or department policy and not reporting it.

Parks's reply, says Chaleff, was essentially "Nope, can't do that." Chaleff needed Parks's permission to grant the immunity. He had asked for and gotten the city attorney's opinion on the subject, and been told that "by city charter statute the power to discipline lay solely with the Chief of Police."

Parks's refusal to temporarily grant immunity for not previously reporting the misconduct of a fellow officer effectively stopped those officers from corroborating Ray Perez's testimony. Their fear of being punished for not coming forth at the time of the offense trumped all other concerns. Bernard Parks's decision was certainly right in tune with his general disciplinary philosophy. But it also played a huge part in successfully limiting the Rampart investigation.

Without the corroboration of those officers, it proved extremely difficult to bring a substantial number of allegedly dirty cops to trial, and harder still to gain convictions for those who were prosecuted. It was a given that any defense attorney cross-examining Ray Perez on the witness stand would say to him: "Tell me, Mr. Perez. You've admitted that you've committed perjury more than a hundred times during previous trials. Why should we believe you now?" It was a situation that seemed designed to fail. But why?

One explanation comes from Connie Rice, who later headed an LAPD-sponsored investigation into Rampart. "They couldn't follow up on widening the investigation into other divisions or grant immunity in order to get corroboration because Rampart meant one of two things. It was either containable to Rampart CRASH, or it was the end of our criminal justice infrastructure, because you can't survive a thousand overturned verdicts. You can survive a hundred, maybe two hundred. Not more than that. The entire system could have collapsed."

Bernard Parks, May 2000, Parker Center

Bernard Parks sat stone-faced during a closed-door meeting with city officials and lawyers from the U.S. Justice Department as a press release summing up the reason for Parks's grim demeanor was being distributed. "The LAPD," read the release, "is engaged in a pattern or practice of constitutional violations through excessive force, false arrests, unreasonable searches and seizures, and . . . management deficiencies that have allowed this misconduct to occur . . . on a regular basis."

The U.S. Justice Department (USJD), it turned out, had been monitoring the LAPD for the past four years. But it was Rampart CRASH, Ray Perez, and the *Los Angeles Times* who'd finally tipped the scales and caused them to fly into L.A. and lay down the law.

In 1994, in the long wake of Rodney King's beating, the federal government had passed a statute permitting the Civil Rights Division of the USJD to sue cities where local police agencies had regularly discriminated against racial and ethnic minorities in enforcing the law. If the city refused, they had to go to trial; if not, the city had to enter into a consent decree or agree to other oversight by the USJD. In the process of addressing police abuse in Los Angeles, lawyers from the USJD had made it abundantly clear that if necessary they would force a trial—a trial that would be embarrassingly revelatory.

Most of the city government quickly saw the writing on the wall. The twenty-year-veteran city attorney, James Hahn, led the city's negotiating team. Hahn was a nice guy, but no one ever accused him of having an excess of vigor in the performance of his duties. He readily, regularly, paid tens of millions of dollars of the city's money to settle police abuse lawsuits against the LAPD, without publicly saying to the LAPD, "What the hell is going on?"

But when it came to Los Angeles signing on to a federal consent decree, James Hahn told the City Council that they couldn't possibly win in court. He may have lacked what it took to stand up to the LAPD for two decades, but he was well aware that lifting the rock that was the LAPD and the Los Angeles criminal justice system in the 1980s and '90s and turning it over in court would reveal the rot beneath it.

Accepting the decree, however, was serious business. It mandated that the LAPD make a series of fundamental structural reforms aimed at permanently ending the department's systemic constitutional violations—a process that would include ongoing monitoring by a federal judge.

Nevertheless, on September 19, 2000, the City Council voted 10–2 to accept the consent decree. It was a stinging, unequivocal rebuke to L.A.'s political establishment, its criminal justice system, and especially its leadership. Both Bernard Parks and Richard Riordan had hated the idea of agreeing to a consent decree, and firmly believed that the decree was the result of a hysteria stirred up in large part by the *Los Angeles Times*. But once the City Council overwhelmingly voted to approve it, Mayor Riordan had little choice but to go along, and he soon signed it into law.

Steve Cooley, Wednesday, November 7, 2001, Parker Center

"With every book, when you read it, you close it," Los Angeles district attorney Steve Cooley said in November of 2001. That was his way of announcing that his office was shutting down its Rampart investigation by the end of December. Cooley, a tall, florid-faced career prosecutor, then added that he expected no new indictments between now and then.

It was a stunning public pronouncement, given the magnitude of what had been left uninvestigated, made more stunning by the fact that Cooley had vowed to take the Rampart probe "as high, wide, and deep as the facts indicated." Back then there was no reason to doubt him.

During Cooley's hard-fought campaign to unseat his predecessor, Gil Garcetti, he'd run as a reformer who was going to come into office and change the widespread assumption that LAPD officers could do pretty much what they wanted without fear of indictment.

But it was not to be. As district attorney, the Republican Cooley had been a good, often principled chief prosecutor, and certainly a vast improvement over the Democrat Garcetti, who never saw a law-and-order political wind to which he did not bend opportunistically rightward. Once in office, Cooley proved to be a stand-up guy, courageously bucking those winds and refusing to prosecute small-time thieves, junkies, and others for petty crimes under California's three-strikes law, as Garcetti had made a public point of doing. But on the issue of comprehensively investigating Rampart and the LAPD, Cooley's loyalty proved to be firmly with L.A.'s political and law enforcement establishment—despite the fact that the anterooms of civil rights attorneys in the city were still filled with victims of Rampart-style LAPD abuse.

But an open-ended investigation of the sort he'd promised would have risked alienating a huge portion of the city's political establishment. And for what? He might have won kudos from civil rights organizations and the press, but any kind of sustained, full-scale investigation would surely have led right back to Cooley's office. Not to him personally, but to many of his office's deputy DAs, who ignored and/or missed the pattern of police abuse that was so evident. For decades the DA's office had allowed itself to be subservient to the LAPD, while its criminal prosecutors became deliberately ignorant or complicit in the lies LAPD officers like Ray Perez were telling on the stand.

Now Cooley's refusal to pursue a wider probe, like Bernard Parks's limiting of the Rampart investigation and the missing pages in Ray's transcripts, smelled like something in that movie *Chinatown*: if you were rich enough, or if the stakes were so big that something *needed* to be covered up, it would be.

****

Richard Riordan got along fine with Steve Cooley, but he disliked James Hahn even before the consent decree. According to then *L.A. Times* editor Tim Rutten, he thought that Hahn was a weak city attorney, that he lost too many cases, and that the city was paying out too much as a result.

So it was ironic that, when Riordan was termed out in 2001 after eight years in office, it was James Hahn who replaced him as mayor, and that after Riordan had a friendship-breaking dispute with his political guru, William Wardlaw, it was Wardlaw who ran Hahn's winning mayoral campaign. Equally ironic was that Wardlaw then helped Hahn manage the big decision about whether or not to rehire Bernard Parks for a second five-year term.

Before Riordan's Police Commission had selected Parks as chief, he had been Wardlaw's favorite candidate. But as it became time to punch Parks's ticket for a second and final five-year term, it had become clear to Wardlaw that Parks had become a liability.

For one thing, Parks would not work cooperatively with James Hahn. He'd become increasingly independent and thought of himself, in Wardlaw and Hahn's view, as having his own political base. Worse, he treated James Hahn like he did most everyone else—with intellectual condescension. "Every time I talk with that guy," Hahn once said, "I feel like I should get college credit."

Secondly, it was highly probable that Parks might never implement the consent decree, or at the very least was going to drag his heels, causing the city to be in court every other month. That, in turn, would very likely cause the federal judge overseeing the implementation of the decree to impose even more intrusive oversight—a potential disaster that any public official would want to avoid.

So Hahn publicly announced to the city, and most especially his Police Commission, that he would not be supporting another term in office for Bernard Parks. And in April of 2002 an obliging Police Commission voted 4–1 not to rehire Parks, and shortly thereafter initiated a nationwide search for a new chief.

Summing Up

In July of 2001 Ray Perez was placed on parole after serving two years of his five-year sentence in state prison. He then signed another plea deal, this one with the U.S. Justice Department for violating the civil rights of Javier Ovando and possessing a firearm with an obliterated serial number, and was sentenced to two additional years in federal prison.

James Hahn was defeated in his second run for mayor, despite the fact that the people of Los Angeles owed him an enormous debt of gratitude. Despite the fact that Bernard Parks had striven mightily to hold LAPD officers accountable for abusing the public for the first time in twenty years, he had been a bad chief. Reform was moving at a snail's pace, officer morale was deep in the tank, officer attrition was mounting, community policing was haphazard or nonexistent, and a federal consent decree that Parks detested and was philosophically opposed to implementing was hanging over the city's head. The survival of the LAPD as a credible and effective law enforcement institution going forward was dependent on Parks's departure.

Matt Lait and Scott Glover wrote about 150 stories on Rampart over a period of more than two years, while, as Lait would later point out, "the number of press releases from the LAPD regarding the Rampart scandal could probably be counted on one hand."

Boyarsky, Rutten, Lait, and Glover were never able to expand their reporting beyond Rampart, although they had hoped to do so. When the *Times* was sold in 2000, a new editor was brought in and the *Times'* coverage of the story essentially shut down. But a federal consent decree enforced by a tough-minded federal judge was now in place—a decree that L.A. may well not have gotten but for the scandal.

As a result of Ray Perez's testimony, over one hundred criminal convictions were overturned, and the city paid over $75 million to the victims of the violence and abuse of Rampart CRASH officers.

Javier Ovando was awarded $15 million of that money, the largest police misconduct settlement in L.A.'s, if not the nation's, history. Later, while en route to Las Vegas, he was arrested near the Nevada state line for drug possession.

To this day Ray Perez and Nino Durden are the only cops who wound up doing any real prison time for the Rampart abuses. In 2002 Durden was sentenced to five years in prison after being convicted on six counts, including conspiracy to obstruct justice, perjury, and filing false reports. Bernard Parks's limiting of the Rampart investigation and his refusal to grant immunity to officers who'd witnessed and failed to report misconduct had its effect, as the case of Brian Hewitt and Ethan Cohan can attest. By all reports, Cohan was one of the good guys in Rampart CRASH, and had not witnessed or even been in the room when Hewitt was banging Ishmael Jimenez around—had not, in fact, even known about the incident until after it was over. Nevertheless, he was fired from the LAPD for failing to promptly report Hewitt for the beating when he'd heard about it. Hewitt too was fired, for the vicious thrashing of Ishmael Jimenez.

L.A. district attorney Gil Garcetti brought criminal charges against three LAPD CRASH members based on Perez's testimony. They went to trial, and a jury failed to convict them. The officers then sued the city and Chief Parks and other defendants for violating *their* civil rights and conducting an improper and negligent investigation. They prevailed at this civil trial, winning compensatory damages of $5 million each, plus their attorneys' fees. In 2008 the U.S. Ninth Circuit Court of Appeals upheld the judgment. In its decision, the Appeals Court quoted Garcetti as testifying that he'd "spoken with Chief Parks six to twelve times about the Rampart investigation," and that his deputy DAs were being "hounded" by the LAPD to file criminal charges. Garcetti also testified that during a telephone conversation, Parks had said the following: "Let's get the case behind us. If we prosecute the case, even if you lose the case, it's over. It's done."

And that's what happened. LAPD investigators sprinted to make a statute of limitations deadline, and Gil Garcetti was left with cases that strongly relied on the word of a crooked cop who was an admitted multiple liar on the witness stand. Garcetti could have stood up to Bernard Parks. But that was not the history between L.A. DAs and the LAPD. "In New York the cops hold the door for the [deputy] DAs," James Fyfe, an ex-cop turned college criminology professor, once observed to a reporter. "In L.A. it's the other way around."

PART FOUR

SOMETHING NEW

SOMETHING NEW

William Bratton and Rikki Klieman,
Summer 2002, Los Angeles and New York

Bill Bratton didn't really know Los Angeles, but he had spent time there. For more than a year after the signing of the federal consent decree in September 2000, Bratton had been flying from his home in New York to L.A. about once every five weeks. There, he was helping monitor compliance with the decree for the mammoth New York–based private-security firm Kroll Associates—which in turn reported its findings to the federal judge enforcing the decree.

Bratton had been intrigued by the LAPD ever since he watched *Drag-net* and *Badge 714* as a kid back in Boston. When the L.A. chief's job opened up in 1992, he had considered applying, and changed his mind only after it became apparent that Tom Bradley and his Police Commission wanted a black chief. Now, with both Willie Williams and Bernard Parks gone, Bratton knew the job was wide open. And he wanted it.

Over the course of his monitoring work he'd met with James Hahn while he was still mayor and discussed the idea of developing an operational action plan for the LAPD. Bratton wanted to address policy issues related to the consent decree, as well as the city's homicide rate, which had fallen significantly but was again rising. Since its peak of almost 1,100 murders in 1992, it had dropped to 419 in1998—reflecting the dramatic decrease being experienced by most of the nation. But by the end of 2002 it had risen again by over 200—to a troubling 647. At the end of their discussions Hahn told Bratton to go ahead with the plan.

After putting it together, Bratton brought it to Martin Pomeroy, the acting chief of the LAPD, whose acquiescence he would need, as Bratton later put it, "to come in and start messing around within the department."

Walking into the chief's office to present his blueprint to Pomeroy, however, turned out to be like "walking into a deep freeze." Pomeroy wasted little time letting Bratton know he wanted no part of his plan, whether it was coming with the mayor's imprimatur or not—a sign that Bratton had yet to learn that New York brashness is rarely a welcome sight in L.A. and that Pomeroy—a true-blue believer in the greatness of the LAPD—would surely find it presumptuous for a back-east professional turnaround man to come in and tell the department how good police work should be done.

But then Bratton needed that chief's job. He was now fifty-four years old and hoped to one day step back onto center stage as the commissioner of the NYPD, or the director of the FBI, or in other positions currently unavailable to him. The LAPD job, at least, was open, and was right up his alley in terms of what needed to be done.

But there was something else: he *wanted* that job. No one was more attuned to the legend of Bill Bratton, or his place in American policing history, than Bill Bratton. But over the last several years he'd begun to feel that the narrative of his spectacular success in the subways and on the streets of New York was being dismissed, rewritten, and devalued by naysayers, while he was lacking a professional law enforcement platform from which to fire back.

In 1999, his frustration would bubble over as he spoke before a fraternal organization of idolatrous former and current NYPD officers known as the Shields.

Suddenly during his speech he'd stopped, "put down his prepared remarks," discarded his reading glasses, and—as writer Rory O'Connor described it in *Boston* magazine—announced to his audience that this was "the best of times and the worst of times. The best of times," he said, because "there's a revolution going on in American policing. . . . Homicides [in New York City] have plummeted by 70 percent—a phenomenal decrease . . .

"And it's the worst of times," he continued, "when the claims of others go unchallenged, claims that take credit for this decrease, [and credit instead] demographic or social changes that mystically caused this decrease in crime. Let me tell you that nothing infuriates me more. In fact," he said, "it drives me crazy!"

Then, comparing the police to the gunmen heroes in the 1960s Western *The Magnificent Seven*, who never got the credit they deserved, Bratton continued: "The only losers in New York City during the '90s were the cops—the very people who made the rest of the city winners!"

Some of that rewriting of history, Bratton would later say, was due to the "anti-Giuliani-ism" that had exploded in New York as Giuliani neared the end of his second term, battling with seemingly everyone in the city. Bratton also blamed his successors as commissioner, Howard Safir and Bernard Kerik, for failing to promote the NYPD as the primary reason for the city's crime decline, and had instead let it come "under attack." It was deeply frustrating for him to watch all of that, he continued, to watch the "gains to the profession, the gains for [him] personally and professionally being undermined."

In short, his legacy was at stake, and Bratton knew it.

****

On the July Fourth weekend of 2002, Bratton, recently returned from Los Angeles, left his Manhattan apartment in fashionable Murray Hill, climbed into his black Jeep Cherokee, drove to the midtown headquarters of Court TV on Third Avenue near 39th Street, and picked up his fourth wife, Rikki Klieman, who was working as an anchor and analyst for the cable network.

A celebrity in her own right, Klieman was a vivacious, quick-witted, fast-talking former Boston defense attorney with a profile high enough to be named one of *Time* magazine's top five "most outstanding women trial lawyers" in the country in 1983.

An only child, she was raised poor in a Chicago suburb by a garment-worker father and housewife mother who gave birth to her after seventeen years of marriage. Her mother, she told Bella English of the *Boston Globe*, "would buy dresses for her at the Salvation Army, three for a dollar. I didn't know why they didn't have money," she added.

After graduating as a theater arts major from Northwestern University, she headed for Broadway stardom in New York City. Waiting on restaurant tables to support herself, she made the young actor's rounds of auditions, without meeting success. Facing reality, she enrolled in Boston University Law School. After graduating in 1975, she worked first as a prosecutor for the Middlesex County (Boston) DA's Office, and then left in 1981 to become a dedicated Boston criminal defense attorney—a hard, financially rewarding job in which she displayed both her brilliance and her near manic will to succeed. They were long and hard workdays and she grew increasingly reliant on Valium, losing fifteen pounds from her slender, five-foot-three, 120-pound frame. A second marriage to a cop turned federal agent went bad—along with other failed romances. One day in court she literally collapsed on the defense table during a trial.

At about this time, however, she'd started appearing on Court TV as a guest analyst during the O. J. Simpson trial. Proving both sharp and telegenic, she was quickly hired as an anchor, moving to New York during the 1994 trial and later being teamed as cohost with Johnnie Cochran.

At age fifty, Klieman had met Bratton one morning in 1998, when she was dining in at a restaurant in Manhattan's Regency Hotel—then a spot for celebratory power breakfasts. Noticing her, Bratton had risen from his seat, walked over, and kissed her cheek. Then, as Klieman later wrote in her autobiography, *Fairy Tales Can Come True*, "he smiled. 'You look so beautiful,' he said. 'If you were single, I'd marry you.' 'You should call me for lunch,'" she replied. "By the time [she] got back to the office, he had called."

Then, as snowflakes fell in February 1999, Bratton, who'd gotten the closed-for-the-winter Central Park carousel opened specifically for the occasion, lifted her up onto a white carousel horse and, as Klieman would tell it many times over, declared, "I want to go round and round with you." The retelling had to it the ring of a true-romance paperback. Still, there was no denying that she and Bratton were mad for each other. Or that Bratton, who loved smart advisors, had married one who was extremely smart—and, equally as important, who understood the liberal mind-set as well as she understood her own, a big assist for Bratton in the years to come.

****

As they headed out to their getaway home in the Hampton village of Quogue, Bratton told his wife he had something serious to discuss with her. Klieman braced for bad news. "I want to go after the job of LAPD chief," he said.

It was bad news—for her. She had survived and recovered from a heart attack, and didn't want the stress of moving from a New York City she loved and from her job at Court TV, where she'd become a star. As one of Court TV's makeup artists told *Boston* magazine in 1999: "When she first started working [here] she wasn't New York enough. . . . Now she's changed her clothes, her look. She's got that sophistication now— hip, chic, and glamorous." And one more thing: Court TV had no studio or facilities in Los Angeles from which she could broadcast.

****

Early that Sunday, after Bratton returned to the house after a morning tennis lesson, she asked him why he wanted the L.A. job so much.

"Nine-eleven," he said. On that calamitous morning Bratton had finished doing a guest appearance on Don Imus's radio talk show and then gone to vote in a municipal election with Klieman. Returning to their apartment afterward to pick up his briefcase for work, he snapped on his television set and saw replays of the first plane smashing into the World Trade Center. "In your life as a police officer," he'd later say, "you live to deal with crisis, to be tested by it. It's very frustrating when you're not in a position to do anything—particularly when you know what needs to be done." Instead, he'd found himself powerless at the moment of supreme crisis in his adopted city, as he imagined all the things he would have done differently than the mediocre, corrupt, and inexperienced Bernard Kerik, who'd been working as Giuliani's NYPD chauffeur/bodyguard before Giuliani had astounded the entire city by handpicking him as his new NYPD commissioner.

He told Klieman that he'd also never really had the opportunity to deal with community policing or significantly improve race relations while leading the NYPD. The flash point for racial tension in America's cities for decades, Bratton believed, had been the police—and if they were ever going to get the consent of the poor people of color they were policing, they'd have to stop being part of the problem. As the most glaring example of that reality, L.A. would be the ideal place to work through the issues surrounding the problem. Those issues, she thought, went to heart of who Bratton was. So she agreed. They'd go after the job together.

****

Sprawled across the dining room table of their house in Quogue were scores of papers, books, newspaper articles, and reports Bratton and Klieman had gathered together to help Bratton compete against the fifty other candidates vying to become the LAPD's next police chief.

Following his long-standing practice of thoroughly researching the police department he wanted to lead, Bratton had obtained reports from UCLA about the department's management that included a series of interviews conducted over the years with the department's top brass; Daryl Gates's autobiography, *Chief*; and two well-researched books about the LAPD after the '92 L.A. riots. He and Klieman also read reams of stories from the *Los Angeles Times* and *LA Weekly*; all the Christopher Commission Reports and everything they could find about L.A. mayor James Hahn.

Then they began to assemble what Bratton would later refer to as his "propaganda package"—a carefully assembled press kit of favorable stories and editorials from his tenure in New York City, his plans for tackling some of the LAPD's problems, and a copy of his 1998 autobiography, *Turnaround*.

The kits were then individually sent to each of the five police commissioners as well as to some of the influential people Bratton had met in L.A. With his record of achievement in fixing broken police departments, Bratton expected to be greeted with open arms once he applied for the chief's job. John Timoney, the craggy-faced, well-regarded Irishman who'd worked for Bratton in New York, was the only other candidate he regarded as serious competition.

He was therefore astounded to discover that he was considered an underdog for the job. All of his and Klieman's diligent preparation, it turned out, was proving surprisingly counterproductive. "Some people," says Bratton, "thought that [the press kits] were showboating, coming from publicity-seeking Bill—'Broadway Bill'—showing off to them who he was. 'Imagine the gall of this guy coming here with all this stuff—who does he think he is?'—that was the attitude, and that had been the issue with Giuliani—the idea that there wasn't enough room on the stage for the two of us."

Particularly offended was the president of the Police Commission, Rick Caruso, a local developer of high-end shopping malls who was then on his way to becoming a multimillionaire. "He made it quite clear through intermediaries," recalls Bratton, "that I shouldn't apply, that I wasn't wanted, that I was too brash." Caruso was worried that Bratton might try to overwhelm Mayor James Hahn, a nice, quiet, unassuming guy, just as Bernard Parks had tried to do. If Bratton thought he could run over the mayor, Caruso believed, he'd try to run over the Police Commission too. And who needed that headache again?

William Bratton, October 2002, Los Angeles

Despite Caruso's efforts, by September 2002 the search for a new chief had narrowed down to Bratton, Timoney, and a Latino chief from the small city of Oxnard, California, who most people assumed had absolutely no chance of being selected, but who had been thrown into the mix because the commission was required to send three candidates to the mayor for final selection, and because it was good politics to include a Latino.

The *Los Angeles Times*, meanwhile, had been running profiles of the three, and both Bratton and Klieman had been outraged when Bratton's appeared. They saw it as playing right into the caricature of him as a cocksure carpetbagger so convinced he had the job all wrapped up that his wife was already in Los Angeles looking for a house in Brentwood— when, in fact, Klieman hadn't stepped foot in L.A. since the selection process began. The article, Bratton later recalled, "nearly killed my candidacy right when I was interviewing with the mayor." In the final days of the process, the *New York Post*'s gossip column, Page 6, published a squib reporting that Mayor Hahn had decided on Timoney as chief. It was entitled, "Bratton Tried Too Hard."

But contrary to the news item, if Bratton had been trying too hard, he'd done so very effectively. He'd paid a personal visit, for example, to John Mack, president of the Los Angeles Urban League and a lion of the black community for decades in its fights against police abuse. Over the course of two hours, Bratton queried Mack about what was wrong with the LAPD and left asking for his support.

By paying Mack a visit, Bratton was helping himself with the mayor as well. James Hahn wanted at least the tacit approval of an African-American leader of Mack's stature for his new chief. Black L.A. had turned out in large numbers to support Hahn in his successful run for mayor and considered him an ally, as they did Bernard Parks.

No matter that Parks was having trouble with Rampart; he was one of their own—a native son who was the most visible and powerful African-American in a city where blacks were losing their political clout to Latinos. So when Hahn finally refused to rehire Parks for a second five-year term, Mack and the rest of the black leadership reacted with bitter, polarizing anger. Getting Mack to at least not *oppose* Hahn's new choice as chief would be a start toward healing their breach.

It was a fight that Hahn had never wanted in the first place. But Parks, as much a believer in an LAPD unaccountable to civilian control as any of the previous white chiefs, had never hidden his contempt for Hahn or for the consent-degree reforms.

Fortunately, Bratton's visit to Mack proved successful. "John Mack had seen anybody who opposed Parks as a personal enemy," recalls Connie Rice. "Yet Bratton completely seduced Mack, who became one of Bratton's biggest supporters. I call that skillful politics."

By the end of the selection process Bratton had won over not just Mack but also Rick Caruso, who after Bratton's interview before the Police Commission became convinced that Bratton's propaganda package was far more a carefully considered plan and a commitment to reforming the LAPD than an advertisement for himself.

"Finally," as Bratton would later recount, "the mayor slid into my camp." But first, one of Hahn's top aides was sent to New York to talk about Bratton with former New York governor Mario Cuomo, with Judge Milton Mollen—whose eponymous commission had critically investigated the NYPD during the department's notorious corruption scandal in the early seventies—and with rank-and-file cops. Hahn's guy came back, as Bratton tells it, "appreciating what I'd done there."

Directly after the announcement of his selection, Bratton, who was in Portland, Oregon, at a board of directors meeting of the Rite Aid Corporation, was flown down to Santa Monica Airport in the company's corporate jet. After being officially sworn in as chief in a private ceremony at City Hall on Monday, October 28, 2002, he was greeted by his officers and the public at a second, huge celebratory swearing in at the Police Academy.

William Bratton, Patrick Gannon, and Gerald Chaleff, Fall 2002, Parker Center

When Pat Gannon first became acquainted with Bill Bratton in late 2002, Bratton's greeting said a lot about where'd he come from and where he hadn't been for the last twenty years. It was always "Hello, Captain," "How are you, Captain?" "Nice to see you, Captain"— because, suspected Gannon, even after six months of weekly personal meetings, Bratton hadn't a clue what Gannon's name was.

Gannon was one of three captains then working Internal Affairs. Each of them began thinking how funny it was that Bratton couldn't— or wouldn't—remember their names. So, after sitting with him every week around the long, darkly stained rectangular table in the chief's office, they'd make a point of saying: "Hey, Pete, what do you think about that?" "Oh, Pat, I don't know," Pete would answer. They'd do it consciously, consistently, and conspicuously, but Bratton never caught on or caught their names.

But nevertheless, Bratton's focus was always on the matters at hand. There was no bullshitting, glad-handing, or jokes from him. And instead of meeting with the three IA captains and no one else, Bratton invited others to listen in as the captains briefed him on current Internal Affairs investigations.

One of those most frequently in attendance was Gerald Chaleff, whose opinions and thoughts, as Gannon later recalled it, Bratton always seemed to find of particular interest. At first the captains were amazed that Chaleff, known within the department as "a card-carrying member of the ACLU," was even sitting in at the meetings. But it quickly became apparent that neither Bratton nor Chaleff thought for one moment that he should be anywhere other than where he was. In fact, Gannon was surprised about how "strong" Chaleff was in expressing his opinion, and refusing to pull his punches.

Chaleff, however, wasn't just stopping by to listen in. He was there in his official capacity as an LAPD bureau chief and commanding officer of the Consent Decree Bureau—i.e., the guy in charge of getting the LAPD in full compliance with the federal decree.

Bratton had first met Gerry Chaleff in 2001, when Chaleff was serving as president of the Police Commission, and the commission was selecting monitors for the consent decree. About a year after Chaleff left the commission, Bratton sent him a copy of his autobiography, along with a note letting him know that he was applying for the chief's job. Chaleff, who also knew Rikki Klieman from her days in L.A. covering the O. J. Simpson trial in 1994, replied by offering to recommend Bratton to people who might have some pull in the selection process, and to call him when he heard any relevant news over the grapevine.

A graduate of UCLA and Harvard Law School, Chaleff had grown up in the liberal, predominantly Jewish Westside of Los Angeles, and in 1968, while still an idealistic young lawyer, had helped found Young Professionals for Kennedy, an organization that campaigned for Bobby

Kennedy's presidential election. Chaleff worked hard for Kennedy. And on the night of the California Democratic primary he was at Los Angeles's Ambassador Hotel celebrating his candidate's upset victory when a woman shouted out the shattering news of Kennedy's fatal shooting. Chaleff, who still keeps a photo of Bobby Kennedy on his office wall, was crushed. About a month later he was informed that he'd been on a list of supporters who'd been selected to go to New York to work on the next leg of the campaign, before it was so tragically aborted.

Instead, he remained in L.A., first coming to public attention in the early eighties when he and his then cocounsel, Katherine Mader (who later became the LAPD's first inspector general), unsuccessfully defended the notorious "Hillside Strangler" serial killer, Angelo Buono. Over the years, he worked for the DA's office, as a public defender, in private practice, and in law firms. He also became active in the Southern California branch of the ACLU, served as president of the Los Angeles County Bar Association, and eventually was president of the Police Commission during Bernard Parks's tenure as chief.

He wore a full beard and had the slightly disheveled appearance of a perpetually distracted literature professor, and was always miscast by Parks and the rest of the LAPD as a radical—as someone who, by reason of his occupation as a defense attorney, his professional affiliations, his ethnicity, and his education—was ipso facto a cop hater. In reality, however, Chaleff was a very politically astute guy skilled in maneuvering within the social and cultural complexity of Los Angeles. If he liked you, he appeared to be a mensch; if he didn't, he could be a ballbuster.

On the Police Commission he got along well with its more conservative members, and worked quietly behind the scenes for what felt like glacial reform. He tried to avoid criticizing Parks publicly, and tried as well to get him to expand the Rampart investigation.

Above all, there was nothing of the embarrassingly sycophantic performance that characterized Edith Perez's tenure as commission president. Gerald Chaleff was a serious man aware of his opportunity to help move LAPD reform forward, who unfortunately was consistently foiled by Bernard Parks's unwillingness to compromise. Nevertheless, in his waning days on the commission, Chaleff would battle back by playing a pivotal role in negotiating the consent decree with the U.S. Justice Department, while Parks was bitterly unsuccessful in convincing the City Council to reject the decree.

But it would be under Bill Bratton—the stranger in town—that Gerry Chaleff would fully blossom as the new chief's indispensable consigliere, who intimately knew both Los Angeles politics and its players within City Hall and the LAPD.

Implementation of the consent decree would be Chaleff's main charge, and of paramount importance to Bratton. If Bratton, with Chaleff's help, could get the LAPD certified by a tough federal judge as in compliance with the decree, then he, Bill Bratton, would emerge with proof that he was indeed the miracle worker he was made out to be in New York. Fail, and his New York legacy—the essence of who he was in the world—could be further challenged.

And the judge in question—Gary Feess—*was* a tough customer, and with reason. He had been counsel to the Christopher Commission during its investigation, and thus had been deeply involved in the rush to reform the LAPD. It had been a good try, but ultimately one not strong enough to bolster an indifferent chief like Williams or thwart an imperious chief like Parks until the damage was done. It had taken a ten-year period—bookended by Rodney King's beating and the Rampart debacle—for the federal government to finally intervene and impose the equivalent of a legal straitjacket. Now, as the judge overseeing a second attempt at finally bringing the LAPD to heel, Feess was determined to bring all of the decree's powers to bear.

Bratton signaled to the department just how important Chaleff was to his plans by elevating him to the civilian equivalent of a deputy chief. He also gave him an office on the sixth floor of Parker Center, right next door to *his* office, and raised the compliance unit's status to that of a bureau, with a staff that would increase from three people under Parks to about one hundred under Bratton.

****

Gerald Chaleff turned out to be like a gift to himself Bill Bratton was able to purchase—one that Willie Williams, to his great misfortunate, never even had the opportunity to shop for. Due to the civil service law at the time, Williams had been unable to hire a civilian like Chaleff, and consequently found himself stuck with the command staff he inherited.

But as result of the 1995 codification of the Christopher Commission reforms into the city charter, Bratton was allowed to hire outside the department and to bring key top staff like Chaleff into it.

Within the LAPD there was a lot of resistance to his second pick, John Miller. He was a reporter, for one. Barbara Walters's partner on the TV newsmagazine program *20/20*. And Bratton was bringing him inside the department *and* making him chief of counterterrorism! But Miller came with a lot of advantages for Bratton. He *did* seem to know a lot about counterterrorism from his reporting, although he possessed no other qualifications in the field. But more important, Bratton trusted Miller—a good reporter who'd served as his loyal press guy and party companion during Bratton's stint as NYPD commissioner. Miller also possessed exceptionally active eyes and ears and liked to get out on the street. Bratton knew he'd go everywhere, watch everything—Miller, in fact, *liked* going to crime scenes, would go to as many as he could, and report back directly to Bratton. And that was very good for Bratton, who needed the unvarnished truth from someone loyal to him.

His third outside hire was Mike Berkow, the chief of police from the small Orange County, California, city of Irvine. Bratton brought him in to head Internal Affairs. He knew Berkow from back when he was a cop in Rochester, New York, had followed his career and saw him as shrewd and ambitious. Naming Berkow deputy chief in charge of Internal Affairs gave Bratton another guy loyal to him who could not be co-opted by anybody else in the department.

★★★★★★★★★★★★★★

It's become almost pro forma for CEOs, managers, and politicians to say that they like smart people around them. But Bill Bratton really did like working with smart people. Ever since his days on the Boston PD, he'd forged and nurtured ties with those whose expertise he could benefit from and who, like him, were passionate about policing and reform. A number of them flew into L.A. on their own dimes to participate in his swearing-in celebration and, more importantly, to assist in his transition process. Each had something distinctive to offer Bratton.

Bob Wasserman's specialty was race and social justice as they related to policing. Bratton had first met Wasserman in the seventies, when he'd been assigned to the Boston police commissioner's office. Wasserman was a civilian who during a brief reform period had been the Boston PD's chief of operations. Soon he became Bratton's colleague, friend, and mentor. In their first meeting together, Wasserman gave Bratton a copy of Herman Goldstein's seminal book on American policing, *Policing a Free Society*. He also assigned him as the department's first liaison to the gay community. Ever since, Wasserman had been Bratton's early-action man, going into a city, quietly observing the department, and then compiling transition books that included profiles on members of the new department's command staff.

Meanwhile, Bratton got John Linder to prepare a "cultural diagnostic" of the LAPD. Bratton had met Linder when he was chief of the New York Transit Police. Linder was then serving as the marketing director for the Transit Authority, when he decided to have Bratton star in a series of Transit commercials about subways and "bringing back New York." Bratton considered Linder "a genius" who'd developed copyrighted cultural analysis of police departments for Bratton and others. The process included a survey of officers within the department, aimed at understanding what they thought the priorities of the department were versus what they thought the priorities *should be*. Bratton and his team would then use the survey as a tool in understanding the values, opinions, gripes, strengths, and weaknesses of the department and utilize the information to move the department in the direction Bratton wanted. Linder's chief finding about the LAPD, recalled Bratton, was "how dysfunctional it was."

Bratton also flew in George Kelling, the Rutgers University criminologist and coauthor of the 1982 *Atlantic* magazine article on "broken windows" policing. He wanted Kelling to explain to captains in the field how to best apply the concept in their divisions while avoiding a backlash from the African-American community. To initiate and train his new command staff in COMPSTAT, he hired former NYPD chief of department Louis Anemone.

Bratton used other consultants as well, all of whom—along with his three insiders—enabled him to establish authority and quickly take hold of the department. Most of the outsiders' work was eventually paid for by the Los Angeles Police Foundation—a private fund-raising organization attached to the chief's office as a kind of booster association. Run independently, it raised money to funnel into projects, studies, and other endeavors the department was interested in pursuing but did not have the budget to finance.

Bratton also moved quickly to foil any attempt by the department to cut him off from the flow of information, as had been done to Willie Williams. He had picked up on such an effort just after he was named chief. Upon flying into L.A. in October, he'd been picked up at the airport in a black Ford driven by a chauffeur/bodyguard in the chief's official security detail—a strapping six-foot-three police officer named Manny Gonzalez. Bratton got in, looked around, and was stunned to see there was no communications radio, no red light, no police equipment of any kind.

"Hey, Manny," he asked, "where's the police radio? Where's the siren?"

"We don't have those in this car, Chief, so there are no disturbances."

"What if there's some kind of emergency?"

"I don't know, Chief; we just don't have any of that."

It said a lot to Bratton, as he'd later recount, about the department's previous leadership. If the official car of the chief of police didn't even have a radio or red lights or a siren, how connected could he be to the world of policing and what was happening on the street?

"Manny," he told him, "get me a car with a radio, a red light, and a siren. I want a full police package."

"What Manny and the chief's office staff were trying do, as they'd done with [Williams and] Parks, was corral me and keep me in the chief's office so I wouldn't see what was happening within the department," Bratton would later say. "The idea was the old guard [brass] would keep me so busy that I wouldn't leave my office and get out and talk to people that they didn't like and didn't want me to listen to. Then, at the end of the day, they would come in and present a document to me, describe the document, get my signature on it, and go about their business. It was just all about them and control. And the one thing I understood about organizations was right from the get-go, you had to let them know who was in control." Bill Bratton had no intention of being Willie Williamsed.

William Bratton and Charlie Beck, Fall 2002, Los Angeles Police Academy, Elysian Park

Charlie Beck was only vaguely aware of Bill Bratton when he heard he'd be replacing Bernard Parks as the fifty-third chief of the LAPD. Nevertheless, hiring another outsider seemed highly problematic to him, given Willie Williams's glaring failure just five years earlier. After reading and liking Bratton's 1998 autobiography, *Turnaround*, however, he wasn't really sure what to expect. Then he attended Bratton's first presentation to the entire LAPD command staff and got his answer.

The event took place within the rustic confines of the old Police Academy in Elysian Park. There, Bratton strode into a small, cramped banquet hall, walked to the podium, and proceeded to read the riot act to about 110 LAPD command officers, about 60 of whom were captains.

"He really chewed ass," recalls Beck, who was then a captain heading downtown L.A.'s Central Division. "He told us he wasn't happy with the way things had been going; that the department was hidebound and unwilling to take chances, and that as leaders we were overly manipulative and weren't allowing the organization to perform up to its potential."

And then Bratton said—and Beck remembered this specifically—"I want you to get results. I want you to reduce crime. And if you have to pull everybody out of patrol one day and put them in plainclothes to do it, I don't care. Do it."

Bratton was talking LAPD heresy with that last sentence, and suddenly his audience began taking notice.

Ever since Bill Parker's "professionalization" of the LAPD back in the fifties, his successors had insisted on following the department manual's mind-numbing "uniform set of rules and regulations" word for word. They had since grown so long, rigid, and complex that they were stifling the efforts of commanders—particularly captains in the field—to deal with situations unique to their divisions or to experiment with new ways of approaching old, intractable problems. Instead, problems were dealt with as per the dictates of the manual.

This gospel had been taken to the penultimate level under Bernard Parks, who, even if he actually said that you could deviate from procedure in a particular situation, was rarely believed. And now here was Bratton standing there and saying to his entire command staff: "Why aren't you guys being creative and thinking about crime reduction, and why isn't that number one on your to-do list?"

****

Long before Pat Gannon started meeting with Bratton, he too had attended Bratton's big initial command staff meeting up at the Police Academy. As a captain and chief investigator for Internal Affairs, Gannon had led the (Parks-limited) investigation into Rampart CRASH. And like Beck, Gannon was smart, curious, and open to change.

White-haired, congenial, and self-assured, Gannon had the look and bearing of a corporate CEO from Utah. But in reality he was an Irish cop from San Pedro, an old, working-class L.A. fishing village turned major port filled with unionized Croatian, Slovenian, Italian, and Mexican workers. Like Beck's, Gannon's family had a history with the LAPD— one that was even deeper and longer: Sergeant Gerald F. Gannon, 1927–1952; Police Officer III Gerald F. Gannon, Jr., 1948–1973; Pat Gannon himself, 1978–2012; and his son Michael P. Gannon, 2005 to the present.

Pat Gannon had gone to the meeting ready for Bratton, or rather ready for *a* Bratton. "I didn't know what to expect," says Gannon. "I just knew I was begging for leadership. There had been such a long leadership void. Parks was smart but he wasn't a good leader. So I was looking for somebody to lead us back, get us out of this situation where we were getting beat up every day."

****

The messages that Pat Gannon would take away from that initial encounter with Bill Bratton were few and simple: One, reduce crime. We are not worried about arrest numbers or other metrics. We are concerned about *crime* numbers.

Message two was that "Bratton wanted to take the shackles off and let us reduce crime in legal ways we thought would work. . . . In the old LAPD," says Gannon, "we were the stenographers recording and reacting to the deeds of the rest of society. So another message I took from the meeting was that the police matter. What you do can make a long-lasting difference, and that the police can change things. Going in and temporarily flooding areas [as was done during Operation Hammer] isn't what reduces crime; we're not just a suppression force."

"Conversely, if things are going bad, you better look at what you're doing, because something isn't right. You might even be contributing to it. I think," Gannon would later sum up, "that this police department was partially responsible for the '92 riots. We treated people very callously and really embraced the philosophy of 'we know best' and that 'the way you solve crime is by making arrests.' I think we should make arrests. But you know there are other things too. We worked really, really hard in the past in ways that just weren't productive."

****

At the Police Academy that day, Bratton introduced the LAPD's command staff to a way of running an organization that wasn't particularly new and certainly wasn't radical. But for a police force that had modeled itself on a military command structure that actively discouraged individual creative thought, it was a whole new way of thinking. And Bratton, always a man in a hurry, didn't bother to persuade his officers of the benefits of this shift. Instead, he let those present know that this was the way it *would* now be.

Everyone, he told them, would have to submit a résumé and a photo and answer a list of questions about himself and his current job. He intended to go through each and every one of them to learn as much as he could. He had a large command staff and wanted a "face with a biography in a book" that he could turn to when hearing about "who was good and who was bad."

The self-evaluative résumés also offered Bratton other advantages. By demanding that all members of the old LAPD hierarchy justify their existence, he could judge them rather than the other way around, as had been done to Willie Williams. Above all, as Beck and Gannon both understood it, he was letting them know that they were applying for their own jobs again, and for promotion or assignment to the boondocks.

Shortly afterward, Bratton did in fact begin his one-sided chess game, demoting and forcing retirements and promoting officers who'd impressed him over candidates next in line for a position. "Hey, we understand force in the LAPD," Charlie Beck would later say. "He used the demotions and forced retirements, and demonstrated his authority, knowing that if you want to keep crows away, you kill one and leave it on the fence."

Nevertheless, implementing a new way of thinking about crime and the way the LAPD treated the public would take a shift in culture. The department had been so small and underfunded and under such intense criticism for so long that it had turned deeply inward, resulting in a calcified groupthink.

Fortunately for Bratton, the consent decree, with its mandatory, legal compliance, demanded a shift in culture. He *had* to carry out all those contentious reforms mandated by the decree, he could argue, because there was simply no way around them.

★★★★★★★★★★★★★★

That day at the Police Academy, the reaction as the command staff filed out of the meeting was "What's with this guy?" Beck never noticed a lack of eye contact during Bratton's fire-and-brimstone introductory address. He didn't recall anybody being actively disrespectful either. But after they had been dismissed, he saw a lot of dazed-looking people who were extremely troubled by the message they had been sent. What he didn't see was the usual groups hanging around the parking lot shooting the shit. Everybody instead was getting into a car and getting the hell out of there. And Beck was thinking: "Well, read his book [*Turnaround*], man. Read the book. We're in the first chapters of the book [establishing the necessity to change], that's where we're at. And those first chapters are not fun."

Alternatively they could have read the transcript of Bratton's speech on the day he was sworn into office at the Police Academy: "The department is not strategically engaged in fighting crime," he said. "We have nine thousand officers smiling and waving as they drive around in their cars"—a statement that really wasn't true at all. LAPD officers were engaged in fighting crime; they just weren't doing so strategically or effectively. It was clear that Bratton wanted something new. What wasn't clear to his command staff, however, was how to deliver it.

****

Years later, when Bratton was leaving the LAPD, much of the press coverage would give him credit for laying the groundwork for the successful implementation of community policing in L.A. "And there were people throughout the department," says Pat Gannon, "who would ask: 'How does Bratton get credit for community policing? There wasn't one program that was instituted throughout the department—not one department initiative that said here is how we are going to institute community policing in Los Angeles.'" And that was true.

But Gannon nevertheless thought the doubters were missing the point, which had to do with Bratton's expectations on reducing crime. "As crime declined, community trust and confidence grew out in the field and within the department's divisions because we'd begun to do things differently—to develop relationships and partnerships within the community [to help make crime reduction happen]. That's what community policing is.

"So, Bratton didn't give us a blueprint. The old LAPD way would have been to take six months to a year, draw up a beautiful program and a beautiful packet, hand it to somebody and say . . . now all throughout the 460 square miles of the city everybody has to do this the same way. Bratton's attitude was that you can't do it that way. Because what is going on in Rampart versus what is going on in Harbor and what's going on in South L.A. are all different. He wanted us to just do it! Develop those relationships, use our imagination, do it legally, ethically, but do it. And as an organization that's what we started to do."

Charlie Beck, 2002, LAPD Central Division and Skid Row

In 2002, the LAPD's Central Division covered what was as close to a traditional, inner-city core as Los Angeles had to offer: a cramped, creaky Chinatown; a sterile, urban-renewed Japanese commercial strip; fish and produce markets; a performing arts center and a famous concert hall; a classic 1930s public-works Art Deco train station and a new bus terminal; a Catholic cathedral and seat of the archdiocese; the headquarters of the *L.A. Times* and the MTA; gleaming high-rise office buildings and hotels and once-glorious movie palaces and commercial structures from the 1920s through the 1950s. At its hub stood a civic center that included City Hall and L.A. County's government offices.

In and around that center were the moving parts of Los Angeles's criminal justice system: the LAPD's soon-to-be-replaced home, Parker Center; a stark, bone-chilling, slit-windowed federal prison; federal and county courthouses; a dungeon-like L.A. County Men's Central Jail; and a few blocks away a newer county lockup—the behemoth Twin Towers jail that served as a "receiving center" that processed both the roughly 20,000 inmates L.A. County had in custody daily and the 165,000 that flowed through its jails every year. It also contained a housing unit that daily confined about 2,300 mentally ill inmates—the largest such mental-health facility in the nation.

Close by was another of Central Division's key defining features: the largest skid row in the western United States, a fifty-block area of prime real estate ripe for gentrification. From the 1920s through the 1960s the district had been home to cheap, single-occupancy hotels and bars for hard-drinking transient laborers working in the city's factories and fields and on the loading docks for the downtown railroads.

By 2002, however, what had once been a seedy last stop for work-ing men had turned into a centralized human trash heap. One that fea-tured a large open-air drug market; people OD'd on the street; and long rows of small tents, discarded brown-cardboard-box bedrooms, faded lawn chairs, and human feces and urine on the sidewalks. Interspersed throughout stood overstuffed shopping carts containing the possessions of the about fifteen hundred degraded, beaten-down men and women who lived their lives in full view, out on the street.

About 40 percent of L.A. County's homeless were mentally ill, with many of them dual-diagnosed as severe drug addicts or alcoholics as well. As Los Angeles County supervisor Gloria Molina would point out at the time: "There are just no facilities for the mentally ill homeless. You can go up and down skid row and you'll see that 95 percent of the people there need mental-health counseling right away."

The homeless population in Los Angeles and California, like those elsewhere in the nation, had begun to rise after 1967, when the state abolished the forced incarceration of the nonviolent mentally ill and closed many of its large, often abusive lockdown mental institutions. The follow-up plan was for the state's mental-health department to open new, community-based clinics and provide housing and other services. But that never occurred. Instead, tax cuts mandated by voter-approved ballot initiatives like the permanently tax-lowering Proposition 13, the recession of the 1980s, and the devastating crack epidemic would all hit L.A. particularly hard. The result was the near collapse of the county's mental-health-care system and the explosion of the population of Skid Row as the homeless and mentally ill were recycled off the streets, into jail for short stays and then out into the streets again. The small num-ber of homeless housing units that were being provided, meanwhile, proved woefully inadequate to keep up with demand.

By 2000 an estimated ninety-one thousand homeless men, women, and children were living in Los Angeles County, with only about eigh-teen thousand beds in shelters across the county and about eighty-three single-room-occupancy hotels for the homeless, most of which were located in Skid Row.

It was as if the powers that be in the city and county had sat around thinking about the looniest solution to the homeless problem, and then decided to just let it happen. As Charlie Beck, who'd been made lead captain of Central Division and Skid Row in 2002, would later put it: "For whatever reason—and I can't really speak to why—the police and society had allowed a different standard of behavior for that area of the city than anywhere else." Then he added something that perfectly illuminated the situation: "It's not so much what the police let you do, it's what everybody else lets you do. Human behavior to me is more about what your neighbor says to you than the random acts of the police department." Beck didn't have to add the obvious: that by concentrating so much human misery into so small a district, L.A. had created a dazed, bedraggled community of severe, untreated addicts and the mentally ill that was disastrous not only for them but for the businesses located in the area, and for a Los Angeles struggling to revitalize its central core— an area that L.A.'s non-homeless currently were avoiding at all costs.

****

The first of the LAPD's twenty-one divisions that Bill Bratton decided to inspect was Central. On a Skid Row walking tour with Beck, Bratton, unsurprisingly, was deeply unhappy with what he was seeing. "How long you been in charge here?" he asked. Beck thought, "I'm going to tell him the truth, and I hope it's not too long." "Six months," he confessed. He could almost hear the wheels clicking in Bratton's brain.

"Have you made any progress?" Bratton finally said.

Beck had his answer ready: "Yes, but not enough. Here's what I've got planned."

After listening, Bratton replied with one word: "Okay." Beck wasn't sure what that meant. Was it good or was it bad? It was neither. What Bratton had meant was "Okay, show me what you've got."

****

Beck's task was to tame the lawless chaos of damaged people who had been left, essentially, to fend for themselves. Establishing a sense of order in Skid Row, Beck reasoned, was, by necessity, his first task. He began by counting the tents and packing-box bedrooms as a way of approxi-

mating the number of people living on the area's streets. Then, in con-
junction with homeless shelter staffers and mental-health workers, his
officers began approaching those camped out and giving them a choice:
sleep on the street or sidewalk in a tent or box during the day and risk
ticketing or arrest, or use the mission services that were being offered.

At the rescue missions, Beck knew he'd have captive audiences right
before lunch, when residents had to first go into the auditorium for a
daily sermon. So he began a series of talks to about four hundred of the
homeless, "many of whom," he says, "had a slim grasp on reality. Some
would listen; some would be talking in tongues."

"You're no longer going to be permitted sleep on the sidewalks before 10 p.m.," he told them, "and you can't block or sit on the sidewalks
during the day. If you do, you'll be ticketed." The same, he added, would
apply to such actions as drinking in public, jaywalking, and littering—
"broken windows" policing straight out of Bill Bratton's playbook.

The missions had rules too: no drinking, getting high, bullying, or
fighting; and mandatory lining up for meals and attendance at daily sermons. Beck's cop-eyed assessment of the situation was this: "Folks that
were lawless liked [L.A.'s] Skid Row because there were no laws. So they
wouldn't abide by the missions' rules either." His solution: get them
into the missions or to leave the area. And many did leave, thus reducing
the Skid Row population to a more manageable number of those need-
ing and wanting services and temporary mission housing.

"People always ask," said Beck later, "'Where'd the homeless all go?'
That question assumes that the situation was insolvable, immutable. But
it wasn't. Some went into treatment; some went back to wherever their
family roots were and became a problem there. But they stopped congregating in huge numbers on Skid Row, reinforcing each other's destructive behavior in the only area of Los Angeles that allowed it. Just
having a routine downtown—roll up your beds at six in the morning and
you can't put them up until ten at night—had a tremendous effect [in
reducing the number of homeless living on Skid Row's streets] because
it's a pain in the ass for them to have to do it. For most of the people that
don't want any rules, that was way too many rules. So many just left."

Bill Bratton labeled Beck's concentrated effort one of his "Safer Cities Initiatives" and gave him fifty additional officers to patrol Skid Row. They proceeded to enforce Charlie Beck's rules while writing tens of thousands of tickets for petty crimes and infractions like jaywalking and loitering, or anything that would drive the hapless homeless off the streets and out of the area. Those actions had an immediate effect, despite the fact that federal courts afterward would at least twice brand key aspects of the department's enforcement policies unconstitutional and order them halted.

Crime fell, for example, and blatant street-corner drug dealing and prostitution were sharply curtailed as was regional hospitals' wickedly venal practice of dumping their just-released homeless and often mentally ill patients onto the streets of Skid Row overnight and clandestinely, leaving them alone and often clueless in their hospital garb.

In the wake of all this came the steady reclamation of key blocks of Skid Row that had been a civic disgrace, and their gentrification and integration into the heart of a surging, redeveloping downtown L.A. Bratton and Beck had acted, and those were the payoffs. None were small accomplishments. But time would prove that the unwillingness of L.A.'s power brokers to provide funding for services and especially for permanent housing for the homeless outside the city's core would ensure that nothing much changed on Skid Row, and that the LAPD and the poor, desperate residents of the streets of Skid would still be dancing to much the same tune over a decade later.

As Bill Bratton told the *Los Angeles Times*, his "responsibility was not [homeless] housing, not their medical care, not their social needs. Those were the responsibility of city and county government, and in those areas, the county and the city and the state have been incredibly deficient in serving that population." Bratton was right. But like rest of L.A.'s city and county agencies, he too had no answers that didn't ultimately just kick the problem down the road while further dehumanizing the lives of the people being kicked.

But it would take Ta-Nehisi Coates, the great *Atlantic* magazine essayist, to express the real heart of the problem. "At some point," wrote Coates in his commentary "The Myth of Police Reform," "Americans decided that the best answer to every social problem lay in the power of the criminal-justice system. Vexing social problems—homelessness, drug use, the inability to support one's children, mental illness—are presently solved by sending in men and women who specialize in inspiring fear and ensuring compliance. Fear and compliance have their place, but it can't be every place."

★★★★★★★★★★★★★★

Several years earlier, in late October of 1999, Kevin Evans, a homeless thirty-three-year-old schizophrenic with cerebral palsy, had died of cardiac arrest during a one-sided fight with a swarm of sheriff's deputies. They quite literally crushed him to death in the strap-down room in the Twin Towers jail.

The incident had begun when Evans refused to relinquish his sole possession: a standard-issue jailhouse baloney sandwich on white, wrapped in plastic. It had then escalated from there into the deputies' pile-on. Kevin Evans's first mental breakdown had also occurred over the issue of food. When he was eighteen, according to his then sixteen-year-old sister, Anntanaea Lambey, she'd been about to exit their apartment to give a hot dog to her boyfriend waiting downstairs when Evans suddenly hissed, "Don't be giving any food away." Then he hit her in the face. His behavior was unprecedented, and she later complained to their mother and godmother, who responded by grabbing Evans and confronting him. "Let me go! Let me go," he wailed in reply. The two women, convinced he was possessed by Satan, lapsed into fervent prayer. "From that day on," Lambey would later say, "my brother was never the same."

The five-foot, seven-inch Evans was more than familiar with the Twin Towers jail, in which he died. He'd been incarcerated there at least four times as a consequence of being cited or arrested on thirteen different occasions over the previous two years—all essentially for being a disturbing-looking homeless black man. On his previous stays at the Towers, the doors would soon slide open and disgorge him. With nowhere else to go, Evans, like hundreds of others, would then simply return to the nearby netherworld of Skid Row.

****

Sometimes Evans would find his way out and back to where his family had moved from South Los Angeles: the movie-set locale where those old John Wayne–John Ford Westerns had been shot in the remote eastern region of L.A. County, near the parched desert cities of Lancaster and Palmdale. There, Kevin Evans would roam the streets with his shoes off, engrossed in deep conversations with himself, despoiling by his presence the shopping areas of the white, conservative people who'd moved from L.A. precisely to get away from those who looked and acted like Kevin Evans.

In Lancaster, the residents paid the county for a six-deputy Los Angeles Sheriff's Department unit whose sole purpose was "to deal with loitering, prostitution and other quality-of-life issues," while the captain in charge of the Lancaster sheriff's station would boast of having "over 100 volunteers—out on patrol, in Neighborhood Watch—all just looking for that suspicious person and calling it in."

But Kevin Evans's story wasn't just about zealous cops and jailers; it was a tale of an overwhelmed, dysfunctional L.A. criminal justice system that didn't know what to do with the homeless and mentally ill, and had no interest in figuring it out. Instead, each step of the way, the criminal justice system focused on how to sweep him off the streets and pass him on to the next cog in the machine.

In May of 1998, for example, Evans was ticketed for loitering in a Lancaster shopping center. Two weeks later he was arrested on an outstanding warrant and brought before a judge. That appearance was one of at least four in which judges declared him mentally "incompetent to stand trial." The result of those findings, however, was not to help Evans with his disease. Rather, it was to sufficiently medicate him so he'd be "competent" to stand before the judge, answer a few questions, and be sentenced to the Twin Towers jail for a few days or weeks before being released.

"For me to find out how he died was just not that surprising," deputy public defender Marlon Lewis, who defended Evans in one of his pro-

ceedings, would later recount. "Seeing the shocking number of proba-
tions he had trailing him, it was clear that the system was not making
any attempt to address his problem, and that its only answer was incarceration, which everyone knew was going to do nothing for this man."

Antelope Municipal Court judge Richard E. Spann would later say
that he could not remember Evans, even though he'd been brought
before him on three separate occasions. In fact, Spann declared him
incompetent to stand trial and, in September 1998, even ordered a psy-
chiatric evaluation. But it was never administered. Nevertheless, as
Judge Spann later admitted, he had "no idea" who Evans was. By the
end of May 2001, Spann had ruled in three thousand custody cases. "I
hate to sound this way," he said, "but I simply have no independent recollection of him."

****

By 2015 there were still fifteen hundred chronically homeless people on
the sidewalks of a Skid Row that was losing a critical number of permanent housing units for the homeless to redevelopment. Meanwhile, tensions between the people living in boxes on the sidewalk and the LAPD
remained as high as they had ever been. Countywide, over half of L.A.'s
fifty-eight thousand homeless had drug and/or alcohol addictions, and a
quarter, like Kevin Evans in the nineties, were mentally ill. "In the summer of 2014," as the *Los Angeles Times* reported, the situation had grown
so bad that the LAPD would feel compelled to "issue an anguished call
for help, declaring Skid Row was in a mental health crisis."

****

Dressed in a black suit and white collar, Father David O'Connell looked
as if he'd just stepped off the set of *The Bells of St. Mary's* for a quick
smoke with Bing Crosby. Ruddy-faced, with gray hair, a full beard,
and a lilting Irish brogue, O'Connell has been a Los Angeles priest for
twenty-three years and was in 2002 the pastor of two Catholic churches
in South Los Angeles.

It was Christmas season—a Monday afternoon—and O'Connell and twenty-four other members of a community federation known as L.A. Metro IAF were seated in a conference room at the headquarters of the Los Angeles Police Department. Priests, rabbis, union and neighborhood organizers—all of them had trekked downtown to meet Bill Bratton, their new police chief. They wanted to tell him—they *needed* to tell him—about their embattled neighborhoods. "A week and a half ago, a member of our parish who owns a store across the street from our church was robbed and killed at six fifteen at night," said O'Connell. "Shot dead. In front of his family. Then, about a month ago, a fifteen-year-old was walking down the street—walking home from an event at church—and he got killed."

Another man told of a bridge by a school in East L.A.'s Lincoln Heights, a place where would-be gang members had been harassing children and women, and how one little girl was raped, murdered, and dumped over the side of the walkway.

The stories tumbled out, one by one. Many were devoid of emotion, as if the tellers had grown numb from the violence, but all were built around a single theme—a question, really, a plea: "Where are the police? Can you give us some protection?"

"People live like cockroaches around here," Barbara Franklin, a public school teacher in Pico-Union, told Bratton. "We don't see the parents. They're the ones working in sweatshops. If the police became involved at the community level, it would encourage the people to come out of their holes."

Franklin was talking about Ray Perez's old stomping ground, but she was not complaining about the Rampart CRASH's actions, which were now no actions at all since the department's eighteen CRASH units had been disbanded by Bernard Parks in 2000 during the height of the Rampart scandal. "Since Rampart CRASH left, there are so many wounds to heal," Franklin would later elaborate. "The parents come around the corner to get their kids from school and walk right by a shooting victim, or witness a shooting. The parents don't want to go to the cops, and don't go to the cops, because they don't trust the police."

Seated in front of the group, one leg of his blue business suit draped over the other, Bratton soon raised his hands, palms out, and took over the gathering. "The most devastating thing this city has experienced in years was the horrendous activities of the officers in Rampart CRASH," he began. "The haunting and the devastating effect of that, however, was that for months, our gang units were not on the street, and the gangbangers were just doing what they wanted. And when the gang units were reconstituted, in greatly weakened form, they had all new people who had to make all new relationships. Why didn't you ask Parks: 'What were you thinking, disbanding all the gang units?'"

Bratton then reminded the group that Parks also stopped the "Senior Lead Officer" community policing program, under which ranking officers in each police division met regularly with local neighborhood groups. Together, Bratton argued, those two decisions by his predecessor dissolved the glue that bonded the community to the police, however tenuously.

Then he used those two decisions by Parks to announce the dawning of a new day. "Under Chief Parks, there was one big stop sign outside his office, and as a result, the division captains at the local level who should have been responding to you became incredibly risk-averse, because nobody could do anything without getting his signature on a piece of paper." He then told the audience exactly what they wanted to hear. "You'll have access to me on a scheduled basis," he said, "so I can get feedback from you and you get feedback from me. But it's really important that you interact with your division captains. They'll be authorized to act, instead of having to go to the chief's office to get permission."

****

Following the meeting, Bratton wound his way through the worn-out basement corridor of Parker Center, emerged in the dingy parking lot behind the building, and slid into the passenger seat of the chief's gleaming black LAPD Ford sedan. He was heading to a private home in Brentwood where he would be speaking to the ACLU of Southern California, a vocal, decades-long critic and adversary of the LAPD's policing, and perhaps the organization most despised within the department.

As the car pulled out, his driver/bodyguard hung up his cell phone and said out of the side of his mouth: "So the wife is living with two daughters away from the father. The father finds out where she lives, shoots her three times—one right in the eye. She's dead at the scene. He turns the gun and shoots himself in the head, but does not die. He's Code Green at the hospital. The nine-year-old witnessed the homicide/ suicide. The four-year-old's in the apartment, but did not. And today's the wife's birthday."

Bratton had ordered his staff to brief him on every homicide that occurred in the city, so that, in his words, he could "feel the pain of the family, of the city."

Grabbing his phone, he began punching in numbers. It was now evening rush hour. As the vehicle inched toward Brentwood, his driver again laid down his cell phone. "Chief," he said. "We got another one. A man is parked, arguing with his wife. [A] suspect walks up to him, shoots him in the head. Suspect flees, the gun is recovered, but the suspect is not in custody. And on top of that, the victim was sitting there with a gun in his lap."

"You need a scorecard to keep track of it all," Bratton said. Finally they arrived at an enormous wrought-iron gate barring the way to a Brentwood enclave surrounded by massive walls, with a guardhouse the size of a bungalow. "Looks like the ACLU's doing all right for itself," Bratton said. Inside a neoclassical mansion, he stood before about forty people seated on metal folding chairs.

"I'm being asked to try to reinvigorate the organization [the LAPD] to get it back into the game, back into policing the city in a way that is constitutional, is lawful, is respectable, and is done under the framework of the consent decree," he said. "I work to change organizations in trouble and turmoil," Bratton continued. "Re-engineer them. So in me, you have somebody who is committed to the idea of reform, but, most importantly, believes strongly that it can be done.

"The consent decree's intent is to reform the culture of this organization," he continued. Its culture can be reformed. Quite frankly, what I'm looking for at the end of this five-year period of time is to have the federal government and, by extension, hopefully you—the ACLU—saying that the LAPD is no longer corrupt."

****

Earlier in the day, when he'd met with the L.A. Metro IAF, Bratton had told them that "one of the great things about this city is that there's no shortage of people who want to get involved. It's a strength that's really not recognized in this city—[just] how many people . . . want to get involved."

Later, on his way back to Parker Center, he told a reporter: "What you see [at these meetings] is a commonality of concern about this department. This trust issue—I'm seizing on that word 'trust' because it's just one that I hear over and over again. That L.A. Metro group had a very realistic understanding of the department—that it has its flaws, but it's an organization that has a lot going for it, and that it's the entity that they have to work with. The group tonight, absent their involvement in the ACLU, would probably never have an interaction with a police officer. Two totally different strata in society. But in some respects they both want the same thing—a police department that they can trust and respect and an awareness that they also need the police."

Bill Bratton was a smart guy, but it didn't take a genius to have figured that out. It was therefore one of the great mysteries of the LAPD that Daryl Gates, Willie Williams, and Bernard Parks never did.

William Bratton, James Hahn, and Clive Jackson, December 2002, South Los Angeles

As two black men in suits held out a large sign reading, "Stop the Killing. Choose Life, Not Death," Bill Bratton stood with Mayor James Hahn in the courtyard of a South Central community center named after Jesse Brewer. Surrounding them were about 120 people, local community organizers, uniformed cops, and a couple of dozen members of the media.

Bratton and Hahn had called a news conference on a grim December morning in 2002 to announce some get-tough anti-gang initiatives they planned on pursing following the death of a fourteen-year-old student named Clive Jackson, Jr., who was standing in front of a doughnut shop when he was shot dead by a member of the Rollin' 40s Crips.

They were hopeful that Jackson's death would finally wake up a city seemingly inured to gang violence—just as Brian Watkins's stabbing death had served as a powerful symbol of violent crime in New York for Bratton.

Nearby, Clive Jackson's father rocked back and forth on his feet, inconsolable. By his side the boy's mother stared at the ground as Bratton stepped toward the microphone. "The gangs of Los Angeles," said Bratton, "are much more of a national threat than the Mafia was, [and] if we don't deal with them effectively, the disease that these gangs represent will spread across this country. We need to enlist the federal government as partners [against them], just as we are seeking to do with [the] probation and parole [departments] and various [other] entities."

Then a letter dated November 13, 2002, and addressed to UCLA was read. "My name is Clive Jackson," it began. "I would like to know how to get into college so I can get ready [to apply]. . . . Who do I have to talk to? . . . How can I get a scholarship? . . . I don't want my mom to pay for everything." The letter continued in the same vein, heartbreaking in its simplicity, in its naïveté and innocence. For a moment even the cops and reporters appeared stunned. Which was exactly the point of having it read.

"It's the whole idea of personalizing this problem," Bratton said after the news conference. "This kid was just a good kid; he could be the one to put a face on crime here in L.A. . . . I describe it as the Rosetta stone effect. I'm looking for that stone that really strikes a responsive chord."

But it wasn't to be. Clive Jackson's tragic death turned out to be just another local black homicide, not a cross-racial killing of a white tourist with which the white middle class could easily identify and thus generate outrage and demands for action. So L.A. did not rise up as had New York following Brian Watkins's death. California governor Gray Davis did not call offering tens of millions of dollars to help, as had New York governor Mario Cuomo. And Bill Bratton didn't find his Rosetta stone.

Bratton would have to find another way to significantly halt the gang wars and violence that had caused an estimated 11,500 "gang-related" homicides in Los Angeles County from 1980 to 2000. It was an astounding number—the result of what Tom Hayden, in his book *Street Wars*, called an "unchecked intra-tribal war." A war that was nothing like a classic Marxist revolutionary rebellion, although it had the key elements: an impoverished black and brown underclass with a history of savage repression and a growing economic inequality, violently suppressed by wars on crime and drugs—that is, wars on them. But in Los Angeles the rebellion had turned inward onto itself, into a movement of what Hayden rightly described as "mass suicide" by generations of young men with a median age in their early twenties searching for power in the powerless world in which they lived.

****

Bill Bratton had come to Los Angeles talking out of both sides of his mouth when it came to gangs. Spouting the rhetoric of war, he called gang members "domestic terrorists," "a disease"—a cancer spreading across America, and "more of a national threat than [was] the Mafia."

In response, the Jesuit priest Father Gregory Boyle, the great East L.A. savior of lost gang souls and founder of the second-chance job program Homeboy Industries, told the *New York Times* that "Al Capone is not what we're dealing with here." He explained that Bratton was engaging in a "shoot-from-the-hip" analysis and bringing up memories of the bad old days of Daryl Gates. And he was.

It may well have been that the heated rhetoric was necessary for the new cop in town, signaling to communities that felt besieged by gang violence that he was going to reduce crime and keep them safe. Or that he was speaking to his first audience—his cop audience—and letting them know he was not some liberal, back-east reformer, and was going to make them safer too while restoring their tarnished image as crime fighters. But one thing was certain: if Bratton wanted to reduce gang violence in Los Angeles and be part of the process of stopping the criminalization of large portions of future generations of young black and brown Angelenos, he'd have to do more than talk—he would have to come up with solutions other than the failed blunt-force, paramilitary tactics of the old LAPD.

George Gascon, 2002,
Los Angeles Police Department Headquarters

Fifty-year-old George Gascon was not a blunt-force kind of a guy. Nor, thought Bill Bratton, was he the kind of a person "who would please you with a lie." Bratton liked that. So it wasn't all that surprising that one day Rikki Klieman approached Gascon—a lawyer and LAPD deputy chief—introduced herself, and, as she would later tell it, asked him if he wanted to do himself a favor. When he of course said yes, Klieman said, "Go into Bill's office and tell him everything you think is wrong with the LAPD." Gascon's face fell. But Klieman insisted. "Do it and you'll get what you want [the much-coveted number two job in the LAPD: chief of operations]."

By then, Bratton had been in office for about nine months. He had made an old friend named Jim McDonnell his operations chief. One reason he'd selected McDonnell was because he'd been impressed by a hundred-page, voluntarily written report that McDonnell had authored that delineated the department's problems and how to fix them. Unfortunately, the laid-back McDonnell—who would later be elected sheriff of Los Angeles County—had turned out to lack the kind of dynamic leadership Bratton was looking for in an operations chief, and hence Bratton was now looking for somebody else.

Following Klieman's advice, Gascon, a veteran of over twenty-five years with the LAPD, met with Bratton. He told him that the changes taking place on a division and street level weren't enough to significantly alter the status quo. Then he laid out the strategies he'd pursue if he were operations chief. A few months later Bratton made Gascon his operations chief.

Atypically for the LAPD, Gascon was a strong proponent of data-based crime prevention and strategies that focused on policing lawfully, with community acceptance and cooperation. In April of 2000, at the height of the Rampart scandal, Gascon had been placed in charge of the department's training division. When the consent decree was signed, he began the decades-overdue revamping of the LAPD's rote-drill, paramilitary training of police academy cadets and officers in the field. Focusing on problem-solving and respect for civil liberties, he linked them, in a new curriculum, to use-of-force and policing tactics. The linkage was so commonsensical and obvious that it was almost ludicrous that Gascon's ideas were looked upon as amazing and innovative. But for the LAPD and police agencies operating in ghettos and barrios across America, they were. Instead of confronting and commanding people, arresting everyone in sight, quickly using force, and alienating entire communities as a way of reducing crime, Gascon instead was success-fully advocating thinking through solutions to crime problems and being nice to the public as a way of getting its cooperation and support. The latter concept was really something straight out of Miss Manners or a self-help book about how to get what you want out of life. But for the LAPD it was somehow something new.

Gascon's deep and abiding respect for constitutional rights was born out of his experience. He arrived in the U.S. with his parents in 1967, when he was thirteen years old, as a political refugee from Cuba. His father, a mechanic at a beer brewery in Cuba, had been a supporter of Fidel Castro's revolution, but became an outspoken critic of his govern-ment when Castro began to shut down all dissent to his policies. "I got to see as a young person what it was like to live in a police state," says Gascon, "where cops could just do what they wanted, and what it was like to be targeted by the police and have an organized neighborhood block club spying for the police. My mother and I were always fearful that when my father left the house he might not return [as had hap-pened to his uncle, a labor organizer who would spend twenty years in a Cuban prison]. One of the things I've always enjoyed about Amer-ica is that the police are subservient to the people, not the other way around."

Struggling to learn English, he quit his Los Angeles high school, joined the army, became a military policeman, earned his GED, and began college. Returning home, he joined the LAPD in 1978. Strug-gling to raise his family, he quit after three years to make twice as much money selling cars before rejoining the department in 1987. Over the years he also earned a degree in history from Cal State, Long Beach, and a law degree from Western State University College of Law. He would go on to first become San Francisco's chief of police and then its district attorney.

George Gascon, in short, was exactly the kind of leader Bill Bratton was looking for.

Bratton, an avid reader of management books and profiles of business and political leaders, took "leadership identification" very seriously. One of the books he'd read was *Good to Great*, in which Jim Collins had written about the importance of "getting the right people on the bus, the wrong people off the bus, and the right people in the right seats." For Bratton that meant not only positioning his LAPD leadership correctly on the organizational flowchart but matching those working out in the field to the right communities.

"Risk taker" was among the highest of accolades Bratton used when describing a colleague or up-and-coming cop, and it was precisely that innovative quality—coupled with multicultural sensitivity and the ability to think innovatively and to build police-community and interpersonal relationships with black and Latino leaders and activists—that he was looking for, and that was essential to executing his brand of "assertive" but not abusive policing. Which, not incidentally, would involve *increasing* the already high number of pedestrian and vehicle stops the LAPD had been making, particularly in its barrios and in the African-American community. There, violent crime and murder numbers were rising, but hyperalertness to police violence and discourtesy still remained intense, and the relationships with the police fraught with mistrust.

Bernard Parks had reduced the use of the LAPD's notoriously abusive stop-and-frisk practices, such as proning out suspects, spread-eagling them against a wall, or forcing them to kneel on the street with their hands clasped behind their necks while some LAPD officer, often using a loudspeaker, barked out orders.

The LAPD would have to significantly reduce those kinds of provocations if Bratton was going to successfully implement the kind of stop-question-frisk policing he had in mind, while convincing the black community that smart, better-targeted crime reduction and not harassment or arbitrary shows of force was the goal.

As all this was occurring, Bill Bratton was also devising a policing strategy known as the "Safer Cities" Initiative. In New York, Bratton had had thirty-eight thousand police officers, enough to flood any trouble spot with cops and keep them there until a problem was brought under long-term control.

In L.A., with a force of about nine thousand officers that would gradually expand to ten thousand, the department's resources were stretched far too thin for him to do anything remotely like that citywide. So he decided to pick and choose his spots, designating five areas (including Skid Row) in which to concentrate police officers, and by so doing demonstrate that he could significantly reduce crime in the process.

But Bratton and Gascon, meanwhile, wanted to model and anchor their crime-reduction and community-cooperation theories within an even deeper, more independent and decentralized project than Safer Cities—one that would have a more immediate payoff, and where bureau chiefs, along with the rest of the chain of command, would be bypassed and division captains would report directly to Gascon.

They called it "District Policing." Gascon picked three divisions. None were in predominately black areas. Two of them—the Hollywood and Harbor divisions—were primarily selected because they already had highly regarded captains leading them. (Gannon was in Harbor.) The third, the Rampart Division, was chosen because it was crying out for immediate attention.

Charlie Beck, 2002, Parker Center

Charlie Beck had just left Parker Center and was walking across the street to buy a deli sandwich when he spotted Bill Bratton in the crosswalk, coming the other way with his security detail. "So, Charlie," he called out, "did you move to Rampart yet?"

"No, Chief," Beck replied. "Next week."

"Make sure you clean up that fucking park."

"I know, Chief. I will."

"And that," recalls Beck, "was the entire extent of my instructions from him."

Pico-Union was, of course, home not only to the disgraced Rampart Division but also to the park that Bratton had been talking about: Mac-Arthur Park, a city oasis surrounding a small, man-made lake located on the easternmost end of the major commercial stretch of Wilshire Boulevard known as the "Miracle Mile." Once an emerald jewel of Los Angeles, by the early nineties the park had turned into a crime-filled, semi-grassless brown wasteland whose deterioration symbolized the LAPD's failure to provide public safety to the district.

When Charlie Beck first toured the park, he remembers seeing people selling drugs beyond the boathouse and the lake on its south side. "Dope dealers would stand there and people would drive up on Wilshire, swing to the curb, get curbside service, and drive off," he says. "That happened hundreds and hundreds of times a day. The park was literally a place that had been taken over by the criminal element." And it wasn't just dope dealers, Beck would add, it was gangsters, prostitutes, people hawking illegal IDs, selling counterfeit money.

"There was literally no grass in the park," recalls Beck. "Parks and Recreation had stopped doing maintenance, because they were afraid to go into the park. Regular people—families—wouldn't come in either." MacArthur Park was important to the LAPD's new strategy in Pico-Union because it defined the area. "Three hundred people were going to jail each month out of the park," recalls Beck, "and nothing was changing. They would just go through the revolving doors of justice and be right back out."

It's also hard to overestimate just how important the park was to the surrounding community. Pico-Union was an extraordinary area of L.A. in terms of its population density. People lived in decaying apartment buildings from a long bygone era, most without yards. There were a couple of other small parks in the area, but not many. Without MacArthur Park, it was difficult for kids and families to find somewhere to go for some recreation and relief from the blighted urban landscape that was their daily reality.

No official plan for revitalizing the park existed, or at least none that Beck could find. Nor had anybody officially conceptualized how the park might be utilized for the community. Instead the city had, in effect, just abandoned it, and refused to put any of the people's tax money into it.

And no one seemed willing to step up, pick up the ball, and provide the organizational commitment to get the game started. Why should they? Pico-Union was a poor, politically and economically powerless community, a place where it was simply easier—far easier—to write off the local, disenfranchised people and their situation and declare it hopeless than to do anything about it.

In some respects the situation wasn't dissimilar to what Beck had faced on Skid Row. But there, in the end—after establishing some necessary rule and order by using quality-of-life policing to force as many of the homeless out of the area as possible—there was only so much that could be done by the police to alter the situation. But MacArthur Park—MacArthur Park was doable for a division captain like Charlie Beck, doable as a stand-alone project with the potential for permanent impact.

****

Among the many realities of MacArthur Park that Beck had to consider was that the park's run-down physical condition in and of itself was a public safety hazard. The trees and bushes were all overgrown because the Parks and Recreation Department refused to go in and trim them—which, in turn, bred more crime as people hid or lay in wait within the foliage. By convincing Parks and Recreation and the National Forest Service that what he intended was not just another sweep of the park but a genuine, long-term commitment to its transformation, Beck got them to agree to trim the shrubbery and trees.

"One of the things we'd always done in the past," says Beck, "was go in there with a bunch of cops, knock them dead for two or three months, then leave. The criminals would just hunker down and then come back. So I said, 'No, I'm not gonna do that. This is our problem, nobody else's problem. You own it,'" he told his officers, "'I own it.'"

In addition to the wild overgrowth, *none* of the park lights worked. The Department of Water and Power would put up lights and they'd be broken by dealers, pimps, and others who preferred darkness, while the electrical wiring would be dug up, torn out, hauled away, and sold for scrap. Again using the promise of permanent change, Beck got the DWP to put in both exterior lights that helped illuminate the street and streetlights that also reflected back into park.

He also convinced General Electric and others to pay for the mounting of surveillance cameras around the park, and had his officers monitor them. Then he had DVDs made of the footage and gave them to prosecutors *and* suspects. "Look," he had his cops announce to everyone they apprehended, "you got arrested because we have cameras all over the park. If you come back here again, you're going to get arrested again."

In addition, his officers began enforcing the city's new shopping cart ordinance, prohibiting the taking of shopping carts out of supermarket areas by outlawing them within the park. As Beck later put it: "Shopping carts were vehicles that enabled homeless people to transport their belongings into the park and set up transient encampments. So the banning of the shopping carts was big for our efforts."

Beck and his officers also did something quite amazing, for LAPD officers. They got the City Council to commit $2 million to redo the park's soccer field and erected stadium lighting; to renovate a once-beautiful band shell; to restock the artificial lake with fish; and to install artificial turf for a soccer field. Their goal was for the park to be open until at least midnight so that people, especially in the summer, could play soccer in a well-lit, safe place. "If you remove crime from a location," says Beck, "you've got to fill it with legitimate activities; if you don't, then crime will return."

****

One day Beck decided to organize a take-back-the-park candlelight vigil and invited gang intervention organizations like Homies Unidos—which were made up primarily of ex–gang members—to participate. "They had some scary-looking guys in these organizations," says Beck. "Most of them had one foot in and one foot out, but were looking for some way out." Getting out was no easy proposition, especially if it was someone who was typically living back in the old neighborhood where he'd grown up and come of age, where his gang was tight-knit and multigenerational and where all the things he'd known—his entire identity—was linked to the gang. Breaking all that—or at least trying to live inside the law—was a very tough proposition.

"But despite that," says Beck, "many of them became involved in the rallies around the park. If I could find somebody who claimed they represented an organization, I'd talk to them, I wouldn't ignore them. We went to their houses or garages—wherever they met—and talked to them on a human level—like 'Hey, this is the change I'm trying to effect, and I'd like to get your input on how best to do that. Forget whatever's gone on in the past, I'm trying to move forward here.'"

Beck had learned over the years that gangs were stratified, and he tailored his approach to reach members of the community who would be more likely to support his efforts. "Everybody isn't the same," he says. "You have the ones who shoot, pillage, rape. I knew I wasn't going to get them. But I tried like hell to get the ones at the other end." At the same time, Beck was trying to eliminate drug-trade violence in the park, and to put a stop to gang wars on the periphery, about who would control sales in the park. Beck officers continued to arrest "hundreds and hundreds of people for dealing, and hundreds more coming into the area to purchase drugs." Then he courted the press so they'd put out the word "that you can't come to MacArthur Park to buy narcotics." He continued to do that until his undercover officers had no more dealers or customers to arrest.

The result, much of which has lasted until the present day, says Beck, "is that you don't see drug dealing in Mac Park anymore; crime in the park is very limited," and every year there are over fifty concerts in the renovated band shell.

In the old LAPD, a lot of what Charlie Beck and his officers engaged in at MacArthur Park would have been considered soft, off-the-reservation, social-work mumbo-jumbo far outside the scope of a real cop's job of arresting "bad guys."

But because Bratton had freed Beck to think and act for himself, he had come to a different conclusion: "There's an old homicide saying that the answer's always outside of the [crime scene] tape. Inside the tape, there's nothing there, everything is outside the tape. That's kind of the way I began thinking about the answers to our problems. That it's always outside the tape."

Connie Rice, December 2003,
Advancement Project Offices, Los Angeles

Connie Rice was on the phone when her secretary handed her a scribbled note: "LAPD Chief Bill Bratton is on the other line." Rice had met Bratton only twice before and they had no personal relationship. Nevertheless, as she would later tell it, "his greeting was breezy and familiar, as if it were our hundredth call." Then Bratton mentioned a comment she'd made about a week earlier when he and Rice had participated in a December 2003 symposium entitled "The Gangs of L.A.," sponsored by the Institute for Justice and Journalism at USC's Annenberg School of Journalism.

The panelists seated with them that day included Los Angeles County sheriff Lee Baca, while to their left stood a moderator at a podium, staring out at an audience of three or four hundred people packed together on folding chairs in a large, gym-like room. Near the panel's end, the moderator had turned to Rice and asked if there were any significant stories about L.A.'s criminal justice system she thought the local media had failed to cover. Two immediately come to mind, Rice replied. The first was about how the LAPD limited the Rampart investigation, and how detectives had not been permitted "to go where the evidence led." Instead, the investigation had been a limited one, shut down by Bernard Parks. As a consequence, she continued, the department had never produced a promised comprehensive "after-action" report examining the full extent of the scandal, as opposed to just the tiny slice of it that Parks had allowed to be scrutinized. The second involved journalists' failure to report on the limiting and shutting down of that investigation.

Now, on the phone with Rice, Bratton told her that he'd asked the Police Commission to appoint a panel of outside experts and investigators to finally produce the report, and that he wanted her to lead the effort.

Rice was astounded, given her background and her well-known antipathy toward the LAPD. But the request had its own logic. The "Blue Ribbon Rampart Review Panel" that Bratton had in mind would be operating under the proviso that nothing it discovered could serve as the basis for any further criminal prosecutions or internal discipline—

thus dampening serious opposition to the idea within the LAPD while enabling the cooperation of the department's rank-and-file union, the Police Protective League. Bratton told Rice that he wanted the investigation to be a "lessons learned" exercise, with recommended reforms moving forward.

For Bratton, the report would provide him with the opportunity to claim that the investigation had finally been done, that the department had finally put it behind them, and that it was now all about the future.

There were also advantages for Rice in chairing the panel, although they were less obvious. On the downside, four dense, little-noted Rampart reports were already sitting in history's dustbin, containing little that the LAPD and the *Los Angeles Times* hadn't already made public, and accomplishing little or nothing. What good would a fifth do?

Nevertheless, Rice was intrigued by Bratton's offer, seeing it as an opportunity to write and shape a report that told Bratton not simply why things had gone so wrong with Rampart CRASH but how policing a different way might lead to different outcomes—something she'd been thinking about ever since her experience a decade earlier with the department's K-9 unit.

No longer the lawyer–cum–fledgling activist she'd been a decade earlier, Rice had been busy reaching out and trying to figure out what she could do—other than suing the LAPD—to pressure the department to change some of its rules and regulations. She had grown to care deeply about fundamental police reform and police-community relations, and wanted to introduce a more comprehensive vision of public safety focused on reducing youth and gang violence through a multifaceted, holistic approach. To do so, she'd come to understand, she needed to find some way to get the LAPD to change its tactics and policing philosophy.

She'd forged relationships with forward-looking former gang members like Darren "Bo" Taylor, a Crip turned peacemaker who'd founded Unity One, a grassroots organization committed to ending gang warfare; and with young black establishment figures like Blair Taylor, who'd replaced John Mack as president of the Los Angeles Urban League.

As a result, by the time of Bratton's call, Rice had come to some basic understandings. One was that white cops—just like her a decade earlier—"weren't fluent in the culture of black, underclass males": didn't know how to read them, and couldn't tell who was a real threat and who wasn't. The result was that they were treating them all the same—that is, badly.

A second was that although the LAPD had contributed to the problems of South Los Angeles—so much so that they'd caused a momentous riot just a decade earlier—the situation nevertheless wasn't principally of its making. And that was because in a race-and-class, stacked-deck society, one of their traditional, *primary* missions was ghetto and barrio containment and suppression. You could not give police officers such a mission and expect them to act significantly differently than the LAPD had, Rice concluded. It was necessary, therefore, to *completely* change the definition of what an LAPD cop did and who a LAPD cop worked for, and worked with.

Rice's third realization was that straightforward litigation—suing the department to make a change—was a "battering ram" that couldn't do the delicate work of solving issues like bad schools, bad policing, and bad public transportation. Suing the cops could change a tactic, like search-and-bite, but except under extraordinary circumstances it couldn't change their cultural and political mind-set.

So, in 1999 Rice left the NAACP Legal Defense Fund, which she felt was resting on its laurels and not addressing the fact that a civil rights organization circa 2003 had very different fights than the integration battles of the past, and had to operate in multiple arenas and deal with unlikely allies. What Rice was after was change—culture change, mindset change. Policy change at a minimum. Ideally she wanted "full-spectrum" transformation of how a public service organization such as the LAPD saw its mission and treated its clients.

So with two longtime colleagues, Rice joined a team of veteran civil rights lawyers and founded the Advancement Project. Over the decade of the nineties she and her L.A. colleagues would partner with the Bus Riders Union—a grassroots coalition of low-income bus riders—to sue the Metropolitan Transit Authority in a landmark case that produced a settlement requiring that $2 billion be spent on a notoriously underfunded, dysfunctional Los Angeles bus system. In 1999, Rice would also play a significant role in a coalition that helped win $1 billion for the construction of schools in poor neighborhoods in Los Angeles and L.A. County.

Now, with Bratton's invitation, she was being offered a chance to influence the LAPD. So, she told Bratton, yes, she'd chair the panel. That was the advantage *she* would get out of the partnership. And her timing couldn't have been better.

Connie Rice, July 2003, Advancement Project Offices, Los Angeles

In July 2003, Connie Rice phoned Charlie Beck at the Rampart Division station house. The Police Commission had just approved the formation of the Rampart Review Panel, Rice told Beck, and she wanted to interview him and his officers, a request to which he readily agreed.

For Beck, the timing was also perfect. What he'd just accomplished in Rampart and MacArthur Park was exactly what a thoughtful department critic like Rice would find impressive: he had analyzed a complex problem, suggested a big-picture solution, and followed it up by bringing together his cops with non–law enforcement governmental and private agencies, community groups, and activists to tackle it.

Beck's achievement was exactly what Rice needed: a model, a piece, at least, of the kind of policing the LAPD should be doing—*had* to be doing if it was ever to both reduce crime and police abuse. And the beauty of it was that it wasn't her plan, wasn't some think tank's plan, but the successfully implemented blueprint of a veteran LAPD captain whom everyone within the department respected.

So, as they proceeded, Rice and the panel decided to feature Beck in their final written report—*Rampart Reconsidered: The Search for Real Reform Seven Years Later*—as a way to document what Beck had done to restore MacArthur Park and give it back as a gift to the people of Pico-Union while holding it and the Rampart Division up as what was in some key aspects a new, alternative way for the LAPD to do business.

Martin Ludlow, Summer 2003, "The Jungle"

Martin Ludlow was a man on the go. Born in 1964, he was the son of an African-American father and a white mother, but was given up for adoption to a white Methodist minister and liberal political activist named Willis Ludlow and his wife, Anne. Raised in Idaho, he moved around the country with his family, attending rallies and walking picket lines with his adoptive parents before arriving in Los Angeles to attend college. Dynamic, articulate, and ambitious, he would rise to become the political director of a powerful local union, the Los Angeles County Federation of Labor, and marry the daughter of one of L.A.'s most prominent black clergymen. When he ran for the Los Angeles City Council in 2003, he was backed by both business and labor and won handily. Two years later, pulled in two directions, Ludlow quit the council to head the labor federation. Soon, the push-pull of two careers proved his undoing. In 2006, Ludlow would be convicted of conspiracy to divert union employee funds to his City Council campaign, ending both his political and union careers.

Before Martin Ludlow resigned from the City Council in 2005, however, he left behind a different kind of legacy, one that was a wake-up slap to L.A.'s political establishment and law enforcement agencies. In 2003, with money left over from his council campaign, Ludlow decided to organize and fund a summer program to keep every kid in his largely black Baldwin Hills council district safe from violence. Known as "the Jungle," the district's street name referred both to the lush vegetation surrounding the area's hundreds of aging, low-story apartment complexes, and the fact that many of the winding paths, alleyways, and garages within them were the home turf of the Blood gang known as the Black P. Stones—reportedly involved in twenty-eight murders and fifteen hundred aggravated assaults between 2000 and 2005. In the summer of 2002 alone, the area had experienced seventeen shootings, including four or five fatalities, as well as a series of gang rapes.

Ludlow called the program "the Summer of Success," coordinated it through the Advancement Project, and partnered with the LAPD and

L.A. County Sheriff's Department, parole agents, and local churches and service providers. Local gyms and parks were kept lit and open until late at night for midnight soccer, basketball games, and singing and talent contests. Teachers were recruited for tutoring classes, and churches organized snacks and meals to feed the kids. Ludlow negotiated with the gangs in the area to keep the peace. By the end of the nine-week program there had been no shootings, no murders, no rapes, and violent crime had dropped 20 percent. The cessation of violence wasn't permanent, because when the program was over, it was over. But it was a taste of what might be accomplished. Chairing the City Council Ad Hoc Committee for Gang Reduction and Youth Development, Ludlow then convened a series of hearings on gang issues in the spring of 2005 that revealed what had been obvious to gang experts for years: that the gang reduction programs that existed were scattered, uncoordinated, and unaccountable, and were not being influenced or run according to evidence-based best practices, research, and evaluation. It took a year before the City Council finally approved a funding request for further investigation and a status report that would include what needed to be done to move forward. Once it was approved, Connie Rice and the Advancement Project won the $500,000 bid to write it. Suddenly—astoundingly—Rice and her nonprofit advocacy group were now centrally involved in the investigation and writing of two prominent city-sponsored reports crucial to L.A.'s criminal justice policies—one about the city's police department, the other about its gangs.

Connie Rice, July 2006, Rampart Division

The first of Connie Rice's city-funded criminal justice reports—the Blue Ribbon Panel's Rampart investigation—took nearly three years to complete. When it was finally released in July 2006, it contained a detailed analysis of what had caused the Rampart scandal; recommendations for reforms; and what the panel called the "New Rampart Leadership and Crime Fighting Model"—a model based on exactly what Charlie Beck had done at Rampart and in MacArthur Park. "This community-savvy model," read the report, "demanded accountability for both supervisors and officers, but above all, it demanded leadership. At the revamped Rampart, supervisors did not evade standards but enforced them. Officers knew that disrespect to the public would be reprimanded, misconduct punished, corruption rooted out and prosecuted. As importantly, leaders made clear that creative problem solving and community work that reduced crime and generated trust would be rewarded as much or more than high arrest tallies."

Bill Bratton immediately embraced the report he commissioned. It represented a big win-win: the acquisition of Rice, a rising liberal activist star on the L.A. political stage, as a new ally; and the presentation of a successful, decentralized community police and crime reduction strategy in a high-profile division, engineered by another handpicked rising star. Plus—*plus* a laudatory report announced to the world by a panel headed by not just an outsider but an outspoken, media-savvy civil rights lawyer.

Included within the report, however, was also a warning for Bratton. "Most rank and file officers interviewed by the Panel did not analyze department progress or continuing problems through the rearview lens of the CRASH crisis," the panel said, "and few saw any connection between the corruption in Rampart CRASH and the department's systems and culture that gave rise to and shielded the misconduct." Instead, the report concluded, the officers "believed the scandal was about a few bad apples and not about systemic failure."

The latter assessment was not only a warning to Bratton, it was also a confirmation of another opinion rendered just two months earlier, in May 2006. At the time Bill Bratton was in the midst of his fourth year in office, and the LAPD's five-year consent decree was about to expire. That earlier warning had come from U.S. district judge Gary A. Feess, who had weighed in on the lack of progress being made by the department. Bratton, the department, and the city were growing increasingly impatient with the burdensome requirements of the decree and wanted it ended.

But if Bratton and the city were impatient, so was Feess, who was un-

happy with the LAPD and its inability to meet some important requirements of the decree having to do with officer accountability. So instead
of ending the decree, he extended it by another three years. "There have
been forty-plus years of debate in this community about how it is policed," he said. "Time after time . . . reports were nodded to and nothing was done. This consent decree is going to effect real reform, and it's
not going to be extinguished until that happens." Which meant that Bill
Bratton wasn't going to leave the LAPD anytime soon.

Charlie Beck, 2006, South Bureau Headquarters

Stepping into the grim, battered lobby of the South Los Angeles headquarters of the LAPD, Charlie Beck was feeling good. And understandably so. Attached to each of his blue shirt collars were two new silver
stars announcing not only his remarkably rapid rise from captain to
deputy chief but also his assignment to the pivotal post of commander
of the sixteen hundred officers assigned to the 57.6-square-mile area of
South Los Angeles that the LAPD called South Bureau.

It was a big job—one of the biggest in the LAPD—and by this day in
August 2006, Beck was ready for it; had, in fact, been working toward
such a challenge for a long time. As a young police officer in South Bureau, he'd been profoundly affected by the violence he saw there, which
he had quickly learned to view through the hard, jaded eyes of the Vietnam vets who were doing his street mentoring and who saw themselves
as still at war.

But he was now in his early fifties, and had come to understand how
circumstances dictated the behavior of many of the people he'd policed
in South Bureau. And the same went for his cops, who in the face of difficult circumstances often felt the pressure to do the wrong thing.

For Beck, such insights hadn't come easily. He'd never learned much
from criminology or sociological theory. His intellect tended to be more
practical. He'd always been the kind of kid who had to grab the plate ten
times while it was hot before he learned not to. What he liked—really
liked—was analyzing and then fixing a problem, whether mechanical or

organizational. He got the same charge from both, the same igniting of the kind of stream of consciousness that kept him awake at night, rolling ideas around in his head, trying to fit the pieces into the puzzle. And now, with command of South Bureau, Bill Bratton had given him the supreme challenge of both reducing crime and changing the historic, notoriously poisonous dynamic between his cops and the area's black community.

Bratton had been preparing Beck for a big job, including him in meetings with the mayor and sending him, along with other departmental up-and-comers, to Harvard's Kennedy School of Government, to the Boston Senior Management Institute for Police, and to view gang intervention programs in Chicago.

The learning opportunities had come at exactly the right time for Beck. He hadn't been a captain or a commander long enough to have an absolute belief in the infallibility of his actions, and thus was open to new concepts and operational approaches. And he'd never been risk averse. As long as the risk didn't conflict with the one absolute he had in mind as he took command of South Bureau, the home of the two biggest disasters in the LAPD's history.

"I am not," he swore to himself, "going to be the [South Bureau] chief that oversees the next riot. That's not going to happen. I am going to do whatever it takes to make sure that never happens again."

****

For decades L.A.'s politicians had delivered little in the way of jobs or anything else to the 640,000 residents of South Bureau, who collectively comprised 16 percent of the city's population. Because of its negative gang and crime connotations, the City Council *had* eliminated the name "South Central" from the city's nomenclature and maps in 2003, folding the sixteen-square-mile area into the wider designation of "South Los Angeles." But when it came to the heart of the matter—those good, union, living-wage jobs that had been lost in the sixties, seventies, and eighties—*nothing* had ever been done to replace them.

While Los Angeles's population had risen by one million residents since the mid-1980s and now stood at almost four million, the number of available jobs outside of the underground economy had actually dipped *below* the 1990 level. In fact, in 2006, South L.A. had just 0.5 percent jobs per worker, versus 1.1 jobs in the rest of the county, and the area's 30 percent poverty rate remained the same as it had been in 1969 and 1986—about twice that of the rest of Los Angeles County.

Meanwhile, the promised revitalization of the area after the '92 riots had never materialized. In the neighborhoods where gang violence remained most frightening, much of what had been burned down during the '92 riots had never been rebuilt in any meaningful manner, and now stood forlorn alongside the rusted factories, auto body shops, junk yards, liquor stores, and fast-food joints that daily symbolized South L.A.'s agonizing history since the Watts riots.

There was one thing that had changed, however, and that was the area's racial makeup. Once 90 percent African-American, by 2006 its black population had dropped dramatically to just 31 percent, while the number of desperately poor, mostly immigrant Mexican and Central American residents had risen to a stunning 62 percent. Beck had noticed it right away. He'd walk outside South Bureau headquarters, look at the kids walking to and from school, and see this "melting pot, this amazing melting pot. It wasn't that way when I was a police officer," Beck would later recall. "All of Watts was black, and there were some small amount of Hispanics. But [by 2006] the younger the age, the more Hispanic it was, until the grade schools were almost entirely Hispanic."

Nevertheless, three times as many blacks still lived in South Los Angeles as in the rest of L.A. County combined; black gangs were waning but still remained a potent force; violent crime in South L.A. was still twice as high as the rest of the county; and of the city's 515 murders in 2006, over 290 were gang-related, many of which had taken place in South L.A.

So, as Beck took charge, seriously decreasing the area's historic gang violence—along with avoiding another riot—became his top imperative. If history was any judge, however, his prognosis for success was not good. From 1979 to 2006, South Los Angeles had been a lodestar of a modern-day, post-1960s gang culture that during those years had produced, as previously mentioned, over eleven thousand gang-related homicides in Los Angeles County alone. From 2000 to 2009 there were 9,917 homicides in the county as a whole (which includes the city of Los Angeles), of which 43 percent were gang-related. Those gang killings were a terrible subcultural fratricide that was costing the people of L.A. County $2 billion a year in police, medical, and other related expenses. Far more important was the terrible cost in the unlived lives of thousands of dead young men.

Nevertheless, the homicide rate wasn't nearly as high as in the nineties. By 2004, in fact, gang-related killings countywide had dropped from a peak of just over 800 in 1995 to 464, and had significantly declined in the city as well. Moreover, the crack wars and widespread street dealing that had caused so much of the violence had largely disappeared. Nevertheless, the homicide numbers were erratic—sometimes up, sometimes down, and still way too high. All one had to do to confirm that was to ask Pat Gannon.

Pat Gannon and Bo Taylor, Autumn 2005, 77th Street Division, South Los Angeles

By the time Charlie Beck arrived, few members of the LAPD were more knowledgeable about gang crime in South Bureau than Captain Patrick Gannon, who had received a crash course on the subject since leaving Internal Affairs. In the autumn of 2005 he'd been tapped to head the 77th Street Division—a gang-plagued section of South Bureau abutting Watts.

It was there, early one afternoon in November of 2005, that a call crackled over Gannon's car radio as he was cruising down the freeway: a drive-by shooting had just occurred near the corner of Manchester and Vermont, not far from his new division's station house.

Immediately changing course, Gannon headed toward the scene, listening as he went to the beat of new information pulsating in over the radio: the victim was seventeen years old . . . a student who'd been shot in an alley . . . wounded in the ankle . . . otherwise not seriously injured.

The alley was right next to a continuation high school. But the shooting had nothing to do with the school and everything to do with the victim being both a gangster and the latest casualty in an ongoing gang war between the Inglewood Family and the Rolling 60s Crips—a conflict that spanned about eleven square miles housing tens of thousands of residents.

Not more than a few minutes passed before another shooting call came in. Over the next four hours there would be nineteen more, for a total of twenty—*twenty*—retaliatory shootings.

That night, black L.A.'s premier football game was scheduled between the city's last two predominantly black high schools: Dorsey and Crenshaw. The schools were historically bitter enemies not only on the football field but also on the street. Dorsey's gangs were Bloods, Crenshaw's Crips.

By early evening two hundred additional cops were flooding the area, but both a drive-by and an officer-involved shooting nonetheless occurred that night.

Just one month into his tenure as the 77th Street Division's commander, Pat Gannon found himself facing an astounding problem, and the responsibility of solving it. Bratton had made that clear during his first command staff meeting at the Police Academy: it's your division; bring down crime legally, but otherwise as you see fit; if there's a problem, you own it, you fix it.

Gannon had reveled in the freedom of that concept when he'd first heard it. But twenty shootings in one afternoon would be no easy fix. The obvious one—overwhelming the area with cops—wasn't a long-term option. The LAPD simply didn't have enough officers to keep hundreds more of them assigned there permanently, in just one of South Bureau's four divisions. They were needed in those other divisions, as well as in Central and Wilshire and East L.A., where the areas' "hot spots" were also being flooded with cops as part of Bill Bratton's all-out effort to bring down gang crime.

Besides, Gannon's officers had already *been* "stopping tons of people," as Gannon later put it, and "using search warrants, and doing parole searches—all of which had changed nothing." Then he remembered once witnessing a civilian gang interventionist successfully halt a similar but much smaller episode, and began asking who was doing that kind of work in South L.A. Not long after, he was put in touch with a former gangster named Bo Taylor.

A thirty-nine-year-old father of four, Taylor was a charismatic U.S. Navy veteran with a powerful personality who'd risen up the hierarchy of a local Crips gang by selling drugs. He skillfully melded his preacher-like persona with what Connie Rice called his "Dr. Phil–like" conciliatory gifts. By 2005 he was out of the gang life and consumed with a born-again spiritual revival in the cause of advancing the gospel of gang-violence intervention through a grassroots organization called Unity One that he'd founded after the '92 riots. Gannon reached out to Taylor—who was already working with Connie Rice—and arranged for him to meet with about thirty mostly self-declared interventionists, some out of active gang life and working with Unity One, some with one foot still in and the other out.

Partnering with civilian gang intervention workers—whose job was to help reduce gang violence—had never been part of the LAPD's playbook. "For most of the past thirty years," as veteran gang interventionist Ron Noblet later explained, "not only were we unwelcome, we were actual *targets* of law enforcement, viewed—if not as gangsters ourselves—then as some kind of radical, militant anti-police scum, or as a social worker, which was just one click above scum."

There'd always been LAPD officers who understood the need to work with grassroots community organizations who weren't part of the department's usual cast of police groupies—including those employing interventionists. But inevitably those officers would be singled out, disparaged for going native, and become persona non grata within the department.

Some community organizers weren't ex-gangsters but people who'd trained in disciplines like social work (or, in the case of Noblet, in Eastern European studies and the region's ethnic animosities at USC) and had been hired by organizations funded by Los Angeles County or private agencies. There were also people like the Jesuit priest Father Gregory Boyle, who created and ran his own comprehensive gang intervention, rehab, and job training programs. But most such organizations had few formal job requirements and, often, no real criteria for evaluating effectiveness.

That unstructured, often ad hoc nature of gang intervention—along with the gangster past of many of the interventionists—had made it inconceivable that an LAPD notoriously unwilling to partner with any "outsiders" would readily collaborate with these groups. Many *were* mixed bags, and the LAPD had every right to be cautious. But others, like Taylor, were genuinely trying to help their neighborhoods and themselves transition out of a self-destructive situation.

They constituted an entire spectrum of men, from those who never did much of anything in gangs, to shot-callers who'd done their twelve years in prison, matured, learned and changed, and were now back on the street. They possessed a unique range of insights into gut-level cultural street values, gang norms, and street psychology—all of which uniquely allowed them to dispel rumors, calm fears, lower passions, and stop a single outbreak of violence from escalating into the kind of tribal retribution Pat Gannon was now confronting.

They understood, for example, that while street-gang violence was sometimes about money and business—as it was during the crack wars of the 1980s and '90s—drugs were not why the participants were gangsters. They might use drugs and sell drugs, but they'd become gangsters because of where they lived, so that they might become part of that neighborhood's most powerful street fraternity. Drugs just happened to be one of the businesses they did, unlike the drug crews on the East Coast, which formed precisely *so* they could deal drugs.

In L.A. it was all far more primal than just money. It was a way of exercising power in a closed, segregated subculture where kids and young men had been exposed to very little other than answering slights and insults with guns. In their world, you had to defend your reputation, and your gang's, to survive. That was the sad, dog-eat-dog reality at the lowest rung of urban America's class and racial ladder. Some of them—some of those ex-gangsters turned interventionists like Bo Taylor—seemed also to have a new, hard-won understanding of their experience—one best summed up by a gangster named Kumasi who, in Stacy Peralta's brilliantly revelatory documentary *Crips and Bloods:*

Made in America, says: "Part of the mechanics of oppressing people is to pervert them to the extent that they become their own oppressors."

****

After Bo Taylor arranged the meeting with the gang interventionists, Pat Gannon was instructed to dress in civilian clothes and show up alone to the basement of a local church. There he met with them three times. During the first two meetings, they hammered him about constantly being stopped, harassed, and arrested. At their third gathering, Gannon finally interrupted them. "Look," he said, "I'm having serious trouble with the Rolling 60s and the Inglewood Family. I've had eight murders in just the last two weeks. I've arrested people and have multiple resources, but I'm not making any headway. Can you help?" After Gannon's request, the running gun battles stopped. Dead cold. That day.

"Nothing was working," says Gannon. "That worked."

****

Many LAPD officers in South Bureau had long viewed themselves as dumped into a hopeless, thankless situation, one caused by a community of people who were alien to them and who, they believed, were in some inexplicable way inherently inclined to criminality. The cops' incomprehension, their frustration, was impossible to hide. The LAPD was an organization with a strong work ethic, and in South Bureau, where the atmosphere was fraught with physical danger and psychic shocks, that attitude played into how officers policed. That, and the fact that no matter how hard they tried, the situation on the street never got any better. It was therefore easy to assume it that it was only going to get worse, and that the present was only a prelude to a *Blade Runner* future.

Consequently, when crime and violence rose in the area, the LAPD would simply up their game and increase their workload, doubling down with all they knew, which was the big stick and indiscriminate arrests. And the more they did, the worse things had indeed gotten in South Bureau—a push-pull catch-22 the department had historically seemed incapable of even questioning.

Instead it employed its own form of zero-tolerance, "broken win-

dows" policing—a harassing, indiscriminate stop-question-and-frisk enforcement that the department referred to not as "stop-and-frisk" but as
"aggressive" or "proactive" or "confront-and-command" policing. What
they'd learned in the process was how to make sure nobody came out
on the street at night, but not how to stop crime once their Operation
Hammers were over.

They, the cops in South L.A., were good at what they did, if one considered it a positive social good to arrest as many people as possible, see
them sent to jail and prison for as long as possible, and then do the same
to their little brothers and sons, on and on, for generations.

Slowly, however, some did start to question that strategy. Gannon
was one of them. Charlie Beck was another. Beck had even developed
an analogy to illustrate his perplexity. A young police officer is standing
at the end of a conveyer belt. He's the last guy on the assembly line,
catching all these guys from South L.A. as they fall off, and then packing them off to jail. And next to him is his older, more thoughtful self,
wondering what's going on at the start of the line that's placing all those
guys—nonstop—onto the conveyer belt in the first place.

There were a few other people who were also asking that question and exploring the astounding, multilayered, complex influences
that defined poor black areas of cities across the country, like Chicago,
Philadelphia, Baltimore, Oakland, St. Louis, and Los Angeles—and law
enforcement's bludgeon-like response to them. Richard Price, in his
uncannily knowing novels about the intersection between cops, crime,
drugs, and race, was one of those voices, as was David Simon in *The
Wire*, his incomparable television meditation on the drug war and the
underbelly of big-city America during the crack years. And there was
David Kennedy, the brilliant activist anthropology professor at New
York's John Jay College of Criminal Justice, whose "lifework," as the
New Yorker once put it, was "designing a modern system of deterrence
that includes a moral component."

And then, from inside law enforcement, there was Bill Bratton. He
was asking a couple of different questions: why are we permitting this
level of crime and violence to continue, and what can we do as cops, as
strategists and managers, to stop it?

A man of ideas, logic, and solutions, Bratton was a true believer in rules and laws. He seemed personally to find manifestations of disorder such as graffiti both disharmonious and disgusting. Considerations of big-picture social and economic injustice needed to be addressed, he believed, but if they didn't directly apply to policing, were beyond his job description. What he prided himself on, what he loved, and *what he did* was develop smart, effective policing strategies that quantifiably drove down crime numbers. That was his mixed gift to modern, big-city law enforcement.

To accomplish that goal in Los Angeles, he had to significantly reduce gang crime and violence. The other values he would espouse about policing within the letter of the law—helping build stronger neighborhoods through community policing partnerships, holding officers accountable for abusing the public, easing racial animosity between his cops and poor blacks and Hispanics—were all things Bratton publicly espoused. But ultimately they were ancillary problems to be unpacked and dealt with in the service of his one overriding imperative of reducing and preventing crime.

Much of Bratton's plan for South Los Angeles and other high-crime areas was what he had depended on in New York—a combination of hot-spot policing based on continuously updated, computerized, detailed mapping of where crimes were occurring, and then flooding those hot-spot areas with more cops; officers aggressively pursuing stop-and-frisk policing; and holding supervisors accountable through COMPSTAT for bringing down crime numbers.

In New York City under police commissioner Raymond Kelly, those strategies had morphed over the years from tight enforcement to stopping and checking out those who looked or acted suspicious, to finally a very wide definition of who was suspicious to include almost any young black or brown adolescent or young man. Unlike under Daryl Gates and the old LAPD, the goal was not arrests but stopping crimes before they occurred, and changing public culture by changing public behavior—just as Malcolm Gladwell theorized had happened with New York's great nineties crime drop under Bratton in his classic book *The Tipping Point*.

At the heart of the strategy, however, lay a crucial question: how do you gain the support, or at least the quiet acquiescence, of a liberal Los

Angeles political establishment, and of African-American leaders and
grassroots black and Latino community organizations, while increasing the stop-question-frisk policies these very people had fought so hard
against?

Charlie Beck, South Bureau, South Los Angeles, 2006

There had been a lot of discussion about placing a new black deputy
chief in charge of South Bureau. While it was true that the area was no
longer predominantly African-American, it still remained the cultural
center of black L.A., and still had a strong African-American influence
with a long tradition of black political representation.

A black deputy chief, it was thought, could tap into a reservoir of
racial solidarity. Consequently, Charlie Beck—who was not black, and
who also carried the burden of having been a ground soldier in Daryl
Gates's Operation Hammer wars—was not a natural fit for the job.

But Beck himself had never bought into that notion. Instead, he was
sure that what was most valued in communities like South Los Angeles,
particularly when it came to cops, was the idea of fairness. Not weak-
ness. Not tolerance. But *fairness*, and "people not feeling they're being
treated," as he put it, "like creatures in the zoo."

And that was exactly the approach Beck intended to bring to South
Bureau. *Had* to bring, in fact, if, he was going to aggressively execute
Bratton's intrusive policing strategies while at the same time avoiding
once again pitting the department against the community.

From day one Beck knew that accomplishing the latter meant depos-
iting a lot of time and resources into the community trust and bank of
goodwill.

"Community partnerships" had been a catchphrase bandied about
by the LAPD for years, mostly as a public-relations palliative that almost always meant the same thing: Partner, if you must, with business-
people, with the neighborhood watch folks, with the older, dwindling,
button-down middle class who would listen and nod in assent when
the department told them the way it would be. Members of grassroots

organizations, on the other hand, or those living in the housing projects, or existing on poverty's edge, or who were both the victims of and the mother or uncle or sister of a gang member, were rarely sought out or included. They were complainers, voices with opinions who asked hard questions considered hostile to law enforcement, and not part of any community policing strategy as it had been traditionally understood within the LAPD.

But they were also the very people who ached to be listened to by the police. Not just to vent, but to be recognized as human beings who also yearned for the cessation of their world's unrelenting violence, but needed to be legitimately and fairly responded to when they'd been physically or verbally abused, disrespected, or otherwise unjustly treated by police officers. In short, to be successful in his bottom-line goals, Charlie Beck and his officers had, at the very least, to be respectful and, like Pat Gannon, build unlikely alliances and be seen in the eyes of long-ignored constituents as "legitimate."

This was not an approach forged by Beck just because he was a good guy. The necessity of cops encouraging such a buy-in from the people they're policing was an evolving, increasingly accepted concept in police and social science circles called "procedural fairness."

The studies of then Yale law professor Tom Tyler, and of Tracey Meares and later David L. Weisburd and Anthony A. Braga, showed that how people were treated in their interaction with the police, and whether or not they were being treated *fairly*, was, in many cases, more important to them than how their police encounter was finally adjudicated.

Deeply intertwined with "fairness" was the concept of "police legitimacy" and the notion, as Tyler puts it, that "people obey the law and cooperate with legal authorities if and when they view legal authorities as legitimate." The fairness of police behavior—not the fear of police force and the threat of punishment—writes Taylor, "creates legitimacy, and through it drives public actions, and has dramatic implications for a range of policing policies such as racial profiling and zero tolerance policing."

The concept resonated with Charlie Beck, who as soon as he got to South Bureau began talking to a lot of people, jotting down names and making a list of where to go and who to speak with. When he stopped at Bo Taylor's name, he did what Pat Gannon had done: called Taylor and told him he'd like to get together. Taylor replied that he was at his house with a group of his homeboys, and asked him to stop by. Beck agreed. It was a good day for him to do it: he was wearing a suit, rather than his uniform, and could go there without making a big production out of it.

Exiting his car in a neighborhood heavy with gangsters, Beck walked to the back of Taylor's house and into a converted garage where Taylor and some other interventionists were gathered. Beck could tell they were amazed that he'd actually shown up. And that he'd come alone, wasn't wearing a uniform, and wasn't carrying a gun that they could see. Grabbing a chair, Beck "sat down," he later recalled, "and talked to them like they were regular people—which they were."

After listening intently for several hours, Beck started discussing how they might work together. Soon they were meeting regularly, with Pat Gannon often joining in. Eventually their discussions started to focus on how to strengthen the interventionists' legitimacy through some kind of certification process, which subsequently led to conversations with Connie Rice about establishing a gang interventionist school.

For Beck, his new partnership with Taylor was—like Connie Rice's Rampart report was for Bratton—all win-win. One, the interventions actually did help reduce violence—especially retaliatory shootings and killings—broker gang truces, and sometimes get kids out of gangs, just as intended. Second, the very fact that the LAPD was partnering with an on-the-edge organization previously considered a pariah by the police was immensely important for the department in terms of starting to establish street legitimacy and neighborhood credibility. At the same time, it balanced out Beck's gang suppression tactics by giving committed gang members a viable exit strategy and important work supported by the other side, by their former enemies, by the cops.

****

About a year later, Charlie Beck, dressed in his LAPD blues, walked into a packed dayroom in Jordan Downs where three or four large-sized, middle-aged resident black women rushed up to greet him with a hug and a peck on the cheek—a display that wasn't just remarkable, given Jordan Downs's history with the LAPD, but positively amazing.

Less amazing, given his goals, was Beck's accepting, comfortable reaction, which, he says, "was really important, because they have to know it's okay. That there's nothing to be afraid of. A lot of police work gets really wrapped around fear and distrust of others. So you can't model that. You can't shun people when they run up and want to talk and shake hands and hug you. It's all part of the job of building faith in the community, of going to the meetings, talking to people, not talking *at* people, listening to what they say, being honest with them, and telling the truth—'I can't do anything about something,' 'I can't fix that for you,' or 'This is what we can do to make it better'—and then following up and asking them for help in return when I need it. I think a lot of it is just normal human interaction. And if you treat people decently, and use all your skills to build relationships instead of force relationships, it makes all the difference. It takes a lot of work because you're not only trying to build community goodwill, you're trying to win your cops over too—modeling for them—'Hey, this is how we do things here.'"

Charlie Beck wasn't the only one trying to build goodwill around the issues of crime and cops in South L.A. And he knew it, and embraced the others, one of whom was Janice Hahn, the sister of James Hahn and then a council member whose district included Watts. She had founded a brilliantly conceived new community organization to reduce gang violence called the Watts Gang Task Force. Beck immediately recognized the group's utility and gave it his and the department's unswerving support.

Among the bedrock participants were the parents and family members of current and former gang members from places like Nickerson Gardens and Imperial Courts as well as Jordan Downs. Packed into a room in Hahn's City Council office in Watts, the parents and relatives were meeting every Monday with LAPD officers and a diverse coalition of grassroots community organization representatives and resident staff and employees of the housing developments. The purpose, says Beck, was to discuss outbreaks of violence and what to do about them, as well as "building community cohesion and strength around the issue."

To do just that, Beck organized a barbecue soon after he was appointed deputy chief in South Bureau. He invited activist groups and organizations and local public officials from the black community and the Latino community, and they all sat down and ate together with Beck and his cops in an open-air patio behind the South Bureau headquarters. "We fed them and we talked about what we wanted to do," explained Beck. "The usual suspects *were* there," he continued, "but there were also a lot of people who'd previously been left out of the decision-making process, because they weren't seen as mainstream. We were really inclusive in that way."

The other thing Beck did was to have LAPD representatives on the scene "when things went wrong" and his cops were involved. Most of the time that meant him and/or a division captain responding to a shooting or other officer-involved incident directly at the scene. "That way," says Beck, "they knew their side of the story would be listened to and that we'd do the right thing about whatever happened."

NYPD Commissioner Raymond Kelly, New York City; LAPD Chief Bill Bratton, Los Angeles; Stop-Question-Frisk

While Charlie Beck was intent on winning support for, or at least minimizing opposition to, his and Bratton's stop-question-frisk strategies, plenty of action was also taking place across the country in New York City. There, Police Commissioner Raymond Kelly was deeply enmeshed in pursuing his own version of the strategy.

By some measures, Kelly's and Bratton's approaches were remarkably similar, but in others they proved crucially different in terms of public perception, although both chiefs focused on the key metric of crime reduction. New York continued its long-standing, double-the-nation's downward crime trend, while in Los Angeles the crime rate would first stabilize and then also continue, as the LAPD would report, on a steady downward path.

Both Kelly and Bratton emphasized the importance of stop-question-frisk in their policing strategy. Scaled to size, in fact, the number of pedestrian stops weren't much different in Los Angeles than in New York—275,000 to the NYPD's 660,000 in 2005. But Los Angeles's population was half that of New York, and L.A. had less than a third the number of police officers. And, as everybody knows, people don't walk much in L.A.—although they do congregate on street corners in black and Latino communities.

Like New York's, L.A.'s pedestrian stops were disproportionally of African-Americans—about 35 to 40 percent, with a black population within the city of a dwindling 10 percent. Not as large as the discrepancy ratio in New York—where 85 percent of the stops were of blacks and Latinos—but highly significant nonetheless.

The LAPD was also making about 700,000 vehicle stops a year. In 2003 and 2004, blacks were ordered out of their vehicles over 2.5 times more than were whites, and Latinos 2.3 times more. And black motorists were twice as likely to be frisked as whites.

The frisked African-Americans, however, were more than *40 percent less likely* to have a weapon than whites. "A lot of the LAPD's initial defense for frisking so many African-Americans," points out Peter Bibring, a senior staff attorney at the American Civil Liberties Union of Southern California, "was that when they stopped African-Americans they were in high-crime areas, and therefore more likely to have weapons on them. But the data showed that wasn't true. If they are searching [blacks proportionally more than whites] they should find weapons on them more often, or at least at the same rate as whites. But the data showed that was over 40 percent less likely to happen."

When Bratton took office in late 2002, the LAPD had made just over 585,000 pedestrian *and* vehicle stops under Chief Bernard Parks. Six years later, under Bratton, that number had risen by a third, to 875,000 total stops. So the LAPD stops on Bratton's watch were constant and steady, not a one-year aberration. Later in the decade a yearly number indicated that just under one-quarter of the stops resulted in a citation and/or a search or arrest.

Nevertheless, the blowback that Beck and Bratton would receive was minimal, given the massive scope of their stop-question-frisk policies. In contrast, Ray Kelly in New York would be pilloried for his.

There were a number of reasons why.

First, Los Angeles and New York had had two very different experiences with their police departments over the preceding forty years. In the early 1970s the NYPD was both abysmal at preventing crime and deeply corrupt. By the eighties most of the corruption had been cleaned up in the wake of the Serpico scandal, but the department had become even more inept at protecting a city obsessed with race, crime, and violence.

Then, in late 1993, the newly elected, law-and-order Giuliani administration chose Bill Bratton as its police commissioner, and Bratton transformed the NYPD into a forceful, efficient police department that would lead the country's crime decline for the next two decades.

Many New Yorkers were understandably more than willing to put up with the NYPD's stricter, more intense enforcement. The city was booming, and previously crime-ridden neighborhoods were blossoming, in part because of that enforcement. And after 9/11, that support only increased. So when Ray Kelly began ratcheting up the number of stop-and-frisks to levels that an entire generation of black and Hispanic young men would find intolerable, most of the rest of the city shrugged, thanked him for keeping the city safe, and gave him the benefit of the doubt.

But questions slowly began to arise in New York as the number and intensity of the stops accelerated. Between 2004 and June 2012 the NYPD would engage in 4.4 million pedestrian stop-and-frisks—85 percent of which were of black and Hispanic young men and teenagers.

The rationale given for the stop-and-frisks was to get weapons off the street and stop people from carrying them. But guns were found in just 0.14 percent of the stops, and other weapons were found in less than 1 percent of the stops. Far more likely, an arrest would come for a fine not paid or for being in possession of an illegal drug—most typically a joint or two of marijuana. Under New York State law at the time, carrying a small amount of grass in your pocket was a "violation," not a crime, warranting a ticket, not an arrest. But when stopped, the target would frequently be asked to empty his pockets. And when he did so, the grass he was carrying would then be "out in public"—a misdemeanor in New York resulting in an arrest and a criminal record. As a result, black New Yorkers were seven times more likely than whites to be arrested for marijuana possession, although they used pot at about the same rate as whites. Abuses such as these struck directly at the heart of the concepts of fairness and legitimacy in policing, and a drumbeat of opposition to the practice began to grow.

Moreover, unlike Bill Bratton—who had courted African-American and other city leaders in Los Angeles—Ray Kelly had settled into an imperious commissionership in New York. Rarely did he engage the media or public about stop-and-frisk. Instead he seemed secure to the point of haughtiness in the knowledge that he had the absolute backing of the only person that ultimately mattered to him—the one who gave him and the only one who could take away his job—multibillionaire New York mayor Michael Bloomberg, who defended Kelly's maximalist stop-and-frisk policies.

Los Angeles, meanwhile, had entered the seventies with a hyperaggressive police department that saw itself as an occupying force in L.A.'s economically destitute black and brown communities. The department believed that they were unaccountable to civilian control. Throughout the eighties the situation had grown ever more tumultuous, with no end in sight until the 1991 beating of Rodney King and the '92 riots finally provided the political consensus to begin the overthrow of the old LAPD order. Nevertheless, throughout the nineties the LAPD had still managed to both defy reform and continue its hostile confront-and-command policing, of which Ray Perez and Rampart CRASH were only the tip of the iceberg.

Bill Bratton then came along, and in effect said to John Mack and the African-American leadership and to activists like Connie Rice and to the city's liberal establishment: I'm here to reform the LAPD. I respect you and will listen and try to cooperatively work with you to make that happen. When Charlie Beck arrived in South Bureau, he essentially gave black and Latino leaders and grassroots activists the same message. And when he did what he did—in terms of the heavy numbers of stops—he had the goodwill he'd been busy banking to now cash in.

For decades the LAPD had been unable to stem gang violence, even as the department implacably refused to reform its brutal ways. Bratton and Beck were offering a new, improved version of the LAPD's old stop-control-command-and-humiliate policy, with the humiliation part reduced as part of the equation. And the fact that it was aimed at a more discrete, although still far-ranging, target—the city's forty thousand alleged gang members, the very group many people felt it *should* be aimed at—was also important.

Stop-and-frisk in L.A., moreover, was being done by experienced cops and not by rookies straight out of the Police Academy, as was the case in New York.

"Twice a year the New York Police Department was graduating fifteen hundred officers [from its academy]," Bratton would later explain. "They were being surged into areas showing growing crime patterns and trends. The flaw was that they were putting their most recently trained and least experienced officers in some of the highest crime areas in the city. Unlike Los Angeles, where every new police officer has to be assigned to a field training officer for one year, in New York ten or twelve of these recruits were being supervised by just one sergeant. So they had six pairs of officers walking in high crime, minority neighborhoods engaging in stop-and-frisks, with, in most instances, no supervision over what they were doing."

By contrast, says Charlie Beck, "we didn't use new recruits to stop people. In the Los Angeles Police Department, people just out of the academy don't get to do anything by themselves. They certainly don't go out and pick people to stop, because they don't have the skill set; that's important, because it's the right stops that are effective. Random stops are not effective. Random stops or stops that are done to meet some kind of quota are of no value, or actually detrimental to the mission, because they break down public confidence and they increase this sense of unfairness rather than developing a sense of fairness."

Moreover, Bratton seemed to have learned from his calamitous political experience with Giuliani and developed an excellent political antenna. One that made him appalled when he heard about the NYPD's "open-display" marijuana arrests. "I could not believe it," he'd later say. "A lot of people unnecessarily ended up being arrested. It was abhorrent."

Nevertheless, Bratton and Beck were also using legal tactics that reeked of dubious constitutionality—even though the courts had ruled them constitutional. Chief among them was the gang injunction, which had a long and vigorous enforcement history in Los Angeles.

One such injunction ran 276 pages, targeted six gangs (including Alfred Lomas's Florencia 13), and covered 13.7 square miles of South Los Angeles. As reporter Scott Gold pointed out in the *Los Angeles Times*, the injunction made arrestable crimes out of gang members simply being together in public—hanging out in a park, for instance, or standing together on a street corner. Moreover, as part of the injunction, officers in the field were authorized to serve gang *suspects* with the injunction—even though their names weren't on it, thereby making the suspects *part of the injunction*—without having to prove any gang affiliation at all in court.

"What's lost in discussion about this method of enforcement," says the ACLU's Peter Bibring, "is that people are targeted who are only tangentially connected to gangs, or not connected at all. The California attorney general uses ten factors for determining if somebody is a gang member and should be put into the state gang database. Someone has to meet just two of the ten criteria. They include 'associating' with a gang member, who could be a cousin, an uncle, or a next-door neighbor with whom you're walking to school, or someone who can be identified as a gang member by an informant—'reliable' or 'unreliable.'" The result, said Bibring, was that once you were identified, and for the length of the injunction, you had *no* right to peacefully assemble with even one other person who had also been so identified and named on the injunction. According to the LAPD, "There are more than 450 active gangs in the city of Los Angeles. Many of these gangs have been in existence for over fifty years. These gangs have a combined membership of over 45,000 individuals." But since some are small offshoots formed to protect their members and not to gangbang, the number of people under injunction at any one time can vary from five to ten thousand.

Charlie Beck, however, saw the injunction as a vital tool in stopping gangsters from congregating in places "where they become targets of drive-by shootings, or stand around developing the enthusiasm to go out and do a drive-by themselves. So you have to move them on so they're not scaring the little old lady across the street or waiting for some guys in a black car to come by and light 'em up. That's what injunctions represent."

Eleven thousand gang-related homicides in Los Angeles County is a terrible number, and the LAPD is right to focus on it. But its solution—using injunctions to ensnare active gangbangers—also ensnares thousands of others who might not be gang members at all; at worst they are peripheral players living in impoverished, multigenerational Latino gang neighborhoods. Injunctions have mostly proven ineffectual in wiping out gang violence. At best they're a quick-fix, Band-Aid solution that changes little in the long term, and may or may not have an effect. To the extent that gang violence has gone down, it's been in large part because of demographic shifts, such as the disassembling of the city's black gangs and their movement into Riverside and other counties east of Los Angeles, and because of the alliance between L.A.'s Latino gangs and Mexican drug cartels—big moneymaking organizations that don't want to see stupid, petty gang wars drawing attention to them and their business in the U.S.

****

Meanwhile, in New York, Ray Kelly was defending his massive use of stop-and-frisk by stressing the undeniably powerful correlation between young, impoverished (black) men and boys and high homicide rates.

"African-American men between the ages of sixteen and thirty-seven, who are just four percent of [New York] city's population, comprise forty percent of those murdered citywide," Kelly would point out in a speech in April 2013. "Eighty-two percent of those young men were killed with a firearm. As a city, as a society, we cannot stand idly by in the face of facts. I believe that this tactic [stop-and-frisk] is lifesaving." At about the same time, Kelly put it another way, writing in an opinion piece in the *Wall Street Journal*: "In the eleven years before Mayor

Bloomberg took office, there were 13,212 murders in New York City. During the eleven years of his administration, there have been 5,849. That's 7,383 lives saved—and if history is a guide, they are largely lives of young men of color."

These numbers too, like L.A.'s gang homicides, were striking in their persistent awfulness, and, like with L.A. gangs, had not yet begun to be addressed except by police repression. So Kelly was right to call attention to them in 2013. But it was impossible to know in 2013 if the massive use of stop-and-frisk had been a key, essential element in New York City's steep and consistent decline in homicides. It may have been. But nobody knew for sure, because there was no real data that proved it one way or the other. And one big reason why was that Ray Kelly had long refused to allow the NYPD to take part in studies that could lead to an answer.

One thing that was certain, however, was that by 2013 stop-and-frisk as practiced in New York had been alienating tens of thousands of young men who'd done nothing wrong and knew it, but were nevertheless being singled out and treated differently by the cops. Often based solely on their race, age, and economic status, these young men had been forced to suffer the constant indignity of a baseless stop and a baseless search in a country where their constitutional rights were being violated by the police and a conservative United States Supreme Court that was largely upholding the searches. Bratton and Beck had worked hard to mute opposition in Los Angeles, and to a large extent had been successful.

But Bratton, like Kelly, saw stop-and-frisk as an essential part of protecting these victims by establishing new behavioral norms and preventing crimes before they occur. "You've got to have it," he would say of stop-and-frisk in 2013. "Many politicians and community activists are thinking of doing away with it. I'm sorry; you do away with it, you might as well move out of [New York] City. The crime will come back faster than the blink of an eye. It is the most frequent, effective and useful tool we have in policing."

And therein lay the essential conundrum faced by Bratton, Beck, and Ray Kelly as they aggressively pursued a policing strategy that on its face, if not in the letter of the law, was antithetical to the spirit of the Fourth Amendment to the Constitution, but which they believed was effective and necessary.

Connie Rice, January 2007,
Los Angeles City Council Meeting

"Gang Interventionists," said Connie Rice to the Los Angeles City Council during a 2007 hearing packed with reporters, "are the people who keep kids safe. . . . We [the city] just spent $7 million for a reptile enclosure. I'm happy for Reggie [the alligator], but we need to save our kids first."

Rice was speaking to the City Council as part of her campaign to get a gang interventionist academy established, a key component of a second report that Rice and the Advancement Project had written following the Rampart report. This one too had a long gestation period, having been commissioned by the City Council in 2005—about a year after City Councilman Martin Ludlow's "Summer of Success" program.

Released in January 2007, this second report on Los Angeles's criminal justice system was more, far more, than the council or really anybody else had anticipated. At one thousand pages, it weighed in at twelve pounds and was exactly what its title declared it to be: *A Call to Action: The Case for a Comprehensive Solution to L.A.'s Gang Violence Epidemic*.

A devastating critique of the status quo, the report excoriated the city and the county's historically siloed criminal justice and social service systems for working independently and often self-servingly in failed attempts to stem gang violence.

"Right now there's $1 *billion* in [city and county] programs for kids, but it's all wasted, because it's not being used to reduce the violence [directed at them]," Rice would say following the report's release. "When a kid comes home from juvenile lockup, there's no reentry team. All these government agencies don't cooperate. Parole doesn't talk to child services. So the kid's gang ends up being his reentry team.

That $1 billion has to be reallocated and placed into one comprehensive program."

Over twenty subject-matter experts—including cops, gang interventionists, sociologists, educators, demographers, and epidemiologists who study violence as a disease—had contributed their expertise to the report. One of them was Wes McBride, a veteran L.A. County Sheriff's Department detective who was among the county's top experts on street gangs. According to Rice, McBride told her that the week before he retired he'd arrested the grandson of the first man he'd arrested when he was just out of the Sheriff's Academy. And that ten years earlier he had also arrested the man's father. His career, concluded McBride, had helped destroy three generations of one family, and hadn't changed a thing. If this could help change that situation, he informed Rice, he was willing to work with her.

Among the report's central critiques was that the gang "suppression" tactics upon which Los Angeles had focused for the past quarter century had failed. Suppression was necessary, the report pointed out, but only as part of the mix, a slice of the pie. By itself, it only strengthened gangs, because they were intergenerational and existed for identity purposes. Attacking them only increased their cohesion. "Twenty-five years of containment-suppression," as Rice would later say, had only "produced twice as many gang members and six times as many gangs, with no end in sight."

Instead, the report recommended, Los Angeles's gang neighborhoods should be viewed as ecosystems—with businesses, NGOs, churches, community organizations, and city and county agencies all joining with law enforcement to treat both the symptoms *and the causes* of gang violence while developing new integrated programs like a gang interventionist academy.

In a perfect world Rice's unified commonsense approach might well have been adopted. But large, self-serving bureaucracies are not the stuff of perfect worlds, and even getting the L.A. City Council to act was going to be a heavy lift. Los Angeles's weak mayoral structure and dithering City Council had historically ensured that citywide public policy moved slowly. It had taken a decade of turmoil prior to the beating of Rodney King and the '92 riots before a consensus had finally been reached on the drastic need to transform the LAPD, and a decade more of floundering and scandal capped off by a federal consent decree before the reform process finally geared up in earnest.

Beyond that, and unbeknownst to Rice or anyone else at the time, the Great Recession was about to hit Los Angeles *hard*, which would dictate a severe financial retrenchment, and not the kind of dramatic and costly program *A Call to Action* required if followed correctly.

Nevertheless, the report would serve its purpose. As UCLA social welfare professor Jorja Leap would later write, "There were many things the report was not. It was not a scientific evaluation . . . an exhaustive survey of gang programs in Los Angeles . . . [or] a document guided by research methodology. . . . However," Leap added, "what the report so importantly did was capture the elements of the problem and illustrate how past efforts had fallen dismally short of ongoing need. Significantly, with a series of 100 recommendations, the [Advancement Project] put the concept of a comprehensive, citywide strategy front and center."

Bill Bratton, May Day 2007, MacArthur Park

"I don't know how," says David Dotson, "they could have been so *goddamn* stupid." Dotson, who'd seen a lot of stupid things in the decades before his retirement from the LAPD, was asking the same question as many Angelenos about what had occurred the previous day: May Day 2007, which would prove to be the most startling and embarrassing day of William Bratton's entire tenure as chief of the Los Angeles Police Department.

May Day, the once great international people's day, the day of revolution and of workers declaring their existence and their rights, had reemerged in L.A. in the years following the turn of the twenty-first century as a day of significance among a Latino immigrant population about to fully flex its political muscle.

Just one year earlier, on April 25, 2006—a week before May Day— over half a million Mexican and Central American immigrants and their supporters had converged downtown, a mammoth sea of white T-shirts, placards, and flags, in the largest protest demonstration in the history of Los Angeles.

They were part of a monthlong series of nationwide immigrant protests, including one in Chicago that numbered four hundred thousand. L.A.'s had been an almost festive affair. Nevertheless, the events driving the extraordinary turnout were absolutely crucial to the lives of many in the crowd.

Causing the immediate crisis was the fact that the passage of the comprehensive immigration reform bill proposed by President George W. Bush to grant eventual citizenship to millions of undocumented immigrants had been blocked by the Republican-controlled U.S. House of Representatives. Instead, the House had counterproposed a bill making it a felony to be in the country illegally, mandating the building of a seven-hundred-mile border fence between the U.S. and Mexico, and explicitly providing no opportunity for undocumented immigrants to become citizens.

Nevertheless, despite the high-stakes nature of the protest rally and the underlying political tension, that huge May Day rally just a year earlier had been remarkably violence-free, given the crush of bodies and the historic propensity of the LAPD to react violently to such demonstrations.

"Get off the streets" had been the LAPD's operational credo throughout the twentieth century. And in policing protests the department would often wait no longer than a minute or so between its initial order to disperse and the baton swinging, bone-crushing attack on those not very, very quick on their feet.

In the 1920s and '30s—when the department had been a creature under the influence of the then ultra-right-wing *Los Angeles Times* and the city's powerful Merchant and Manufacturers Association—using billy clubs to break up union rallies had been a routine occurrence. The same mind-set had continued during antiwar marches in the 1960s, a Justice for Janitors union organizing demonstration in 1990, and the protest demonstrations during the 2000 Democratic National Convention.

Now, as May Day 2007 approached, no one was expecting anything different from 2006. The old days were gone, and a new, practical-minded reform chief was firmly in the saddle.

Bill Bratton, in fact, was in the middle of a very good run. With his first five years in office now coming to an end, he was deep in the process of campaigning for reappointment to the second term he needed to complete his reform agenda—a task that in his mind would be at an end on the day federal judge Gary Feess lifted the consent decree.

But for now, at the very least Bratton had virtually disarmed his critics. The mayor and the Police Commission had become some of his strongest supporters, and so had most of the City Council. Just the night before, at his last public confirmation hearing prior to his reappointment, the occasion had turned into what he'd later describe as "a love fest." Little to no opposition had been expressed—a remarkable achievement, given the LAPD's historically fractious relations with nearly everyone. As David Dotson would put it at the time: "He's managed to walk a tightrope between forging ties with the black community and activist groups like the ACLU, while improving troop morale and making everybody relatively satisfied." Relatively satisfied—despite the fact that his officers had made almost one million stops in one year, and hundreds of black motorists and pedestrians would file racial profiling complaints against his department.

So satisfied that John Mack, now president of the Police Commission, would say *this* in announcing his support for a second term: "Chief Bratton [has] provided visionary and progressive leadership for the department. His efforts have greatly benefited the City of Los Angeles and advanced effective policing. . . . He has aggressively reached out to individuals, victims, immigrant rights organizations, Latino leaders, members of media, civil rights and civil liberties leaders and organizations."

Meanwhile, the ACLU would also release its own statement of support for Bratton's rehiring. This too was a remarkable occurrence engendered by Bratton. The ACLU had commissioned a Yale researcher who made an overwhelmingly strong case against Bratton's stop-and-frisk policies, declaring not only that the department was engaged in an extraordinary number of stops but that the LAPD was engaged in racial profiling. The organization also criticized Bratton's heavy enforcement actions in Skid Row. Then it said this in a letter supporting Bratton's rehiring: "Without minimizing the importance of [our] disagreements, we recognize Chief Bratton's firm commitment to and leadership in reforming the LAPD, preserving open and accountable policing, policing with respect for the constitutional rights of the residents of Los Angeles, and making the LAPD responsive to the concerns of the community whose trust he recognizes his Department requires." The letter was signed by the ACLU's Southern California executive director, Ramona Ripston, who, like Mack, had for decades been one of the LAPD's most outspoken and unstinting critics. Like Mack and Ripston, Connie Rice would also strongly support Bratton's rehiring.

At the same time, Bratton's personal bottom line, his ace in the hole—those declining crime statistics for which he'd built up such expectations—were right there for him to boast about. From 2002 through 2006, serious crime had fallen by almost 35 percent, and homicides by over 35 percent. A good case, and one that Bratton would vociferously make when challenged, was that those declines were due to aggressive enforcement of the combination of policing strategies he'd employed in areas like South Los Angeles.

But equally good, and certainly at least complementary, factors that might also have influenced the decline were minimized or dismissed by Bratton. Among them were the racial transformation of much of South Los Angeles and the cyclical nature of gang crime in the city. In 1992, there had been over 1,000 homicides in Los Angeles. By 1998, under Willie Williams and Bernard Parks, that number had fallen by nearly *60 percent* to 419. By the time Bratton had been named chief in late 2002, homicides had risen again by over one-third to 647 before dropping by almost one-third under Bratton to 480 in 2006. The truth was nobody yet knew for sure why crime had dropped so significantly under Bratton's first four full years in office. It could well have been because of his heavy police-saturation policies, or those policies in combination with any number of other factors. The proof would be in the long-term sustainability of the decline.

In any case, as May Day 2007 rolled around, radiating from Bill Bratton was the shine of success. And then the people whose stupidity David Dotson never could understand made their move.

★★★★★★★★★★★★★★

Bratton arose on May Day morning scheduled to fly down to El Salvador to join Los Angeles mayor Antonio Villaraigosa on a six-nation tour of Latin America. But he wanted to remain in L.A. until the end of the day to make sure everything unfolded as planned. And for most of the day it did.

The demonstration turned out to be small compared to the preceding year—very small: between fifteen and twenty-five thousand people peacefully assembled in downtown L.A. for an uneventful rally. At its end, an estimated six to seven thousand then trekked a couple of miles west to MacArthur Park, where they arrived at about 5:00 p.m. accompanied by a contingent of Spanish-language reporters.

★★★★★★★★★★★★★★

Early that evening Bratton decided to leave the demonstrators' closing rally at the park and return to his home in the old, stately neighborhood of Los Feliz. There he prepared for the flight he was taking later that night to El Salvador, keeping one eye on the television as he packed. At one point he noticed the station was broadcasting helicopter shots of a rock- and bottle-throwing disturbance on Olvera Street, a major thoroughfare bordering MacArthur Park. But there were a lot of cops down there, and he wasn't getting any calls to alert him of serious trouble, so he assumed it would easily be handled, and continued going about his flight preparations.

On his way to the airport, however, he received a phone call bringing news of just how wrong his casual assessment had been. And it was coming not from his command staff at Parker Center, or his commander at the park, or even anybody in L.A. Instead it was from the mayor of Los Angeles, Antonio Villaraigosa, who had just deplaned in El Salvador. "I'm surrounded by the Spanish-language press," he told Bratton. "They've been showing me live shots of LAPD officers break-

ing up the crowd in MacArthur Park. The journalists there are reporting that live [non-lethal] rounds have been fired by the officers and that
they're beating up people."

Bratton immediately phoned LAPD assistant chief Earl Paysinger,
who was in his office at Parker Center. His response was at once both
reassuring and disconcerting. "No," he told Bratton, "there's nothing
going on that I'm aware of."

"Well, check into it," Bratton told him.

A few minutes later, Paysinger got back to Bratton. "It appears," he
said, "that [Deputy Chief Lee] Carter [who was directly in charge of the
operation] ordered the park cleared, and then less-than-lethal rounds
had been fired."

"Immediately," Bratton later recalled, "the hair shot up on the back
of my neck."

****

The gut instinct that had caused Bill Bratton's surge of alarm would
prove more than justified. Not because anybody would die that day, or
even be critically, life-threateningly injured, although that was a fortu-
itous occurrence, given what occurred.

A few plastic bottles and rocks had been hurled at a few cops, and
suddenly 150 Los Angeles police officers had been ordered to form a
skirmish line in response, after which they'd strutted onto the lawn of
MacArthur Park. Simultaneously, a dispersal order to the crowd was
blaring from a helicopter hovering above—in English, not Spanish—but
nobody could hear it in any case.

Clad in riot helmets, hard plastic face masks, bulletproof vests, radio
headsets, and full military gear, and wielding either two-foot-long batons or surreal-looking rifles that shot rubber bullets or beanbags, the
officers had then descended on the peaceful, festive crowd. In the process they indiscriminately fired off rubber bullets and other projectiles
at close range, into a crowd that included women wheeling baby strollers and dozens of reporters—most of whom were in a section of the
park located away from the area where the bottles had been thrown,
and who were utterly unaware that anything was amiss.

It was not a cop riot, like, for example, the beatings administered by enraged Chicago police officers in Grant Park in 1968 during the Democratic National Convention. It was something different. Something surreal. Marching in tight, disciplined formation, the LAPD officers moved in an undulating wave, swinging their batons like machetes in a field of sugarcane to cut shocked reporters and civilians to the ground.

Anyone familiar with the LAPD instantly knew by their arrogant, focused manner that they were members of the department's "elite" Metro Division. An officer's road into Metro was well known and well worn: work in the toughest divisions and get promoted by becoming known for being tough, being aggressive, taking no shit, and racking up arrests. That was what the department valued and what Metro symbolized.

Metro was also emblematic of another pillar of the LAPD's existence, particularly under Daryl Gates: that the department existed for the convenience of its members, not the public good. The division, in fact, was a macho man's dream. But maybe not a good cop's. Patrol—the heart of policing—was scorned by many cops under Gates, something to get out of while retreating to a specialized unit like Metro with all its perks and comforts. Metro's members had take-home city cars. Their typical day, as David Dotson would later relate it, consisted of arriving at 9:30 in the morning, lifting weights for several hours, and then going out to the shooting range for the afternoon, or to train with the air support guys, or to practice rappelling down some cliff.

"The Metropolitan Division," said Bill Bratton afterward, "was the heart and soul of the LAPD culture that people had always been complaining about—the insensitivity, the brutality and the use of force, particularly against minorities, and the idea that [Metro] could use force without consequence and not have to explain it, the feeling that they were divorced from the community, and were not part of it. It was also the component of the department that had the least responsibility for interacting with the community—and was normally only sent in to deal with a crime or crowd control."

In 2000, during the Democratic National Convention, Metro had acted in much the same way it had in MacArthur Park, including attacking reporters. Afterward media guidelines had been drawn up with the help of the ACLU, describing what the rights of the media were and the responsibility of the media in dealing with those rights. *All* of which were violated by the LAPD during this incident—which was captured on tape and film from twenty-five police cameras and a couple of dozen news cameras that would record hundreds of hours of video.

****

When he finally got Deputy Chief Lee Carter on the phone, Bill Bratton was surprised by how blasé he seemed about the whole event. "Well, we had some incidents [of rock and bottle throwing]," Bratton recalled Carter telling him, "and we cleared the park." When Bratton asked if the officers had fired off less-than-lethal rounds, Carter replied that they had, about thirty or forty. That sounded like a lot to Bratton, who immediately ordered his driver to turn around and head to MacArthur Park.

On the way, he called Mark Perez, who was the head of professional standards in the Bureau of Internal Affairs, and ordered him to the scene at the park and to notify the LAPD's inspector general, André Birotte, about what had occurred and that he should come to the park as well.

Bratton wanted Internal Affairs to immediately begin the investigation, and wanted Birotte, in turn, to monitor the Internal Affairs investigation. There had been a lot of officer use of force, Bratton understood, and they were going to have to deal with it.

Unlike his predecessor, Bernard Parks, who'd tried to cut off the civilian watchdog inspector general at the knees, Bratton had wisely embraced him and was now using the IG to ensure that there would be no confusion, no cover-up, and no accusations of a cover-up.

Throughout much of the twentieth century the tradition in the LAPD and other police organizations was that when an obvious screwup like this occurred, the best way to proceed—the only way to proceed—was to close ranks, back the troops, and restrict access to information. Bratton's instincts and managerial philosophy led him to precisely the opposite conclusion. "I've always told my cops," he'd later explain, "you give me a good story and nobody will tell it better than me. You give me a bad story, and I'm going to tell that bad story. This old thing that's been policy for years, that you need to 'protect the department' and sweep it under the rug—well, I grew up in an era when it was all about [that attitude]. But I've never been part of that school."

But Bratton also understood this: in this day and age, there are no secrets—none. He'd been around long enough to know that this was going to be a *big* story, no matter what he did. The mayor of Los Angeles had, after all, called him from a foreign country, telling him that an overwhelmingly peaceful crowd was being peppered with hard rubber bullets, and that the media—the very entity that was *reporting* the story—was being assaulted, and on tape.

Covering up such incidents by making them the fault of the victims had been standard operating procedure for the LAPD for decades. But that was before the beating of Rodney King. Los Angeles simply wasn't ready for another such don't-believe-your-lying-eyes incident. And to his credit, Bill Bratton understood that as well.

****

By the time Bratton arrived back at MacArthur Park, his press rep, Mary Grady, was already there, as was the IG, Deputy Chief Carter, a lot of reporters, and a substantial number of community activists being interviewed by the media. But the officers who'd been on the attack line were nowhere to be found. Carter, clueless as he was, had sent them home, and so they couldn't be immediately interviewed.

In fact, when Bratton started asking them how many rounds they'd fired off, Carter had a hard time making a determination, because there was no requirement at the time that an officer account for rounds that were fired. So they didn't know how many rounds had been expended in total. When Bratton first posed the question, he was told thirty or forty—but it was one of those "How many?" questions where each time he asked, the number grew higher. (The final tally was 166.)

The spark igniting the chain of events that culminated with the police taking large-scale action, Bratton began to learn, occurred at about 4 p.m. that afternoon, when some motorcycle officers tried to disperse a section of the crowd, a tactic Bratton disapproved of—a "procedural mistake," he called it—and the bottles were thrown. "You don't use a fifteen-hundred-pound machine to try to maneuver through a crowd and push people around. People will push back, officers will get knocked off bikes—it just increases the tension level."

After speaking with Carter, Bratton approached a group of demonstration leaders talking to the media and found them to be a very "legitimate, very rational group thoroughly concerned, confused, shocked, and angry." He promised them a comprehensive investigation and left the scene.

That evening he went back to Parker Center and met with all of his senior staff to map a strategy moving forward.

He had a lot of people to deal with, and all at the same time: his rank-and-file cops and their union, the media, the immigrant community, the Police Commission and inspector general, civil liberties and other police watchdog groups, and all the people in the general public who were angry. It was like, thought Bratton, "trying to change a flat tire while racing down a highway at sixty miles an hour."

Over the next days and weeks he expanded the investigation, ordering Internal Affairs to gather all video of the event and conduct interviews with the participants, the victims, and the department's senior leadership. Meanwhile, he was meeting with community groups, the ACLU, the Police Commission, the City Council, newspaper editors, and broadcast news directors, and appearing on local television and radio stations—particularly Spanish-language stations—talking with anybody he felt could help "calm the waters."

The history of LAPD malfeasance had been the subject of special "blue-ribbon" outside investigations like the Christopher Commission. Bratton didn't want that. He was a make-a-positive-out-of-a-negative guy, both by temperament and managerial philosophy, and in the May Day debacle he saw two opportunities to do exactly that.

The first was to show that the department had advanced far enough under his leadership that it was now capable of investigating itself and coming to an objective, truthful conclusion.

The second was to "break the back of the culture of the department that existed in the Metropolitan Division," an opportunity that was important and, to Bratton's discredit, long overdue. He'd already begun chipping away at "the insensitivity that the whole department was accused of," and felt that "the officers on the street were interacting much better with the community" and *looked like* the community: 45 percent Latino, 15 percent black, over 20 percent female. But Metro was still the last remnant of the old LAPD, and had badly embarrassed him and the department.

Once Bratton had assessed the situation, he made all the right moves. He started by having the department do a follow-up investigation that was accepted by the press, civil liberties organizations, and the public as being honest, fair, and accurate in its criticism of itself. Then he met with everybody he could and ordered the transformative retraining of Metro. The latter move was late in coming, and could have been tragic had there been deaths or life-threatening injuries that day. Nevertheless, the city wound up paying nearly $13 million to settle lawsuits resulting from the incident.

****

Six weeks later, Bill Bratton moved through a ballroom of the San Jose Marriott Hotel as a scrum of reporters and camera crews circled around and moved as one with him. Dressed in a well-tailored navy blue suit, crisp white shirt, and red tie, Bratton was nothing if not cool and collected as he was peppered with questions, so much so that occasionally he allowed a slight smile of amusement to cross his face.

He'd come to San Jose, California, on a sunny June morning to participate in a panel discussion sponsored by the National Association of Hispanic Journalists at their annual convention. Entitled "MacArthur Park and Beyond: Can the LAPD, Immigrant Groups, and the Media Trust Each Other Again?" the panel began with Bratton and three co-panelist reporters taking their seats behind a long rectangular table on the stage. Packed in front of them were about three hundred journalists and editors seated on folding chairs, and scores more hugging the walls in a long, cramped line.

Suddenly the lights dimmed, and everyone turned to a large white screen behind the panelists as a compilation of television footage of the Metro officers attacking demonstrators and reporters unwound before them. As the tape ended and the lights flashed on, Bratton squared his narrow shoulders and allowed a noncommittal expression to float across his face, ready for what was to come.

But remarkably, given an audience that included many from a Spanish-language media passionately committed to its immigrant constituency, and the presence of a contingent of the very journalists who'd been knocked down and roughed up at MacArthur Park, there was little animosity directed at Bratton.

And for a number of reasons. For one, he'd accumulated a wellspring of goodwill among Latinos by steadfastly supporting a long-standing department directive ordering officers not to arrest anyone because of their immigration status. He had also lobbied for undocumented immigrants to obtain driver's licenses, and publicly dismissed the notion of terrorists streaming across the Mexican border to harm Americans. ("Go to a Home Depot and what to do you see?" he once asked. "Hundreds of guys standing there, looking for work, not raping and pillaging.")

But more to the point, Bratton had also defused the uproar over the department's actions by shrewdly and swiftly becoming its most outspoken critic. Declaring the rampage "the worst incident of this type I have ever encountered in my thirty-seven years of policing," he demoted and reassigned Lee Carter, the highest-ranking officer at the scene, reassigned the second-ranking officer, and ordered retraining in crowd control and rules for dealing with the media.

****

In the subways and streets of New York, Bill Bratton had shown what a remarkable, strategically gifted cop he was while overlooking the wider game and the fact that Rudolph Giuliani considered himself, not Bratton, the unquestioned star of the stage. It was a mistake of hubris, a young man's mistake, even though Bratton had been middle-aged.

This time, both in his massive use of stop-and-frisk, and during his response to the May Day fiasco, his careful nurturing of political support both personally and in terms of his otherwise progressive, reformist policies had paid off. And instead of May Day becoming a major black mark on his tenure in L.A., it became a mere footnote.

Not long afterward, the Police Commission voted unanimously to rehire him for a second term.

Laura Chick, February 2008, Office of City Controller; Los Angeles Mayor Antonio Villaraigosa, City Hall

The reaction of the Los Angeles City Council to Connie Rice's *Call to Action* report was to commission yet another study, a kind of second opinion from the Los Angeles city controller. It took eight months, but on Valentine's Day 2008, city controller Laura Chick released her own *Blueprint on Ending Gang Violence*. Echoing the Advancement Project's critique, it focused more narrowly on the city and county's current youth-violence reduction programs, blasted them as shapeless, unconnected, and ineffective, and called for their centralization within the mayor's office. Chick was a highly respected former council member from the Valley, and her confirming report put enormous pressure to act on both the council and the city's mayor, Antonio Villaraigosa.

A liberal Democrat and former speaker of the California State Assembly, Villaraigosa had defeated James Hahn for mayor in 2005. Young and still hungry, he was a self-made man who'd grown up poor and troubled on the streets of East L.A. Short, brown-skinned, and handsome, he was a smooth but self-preoccupied politician of the kind who'd warmly ask a question, appear to be listening intently, and then break away as you were in mid-sentence upon spotting someone higher on the political-opportunity food chain to chat up. He also had an eye for the ladies, and early in his administration had been caught having an extramarital affair with a Spanish-language TV reporter, which was then followed by a high-profile separation from his wife. It had been a searing experience, a kind of baptism by fire filled with head-shaking snickering and nasty vitriol from local right-wing talk radio. But to his credit, Villaraigosa worked hard to correct himself, and would prove to be an able and accomplished leader over his eight years as mayor.

He hadn't, however, run on a gang platform, and now the idea of him taking leadership and ownership of L.A.'s gang problem was thrust upon him. The easy call was to stick with the status quo and not risk a backlash if it didn't work out.

"There was a lot of debate about what we would do about street gangs and violence in our city," says Jeff Carr, an ordained minister who would become Villaraigosa's first "gang czar." "The [*Call to Action*] report that Connie Rice did really lambasted the city and county. It said we were at a crossroad and had to move in a different direction.

"But," continued Carr, "there was no guarantee we were going to do that. There were lots of voices saying Connie was crazy, that youth violence was a law enforcement problem and that what we needed was to [just] further suppress gangs.

"The day the city controller's report came out, we had a meeting about how we should respond. About ten mayoral advisors were at the meeting. And almost all of them argued that it was political suicide to take responsibility, that the violence was ingrained into the social fabric of the city, and that the mayor should stay as far from the issue as possible."

And then, as Carr later told it, he spoke up. "This is why you were elected," he told Villaraigosa. "You're the first Latino mayor in 137 years in this city's history. If you don't take on this issue at this moment, who's ever going to take it on?"

And, according to Carr, Villaraigosa looked at him and said, "You know, you're right, and we're gonna do it."

****

With a unified approach to gang-violence prevention overseen by Carr now established in the mayor's office, the stage was set for Connie Rice, Charlie Beck, and others to create a school for gang interventionists run by Rice's Advancement Project.

Earlier city-financed intervention programs had run into trouble—large amounts of city money unaccounted for, an arrest on federal racketeering and conspiracy charges, accusations of thievery. Ensuring that there be no reoccurrence would require a powerfully reinforcing, comprehensively structured curriculum. And the "Urban Peace Academy," as it would be named, would have one, involving a carefully screened selection process, over one hundred hours of training, and a graduation and certification process. For their efforts, interventionists would be deployed to the city's hot spots and earn a minimum of $30,000 year and health insurance. Schools in those hot spots would identify at-risk students for counseling and services, and the city would continue to fund a version of Martin Ludlow's "Summer of Success" program, called "Summer Night Lights," in local parks and recreation centers.

Thanks to the backing of Bratton, Beck, Bo Taylor, L.A. County sheriff Lee Baca, city controller Laura Chick, and finally the mayor, Rice and the Advancement Project were finally able to achieve two bedrock tenets of their *Call to Action* report: a gang interventionist program, and a centrally coordinated "Gang Reduction and Youth Development Program" (GRYD), within the mayor's office—where power and accountability were consolidated under his auspices.

Prevention and intervention organizations and programs within the GRYD would receive $21 million in 2010, a figure which Villaraigosa and the City Council would protect throughout the Great Recession despite severe cuts in other parts of the budget, including to the City Attorney's Office and the LAPD's counterterrorism task force.

The bigger, independent state and county social service agencies never bought into Rice's wraparound approach, nor did the probation and parole departments. They were too busy fighting each other for funds and ensuring their self-perpetuation.

Nevertheless, the City Council and key philanthropic organizations would allocate $700,000 for the first year of the gang academy's funding and then raise its budget to over $1 million. The LAPD, other city departments, and some of Los Angeles's most liberal philanthropic organizations were now working together to reduce gang and youth violence. Bill Bratton didn't make that happen. But he supported Connie Rice and gave Charlie Beck the independence to facilitate it.

Bill Bratton, August 2009, Parker Center

Flying into Los Angeles from New York in early August of 2009, Bill Bratton was in possession of news already beginning to leak out.

He was resigning.

Neither the mayor nor the Police Commission nor his assistant and deputy chiefs had been notified. But the man who'd been charged with the day-to-day monitoring of the department's consent decree, Michael G. Cherkasky, knew, because he was about to become Bratton's new boss.

From 2001 through the previous month of July of 2009, Cherkasky had been *the* independent monitor, overseeing compliance with every aspect of the consent decree and then reporting his findings to federal judge Gary Feess. Bratton had wanted his decision to leave the LAPD to coincide with Feess terminating the consent decree.

Prior to becoming the decree's monitor, Cherkasky had been an executive at the giant New York–based private security firm Kroll, Inc., during the nineties, and had been named the decree's independent monitor when the firm was awarded the job in 2001. Shortly after taking the helm, he'd then named Bratton as one of his monitors.

And now, Cherkasky, who had recently become the chief executive of Kroll's global parent company, Altegrity, Inc., was hiring Bratton *away* from the LAPD to become chairman of Kroll.

It all seemed a bit incestuous, but few questions were raised. Cherkasky had been the independent monitor before Bratton had been hired as chief; he'd had nothing to do with Bratton's hiring, had filed critical reports about the slow pace of the department's compliance, and was not the ultimate consent-decree-ending decision maker in any case. That was Judge Feess. He was, however, the ultimate *recommender* to Feess on when the decree should be terminated. And now he was recommending termination.

****

Bill Bratton had been chafing under the consent decree since at least 2006, when Feess had not only refused to end it but had extended it for another three years. And in late June of 2009, he'd told *Los Angeles Times* reporter Patt Morrison on her local KPCC radio show that the decree was an albatross wrapped around his and the department's neck. That was why it had to be ended. "We are arguing," said Bratton, "that if you continue the consent decree, symbolically, that basically is a slap in the face of the department. The polling by the *L.A. Times* shows that a majority of the people in this city feel this department is really doing a good job."

If Feess didn't terminate the decree, Bratton continued, "The judge would effectively be saying, 'Well, you worked hard over the last eight years [on the decree, but] it doesn't count. We're going to keep you in this consent decree for three more years.'"

Back in 2006, Judge Feess had forcefully told the city and the department that the LAPD had defied reform for forty years and that, in essence, he was going to make damn sure that that didn't happen again.

But by the summer of 2009 Bill Bratton was equally damn sure that *he* wasn't going to wait around another two or three years for Feess to lift the decree. He was never good at, and in fact prided himself on not, hanging around longer than necessary. He told the *Los Angeles Times* in 2008 that he "never wanted to go and just maintain something" but wanted instead "to be able to fix something." And in his mind the LAPD was fixed, at least to the extent that he wished to take it.

All he had needed was for Gary Feess to declare it so and enable him to move on to the greener, more lucrative pastures of New York—the adopted home of both him and his wife, Rikki.

So when Feess appeared not to be budging on the issue, Bratton launched a campaign to generate some buzz in the press as a way of persuading Feess to unburden him and the department of the decree.

To buttress his crusade, Bratton decided to use money from the privately funded LAPD booster organization the Police Foundation to commission a report that would be called *Policing Los Angeles Under a*

Consent Decree: The Dynamics of Change at the LAPD. And he would go to the very top to get the authors he wanted to conduct the study—straight out of the Harvard Kennedy School and its groundbreaking Criminal Justice Policy and Management Program, a program with which Bratton had had a long, fruitful relationship going back two decades.

Released in May 2009, the report was a generally favorable evaluation of the department. It pointed out how "serious crime" had dropped by almost 35 percent from 2003 to 2008 (after dropping 52 percent from 1992 to 1999 under Williams and Parks, before rising by 5 percent from 2000 to 2002). It also noted a 30 percent drop in officer-involved shootings and the use of choke holds and strikes to suspects' heads with a baton or flashlight. The report also showed that the number of Angelenos who thought that the LAPD treated "all racial and ethnic groups fairly" had risen from 39 to 51 percent over the past four years; and that pedestrian and vehicle stops had risen by almost 50 percent between 2002 and 2008, which they considered a good thing. The report's authors, however, also wrote that they "saw a lot of force displayed in what seemed to be routine enforcement situations."

Overall, however, the report's principal author, Christopher Stone, would point out that "we're talking about a department that has been able to reduce crime, increase satisfaction with the community, while increasing law enforcement activity." Stone then presented the report to the decree's monitors; Cherkasky in turn presented it to Feess, who in August of 2009 approved a transitional plan that allowed the Police Commission to continue to oversee the last years of the decree's existence.

As badly as Bill Bratton wanted out of the consent decree, however, the truth is that it had cut both ways for him. Its carefully crafted metric-based provisions may well have been annoying, time-consuming, and burdensome to implement, but they provided a structural blueprint for cultural and operational reform of the department that was extremely beneficial. And the reality was that he wasn't asking out of the consent decree because he had nothing to show for it. He'd placed his extremely well-connected civilian, Gerald Chaleff, in charge of getting the consent decree *done*. And Chaleff, for the most part, *had* gotten it done.

****

Having accomplished what he set out to do, which was to rekindle his career and lay the groundwork for the reformation of the LAPD, Bill Bratton left Los Angeles a far better politician than he'd been in New York. He now understood how to work with the city government. The first L.A. mayor he served under, James Hahn, was soft-spoken, introspective, and unassuming. The second, Antonio Villaraigosa, was outgoing and engaging, a big personality who loved the spotlight. Neither was as egomaniacal as Giuliani; they both pretty much left Bratton alone to do his job, and he never really clashed with them. Never a man to suffer fools gladly, he would have his run-ins with the City Council, but ultimately even that wasn't an issue.

For more than two decades before Bratton's tenure in Los Angeles, the LAPD's chiefs had been locked in often bitter conflicts with their mayors: Daryl Gates's battles with Mayor Tom Bradley had been both legendary and destructively divisive; Willie Williams's refusal to work with Mayor Riordan to hire thousands more officers killed their working relationship before it ever got started; and Bernard Parks's contemptuous treatment of Mayor Hahn had ensured his own downfall.

But after a few tin-eared false starts of the sort made by many pushy northeasterners newly arrived in L.A., Bratton had settled in and restored a stature and legitimacy long lost to the office of the Los Angeles chief of police. At the same time, he also brought the department's Police Protective League, which had been furiously hostile to Parks, into his decision-making processes while stabilizing and rationalizing the disciplinary system.

Beyond the changes mandated by the consent decree, Bratton also started the conversion of the LAPD's culture by altering the way the department's patrol officers thought about their jobs. Under him and commanders like Charlie Beck, George Gascon, and Pat Gannon, there was a much wider focus on having a positive community impact as opposed to just racking up arrest numbers.

Charlie Beck's reform of the Rampart Division and his multipronged, community-engaged revitalization of MacArthur Park had taken place because Bratton had allowed him to experiment by giving him just five words of instruction: "Clean up that fucking park!"

Beck and Pat Gannon would embrace a gang interventionist academy and develop the kind of strong relationships with grassroots community organizations and activists that would help grow the concepts of legitimacy and fairness within the LAPD—again because Bratton gave them the freedom to do so.

Bratton was also successful as chief because he cultivated key members of L.A.'s police-focused political establishment. His support for the concepts that came out of Connie Rice's *Call to Action* report—especially the gang-interventionist academy and the mayor's Gang Reduction and Youth Development office—were key to their passage.

In addition, Bratton had spotted Rice as someone with ideas, just as he spotted Jack Maple in New York, and entered into a partnership with her, giving Rice the imprimatur of the LAPD and the opportunity to get reforms instituted within and around the LAPD that directly advanced both her agenda and his own.

Bratton also began the process of making the LAPD a far more efficient and accountable department while—at least according to the department's own numbers—starting a record of crime decreases that lasted for eleven straight years.

Then, among his last acts in office, he successfully campaigned for Charlie Beck to succeed him. Soon after, among *his* first acts in office as chief, Charlie Beck walked a beat in Jordan Downs—where Andre Christian was now working as a gang interventionist—while shaking hands and introducing himself to the residents.

But he had also greatly ratcheted up the number of gang injunctions and legitimized stop-and-frisk in Los Angeles.

Pat Gannon, Ron Noblet, and Alfred Lomas, December 2010, Magnolia Place Community Center

Standing unobtrusively at the back of a large, unadorned meeting hall in a low-slung South Central community center, Pat Gannon was busy chatting with a reporter as mingling clusters of black and Latino men and women ambled into the room. Some were young, but many were approaching or settling into middle age, and had the weathered look of lives hard lived. Stopping to grab a cup of the coffee and some doughnuts or bagels on a table behind Gannon, they then took a seat in one of the metal folding chairs facing the podium at the front of the room.

It was a rainy mid-morning in December 2010—graduation day at the Urban Peace Academy, the second since the opening of the gang-interventionist program the previous summer—and twenty-five men and women were about to receive their graduation certificates.

Not far from Gannon stood Ron Noblet, pale-vanilla face expressionless, arms folded, absolutely still. Tall, broad-shouldered, his gray hair crew-cut, he looked like some white-socks-wearing, plain-clothes Irish cop from the Bronx, circa 1972. But in fact he was a half-Mexican-American, half-Eastern-European ex-marine and native son of Los Angeles. A Slavic studies major at USC, Noblet had been working with gangs as a consultant and interventionist for forty years and had become a key part of the academy's management team. He'd grown up with an alcoholic father who'd raised and disciplined him with terrible beatings and berating. His life quest subsequently became trying to understand what violence was about, and how it might be mitigated.

When Noblet heard that the Advancement Project was creating the UPA, he called Connie Rice and introduced himself with one sentence: "You don't know me, but you need me." It turned out she did. Rice had spent a great deal of time working with and understanding gangs and intervention through the prism of black interventionists in South L.A., but she knew little about Mexican and Central American gang culture. Ron Noblet knew a lot.

"Ron was very important," recalls Rice. "He was all but a member of the Latin Kings and El Sereno when he was growing up, and went on from there to study the blood feuds of Eastern Europe at USC. And as a half-white, half-Latino kid he didn't belong anywhere, and consequently was geared to really soak up what he was learning in a uniquely impartial and academic way."

During his decades as an interventionist, Noblet dealt with serious, deadly people, and had to figure out a way to gain the trust of both gang members and cops and not be considered a creature of either. The way he found was to walk a tightrope between rival gangs and between gangs and the police, intervening or brokering deals whenever he could while being so boldly transparent that everybody could see him in action and watch as he kept his word.

"The difference in gang work now," Noblet would later say, "is there's real cooperation between blacks and browns, and interventionists and the police. I don't mean snitching. I mean a mutual understanding that both sides want to lower the level of violence. Gang workers don't help the police investigate the last killing, they help to stop the next killing."

Meanwhile, just as the graduation ceremony was about to get started, Alfred Lomas rushed in. Looking like a lawyer late for court, he was dressed in a blue suit, white shirt, and red tie that somehow managed to conceal the amazing maze of gang tattoos spread across his arms and upper body, including vivid flames running up the collar line of his neck.

Lomas, it turned out, was one of the Urban Peace Academy's first graduates, brought into the fold by Noblet.

In 2005, Lomas's obsession with getting high had again landed him in L.A. County Jail. Once released, he found himself wandering the streets of Skid Row. There he met members of a church ministry called the Dream Center, looking to save lost souls. He agreed to accompany them back to the church's large social-welfare center west of downtown, in Echo Park. There they enrolled him in an in-house drug treatment program. Once sober and off drugs, Lomas proved a remarkably articulate, coiled ball of energy, working for the ministry's food distribution program, operating a mobile food bank.

One day in 2007 he received a phone call from an LAPD captain

named Mark Olvera, who was then the commanding officer of the
Newton Division. Olvera asked for a favor, much like the one Pat Gannon had asked Bo Taylor for in South L.A. two years earlier: help in
averting an explosive situation between the black and brown residents
of the Pueblo del Rio housing projects. A Mexican kid had been found
dead, and rumors were flying that he was a victim of the project's black
Bloods gang, the Pueblo Bishops. Neither the LAPD nor the coroner's
office had yet determined the cause of death, however.

Prospects for retaliatory violence were nevertheless running high
and Olvera asked Lomas if he'd try to head it off. Lomas agreed. Fortunately, he knew the dead kid's parents and some of their friends and
told them that, despite the rumors, he had firsthand knowledge that law
enforcement had not yet determined what had killed their son.

He also gave the Florencia gangsters living in the projects the same
message, adding that whatever the truth was, he'd let them know face-
to-face as soon as he learned it. That bought Lomas and the LAPD a
twenty-four-hour window to "keep everybody calm and all the rumors
from spreading." And it worked. "It could have turned into a huge retaliatory black-and-brown gangbang," says Lomas. "Instead, it turned out
the kid had died of an aneurysm, and that was the end of it."

★★★★★★★★★★★★★★

Being out in the open about both his old life as a gangster and his new
life on the square, Lomas was duty-bound to live life as he was proclaiming it to be, a credo taught and reinforced within the bond he'd forged
with Ron Noblet. "Al was a generation behind in age of some of the
really heavy shot-callers in various organizations," Noblet would later
say. "With Chicanos and Mexicans there is a hierarchy. And part of that
hierarchy is age difference. The older guys knew what he was trying to
do now, and gave him a pass. Even though they themselves were stone
criminals and gangsters, if you say you're trying to do the right thing,
and you do it, they'll give you a chance. But if they find out you're playing both sides, you're dead. They don't like hypocrisy."

If his fellow gangsters were giving Alfred Lomas a pass, however,
law enforcement definitely was not. And in 2007, two years before the

birth of the Peace Academy, he started getting squeezed. The LAPD, the Sheriff's Department and the feds had launched a two-year gang investigation including a sweeping injunction against six gangs that included Florencia 13.

For Lomas, this was deeply disturbing news. All that was needed for him to effectively spend the rest of his life behind bars was to get caught up in some mad-ass lawman's supposition that he was still a muscleman for drug dealers, and then see to it that a federal RICO conspiracy indictment was slapped on him. And that's exactly what almost happened. Three times—with the last incident occurring during Bratton's last year in office, 2009.

Lomas was then working with the Pueblo Bishops in the projects, where he was also establishing himself as a God-fearing, evangelizing interventionist.

Early one morning the gang task force suddenly raided Pueblo del Rio, arresting eighty Bishops for drug dealing and then putting heavy pressure on some of those arrested, according to Lomas, to implicate him. Claiming to have suspicious surveillance pictures of Lomas at the projects and at gang funerals, the cops told him they believed that his work in the projects was simply a front, and that in reality he was a drug connection between Florencia—which was a transnational gang with access to drugs from Mexico and Colombia—and the Bishops.

It was not an unreasonable assumption. A Mexican-American ex-gangster going into black gang territory claiming to be doing good works, and being permitted to do so, was unheard-of. And the cops, who were not buying it, started, as Lomas later told it, to put fierce pressure on Lomas to confess, and on the Bishops to roll over on Lomas. Neither happened. But Lomas believes that the only thing that eventually saved him was the fact that he'd already established his bona fides with the LAPD.

One of those who wound up vouching for him was LAPD sergeant Curtis Woodle, who had arrived at the day's graduation shortly before Lomas. One of Woodle's jobs, says Lomas, was establishing "who was real and who wasn't" during the Peace Academy's selection process.

Woodle became Charlie Beck's point man on a lot of issues dealing with gangs. Beck had first met Woodle when he was commanding the Rampart Division. Curtis Woodle had been revolted when he'd once pulled up to a drive-by shooting and discovered the bullet-riddled dead bodies of two girls, one thirteen, the other sixteen, sprawled across the seats of their car, each looking, in Woodle's eyes, like his daughter, Veronica. That day he vowed to do something other than be just a hard-nosed gang cop.

That's what he was trying to be when Charlie Beck first noticed him. Woodle had chosen a local middle school as a personal project to try to keep kids out of gangs, and one day Beck had stopped by to check him out. He liked what he saw—which was the kids flocking around LAPD cop Curtis Woodle and his astounding superhero physical presence.

When Beck was subsequently assigned to South Bureau, he decided to bring Woodle along with him to run similar antigang youth programs. Then, as the Peace Academy was developing, he assigned Woodle as his liaison to smooth out any problems between this new, odd mix of cops and interventionists. "And Curtis," as Beck would later tell it, proved "very good at figuring out how to do that, how to make strong relationships with people, and he became a big piece of that program."

Lomas's other savior was the very same Captain Mark Olvera whom Lomas had helped out during the episode when the Latino kid was found dead in the projects. Olvera too was involved with the Peace Academy, having served on UPA's Law Enforcement Curriculum Development Work Group. The five words that might well have quasi-officially saved Alfred Lomas came from Olvera in an article in the *Los Angeles Times*: "He is the real deal."

****

When Pat Gannon was called up to the graduation podium to speak, Connie Rice, acting as the day's MC, introduced him as the "deputy chief in charge of South Bureau—which Peter Jennings of ABC News had called the deadliest beat in America."

It proved a good segue for Gannon. "Well, I've got to tell you," Gannon replied as he gripped the podium, "because of the work you've done, South Bureau is no longer the deadliest beat in America.

"This year, right now, the city of Los Angeles has had 287 murders. In 1992 we finished with 1,100. And in my nearly thirty-three years on the LAPD I can't think of one thing that has done more to impact those numbers than gang interventionists. What you've done to stop indiscriminate street crime and retaliatory shootings has been a huge benefit. In the nineties, one shooting led to ten retaliatory shootings. We simply don't see that today.

"In 2009," Gannon continued, "Chicago had 458 murders; we had 314. They're smaller than L.A. And it's twenty-one degrees there today. If it was twenty-one degrees in L.A., we wouldn't have *any* crime. We should finish 2010 under 300.

"So when I meet with my staff every Tuesday morning," Gannon said, "or get notified of a shooting at night, my first question is, 'What did gang intervention have to say?' And I thank you for that."

★★★★★★★★★★★★★★

A number of other people would also speak that day. Connie Rice was the last. And given the newness of the Urban Peace Academy and the nature of the event, what she had to say was in the form of a pep rally for all concerned.

But what she told the *Chicago Reader* several years later best summed up what she, Gannon, Bratton, Beck, Taylor, Villaraigosa, and many others were trying to achieve.

"If your goal is not gang eradication, which none of us knows how to do, but instead is violence reduction, and you enlist [former gangsters to help you], then you begin to change the physics of the neighborhood. We're doing it with the cooperation of the gangs because they're so powerful that they control some of the neighborhoods. We get them into classes and training, and we say if you help us stop the violence, we're not going to hold the past against you. Everyone agrees we should keep the kids safe. [But] if you don't give [gangsters] a way to exert power legitimately, they'll do it another way. . . . Some of the cops are saying, 'We don't like you treating the gangsters with respect.' But once you create a different kind of momentum, people find it impossible to ignore."

****

That momentum for reform has indeed been created in Los Angeles—spearheaded by Bratton and deepened by Beck. Most remarkable is the dramatic drop in the level of animosity between the city's poor black and brown communities and the LAPD.

Equally as notable, homicides by 2013 would drop to 250. Pat Gannon had both predicted and rightly boasted that the year 2010 would end with under 300 homicides, and it did, with 297. But for it to then decline by almost 50 fewer murders in 2013 was truly a triumph for which the LAPD deserved significant credit.

There were, of course, factors other than Bratton's and Beck's contributions that led to the decline in homicides. For one, drug distribution has shifted dramatically. The old method of street-corner dealing by young black guys in open-air, very violent marketplaces had greatly diminished. The market for crack cocaine had collapsed due to its terrible destructiveness. A lot of drug dealing was now being done through call-up, cell-phone distribution delivered by unlicensed taxis. Statewide, possession of small amounts of marijuana became an infraction punishable by a $100 fine, with no arrest and no record, and medical marijuana cards were plentiful.

The Bloods and the Crips, in addition, simply weren't as well organized as the Mexican gangs, and couldn't sustain their business viability—which required discipline, organizational skills, and, on an ongoing basis, the social cohesiveness that the Mexican-American gangs have developed in abundance because of their multigenerational existence.

The demographic shift in Los Angeles has also been a huge factor in the city's crime decline. In L.A. the immigrant family unit is strong, their work ethic is pronounced. The huge concentration of African-Americans in the housing projects has given way to Latinos, who are less involved in criminal conflict now that the cartels are keeping the lid on gang fights over distribution, and because there's also been a big lessening of racial tension on the streets of South Los Angeles.

"I'll tell you how positive the change has been," Ron Noblet told a reporter in 2010. A couple of hard-core guys—one of whom is Andre Christian—have been running a fatherhood project paid for by the housing authority in Jordan Downs. Every Wednesday I go over there. Recently I have been bringing a young Chicana as a co-facilitator.

"She's the first person in her family to go to college, and the first to graduate, and is beautiful beyond belief. And not one person reacted to her negatively. Five or ten years ago she would have been hit on, beaten, or raped by either males or females—females because of jealousy, males because they wanted sex. Now everybody comments on her beauty and helpfulness. That's because outsiders are no longer seen as the enemy to be preyed upon, and because three-quarters of the projects are now Latino."

Daryl Gates and Charlie Beck, April 2010, San Clemente, California

Propped up in a hospital bed, Daryl Gates was looking out onto a panoramic view of the Pacific Ocean when LAPD chief Charlie Beck strode into his hilltop condominium in San Clemente, California. Beck knew Gates was dying of cancer. But he was still startled by how frail he looked. He'd known the older man for decades as an ardent surfer, superbly conditioned marathon runner, and devoted jogger who had taken immense pride in his fit and tanned appearance.

But on this bucolic Southern California day in April 2010, the evidence of his physical decay was undeniable. His pale skin hung from his bones, his once powerful legs were shriveled, and he'd been released into hospice care at home because there was nothing more to be done.

Beck had forgone wearing his usual long-sleeved chief's uniform and tie for the visit and dressed instead in the comfortable, short-sleeved, open-at-the-collar LAPD blues favored by his street cops. Gates had been the first LAPD chief to wear that uniform style as a way of saying to the troops, "Look, I'm one of you." By his dress choice, Beck was signaling to Gates their shared past.

Beyond that act of grace, Beck understood that despite being reviled by those outside the LAPD, within it and among the retired, Gates remained a revered, legendary figure who'd stood up for them until it all came crashing down.

Lost in a time warp, Gates and his men had railed against change in a radically transformed city no longer theirs, and yearned for the days when the L.A. media was their lapdog, they were heralded, publicized, and glamorized as the Golden Boys of American law enforcement, and portrayed in dozens of television series as the epitome of a cutting-edge crime-fighting machine.

That legend now lay on history's scrap heap, killed in the 1980s and '90s by the LAPD's destructive policing and black and brown L.A.'s retaliatory fury. Yet for another decade, Daryl Gates and his tenure had lived on as a rallying cry for the faithful who believed in their hearts that there had been nothing about their department that needed reform.

It had been precisely that reverence for that legacy, for that *attitude*, that Bill Bratton, Judge Gary Feess, and so many others had to work so hard to bring under control—and now the task was in the hands of Charlie Beck to complete.

At fifty-six years old, and after thirty-two years in the department, Beck had been sworn in as Los Angeles's fifty-fifth police chief in November of 2009, nearly three months after Bill Bratton had announced his resignation. And now, as Beck sat next to him, Gates spoke with pleasure about Beck's rise to the top. And about his joy that the department had been given over to a brother in the LAPD fraternity—to a man he had known since he was a little boy running around at LAPD picnics with his father, Gates's friend and one of his deputy chiefs. And about his deep relief that his department was no longer being led by a despised interloper who'd understood nothing about the soul of their organization. "I feel I can go now," he told Beck. "That it's okay to leave."

They talked a little more, Charlie Beck showing his respect for Daryl Gates, and undoubtedly a certain affection as well. But Beck had no intention of restoring what Gates considered the good old days. He'd made that clear while speaking to the City Council during his nomination hearing, saying, as the *Los Angeles Times* would report, that "his top goal was to extend the reforms begun by [Bill] Bratton and moving them down into the rank and file . . . [and] into the mindset of the thousands of officers who are the heart of the organization." That effort, Beck added, will be the "hallmark of my administration."

Today, however, that goal wasn't figuring into the conversation. It was highly unlikely that Gates had any real conception of Beck's plans. And what would have been the point of telling him, in any case?

Suddenly an LAPD helicopter appeared against the blue waters of the Pacific and hovered in clear view through the condo's picture window. After a moment, Daryl Francis Gates struggled to sit up in his bed and, once he'd managed it, snapped off his final salute.

EPILOGUE: 2015

I **STARTED THIS** book with great admiration for Bill Bratton and Charlie Beck. And as I closed out the writing of this epilogue in the spring of 2015, I still found myself admiring them for many of the things they've accomplished, as well as for their personal drive, media savvy, refusal to defend the indefensible, and ability to garner support for their policies from liberals in a liberal Los Angeles, and from a previously highly critical African-American community. But perhaps most of all I came to respect their success in bringing change to moribund police departments while putting their engineer's problem-solving minds to the vital work of improving public safety.

Now, four years later, people continue to ask me if the LAPD is really reformed. To that I answer, "Compared to what?" If they mean compared to Daryl Gates's arrogant, combative fourteen years as chief in the eighties and early nineties, or the decade adrift under Williams and Parks, or to many other police organizations, my reply is yes, emphatically yes. In addition to what I've already mentioned, Bratton and Beck refocused officer training away from its singular obsession with creating instruments of repression by also committing the LAPD to real, innovative community service.

And with that has come a notably less hostile attitude toward the public, far more transparency in dealing with the media, and a willingness to listen and be open to their critics' concerns. And, finally, they reduced crime—dramatically in the case of Bratton in New York in the early and mid-nineties, and steadily in Los Angeles (although the latter would be open to question, as we shall see). In all, their accomplishments have not only been steps in the right direction but also rare, hopeful advances in the world of criminal justice, where progressive reform moves at a snail's pace.

But halfway through the writing of *Blue*, I began to understand far more clearly the terrible ramifications of stop-and-frisk and broken-windows policing in poor communities throughout America; and as a result, my view of both men, based on their strong support for these tactics, became more nuanced. It all crystallized for me when the news that would mesmerize America in 2014 started surging in, announcing that American policing was in deep crisis—in large part because of the practice of these tactics across the country.

The first signal came on a mid-July day from a Staten Island sidewalk in New York City. There, a 350-pound unarmed black man named Eric Garner was being cuffed and arrested by an NYPD officer for selling single, untaxed cigarettes known as "loosies," when suddenly he made the fatal mistake of pulling his wrists apart. A split second later a tall, burly white cop standing directly behind him locked a forearm in a choke hold around Garner's windpipe, pulling tight and ferociously yanking him by his neck to the ground. Several other cops instantly piled onto his back, choking and smothering the life out of Garner while ignoring the dying plea he would utter eleven times before he died: "I can't breathe."

Soon a vivid cell-phone video of the incident, captured by a bystander, made Garner a cause célèbre on the Web and TV news shows, spotlighting long-standing grievances over police abuse and sparking the beginning of a widespread public discussion of the issue not heard as intensely since the 1991 beating of Rodney King and the '92 Los Angeles riots.

One month later, in a Midwestern backwater called Ferguson, Missouri, that discussion heated up exponentially. Demonstrators there were protesting the recent shooting death of an unarmed black teenager named Michael Brown by a white officer when a large contingent of local police suddenly arrived at the scene in army Humvees and armored vehicles. Dressed, armed, and equipped like combat marines ready to fight insurgents in the Second Battle of Fallujah, many of the officers then took positions on a skirmish line or atop their vehicles and aimed red laser beams from their assault rifles directly at the chests of stunned protesters.

Broadcast live, the spectacle ignited public shock and outrage and inspired scores of sympathy demonstrations throughout the country. Many were led by young black grassroots community organizers and focused on killings of unarmed black men by white police officers. Some, however, were also directed at ending mass incarceration, stop-and-frisk policies, tight broken-windows policing, and the war on drugs, all of which were becoming *the* civil rights issues of the twenty-first century for African-Americans.

To the protesters' popular rallying cry of "I Can't Breathe" were swiftly added two others: "Hands Up, Don't Shoot," in solidarity with an alleged gesture of surrender—later disproven—Brown was making when he was shot and killed; and "Black Lives Matter," a retort to the seemingly reckless manner in which cops were killing men like Garner and Brown in cities throughout the nation.

****

Six months earlier—on the very first day of 2014, in fact—Bill Bratton, amazingly but not unpredictably, was once again being sworn in as the new commissioner of the New York City Police Department. That July, the killing of Eric Garner and other events would plunge him, the NYPD, and the city's new mayor deep into the thick of the national crisis of confidence in the police that, with Garner's death, was arousing long-pent-up rage, as well as old fears of the city reverting back to the crime-filled years of the past.

Meanwhile, back in Los Angeles, Charlie Beck was entering his fifth year as LAPD chief, all but assured of reappointment for a second five-year term that summer, and unaware that his department too would become part of policing's tribulations in 2014.

****

Charlie Beck began his tenure as chief with amazing skill, avoiding repetition of the department's past sins and with great instincts saying and doing the right, fair, decent things while building on Bill Bratton's legacy.

Beck would signal the best of his intentions on his first full day in office by going to Watts's Jordan Downs housing project and symbolically walking patrol, greeting residents and shaking hands with people he'd once felt he had to get away from to save his humanity.

Soon he formed a special unit staffed only with LAPD officers who'd volunteered to work in Jordan Downs and other high-crime housing projects in an innovative community-policing program called Community Safety Partnership Police.

The unit's cops would be judged not by arrest numbers but by how effectively they strengthened and stabilized each of the housing projects; kept crime and violence low through gaining the community's trust, partnership, and support; and worked with the projects' kids and families to keep the kids out of jail. Like the Urban Peace Academy Beck also helped found, it remains today a community-building police mission that could never have existed in the LAPD before Beck and Bratton.

In addition, Beck began forging ties with the city's Latinos and other immigrant communities, lobbying for driver's licenses for undocumented residents and stopping impounding cars driven by those license-less immigrants, saving them hundreds or thousands of dollars in towing and impoundment fees in the process.

At the same time the LAPD's gang-injunction policing would continue unabated under Beck. According to the Los Angeles City Attorney's Office, as of 2015 there were "more than forty-six permanent gang injunctions in place in the city of Los Angeles, enjoining the activities of seventy-nine criminal street gangs." Some of the injunctions dated back to 2000.

****

As all this was occurring, officer-involved beatings, shootings, and killings across the country were starting to make persistent national headlines, and, thanks to cell-phone videos and ubiquitous street and building cameras, had begun to cumulatively settle into public conspicuousness, and would carry over well into 2015 to become a long list indeed. Among the many recorded were the routine, the chillingly deadly, and the stupidly fatal.

The first featured a man so scared of San Bernardino County sheriff's deputies that he mounted a nearby horse and fled from them, only to be viciously, gratuitously gang-beaten by a swarm of deputies once they caught up with him—all of which was captured by a news helicopter whirling above.

A second involved a middle-aged black man in North Charleston, South Carolina, whose vehicle was bullshit-stopped by a white officer. When the unarmed man decided to run away because he didn't want to again be jailed for back child-support payments, the officer casually and fatally shot him multiple times in the back. This incident too was recorded, on this occasion by the cell phone of a passerby.

A third, captured by a body camera worn by a sheriff's deputy in Oklahoma, focused on a white seventy-three-year-old insurance company executive and armed and uniformed Tulsa County Sheriff's Department volunteer who was also a generous giver of gifts to the department. Working with deputies on a stakeout, he accidentally pulled out his gun instead of his Taser and killed the unnamed black suspect.

The LAPD too was having its share of controversial shootings. According to the *Homicide Report*—the extraordinary blog written by veteran *Los Angeles Times* reporter Jill Leovy—there were 605 officer-involved homicides in all of L.A. County from January 1, 2000, through late April of 2015, of which almost 40 percent, or 228 deaths, were at the hands of LAPD officers. Meanwhile, a 2014 investigation by the *New York Daily News* found that the NYPD, with more than three times the number of police officers as the LAPD, had killed "at least 179 people" over almost exactly the same time frame: January 1, 2000, to September 2014.

In 2014 the *Wall Street Journal* also analyzed officer-involved killings from 105 of the nation's largest police departments and found there had been "at least 1,800 killings in those 105 departments between 2007 and 2012." (About 18,000 law-enforcement agencies "didn't report any [officer-involved killings to the FBI].")

During those years the LAPD reported 111 officer-involved homicides, and Chicago—the city closest in population to L.A., and with similar gang problems—reported 87, and New York City 68. Officer-involved killings have always been high in the LAPD and in the Southwest in general, and under Bratton and Beck they remained comparatively so; and, as of June 2015, have again become a fiercely contentious issue in Los Angeles.

Nevertheless, as the summer of 2014 progressed, Charlie Beck seemed to be cakewalking to a second five-year term as LAPD chief. Then a bombshell hit.

On August 9, just three days before Beck's scheduled reappointment, a *Los Angeles Times* investigation revealed that from early October 2012 through September 2013, the LAPD had misclassified nearly twelve hundred aggravated assaults (violent felonies) as simple assaults that consequently didn't appear in the department's annual report of serious (felony) crimes. (The paper had requested data for the past decade, but in the end had to settle for just one year.) The misclassifications included "hundreds of stabbings, beatings and robberies"—the very crimes that people fear the most. Had those crimes been properly classified as the aggrieved assaults they actually were, the *Times* concluded, "the total aggravated assaults . . . would have been almost 14 percent higher than the official figure [released by the LAPD]."

Beck responded by essentially saying that mistakes are inevitable when you're dealing with 97,000 crimes in a single year. But when *Times* investigative reporters Joel Rubin and Ben Poston then reviewed their findings, they discovered a pattern that only magnified the seriousness of the problem: almost all of the misclassified crimes had "turned serious crime[s] into minor one[s]"; almost none had been misclassified the other way around, so it was hard to believe they were simply random mistakes.

No one believed Charlie Beck was directly responsible for the misclassifications. Beck later said that the misclassification of assaults is common in many police departments because of the vague definitions used to categorize simple and aggravated assaults. Even so, the pressure on commanding officers, division captains, and investigators to constantly report reductions in serious felonies appeared intense enough to cause some of them to respond by deliberately misclassifying the crimes.

Despite the revelation, Charlie Beck's accomplishments were real enough that on August 12, 2014—just three days after the *Times* released its exposé—the Los Angeles Police Commission voted 4–1 to rehire him.

Acting to contain the damage, Beck released a major reform plan in mid-December to ensure the misclassifications would not occur again. Nevertheless, the *Times* story would not go away.

Later, at 2014's end, the LAPD's new major-crime report showed a 14 percent increase in violent crime, the first in twelve years.

The increase was driven by—guess what?—a soaring rise of over *28 percent* in the very category of aggravated assaults the *Times* exposé had first pinpointed.

When Bill Bratton came to Los Angeles as chief, he brought with him Jack Maple's policing-by-the-numbers COMSTAT system of judging command officers' effectiveness and promotion potential, thus providing a particularly strong incentive for officers to cheat to meet production goals: live by the numbers, die by the numbers.

The same seems true in Chicago, where a similar phenomenon had also been discovered in 2014. There, *Chicago* magazine journalists David Bernstein and Noah Isackson investigated Chicago's major violent crime statistics for 2013. In the process they "identified 10 people . . . beaten, burned, suffocated, or shot to death in 2013 whose cases had been reclassified . . . or downgraded to more minor crimes; or closed as noncriminal incidents." They also discovered "serious felonies such as robberies, burglaries, and assaults" that had received the same treatment.

Of particular interest was the fact that Gary McCarthy, Chicago's reform superintendent of police since 2011 and a Bill Bratton acolyte, had led the NYPD's COMPSTAT meetings in New York as deputy commissioner of operations.

New York City's COMPSTAT-driven felony crime numbers, it turns out, had also been questioned in 2012 by John A. Eterno—a former NYPD captain—and the highly respected criminologist Eli B. Silverman in their book *The Crime Numbers Game*. Within the New York

Police Department, they charged at the time, "crimes are being downgraded, crime scenes revised, and the seriousness of the crime downplayed."

There was plenty of smoke in both Chicago and New York over the accusations, but no smoking gun as there was in Los Angeles. Nevertheless, according to Chicago police statistics, major violent and property crimes dropped 56 percent from 2010 to 2013—a number that Bernstein and Isackson describe as bordering on "the miraculous." Little or nothing of this, however, made its way onto the national stage. But other events with far more sizzle soon would.

****

That summer Bill Bratton was dealing with his own problems in New York City. He'd been rehired as NYPD commissioner in January 2014 by the city's new mayor, Bill de Blasio.

At first they appeared a very odd couple indeed.

An unabashed progressive populist, the white, underdog de Blasio had deep ties to the city's black, left-wing political activists—a group that included his African-American wife—and had run for mayor in 2013 as a sharp critic of stop-and-frisk, a key issue in the race. He'd even employed his charming biracial teenage son, Dante, in a highly effective campaign commercial in which he labeled his father "the only one who will end a stop-and-frisk era that unfairly targets people of color." De Blasio's candidacy soon caught fire, and he went on to win a resounding victory significantly propelled by an astounding 95 percent of the African-American vote.

Bratton, on the other hand, was mistrusted by many of de Blasio's most ardent supporters for introducing and championing stop-and-frisk in New York City and never disavowing it.

But after meeting together over a dozen times, he and de Blasio apparently reached an agreement that at the very least stop-and-frisk would have to be dramatically scaled back, and throughout 2014 they would publicly speak as one on the issue.

De Blasio's reasons for hiring Bratton were obvious and would become far more so as Bratton's stature among conservatives, older cops, and bellicose police unions helped de Blasio recover from ugly attacks that would come his way later in the year.

That stature was, of course, the product of experience derived from successfully transforming the New York City Transit Police—and police departments in Boston, New York City, and Los Angeles—and learning key political lessons—like how to work well with mayors—along the way.

Bratton's desire for the job was more complex: money; status; vindication after being forced out as commissioner back in '96 by Giuliani; an *absolute* love of the reform game and playing it out again on America's biggest stage; and a legacy that he was very much aware could be tarnished if he himself didn't fix it.

Now, in New York, under a new, progressive mayor, Bratton would have the opportunity to end the NYPD's repressive policing tactics and remake its culture into a community-policing model without undoing his "broken windows" strategy.

Done right, done judiciously as part of a wider community-policing strategy, broken-windows enforcement can be a useful tool in decreasing the kind of quality-of-life crimes like public urination and intoxication, aggressive street prostitution, and panhandling. Done wrong, however, the practice can often lead to police confrontations with people who feel they're simply being harassed by police acting out yet another variation of stop-and-frisk. After an interview with Bratton, *Politico* summed up his vision of broken-windows policing as "Most of the time, the level of enforcement [of] broken windows [will now be guided] by the complaints and standards of the neighborhood."

But he'd start the process by tackling stop-and-frisk. By 2014, New York was no longer the high-crime, sometimes out-of-control city it had been in the eighties and early nineties, and hadn't been for close to twenty years. Nevertheless, the NYPD's stop-and-frisk enforcement in the city's ghettos, barrios, and housing projects had grown ever more intense, becoming so omnipresent, heavy-handed, and racially divisive that by 2014 it seemed to be no longer politically sustainable.

When Bratton's predecessor, Ray Kelly, was named commissioner by Mayor Michael Bloomberg in 2002, for example, the NYPD stopped-

questioned-and/or-frisked over 97,000 New Yorkers. By 2011, that
number had exploded to over 685,000. That same year the total number of black males aged fourteen to twenty-four who were stopped
would *exceed* the entire population of the city's young black men in
that age group by ten thousand—that is, a large portion of the 158,000
black males in that age group were stopped more than 168,000 times.

In the summer of 2013, criticism peaked when a federal judge ruled
that New York's stop-and-frisk policy was unconstitutional racial profiling. The ruling was then underscored in 2014 by de Blasio's decision as
mayor to drop the Bloomberg administration's appeal of the judge's verdict and by his agreement to make all the changes the judge had ordered.

As he did so, de Blasio described his actions as "a defining moment
in [New York] history . . . for millions of our families, especially those
with young men of color."

Bratton too had something to say on that day.

Making a "solemn promise to every New Yorker regardless of where
they were born . . . live, or . . . [what they] look like," Bratton declared
that NYPD officers would no longer "break the law to enforce the law."
"These values," he added, "aren't at odds with keeping New Yorkers
safe, they are essential to long-term public safety, [and] we are committed to fulfilling our obligations under this agreement."

****

In July of 2014 Bill Bratton was forced to momentarily set aside his
focus on stop-and-frisk when broken-windows policing came under attack. Both Bratton and Kelly were strong proponents of the policy. But
the death of Eric Garner over an insignificant broken-windows/quality-
of-life crime—which, not incidentally, had been caused by a choke hold
banned by the NYPD since 1993—had changed the dynamic.

In response to Garner's death, Bratton ordered three days of retraining for all thirty-five thousand NYPD officers, focused on avoiding physical and verbal confrontations when making arrests. Bratton described
the program as similar to the firearms retraining that all officers are
required to periodically undergo. But he made no bones about where
he was headed.

"It was evident," Bratton said at the time, "that there was the need for a fundamental shift in the culture of the department, from an over-arching focus on police activity [i.e., stops and arrests], to an emphasis on collaborative problem-solving with the community."

****

December 1, 2014, was an all-good-news day for Bill Bratton, a stop-and-frisk announcement day. The groundwork for the stop-and-frisk news conference that he and Mayor de Blasio were holding had been laid that November, when they'd banned one of stop-and-frisk's most notorious arrest subterfuges: ordering a person stopped by an officer to empty his pockets and, as previously pointed out, then arresting him for *"displaying"* marijuana in public. Following tough public criticism, Ray Kelly had ordered the practice ended in 2013, but Bratton and de Blasio had *codified* it, making possession of less than twenty-five grams of marijuana (fifty to sixty joints) a simple violation punishable by a $100 fine. Period. No jail time or criminal record involved.

Today, however, they intended to announce something far bigger. In 2013 Ray Kelly had also reduced stop-and-frisks by one-third following the federal court's damning stop-and-frisk ruling. And as they decreased, so did the city's homicides, which fell to 335, a new record low. That was good but tentative news for opponents of stop-and-frisk.

Facing reporters now, Bratton and de Blasio had far bigger news. Through December 1, 2014, homicides in the city had dropped yet again to a new record low (that by year's end would total 328). Robberies, meanwhile, had fallen by 14 percent, and burglaries, rapes, and grand larcenies had declined as well—all good, solid numbers right in line with the similar decreases of recent years.

Viewed, however, as a gauge of just how important stop-and-frisk had been in suppressing crime, they were spectacular. As crime was decreasing, stop-and-frisks had plunged 79 *percent* in the first nine months of 2014. By year's end, Bratton predicted, the department would record fewer than 50,000 stops—a fraction of the more than 685,000 its officers had made in 2011.

For over a decade as commissioner, Ray Kelly had insisted that the intense, targeted stopping-and-frisking of poor, young black and brown men was crucial to maintaining New York's low crime rate and could be scaled back only at the city's peril. The biggest beneficiaries of New York's crime decline, Kelly had insisted, were the young black and brown men whose lives had been saved by the tactic—and some of them might well have been.

But the young men allegedly benefiting from Kelly's brand of intense stop-and-frisk were also being crushed not just by harsh, stagnant economic truths and the dog-eat-dog violence of ghetto and barrio life but also by cops bent on stopping and busting them for whatever they could and saddling them with criminal records. Ray Kelly rarely mentioned that part of the equation. In 2014, Bill Bratton, the father of the modern use of stop-and-frisk, had the guts and fortitude to prove Ray Kelly and himself wrong—at least for 2014.

****

As December was closing, other news also augured well for the city's reform activists. A follow-up survey revealed that two-thirds of New Yorkers believed that Daniel Pantaleo—the officer whose choke hold had killed Eric Garner—should have been indicted.

Bill de Blasio, meanwhile, was defending the protesters rallying against the killings of Eric Garner and Michael Brown. At one point he emotionally explained how he and his African-American wife—like so many parents of black and mixed-race boys—had had to engage their son, Dante, in "painful conversations [about] taking special care" when dealing with the police.

At the same time, however, the pattern of largely nonviolent behavior by New York demonstrators and police, established that summer following Eric Garner's death, would grow far more intense in late November and early December when the Brown grand jury in Ferguson and the Garner grand jury in Staten Island both announced their refusals to indict the officers responsible for the two men's deaths.

During those demonstrations there were scuffles, an officer had his nose broken, Bratton had fake blood thrown on him as he monitored a demonstration in Times Square, and some protesters vociferously cursed and taunted the city cops monitoring them.

What was important and often overlooked was that the NYPD's actions during the demonstrations had not become the focus of the events, as they had in 2010 when officers angrily manhandled and pepper-sprayed Occupy Wall Street demonstrators.

In the days that followed there were protests in Philadelphia, Chicago, Oakland, Seattle, San Francisco, and many other cities, and at colleges and universities. Harvard and about forty other medical schools across America held demonstrations protesting Brown and Garner's deaths, and NBA superstars LeBron James and Kobe Bryant wore "I Can't Breathe" T-shirts as they warmed up for games.

The momentum, both in New York and nationwide, seemed to be with the reformers.

Until it wasn't: until December 20, 2014, when a deranged black man named Ismaaiyl Brinsley shot and killed NYPD officers Rafael Ramos and Wenjian Liu in broad daylight as they sat unsuspecting in a patrol car in Brooklyn. Their murders, it turned out, would do more than end their lives. They would also radically change the conversation from de Blasio and Bratton's apparent success in dramatically reducing stop-and-frisks while lowering the homicide rate to visceral, tribal outrage from the city's cops and conservatives aimed not at the killer of the police officers but at both de Blasio personally and at the reforms he and Bratton had been initiating in general.

Most stunning was their use of Brinsley's declared motive of revenge for Brown's and Garner's deaths to try to draw a causal link from de Blasio and the protesters to the officers' murders.

"A predictable outcome of divisive anti-cop rhetoric by de Blasio and Attorney General Holder," tweeted George Pataki, the Republican former governor of New York, after the officers' killings.

On ABC News, meanwhile, Ray Kelly asserted that de Blasio had run on an "anti-police campaign" in 2013, and that the mayor's conversations with his son about taking care when dealing with the police had been what "set off this [post-murder] firestorm."

Pat Lynch, the head of the NYPD's twenty-five-thousand-strong rank-and-file patrol officers' union, the Patrolmen's Benevolent Association (PBA), went even further, declaring that the dead officers' blood "starts on the steps of City Hall, in the office of the mayor."

Earlier, at the hospital where the two officers had been taken, well over a dozen cops in and out of uniform had turned their backs in unison in a show of disrespect as de Blasio and Bratton walked down the hallway. Thousands of police officers from around the country would attend the funerals of Ramos and Liu, and would then join thousands more active and retired NYPD officers in full uniform in open disrespect as they too turned their backs to the mayor as he rose to speak.

****

From the hindsight of 2015, it's evident that Bill Bratton did an enormous amount of heavy lifting in the struggle to move American policing away from the repressive tactics he once championed and that the nation witnessed in Ferguson, Cleveland, and other cities in 2014.

Ever since the fugitive slave laws and Reconstruction, that kind of policing has had as one of its primary missions—in the North, the South, and the West—the suppression of black Americans and the maintenance of Jim Crow as an alternative to doing the hard work of truly dealing with America's obscenely cruel racist legacy.

In February 2015 James B. Comey gave a speech remarkable for an FBI director, saying that "all of us in law enforcement must be honest enough to acknowledge that much of our history is not pretty. At many points in American history, law enforcement enforced the status quo that was often brutally unfair to disadvantaged groups. . . . That experience should be part of every American's consciousness, and law enforcement's role in that experience, including in recent times, must be remembered. It is," he summed up, "our cultural inheritance."

****

Meanwhile, the scenes from Ferguson reminded us that "recent times" means the last thirty years of America's unprecedented, never-ending wars on drug crimes—which law professor Michelle Alexander, in exploring the connections of those wars to past repression, quite rightly called "the New Jim Crow."

And springing out of those wars has been the stunning militarization of American policing.

In the early seventies President Richard Nixon officially declared America's drug policy a "war on drugs." What we got was a war on us. By the mid-1980s two to three thousand drug raids a year were taking place. By 2010 the number had soared to seventy to eighty thousand per year. An ACLU study of SWAT teams in 2011 and 2012, reported in the *Los Angeles Times*, revealed that of the twenty police agencies examined, "eight to ten SWAT team deployments were to . . . serve search warrants primarily in drug cases," and that "two-thirds of the deployments involved breaking down doors," often using terrifying combat-style flash-bang grenades; were focused on small-time dealers or users; and were based on unsubstantiated tips from informants. Since 2000, at least fifty Americans have been "seriously injured, maimed, or killed by such flash-bang [grenades]."

At the same time, civil asset forfeiture laws, originally aimed at organized crime and drug kingpins, were increasingly being used against ordinary citizens who had never been charged with a crime by police departments looking for extra money to supplement their budgets. The money, vehicles, and other goods seized by them would skyrocket from a value of $27 million in 1985 to almost $4.2 *billion* in 2012. In the spring of 2014, in fact, the U.S. Justice Department, in a searing condemnation of the Ferguson, Missouri, police department, found that its officers had for years been singling out the city's black motorists to disproportionately stop, ticket, arrest, and fine as a way to finance the police department and the criminal justice system.

Greatly accelerating the drug war's militarization was $4 billion in surplus military equipment donated by the U.S. Defense Department to police forces around the county since the mid-1990s and $34 *billion* in "terrorism grants" made by the Department of Homeland Security since 9/11. By 2014 over one thousand such programs existed, giving away surplus military guns, uniforms, helicopters, and other combat gear and equipment to America's police forces.

****

As I write this, it's far too early to know if America's law enforcement establishment will take the lessons of 2014 to heart.

President Barack Obama has tried to drive home some of these messages. During his tenure, the number of police organizations placed under some form of federal oversight has grown dramatically and now includes more than twenty cities, as diverse as Seattle, New Orleans, Oakland, Cincinnati, Cleveland, New York, Detroit, Albuquerque, and Newark. Following the killings of Michael Brown and Eric Garner, Obama also created a "Task Force on 21st Century Policing" focused on the kind of community policing Bill Bratton has been spearheading in New York.

Both are steps in the right direction. But small steps. It's a mistake to think the problem is simply limited to bad or indifferent police agencies. They have to be viewed against a backdrop of a much larger societal dysfunction indisputably—and historically—tied to inequities of race, class, income, and opportunity; the politics and the business of crime and guns; the politicized state of our courts; the cruel recklessness of our sentencing laws; and the disastrous state of our public schools. All these seemingly disparate forces together keep doing one thing well: feeding generation after generation of young American men into the world's largest prison system, with no end in sight.

In 2014 both the American people and the American press started asking hard questions about the current state of American policing. Those questions need to continue even as others are asked. Such as, when will our police departments be relieved of many of the ancillary tasks they have been charged with carrying out over the last thirty years, like being responsible for the homeless and mentally ill—tasks to which, as Ta-Nehisi Coates points out, they are ill-suited by training, mission, and inclination to perform? And as we inch toward defining what a new paradigm for our police should be, we need to ask how we can begin shaping that goal in our violent, racist, gun-loving society. And when will we start recruiting and training police officers who are genuinely committed to community-building and service and don't want to run around like gung-ho marines in our nation's poorest neighborhoods?

Increasingly, the answers to these and dozens of other similar questions are out there—the data is in, the pilot projects are done, and enough is known to start a true transformation of a notoriously risk-averse, blindly resistant police establishment whose leaders mostly think alike and reinforce one another's prejudices and often willful ignorance.

Those answers are coming not just from criminologists and the relatively few thoughtful, committed reformers within the criminal justice system. They're coming as well from behavioral and social scientists, from anthropologists, from public health experts, from neuroscientists and experts in pre- and postnatal care—from disciplines that are exploding with new revelations and information almost daily. If applied correctly and over a long term, this information could almost certainly dramatically scale back both crime and the millions of broken, impoverished lives we help produce and then imprison for decades in numbers so much higher than those of any other industrial nation that it boggles the mind.

The title of Ta-Nehisi Coates's essay is "The Myth of Police Reform." In it, he concludes by pointing out that "a reform that begins with the officer on the beat is not reform at all." He's right. American society is now in a major crisis centered on our deeply corrupted politics and institutions and propelled by our New Gilded Age disdain for and dehumanization of the poor and powerless. There's no denying it, because it's undeniable. Nevertheless, you have to start somewhere in a multifront struggle, and American policing is a good place to begin.

ACKNOWLEDGMENTS

I've been writing about the LAPD for over twenty-five years, and this book—my second about the department—is the culmination of what I've learned.

During those years I accrued an enormous debt to scores of L.A. police-beat reporters, first at the long-defunct *Los Angeles Herald Examiner* and then for decades at the *Los Angeles Times*. Their methodical work of daily holding the LAPD accountable (when L.A.'s politicians didn't dare) has enormously enriched my own reporting, both in the writing of *Blue* and in my earlier, character-driven narrative history of the LAPD, *To Protect and to Serve*.

Much of *Blue* is based on historical research, interviews, and other original reporting I did exclusively for this book, but some is based on my original reporting for other publications over the decades, including *To Protect and to Serve*. Some passages from that book and from my previously published material have been rewritten and integrated into *Blue*, and on several occasions I've included them verbatim, or nearly verbatim.

Among the L.A. reporters who covered the LAPD, I'd particularly like to thank the fearless David Cay Johnston, Bill Boyarsky, Tim Rutten, Joel Rubin, Scott Glover, Matt Lait, Richard Winton, Andrew Blanstein, Joel Sappel, Wayne Satz, Lennie LaGuire, and Mark S. Warnick. I'm also indebted to Kit Rachlis, my editor at both the *LA Weekly* and *Los Angeles* magazine, and to Gary Speaker, my longtime op-ed editor at the *Los Angeles Times*.

Much of *Blue* is about cops and police leadership, and many LAPD officers—past and present—have been extremely generous in helping me understand how and why big-city police organizations—and particularly the LAPD—function as they do.

Over the years no police officer has been more helpful than former LAPD assistant chief David Dotson, who had the audacity to buck the *omertà* that saturates cop culture and critically testify against his department at the 1991 Christopher Commission hearings, earning himself a forced retirement for his trouble.

For the writing of *Blue*, however, I'd particularly like to thank LAPD chief Charlie Beck for his generous time, and for teaching me what it was like to be him as a street cop operating in hostile territory and as he rose through the ranks to become chief.

Bill Bratton—who is second only to the LAPD as a character in *Blue*—was also a key source for this book. The detailed interviews I conducted with him and his wife, Rikki Klieman, were invaluable in writing about the Bratton eras in Los Angeles and New York.

Similarly, Alfred Lomas, Andre "Low Down" Christian, and Ron Noblet were essential to the writing of *Blue*. Ron was key in helping me understand L.A. gangs and in introducing me to Alfred and Andre—who in turn were extraordinarily generous in sharing their life stories as a framework to tell the larger tale of Los Angeles gang life in the era of crack wars and record homicides.

Over the years I've spoken with so many cops it's impossible to mention them all. For the writing of this book, however, I particularly want to thank Sergeant Curtis Woodle, former LAPD assistant chief George Gascon, Deputy Chiefs Pat Gannon and Michael Berkow, and, going back to the 1990s, Chief Willie Williams, Officer Ray Perez, the late Assistant Chief Jesse A. Brewer, and Brien Chapman.

The same holds true of all the non-cops I spoke with who worked within and around the department. Especially helpful were Connie Rice, Peter Bibring, Mike Yamaki, Rabbi Gary Greenebaum, Gerald Chaleff, Anthony De Los Reyes, Johnnie Cochran, Jack Weiss, Katherine Mader, Ann Reiss Lane, Steve Cooley, and Merrick Bobb—a man of astounding grit and courage and a pioneer in monitoring law enforcement organizations, who taught me how to view police departments as living, breathing institutions.

Over the years it took me to write *Blue* I was fortunate to be working at John Jay College's Center on Media Crime and Justice and on the Center's daily Criminal Justice news site, *The Crime Report* (*TCR*). My friends and colleagues there—Ted Guest, Cara Tabachnick, Ricardo Martinez, Graham Kates, and Katti Gray—were a joy to work with and learn from. This was especially true of the center's director and *TCR*'s executive editor, Steve Handelman, an award-winning former foreign correspondent who, as the soul of both our center and *TCR*, has kept our small crew always striving for excellence.

At Simon & Schuster, there a lot of people to thank: Roger Labrie, who bought my book; Karyn Marcus, who as my editor championed *Blue* and always gave me sage advice; Emily Graff, a young editor who picked up where Karyn left off, and with great skill and tact successfully completed the editing of this book, despite having to work with an often crotchety old journalist; and S&S's attorney Eric Rayman, who vetted this book. I also grew to deeply respect S&S's publisher, Jonathan Karp, who on a number of occasions personally assured me of his support for *Blue*, and then kept his word.

Additionally, I'm deeply indebted to the extraordinary Emily Maleki, who, in the midst of giving birth to and then raising twins, never once faulted in her expert researching, fact-checking, and manuscript preparation for *Blue*; to Dr. Benjamin Bloxham; and to the late A. J. (Jack) Langguth—not only for his suggestions in the writing of *Blue* but also for his friendship and mentoring for over thirty years.

Finally, I'm most grateful to my wonderful family: Judy Tanka, Andrea Domanick, Ashley Hendra, Teresa Tanka, Carol Domanick, David Deitch, Anthony Domanick, Cynthia Domanick, and Jason and Avram Deitch.

NOTES

Abbreviations

AP: Associated Press
CNS: City News Service
LADN: Los Angeles Daily News
LAHE: Los Angeles Herald Examiner
LAT: Los Angeles Times
NPR: National Public Radio
NYDN: New York Daily News
NYT: New York Times
PRI: Public Radio International
SCPR: Southern California Public Radio
UPI: United Press International
WSJ: Wall Street Journal

PART ONE: SOMETHING OLD

Alfred Lomas, Wednesday, April 29, 1992

3 *sitting in a Florencia 13 crack house*: Alfred Lomas interview.
4 *Reginald Denny beating*: Hazen, ed., *Inside the L.A. Riots*, 50; "The Untold Story of the LA Riot," *U.S. News & World Report*, May 23, 1993; *Los Angeles Times*, *Understanding the Riots*, 49; "Fit Punishment for the L.A. Mayhem," *NYT*, December 9, 1993; "Bad Cops," *New Yorker*, May 21, 2001.
4 *fifty-six times in eighty-one seconds*: "Juror Says Panel Felt King Actions Were to Blame," *LAT*, April 30, 1992; "The Police Verdict; Los Angeles Policemen

Acquitted in Taped Beating," *NYT*, April 30, 1992; "National Guard Called to Stem Violence After L.A. Officers' Acquittal in Beating," *Washington Post*, April 30, 1992; *Los Angeles Times, Understanding the Riots*, 33. Various accounts of the length of the beating have been given, ranging from eight-one to ninety seconds, depending on the point at which the action on Holliday's tape becomes discernible.

4 *Monadnock PR-24 batons*: "Training: A Casualty on the Street," *LAT*, March 18, 1991; "Friend Relives Night of Police Beating," *NYT*, March 21, 1991; "Police Get a Handle on New Stick," *Philadelphia Inquirer*, January 26, 1992.

4 *[LAPD] officers . . . acquitted of all ten accounts against them but one*: *Los Angeles Times, Understanding the Riots*, 6.

4 *Rodney King beating/injuries*: "The Man Swept Up in the Furor: Friends, Family Say King Was Sometimes Lost but Never Violent," *LAT*, March 17, 1991; "Tape Forever Ties Victim to Beating," *NYT*, March 20, 1991; *Los Angeles Times, Understanding the Riots*, 33.

4 *"jam your toe"*: " 'I Was Just Trying to Stay Alive,' King Tells Federal Jury," *LAT*, March 10, 1993; "Rodney King Testifies on Beating: 'I Was Just Trying to Stay Alive,' " *NYT*, March 10, 1993.

4 *Simi Valley . . . with a black population of 2 percent*: U.S. Bureau of the Census, census of 1990; "King Case Shifts to Courtroom in Simi Valley," *LAT*, February 4, 1992. "Poverty Rate Fell in 1980s, Figures Show," *LAT*, May 12, 1992, lists the 1990 ethnic breakdown of Los Angeles County, quoting the census, as 66 percent white, 26 percent Latino, 5 percent Asian, and 2 percent black.

4 *Simi Valley . . . 4,000 active police officers*: "NAACP to Monitor Trial of 4 Officers," *LAT*, January 9, 1992; "Days of Rage," *U.S. News and World Report*, May 11, 1992.

4 *LAPD's 7,900-member force*: *Los Angeles Times, Understanding the Riots*, 74; "Where Were L.A. Police When the Rioting Began?" Times News Services, May 1, 1992.

4 *Judge Stanley Weisberg moves Rodney King trial to Simi Valley*: Hazen, ed., *Inside the L.A. Riots*, 46; "King Case to Be Tried in Ventura County." *LAT*, November 27, 1991.

5 *Verdict-day TV helicopter shots of the still unrescued Reginald Denny*: Alfred Lomas interview.

5 *chunks of concrete*: *Los Angeles Times, Understanding the Riots*, 49 and 50.

5 *"Rodney King! Rodney King!"*: "Bad Cops."

5 *"Fuck y'all, we killin' . . . Cops gonna die tonight . . . it's Uzi-time"*: "Uprising: Hip Hop & the LA Riots," VH1, first aired on May 1, 2012; photographer Bart Bartholomew's observations; *Los Angeles Times, Understanding the Riots*, 52.

5 *looting and burning of Tom's Liquor and Deli*: *Los Angeles Times, Understanding the Riots*, 52.

5 *Lomas, a Chicano U.S. Marine Corps veteran:* Alfred Lomas interview.

5 *enforcer:* Ibid.

6 *smashing a concrete block:* "Bad Cops."

6 *dancing around:* Ibid.

6 *stealing his wallet:* Hazen, ed., *Inside the L.A. Riots,* 43; "After the Riots: Four Held in Attack at Riots' Outset," *NYT,* May 13, 1992.

6 could *relate:* Alfred Lomas interview.

6 *semi-illiterate high school dropout:* "Rodney King Unsure on Beating Details," *NYT,* March 11, 1993; "Rodney King Seen as Catalyst for Policing Change," AP, June 18, 2012.

6 *worked at Dodger Stadium:* "Profile: Rodney G. King," *LAT,* April 19, 1993; *Los Angeles Times, Understanding the Riots,* 33.

6 *Baby Huey image on the street:* "The Man Swept Up in the Furor: Friends, Family Say King Was Sometimes Lost but Never Violent"; *Los Angeles Times, Understanding the Riots,* 34.

6 *$200 robbery of a 99 Market: Los Angeles Times, Understanding the Riots,* 34; "The Man Swept Up in the Furor"; "Tape Forever Ties Victim to Beating."

6 *on parole:* "Tape Forever Ties Victim to Beating."

6 *Forty-ounce Olde English 800 malt liquor:* "All you could hear was . . . bones being broken," *New York Times News Service,* May 21, 1991; "Friend Relives Night of Police Beating."

6 *speeding down the freeway:* "No Charges Filed Against Suspect Beaten by Police," *LAT,* March 7, 1991.

6 *Scared of being sent back to prison:* "Excerpts of Testimony on Chase and Beating," AP, March 10, 1993.

6 *white economy-sized Hyundai:* "The Man Swept Up in the Furor"; "The Rodney King Affair," March 24, 1991; *Los Angeles Times, Understanding the Riots,* 33.

6 *twice zapped with 50,000-volt Taser darts:* "The Man Swept Up in the Furor"; "Rodney King Testifies About Night of Beating," *NYT,* January 22, 1993; Independent Commission on the Los Angeles Police Department, *Report of the Independent Commission on the Los Angeles Police Department,* 6.

6 *hog-tied:* "King Suffered Only Cuts, Paramedic Tells Court," *LAT,* March 19, 1992; "Videotaped Beating by Officers Puts Full Glare on Brutality Issue," *NYT,* March 18, 1991.

6 *Twenty-seven other responding cops:* Independent Commission on the Los Angeles Police Department, *Report of the Independent Commission on the Los Angeles Police Department,* 11; Domanick, *To Protect and To Serve,* 375; *Los Angeles Times, Understanding the Riots,* 33.

7 *George Holliday, wielding a handheld video camera:* "Videotaped Beating by Officers Puts Full Glare on Brutality Issue"; "Cameraman's Test Puts Him in the Spotlight," *LAT,* March 7, 1991; *Los Angeles Times, Understanding the Riots,* 33.

7   *The crack-house crew, in short, understood*: Alfred Lomas interview.
7   *"basically consisted of three or four cops"*: Ibid.
7   *"supposed to work"*: "Their Lives Consumed, Officers Await 2d Trial," *NYT*, February 2, 1993.
7   *"Wow! The cops are beating his ass"*: Alfred Lomas interview.
8   *"a lot more than just whack Rodney"*: David Dotson interview.
8   *"And once their report was handed in"*: Ibid.
8   *Reginald Denny's battered body*: "Days of Rage"; *Los Angeles Times, Understanding the Riots*, 49; "Fit Punishment for the L.A. Mayhem"; author's observations.
8   *report to a police command center thirty blocks away*: *Los Angeles Times, Understanding the Riots*, 50.
8   *LAPD leaves Florence and Normandie*: Hazen, ed., *Inside the L.A. Riots*, 51; "Where Were L.A. Police When the Rioting Began?"; *Los Angeles Times, Understanding the Riots*, 50, 52, and 61; Marika Gerrard, Los Angeles News Service, Bart Bartholomew's observations; "Uprising: Hip Hop & the LA Riots"; *ABC 7 Live* aerial shot, April 29, 1992.
8   *"Where the fuck are the cops?"*: Alfred Lomas interview.

Tom Bradley, Wednesday, April 29, 1992, First African Methodist Episcopal Church; Bill Parker, Present in the Ether

9   *two thousand people . . . First African Methodist Episcopal Church*: *Los Angeles Times, Understanding the Riots*, 52.
9   *"Come Help Us Stop the Madness"*: Hazen, ed., *Inside the L.A. Riots*, 31.
9   *First AME Church in Los Angeles/response to Rodney King verdict*: Hazen, ed., *Inside the L.A. Riots*, 31, 35, 44, and 108–9; *Los Angeles Times, Understanding the Riots*, 52 and 59; "Uprising: Hip Hop & the LA Riots"; author's observations.
9   *Tom Bradley at First AME Church*: Author's observations; Domanick, *To Protect and To Serve*, 3–4.
9   *Tom Bradley was seventy-four years old on April 29, 1992*: Bradley's date of birth: December 29, 1917.
9   *Passion of the Christ stained-glass windows*: Hazen, ed., *Inside the L.A. Riots*, 31; author's observations.
9   *born the son of a humble, churchgoing housemaid*: Galm, *The Impossible Dream*, 15–17, 47, and 50.
9   *integrated Los Angeles public schools*: Ibid., 25.
9   *track star*: Ibid., 23.
10   *UCLA/joins LAPD/law school/lieutenant*: Ibid., 24, 39, 62, and 69–70.
10   *Bradley elected Los Angeles city councilman in 1963*: *Los Angeles Times, Understanding the Riots*, 21; Galm, *The Impossible Dream*, 119. Bradley was one of three African-American men elected in 1963, but he was not the first. Gilbert

Lindsay was the first. Tom Bradley was elected three months later, in April 1963. Billy Mills was the third.

10 *Bradley-Parker confrontation*: "Riot Hearings Boil, Parker, Bradley in Row over 'Mystery Man,'" *LAHE*, September 14, 1965; "Bradley Struggles to Overcome His Anti-LAPD Image," *LAT*, October 14, 1986; "Gates on Gates," *LAT*, October 24, 1992; *Los Angeles Times, Understanding the Riots*, 13.

10 *Badlands of South Dakota*: Webb, *The Badge*, 245; *L.A. Police Beat*, September 1966; "Shadow Caster," *Los Angeles Magazine*, April 2010.

10 *alcohol*: Gates, *Chief*, 32.

10 *Parker basis for Spock*: "Daryl Gates' Real Legacy," *LA Observed*, April 16, 2010; "Shadow Caster."

10 *bad heart*: "L.A. Chief Overlooked a Bad Heart to Serve," *Washington Post*, July 18, 1966; "Last Man Out of Parker Center Turns Off the Lights," *LA Observed*, January 15, 2013.

11 *465 square miles*: City of Los Angeles Department of Public Works.

11 *top-down paramilitary organization*: "Leave Chief Parker Behind," *LAT*, April 11, 2009; NPR, January 12, 2012.

11 *170,000 by 1950*: *Los Angeles Times, Understanding the Riots*, 11.

11 *"45 percent of Los Angeles will be Negro"*: "Gates's Hell," *Vanity Fair*, August 1991; Dunne, *Another City, Not My Own*, 62; Hazen, ed., *Inside the L.A. Riots*, 23; "Chief Parker Molded LAPD Image—Then Came the '60s," *LAT*, May 25, 1992.

11 *UCLA study . . . fifty thousand people . . . Watts Riots*: "In L.A., Burning All Illusions: Urban America Sees Its Future," *Nation*, June 1, 1992; Hazen, ed., *Inside the L.A. Riots*, 98.

12 *Bradley was addressing a throng*: Author's observations.

12 *Tom Bradley at First AME Church at podium*: Domanick, *To Protect and To Serve*, 3–4; author's observations.

12 *TV monitors . . . shots of Reginald Denny*: Hazen, ed., *Inside the L.A. Riots*, 31.

12 *"I was shocked, I was stunned"*: "The Reaction," *LAT*, April 30, 1992; "Ashes of a Mayor's Dreams," *LAT*, May 1, 1992; "Understanding the Riots, Part 1," *LAT*, May 11, 1992; author's observations.

12 *"certainly weren't watching that videotape"*: Author's observations.

12 *Defeated in his first run for mayor in 1969*: Jesse Brewer interview; Galm, *The Impossible Dream*, 159.

12 *labeled an enemy of the LAPD*: "Bradley Accorded Edge Over Yorty," AP, May 27, 1973; "Bradley Struggles to Overcome His Anti-LAPD Image."

12 *1969 Los Angeles mayoral campaign*: ABC, April 2, 1969; CBS, May 6, 1969.

12 *background*: "Yorty's Eye Is on the Big Apple," *New York Times Magazine*, September 17, 1967.

12 *1973 Los Angeles mayoral campaign*: CBS, May 29, 1973; NBC, June 31, 1973.

12 *liberal political majority:* "Recalling Sleepy Lagoon," *LAT*, May 10, 1991; "Tom Bradley Topped Dinkins in White Vote," *NYT*, September 28, 1989; "Bradley Wins in Los Angeles," *Chicago Tribune*, May 31, 1973.

13 *American Nazi Party picketing:* Herald Examiner Collection, Los Angeles Public Library.

13 *Bill Parker would die in office in 1966:* "Widow of Former Police Chief Parker Eulogized," *LAT*, February 24, 2000; "The LAPD: Chief Parker," Los Angeles Police Department website, accessed February 6, 2015, http://www.lapdonline.org/history_of_the_lapd/content_basic_view/1110.

13 *ironclad civil service statutes:* Domanick, *To Protect and To Serve*, 151–52.

13 *In six days of rioting (statistics):* "Watts Riots, 40 Years Later," *LAT*, August 11, 2005; *Los Angeles Times, Understanding the Riots*, 10.

13 *In 1967 . . . riots had broken out in 150 American cities:* "After the Riots: From Riots of 60's to Riots of the 90's, a Frustrating Search to Heal a Nation," *NYT*, May 8, 1992.

13 *rioting in over a hundred American cities:* "Facts About Martin Luther King Jr.," Reuters, April 4, 2008; "Shoot to Kill . . . Shoot to Maim," *Chicago Reader*, April 4, 2002.

14 *lost both his bids for governor in the 1980s:* "Tom Bradley, Mayor in Era of Los Angeles Growth, Dies," *NYT*, September 30, 1998.

14 *blue ribbon commission:* "Rodney King's March 2, 1991, Traffic Stop and Beating Turned LA into a Riot Zone; Then Changed It," *LADN*, March 2, 2011.

14 *"a significant group of officers":* Independent Commission on the Los Angeles Police Department, *Report of the Independent Commission on the Los Angeles Police Department*, 2 and 4.

14 *Findings of the Christopher Commission report:* Ibid., iv, xiv, xix, 98, and 204.

15 *live footage of an LAPD guard shack:* Author's observations, April 29, 1992.

15 *Finally finished with his weary speech:* Author's observations.

15 *the riot was spreading . . . protesters screamed and pounded their fists:* Hazen, ed., *Inside the L.A. Riots*, 108–9.

Charlie Beck, Wednesday, April 29, 1992, Parker Center

15 *"Where are all your patrol units?":* Charlie Beck interview.

16 *"it would have consumed and squeezed the life out of [him]":* Ibid.

16 *charter member . . . CRASH:* Rice, *Power Concedes Nothing*, 255; CNN, November 3, 2009.

16 *his father was a retired LAPD deputy chief:* Connie Rice interview; "Three Generations of Cops LAPD Dynasty," *People*, February 22, 2010; "Cops Count. Character Counts," *LADN*, November 3, 2009.

16 *his sister an LAPD officer . . . detective:* CBS, November 17, 2010.

16 *his wife a Los Angeles County sheriff:* CNN, November 3, 2009.

16 *son and daughter would also both join the LAPD*: Connie Rice interview; "Cops Count. Character Counts"; CNN, November 3, 2009.

17 *Charlie Beck . . . professional motocross racer*: Charlie Beck interview; "LAPD Chief Charlie Beck's One-Time Dream Career: Dirt Bike Racing," *Orange County Register*, April 16, 2014.

17 *"Fuck Tha Police"*: Niggaz Wit Attitudes (N.W.A), "Fuck Tha Police," recorded 1987–88.

17 *Southeast Division*: Charlie Beck interview.

17 *"They weren't evil people"*: "An Epiphany, and an Evolving Philosophy of Policing," *LAT*, November 15, 2009.

17 *"That . . . was the LAPD's crack-war strategy"*: Charlie Beck interview.

18 *drove his Ford Bronco west, back to Parker Center*: Ibid.

18 *1988 raid on . . . South Central's Dalton Avenue*: "Police Power: Why No One Can Control the LAPD," *LA Weekly*, February 16–22, 1990; Hazen, ed., *Inside the L.A. Riots*, 21; *Los Angeles Times, Understanding the Riots*, 31.

18 *Red Cross . . . temporary shelter*: "The Raid That Still Haunts L.A.," *LAT*, March 14, 2001; "Many Laud Police for Drug Raid on Dalton Ave.," *LAT*, November 13, 1990.

18 *the city paid $3.8 million*: "The Raid That Still Haunts L.A."; "Award in Final Dalton Case OKd by Court," *LAT*, January 23, 1992.

18 *"poorly planned and executed field operation"*: Domanick, *To Protect and To Serve*, 352.

18 *"like having the Marine Corps"*: "Gates Blames Drugs, Gangs for 4% Rise in L.A. Crime," *LAT*, December 25, 1986; "Major Crimes Increase in L.A.," AP, December 26, 1986.

19 *eighty LAPD officers*: "City Won't Have to Pay Dalton Case Legal Fees," *LAT*, January 1, 1993; "Raid of the Day: The 39th & Dalton Edition," *Huffington Post*, February 5, 2013.

Daryl Gates, Wednesday, April 29, 1992, LAPD headquarters

19 *"back to business as usual"*: Charlie Beck interview.

19 *$1 million for police overtime*: "King Jury Still Out; Police Chief Has Big 'Trouble' Fund," Times News Services, April 28, 1992; "Where Were L.A. Police When the Rioting Began?"

19 *"There never was a riot contingency plan"*: Hazen, ed., *Inside the L.A. Riots*, 51.

19 *"The jury was still deliberating in Simi Valley"*: Anthony De Los Reyes interview.

19 *"Nobody believed those officers were going to be acquitted"*: Ann Reiss Lane interview.

20 *"as ready as we ought to be"*: Daryl Gates, City Hall press conference, April 30, 1992.

20 *news release issued by 10 a.m.*: Domanick, *To Protect and To Serve*, 426; Hazen, ed., *Inside the L.A. Riots*, 51.

20 *one thousand detectives . . . go home*: Los Angeles Times, *Understanding the Riots*, 74; Hazen, ed., *Inside the L.A. Riots*, 51; "Where Were L.A. Police When the Rioting Began?"

20 *forty miles away, attending a seminar*: Rothmiller and Goldman, *L.A. Secret Police*, 4; Los Angeles Times, *Understanding the Riots*, 135.

20 *Dotson . . . persona non grata*: David Dotson interview; Webster and Williams, *The City in Crisis*, 15.

20 *Assistant Chief Robert Vernon . . . pending his retirement*: Author interview with police commissioner, May 2, 1992; "Vernon Reveals Plans to Retire This Month," *LAT*, April 16, 1992; Hazen, ed., *Inside the L.A. Riots*, 51.

20 *overseeing of about 85 percent of the department's cops*: "Vernon Injected Religious Views on Job, Officials Say," *LAT*, February 5, 1992.

21 *poor relationship with the Police Commission and Mayor Bradley*: Independent Commission on the Los Angeles Police Department, *Report of the Independent Commission on the Los Angeles Police Department*, 202 and 204; "As Rioting Mounted, Gates Remained at Political Event," *NYT*, May 5, 1992; Los Angeles Times, *Understanding the Riots*, 85.

21 *Gates and Bradley not speaking*: "Bradley and Gates Simply Weren't Speaking When the City Erupted," *LAT*, May 8, 1992; "Los Angeles Mayor Criticizes Chief for Slow Action on Riot," *NYT*, May 4, 1992; Los Angeles Times, *Understanding the Riots*, 85.

21 *no coordination with the Los Angeles Fire Department*: "Top LAPD Officer, Fire Chief Cite Flaws in Police Response," *LAT*, May 8, 1992; "Riots in Los Angeles: The Blue Line; Surprised, Police React Slowly as Violence Spreads," *NYT*, May 1, 1992.

21 *Six hundred buildings*: "King Case Aftermath: A City in Crisis: Officials Discern No Pattern in 4,000 Arson Fires," *LAT*, May 2, 1992; "Watts Riots, 40 Years Later."

21 *"One of the things that overwhelmed us"*: Chief Daryl Gates, City Hall press conference, April 30, 1992.

21 *"not a top priority"*: "Top LAPD Officer, Fire Chief Cite Flaws in Police Response"; Los Angeles Times, *Understanding the Riots*, 135.

21 *"support a strong police department"*: "Chief Parker Molded LAPD Image— Then Came the '60s"; Dunne, *Another City, Not My Own*, 62; Hazen, ed., *Inside the L.A. Riots*, 23.

21 *Morale in the department was at an all-time low*: "10 Years After Rodney King," AP, March 3, 2001; Los Angeles Times, *Understanding the Riots*, 39.

21 *"I think there was a lot of discussion"*: Chief Daryl Gates, City Hall press conference, April 30, 1992.

22 *"I'm elated"*: "Verdict Greeted with Relief and Elation Among LAPD Officers," *LAT*, April 30, 1992.

22 *"I don't think [Daryl Gates] understood the ramifications"*: Hazen, ed., *Inside the L.A. Riots*, 51; Stanley Sheinbaum interview.

22 *"The people who get promoted"*: Thomas Windham interview.

22 *"a certain bunker mentality"*: Stephen Reinhardt interview.

Charlie Beck, Wednesday, April 29, 1992, Parker Center

23 *Arriving at Parker Center*: Charlie Beck interview.

23 *Civic Center protests/riots*: *Los Angeles Times*, *Understanding the Riots*, 63; Hazen, ed., *Inside the L.A. Riots*, 31; author's observations.

23 *"No justice, no peace"*: Hazen, ed., *Inside the L.A. Riots*, 31 and 35.

23 *Parker Center riots/protests*: Ibid.; *Los Angeles Times*, *Understanding the Riots*, 63 and 47–49.

23 *"You should be out here with us throwing stones"*: Hazen, ed., *Inside the L.A. Riots*, 35.

24 *"It was . . . the most sobering, somber experience"*: Anthony De Los Reyes interview.

Daryl Gates, Wednesday, April 29, 1992, Brentwood, California

24 *Gates heads to Brentwood fund-raiser*: "Where Were L.A. Police When the Rioting Began?"; *Los Angeles Times*, *Understanding the Riots*, 49 and 74; Hazen, ed., *Inside the L.A. Riots*, 43.

24 *amendment to limit an LAPD chief's lifetime tenure*: "As Rioting Mounted, Gates Remained at Political Event"; "What Could Be More Political Than Gates?" *LAT*, May 27, 1992; "After the Riots: The Day L.A. Changed," *LAT*, May 31, 2012.

24 *Calls for Gates to resign*: "Group Seeks Gates' Apology for Remarks," *LAT*, February 15, 1991; "Chief Gates Should Quit, Sen. Biden Says," *LAT*, March 18, 1991; *CBS Evening News*, March 19, 1991; "The Times Poll: 31% of Angelenos Say Gates Should Quit Now," *LAT*, March 22, 1991; "3 Congressmen Call for the Resignation or Removal of Gates," *LAT*, March 23, 1991; "L.A. Mayor Asks Police Chief to Quit," *LAT*, April 3, 1991; "Crisis in the LAPD: The Rodney King Case," *LAT*, April 5, 1991.

25 *"I don't want to be mayor of Los Angeles"*: "Ed Davis Calls It Quits: 'I Have Served Long Enough,'" *LAT*, January 29, 1992; Hazen, ed., *Inside the L.A. Riots*, 23.

26 *eight hundred thousand immigrants from the developing world*: Fix and Passel, *Immigration and Immigrants*, 29.

26 *By 1990, 87 percent . . . were Latinos and/or other minorities*: California Department of Education, Educational Demographics Unit—CBEDS.

26 *By the late eighties . . . 40 percent of the city's population*: *1990 U.S. Census of Population and Housing Summary*, cited in Independent Commission on the Los

Angeles Police Department, *Report of the Independent Commission on the Los Angeles Police Department.*

27 *Named chief in 1978, Daryl Gates:* "A Chronology: Key Events in the Life of Former LAPD Chief Daryl F. Gates," *LAT*, November 11, 2011; "Daryl Gates' Downfall," *LAT*, April 28, 2010.

27 *Gates was raised in abject poverty:* "Daryl F. Gates and 'the Sting of Poverty' That Followed Him to Grade School," *LAT*, April 16, 2010; "Report on King Beating May Alter Gates' Legacy," *LAT*, July 8, 1991.

27 *son of an alcoholic and absentee father:* "Controversial LAPD Chief," *LAT*, April 17, 2010; "Report on King Beating May Alter Gates' Legacy."

27 *"the last stand of native-born Protestant Americans":* "A Mayor Who Stood for Reform," *LAT*, November 16, 1997.

29 *"thin blue line":* "Chief Parker Molded LAPD Image—Then Came the '60s"; "Understanding the Riots—Six Months Later," *LAT*, November 17, 1992; *Los Angeles Times, Understanding the Riots*, 15.

29 *"Man, the most predatory":* Blue Ribbon Review Panel et al., "Rampart Reconsidered: The Search for Real Reform Seven Years Later," 17.

29 *"the most lawless nation on Earth":* " 'Wild Bill' Parker, Scrappy Lawman of the New West," *Eugene Register-Guard*, May 24, 1964.

29 *"Now, look at him":* Tom Reddin interview.

30 *"Spacco il capo":* "Philadelphia's Electoral Surprises," *Baltimore Sun*, June 1, 1991; "Rizzo Claims He Could Stop Italy's Red Brigade," AP, July 1, 1978; "Rizzo Boasts Philadelphia's Police Are 'Toughest' in World," *Toledo Blade*, August 13, 1979.

30 *"Make Attila the Hun look like a faggot":* "The Nation: Thoughts of Chairman Rizzo," *Time*, October 24, 1977.

30 *"Casual drug users should be shot":* "Casual Drug Users Should Be Shot, Gates Says," *LAT*, September 6, 1990.

30 *"Who would want to work with one?":* "Requiem for Daryl Gates," *Crime Report*, April 18, 2010.

30 *"lucky that was all he had broken":* "Police Power: Why No One Can Control the LAPD"; "Gates Defends His Officers' Search Methods in Court," *LAT*, November 30, 1988; "A Question of Respect: Judgment Against Gates Makes Statement for Minority Rights," *LAT*, December 7, 1988.

30 *"an inspiration to the nation":* Face the Nation, CBS, May 19, 1985; "The Region: Review of L.A. Police Tactics Requested," *LAT*, May 23, 1985; "Philadelphia Action Called 'Last Resort' Against Move's Threats," *NYT*, May 20, 1985; "Mayor Releases Threatening MOVE Letter," AP, May, 20, 1985.

30 *"jumped on [his] heroes list":* Domanick, *To Protect and To Serve*, 297; "Philadelphia Action Called 'Last Resort' Against Move's Threats."

30 *"Battering Ram":* "L.A. Police Battering Ram," *LAT*, February 8, 1985; "Uprising: Hip Hop & the LA Riots"; *Los Angeles Times, Understanding the Riots*, 29.

31 *two terrified black women and a couple of kids:* "L.A. Police Battering Ram."

31   *"To fire a police chief"*: Gates, *Chief,* 31.

32   *A competitive runner, Gates:* Tim Rutten interview.

32   *"In a lot of cases . . . an officer will appeal to the Chief"*: Independent Commission on the Los Angeles Police Department, *Report of the Independent Commission on the Los Angeles Police Department,* 165.

32   *"the essence of the [LAPD's] excessive force problem"*: Ibid., ix and 32.

33   *unwritten LAPD credo:* "Brutality: Hard Issue for Police," *LAT,* April 4, 1991.

33   *"Gates made himself a martyr within the Los Angeles Police Department"*: Charlie Beck interview.

33   *luncheon rally for Gates:* "Gates Jokes with Man Who Taped Beating," AP, April 6, 1991.

34   *"patsy for the police"*: "Onetime Allies: Press and LAPD," *LAT,* May 24, 1992.

35   *In 1976, newly arrived KABC reporter Wayne Satz:* Letter from Wayne Satz, October 1, 1990.

35   *"They didn't think they had any public accountability"*: "LAPD Sins Are Old Hat to KABC," *LAT,* August 5, 1991.

35   *Eulia Love:* Los Angeles Board of Police Commissioners, *The Report of the Board of Police Commissioners Concerning the Shooting of Eulia Love and the Use of Deadly Force,* 1–56.

35   *David Cay Johnston stories:* "Daryl Gates' Real Legacy."

36   *Times . . . broke the Brentwood fund-raiser story:* "Gates' Absence Early in Riot to Be Examined," *LAT,* May 4, 1992.

36   *ten minutes:* "Los Angeles Mayor Criticizes Chief for Slow Action on Riot"; "Gates' Absence Early in Riot to Be Examined"; "As Rioting Mounted, Gates Remained at Political Event."

36   *about twenty minutes:* "Gates' Absence Early in Riot to Be Examined"; "As Rioting Mounted, Gates Remained at Political Event."

36   *"There are going to be situations where people are without assistance"*: "Another Video Dogging LA's Chief Gates," AP, May 3, 1992; "Gates' Absence Early in Riot to Be Examined"; "Gates Hammered by Media over LAPD Riot Response," *LAT,* May 28, 1992.

Bill Bratton, New York City, Early 1990s

36   *three and a half million daily riders of New York's . . . subway system:* "Bratton: The Making of a Police Visionary," *Crime Report,* December 6, 2013.

37   *Transit crime had risen by 25 percent:* Ibid.

37   *robberies were growing at two and a half times:* Ibid.; Bratton and Knobler, *Turnaround,* 143.

37   *3,500 officers:* "Defense Attacks Arrest in Transit Police Case," *NYT,* March 24, 1988; "Bratton: The Making of a Police Visionary."

37   *170,000 a day:* Bratton and Knobler, *Turnaround,* 143; Gladwell, *The Tipping Point,* 144; "Bratton: The Making of a Police Visionary."

37 *The city's 1989 homicide rate of 1,905*: "Number of Killings Soars in Big Cities Across U.S.," *NYT*, July 18, 1990; "New York, Nation Faces Rise in Crime," *Christian Science Monitor*, April 9, 1990; "Mayor Bloomberg and Police Commissioner Kelly Announce 2012 Sets All-Time Record for Fewest Murders and Fewest Shootings in New York City History," Office of the Mayor, December 28, 2012.

37 *2,245 murders . . . 1,946 killings*: "Reported Crimes Continue to Show Decline," *NYT*, October 2, 1996.

38 *In 1972 . . . inside a Black Muslim mosque*: "Harlem Split on Plan to Honor Officer Killed in Mosque in '72," *NYT*, May 11, 2012; "Nation of Islam Mosque Killing of NYPD Cop Still a Mystery, 37 Years Later," *NYDN*, March 22, 2009.

39 *"the Central Park jogger"*: "Central Park Jogger Case (1989)," *NYT*, October 3, 2012; "Central Park Horror, Wolf Pack's Prey, Female Jogger Near Death After Savage Attack by Roving Gang," *NYDN*, April 21, 1989.

39 *the defendants were declared innocent*: "5 Exonerated in Central Park Jogger Case Agree to Settle Suit for $40 Million," *NYT*, June 9, 2014; "NYC Is Pressed to Settle Central Park Jogger Case," AP, April 6, 2013.

39 *Brian Watkins*: "Tourist Slain in a Subway in Manhattan," *NYT*, September 4, 1990; "Utah Tourist Murdered on Subway Spurred NYC to Get Tough on Street Crime," *NYDN*, September 4, 2011.

39 *black .38-caliber revolver*: "All About Crime," *New York*, September 3, 1990.

40 *New York cover story*: "The Rotting of the Big Apple," *Time*, September 17, 1990.

40 *addressed then Mayor David Dinkins*: "Dave, Do Something!" *New York Post*, September 7, 1990.

40 *Bernhard Goetz*: "A Gunman's Tale of Fear, Hatred and Drugs," *NYT*, April 13, 1996; "The Little-Known World of the Vigilante," *NYT*, December 30, 1984.

40 *Bernhard Goetz armed himself with a handgun*: "Bernhard Goetz: NYC's Most 'High'-Minded Citizen," *New York Post*, November 7, 2013; "Why Goetz Got Off," *NYT*, August 14, 1988; "Taking Both Sides of a Heated Issue," *Philadelphia Inquirer*, July 8, 1988.

40 *Goetz . . . found not guilty*: "Not Guilty," *Time*, June 29, 1987; "Goetz Is Cleared in Subway Attack," *NYT*, June 17, 1987.

40 *later was sentenced . . . for illegal gun possession*: "Goetz Is Cleared in Subway Attack."

40 *"Watkins's murder became a cause célèbre"*: William Bratton interview; "The Reformer, on Honeymoon," *LAT*, January 19, 2003.

40 *"great back-slappers"*: Ibid.

41 *all-white Irish district known as Dorchester*: Bratton and Knobler, *Turnaround*, 7; "Bill Bratton Is America's Most Wanted," *Boston Globe*, March 8, 2013; "The Commish," *NYT*, February 1, 1998.

41 *high school sweethearts*: Bratton and Knobler, *Turnaround*, 3.

42 *chrome-plating factory . . . mail sorter*: Ibid., 5.

42 *"Somewhere along the line"*: Ibid., 9.

42 *Boston Latin*: Ibid., 16 and 17.

42 *sentry dog unit*: Ibid., 27.

42 *Boston PD*: Ibid., 38.

42 *Irish Alzheimer's*: Ibid., 115.

42 *2,800 cops . . . Boston PD*: Ibid., 38 and 55.

42 *fifty-five minority officers*: Ibid., 38.

42 *Fewer than twenty-five officers had college degrees*: Ibid., 48.

42 *Boston State University*: Ibid.

43 *"loved our system of government"*: Ibid., 36.

43 *"Blue Cocoon"*: Ibid., 48.

43 Boston Magazine: Ibid., 114–15.

44 *"wiped out graffiti"*: Ibid., 151.

44 *T.A. focus groups*: Ibid.

44 *3 percent of felonies*: Ibid., 171.

44 *transit officers . . . demoralized*: Ibid., 151 and 152.

45 *decreased by over 20 percent*: "Bratton: The Making of a Police Visionary."

45 *"broken-windows" theory of crime*: "Broken Windows," *Atlantic Monthly*, March 1, 1982; Bratton and Knobler, *Turnaround*, 152.

Charlie Beck and Mike Yamaki, Wednesday, April 29, 1992, LAPD Command Post, South Los Angeles

45 *Charlie Beck pulled into . . . Parker Center*: Charlie Beck interview.

46 *"holocaust of fire-gutted buildings"*: "Anger Smolders Along Vermont Avenue," *LAT*, May 2, 1992.

46 *L.A.'s first Asian-American police commissioner*: "Bradley Names Defense Lawyer to Police Board," *LAT*, April 10, 1991; Michael Yamaki interview.

46 *parents had spent the Second World War in an internment camp*: Michael Yamaki interview.

46 *father . . . insurance industry . . . Democratic Party politics*: Ibid.

47 *hiring more Asians was not only a matter of fairness*: Ibid.

47 *"nobody in the LAPD"*: Ibid.

47 *phone calls to local hotels*: Ibid.

47 *Beck . . . ashamed*: Charlie Beck interview.

Andre Christian, Wednesday, April 29, 1992, Riverside County; Jordan Downs Housing Project, Watts

48 *sat down to catch some news*: Andre Christian interview.

48 *Christian had moved from Jordan Downs to Riverside County*: Ibid.

48 *"all that open land"*: Ibid.

49 *"getting young cats"*: Ibid.

50 *Twenty-five hundred people . . . seven-hundred-unit*: "Jordan Downs to Get Police Substation," *LAT*, November 22, 1992; "L.A. Officials Envision Revitalization for Jordan Downs Housing Project in Watts," *LAT*, February 28, 2009.

50 *1,054-unit Nickerson Gardens*: "Nickerson Gardens Targeted for Redevelopment," *Los Angeles Sentinel*, March 25, 2004; "Willowbrook/Avalon Project Hearing Appeal Lost (Was It a Sham?)," *LA Watts Times*, October 11, 2012.

50 *"You could show no inferiority"*: Andre Christian interview.

51 *caught in a gang ambush*: Ibid.

51 *"Killer King"*: "King Plan Nurtures a Fragile Hope," *LAT*, March 15, 2009; "Los Angeles Hospital to Close After Failing Tests and Losing Financing," *NYT*, August 11, 2007.

52 *gang-related killings in L.A. County*: "Gang-Related Killings in County, City Set Record in '89," *LAT*, January 12, 1990.

52 *California's three-strikes law . . . stealing a steak . . . AA batteries*: "Proposition 184: Nonviolent 'Three Strike' Crimes Detailed," *LAT*, October 19, 1994; "County Chaos Is Beyond One Man," *LAT*, October 22, 1998; "Supreme Court Roundup; 'Three Strikes' Challenge Fails, but Others Are Invited," *NYT*, January 20, 1999; "They Changed Their Minds on Three Strikes. Can They Change the Voters?" *LAT*, September 19, 2004.

52 *introduction of crack into Los Angeles*: *Los Angeles Times, Understanding the Riots*, 30.

53 *Powder cocaine . . . $100 a gram*: "Price, Purity of Cocaine Vary Widely Across Nation," *LAT*, October 22, 1989; "Crack: A Disaster of Historic Dimension, Still Growing," *NYT*, May 28, 1989.

53 *$5, $10 . . . size of the rock*: "South Central Cocaine Sales Explode into $25 'Rocks,'" *LAT*, November 25, 1984; Nadel, *The Crack Cocaine Epidemic*, 1.

Andre Christian, Wednesday, April 29, 1992, Jordan Downs

54 *Florence and Normandie, where things had already turned ugly*: FOX 11 live aerial, April 30, 1992.

54 *eighty-eight rounds in defense*: "Faces of Death: 10 Men Slain by Officers in Riots," *LAT*, May 24, 1992; "Quiet Tension Has Replaced Rage That Exploded in L.A.," AP, May 27, 1992.

54 *"It was anarchy"*: "Faces of Death: 10 Men Slain by Officers in Riots"; *Los Angeles Times, Understanding the Riots*, 63.

Alfred Lomas, Thursday, April 30, 1992, Huntington Park, One Block East of South Central L.A.

55 *glued to his crack-house TV*: Alfred Lomas interview.

55 *"On south Western Avenue"*: "Under Fire: Guns in Los Angeles County: Proliferation of Guns May Be Bloody Legacy of Riots," *LAT*, May 17, 1992.

55 *fat, middle-aged Latina*: Alfred Lomas interview.

55 *"At four in the afternoon"*: Hazen, ed., *Inside the L.A. Riots*, 33.

56 *51 percent of those arrested during the peak of the rioting were Latinos*: "51% of Riot Arrests Were Latino, Study Says: Unrest: RAND Analysis of Court Cases Finds They Were Mostly Young Men. The Figures Are Open to Many Interpretations, Experts Note," *LAT*, June 18, 1992; Hazen, ed., *Inside the L.A. Riots*, 46.

Thursday, April 30, Across L.A.

56 *two big-bellied Latino men*: Author's observations and interviews, April 30, 1992.

56 *"Fuck respect," Miami Heat shot back*: Entire conversation, heard, observed, and recorded by the author, April 30, 1992.

57 *riots/looting spread*: Los Angeles Times, *Understanding the Riots*, 84 and 88–91; Hazen, ed., *Inside the L.A. Riots*, 97–98 and 100.

57 *Frederick's of Hollywood*: Los Angeles Times, *Understanding the Riots*, 90; Hazen, ed., *Inside the L.A. Riots*, 98.

57 *"the crush of looters"*: Los Angeles Times, *Understanding the Riots*, 69.

Michael Yamaki, Thursday, April 30, 1992, Koreatown

57 *Korean-owned mom-and-pop convenience stores*: Hazen, ed., *Inside the L.A. Riots*, 99–100 and 109; Los Angeles Times, *Understanding the Riots*, 59, 72, 74, 77, and 106; *LAT*, photographs by Hyungwon Kang.

57 *"We trusted them"*: "Big Mike" Cummings interview.

58 *Latasha Harlins*: Author's observations and interviews, April 30, 1992; Los Angeles Times, *Understanding the Riots*, 38, 40–41, 68, 72, and 77; Hazen, ed., *Inside the L.A. Riots*, 99; "Uprising: Hip Hop & the LA Riots."

58 *An eighteen-year-old Korean man was killed*: Los Angeles Times, *Understanding the Riots*, 88.

59 *spotted the very same eyeball*: Michael Yamaki interview.

59 *"We can't give anyone protection"*: Ibid.

Michael Yamaki, Thursday, April 30, 1992, Watts

59 *Watts Labor Community Action Committee*: "From Watts Riot Ashes: Bright Hopes, Heartaches," *LAT*, May 10, 1992; "Watts Organizer Feels Weight of Riots, and History," *NYT*, June 24, 1992; Los Angeles Times, *Understanding the Riots*, 81.

59 *"helped pay for a homeless shelter, job training center"*: "Born from the Ashes of Watts, Center Dies in Flames of Riot," *LAT*, May 2, 1992.

59 *"We [the LAPD] didn't have anything ready"*: Michael Yamaki interview.

60 *address the troops*: Ibid.

60 *"The cops, they'd waited just too long to respond"*: Andre Christian interview.

60 *"If someone looked out of place"*: Gates, *Chief*, 34.

61 *"pounding the fear of God into people"*: David Dotson interview.

61 *"super-aggressive twenty-two-year-olds"*: "Los Angeles Times Interview: Joseph Wambaugh: What LAPD Needs Is Women to Combat Testosterone Level," *LAT*, July 14, 1991.

61 *"He is facing, daily and nightly"*: Baldwin, *Nobody Knows My Name*, 62.

62 *"aggressively identify"*: Independent Commission on the Los Angeles Police Department, *Report of the Independent Commission on the Los Angeles Police Department*, 99.

62 *"blunt-force military tactics and assaults"*: Charlie Beck interview.

62 *"no shooting policy"*: Jack White interview.

62 *LAPD ranked number one in killing or wounding*: Independent Commission on the Los Angeles Police Department, *Report of the Independent Commission on the Los Angeles Police Department*, 170.

62 *virtually nothing had changed*: Los Angeles Urban League, American Jewish Committee, and the National Conference of Christians and Jews, "Joint Task Force on South Central Los Angeles—Fifteen Years Later."

63 *"hard-charging street army"*: "Why Chief Willie Williams Deserves Five More Years," *LAT*, December 22, 1996.

63 *Bell Jet Ranger*: "Sky Patrol: Arm of the Law Goes to New Heights Through Helicopter Units in LAPD's Air Support Division," *LAT*, April 3, 1988.

63 *"roust anything strange"*: Gates, *Chief*, 112–14.

63 *Karen Toshima's murder*: "The Legacy of a Slaying: Westwood Gang Shooting Alters Public Attitudes, Police Tactics," *LAT*, September 11, 1989; *Los Angeles Times, Understanding the Riots*, 31.

64 *"Operation Hammer"*: "1,000 Officers Stage Assault Against Violent Youth Gangs," *LAT*, April 9, 1988; "237 Held in Sweep; Violence Continues," *LAT*, August 20, 1989; "LAPD Nails 352 in Operation Hammer," *LAT*, August 21, 1989; "Police Arrest 1,092 in Weekend Sweeps; Gang Killings Continue," *LAT*, October 2, 1989; "700 Seized in Gang Sweep, 2 More Die in Shootings," *LAT*, September 19, 1988; "The Bum Blockade, Zoot Suit Riot and Bloody Christmas," *LA Weekly*, September 4, 2002; "Behind the Bunker Mentality," *LAT*, June 11, 2000; Hazen, ed., *Inside the L.A. Riots*, 15 and 98; *Los Angeles Times, Understanding the Riots*, 31.

64 *twenty-five thousand overwhelmingly black men of all ages*: "Behind the Bunker Mentality."

64 *"Pick 'em up for anything and everything"*: "1,000 Officers Stage Assault Against Violent Youth Gangs"; "The Bum Blockade, Zoot Suit Riot and Bloody Christmas."

64 *motorcycle and patrol officers multiplied their justification*: Steve Fisk interview; David Dotson interview.

65 *the DA filed just 103 cases*: "NAACP Raps Police over Gang Sweeps," *LAT*, April 15, 1988.

65 *"What the LAPD was missing"*: Charlie Beck interview.

65 *California . . . annual corrections budget top $11 billion*: "Gov. Brown Tries to Justify Unconstitutional Prison Overcrowding, Backslides on Corrections Budget," *San Francisco Bay View*, January 11, 2013; "Inside Criminal Justice," *Crime Report*, January 10, 2011.

66 *More than one in three young black men*: Alexander, *The New Jim Crow*, 9.

66 *Special Investigation Section, or the SIS*: "Experts Elsewhere Criticize SIS Record of Few Arrests, Frequently Deadly Shootings," *LAT*, September 25, 1988; "Special Police Unit Is Under Review," *LAT*, November 11, 2003.

67 *One in three people involved in armed robberies got hurt*: "'The Risk Is Too Great,'" *LAT*, September 27, 1988; Reaves, *Using NIBRS Data to Analyze Violent Crime*, 16.

67 *SIS would shoot and kill twenty-three people*: "Experts Elsewhere Criticize SIS Record of Few Arrests, Frequently Deadly Shootings."

67 *"SIS detectives over the years had shot 13 unarmed people"*: Ibid.

67 *excessive-force lawsuit settlements*: "$11.3 Million Paid in 1990 to Resolve Police Abuse Cases," *LAT*, March 29, 1991.

67 *Rodney King was awarded $3.8 million in a civil suit*: "Rodney King Is Awarded $3.8 Million," *NYT*, April 20, 1994; "King Gets Award of $3.8 Million," *LAT*, April 20, 1994.

67 *Joe Morgan won $540,000 in another federal lawsuit*: "Morgan Awarded $540,000 by Jurors," *LAT*, February 15, 1991; "Morgan Wins Judgment," AP, February 16, 1991.

67 *"large third degree burns"*: Independent Commission on the Los Angeles Police Department, *Report of the Independent Commission on the Los Angeles Police Department*, 58.

67 *"lost two teeth and suffered multiple concussions"*: Ibid.

67 *"Received seven [more] complaints"*: Ibid., 59.

68 *"the sweetest, gentlest things"*: "A Biting Controversy," *Los Angeles Times Magazine*, February 9, 1992.

68 *"only bite if attacked"*: David Dotson interview.

68 *eight thousand unsolved murders*: "Old, but Never Totally Cold," *LAT*, May 23, 2005; "An LAPD Critic Comes in from the Cold," *Crime Report*, January 18, 2012.; "A Few Warm Bodies Can Solve a Lot of Cold Cases," *Houston Chronicle*, May 31, 2005.

Charlie Beck, Late Eighties to Early Nineties, Watts

68 *"wild and chaotic"*: Charlie Beck interview.

68 *Once Beck was on a robbery stakeout in Watts*: Ibid.

69 *"the Vietnam vets"*: Ibid.

69 *"use each occasion"*: "Throwing the Book: Reiner Will Seek Maximum Jail Sentence for Gang Members," *LAT*, September 20, 1989.

69 *over seventy thousand . . . gang members*: "New Anti-Terrorism Law Used Against L.A. Gangs," *LAT*, April 21, 1989.

69 *"Well under five percent [of gang members] . . . engaged in serious criminal violence"*: "If Police Call It Gang Crime That Doesn't Make It True," *LAT*, September 28, 1989.

Curtis Woodle, Thursday, April 30, 1992, Los Angeles Police Academy, Elysian Park

70 *Early Thursday morning*: Curtis Woodle interview.

71 *"Watch any episode of . . . Cops"*: David Dotson interview.

71 *"to find a reason . . . to kick your ass"*: Curtis Woodle interview.

72 *Rodney King . . . "had just led officers on a high-speed chase"*: Ibid.

72 *"choke him out"*: Ibid.

72 *LAPD choke hold banned*: "Los Angeles Police Reconsider Using Choke Hold," *LAT*, September 3, 1991; "Chokehold Ban Cited as Reason King Was Beaten," *LAT*, March 25, 1992; "Final Suit over LAPD's Use of Chokehold Settled," *LAT*, September 29, 1993; "Finding a Safe Way to Subdue Violent Suspects," *LAT*, June 14, 1994.

72 *Departments . . . one choke hold death each*: "The Bum Blockade, Zoot Suit Riot and Bloody Christmas."

72 *from 1975 to 1982 . . . LAPD . . . fifteen such deaths*: "Eric Garner's Killing and Why the Police Chokehold Is So Racially Charged," *Washington Post*, December 4, 2014; Hazen, ed., *Inside the L.A. Riots*, 22.

72 *"would have been okay"*: Curtis Woodle interview.

73 *watched on his TV screen as an L.A. County Sheriff's Department bus*: Ibid.

Alfred Lomas, Thursday, April 30, 1992, Florencia 13 Crack House

73 *felt like he was at a swap meet*: Alfred Lomas interview.

74 *"fearsome dope fiend"*: Ibid.

74 *Maravilla Projects*: Ibid.

75 *it "was just an honor to be a member"*: Ibid.

75 *"earning a Harvard MBA with honors"*: Ibid.

75 *"super" or "regional" gang*: National Drug Intelligence Center, *Attorney General's Report to Congress on the Growth of Violent Street Gangs in Suburban Areas*.

Charlie Beck, Thursday, April 30, 1992, Los Angeles Coliseum

75 *twelve-hour midnight shift*: Charlie Beck interview.

Tom Bradley, Thursday, April 30, 1992, Los Angeles

76 *federal troops*: Los Angeles Times, *Understanding the Riots*, 63, 72, 76, 85, 92–93, 95, 102–3, and 120; "Where Were L.A. Police When the Rioting Began?"; "Riots in Los Angeles: The Overview; Cleanup Begins in Los Angeles; Troops Enforce Surreal Calm," *NYT*, May 3, 1992.

76 *three thousand soldiers . . . fifteen hundred U.S. Marines*: "Riots in Los Angeles: The Overview; Cleanup Begins in Los Angeles; Troops Enforce Surreal Calm"; "U.S. Army, Marine Troops Withdraw from Los Angeles," *LAT*, May 10, 1992.

76 *one thousand FBI agents, U.S. Marshals . . . border patrol agents*: Los Angeles Times, *Understanding the Riots*, 98; "Bush Pledges Enough Force to Quell Riots," *LAT*, May 2, 1992.

76 *"a halting plea for peace"*: Los Angeles Times, *Understanding the Riots*, 98.

Andre Christian, Saturday, May 2, 1992, Jordan Downs

77 *pulled his car into Jordan Downs*: Andre Christian interview.

77 *it was cleanup time*: Los Angeles Times, *Understanding the Riots*, 120–23, 131–32, 137, and 140–41; Hazen, ed., *Inside the L.A. Riots*, 148.

77 *self-congratulation time, party time*: Charlie Beck interview; Los Angeles Times, *Understanding the Riots*, 139 and 142; "Uprising: Hip Hop & the LA Riots."

Curtis Woodle, Saturday, May 2, 1992, Florence and Normandie

78 *through the intersection of Florence and Normandie*: Curtis Woodle interview.

78 *"What's with this guy?"*: Ibid.

79 *"Hey, man"*: Ibid.

Charlie Beck, Saturday, May 2, 1992, Coliseum

79 *shutting down the Coliseum command post*: Charlie Beck interview.

79 *over 125 cities*: "40 Years After the Riots, King's Vision 'Unfinished,'" *USA Today*, January 20, 2008; "The Legacy of the 1968 Riots," *Guardian*, April 4, 2008.

79 *President George H. W. Bush . . . flew out to L.A.*: Los Angeles Times, *Understanding the Riots*, 72 and 134.

Connie Rice, Saturday, May 2, 1992, Jordan Downs

80 *a "coal black" classmate . . . "marched right up"*: Rice, *Power Concedes Nothing*, 7.

81 *"hope and achievement"*: Connie Rice interview.

81 *Phillip Leon Rice, Sr.*: Rice, *Power Concedes Nothing*, 8 and 23.

81 *Condoleezza Rice*: Rice, *Extraordinary, Ordinary People*, 184–88.

81 *Judge Damon J. Keith*: Rice, *Power Concedes Nothing*, 82.

81 *"I wanted to be a civil rights lawyer"*: Connie Rice interview.

81 *"when you sit down with the Bloods and Crips"*: Ibid.

81 *"a research assistant"*: Ibid.

81 *stories . . . about the dogs of the LAPD's sixteen-man K-9 Unit*: Ibid.

82 *bitten nine hundred people*: "A Biting Controversy"; "LAPD, Dogs and Video-tape: Police Commission Must Fully Examine Allegations About Police Dog Attacks," *LAT*, December 27, 1991.

82 *Philadelphia . . . bitten totaled just twenty*: "LAPD, Dogs and Videotape: Police Commission Must Fully Examine Allegations About Police Dog Attacks."

82 *LAPD dogs sunk their teeth into 80 percent of the suspects*: "An LAPD Critic Comes in from the Cold"; Connie Rice interview.

82 *"None of us opposes"*: "Police Commission Rejects Activists' Call for Police Dog Ban," *LAT*, January 8, 1992.

82 *Gates had "fiercely defended" the K-9 Unit*: Ibid.

83 *"these beautiful German shepherds"*: Connie Rice interview.

83 *"feeding time"*: "Give Us Hard Data on DWB Stops," *LAT*, May 3, 2000.

83 *"one of the greatest experiences ever"*: "Video of Police Dog Attack on Unarmed Theft Suspect Prompts Panel Inquiry," *LAT*, December 12, 1991.

84 *"If you get the bite rate down from 80 percent to below 10 percent"*: Connie Rice interview.

84 *"sadomasochistic behavior"*: Ibid.

84 *"Give me the bad news"*: Ibid.

85 *"underclass discount"*: Ibid.

Anthony De Los Reyes, May 1992, Los Angeles

85 *Gates . . . "very, very powerful"*: Anthony De Los Reyes interview.

85 *"It was unbelievable"*: Ibid.

85 *"I was there"*: Michael Yamaki interview.

86 *45 dead . . . 2,300 injured*: Los Angeles Times, *Understanding the Riots*, 130.

86 *Insured losses totaled $1 billion*: Ibid.

86 *deadliest and costliest U.S. civil disturbance of the twentieth century*: Ibid., 49 and 130; "The Bum Blockade, Zoot Suit Riot and Bloody Christmas."

86 *federal consent decree*: "Federal Judge Ends LAPD Consent Decree," AP, July 17, 2009; Stone, et al., *Policing Los Angeles Under a Consent Decree*, Executive Summary.

87 *by a two-thirds majority L.A. voters approved the charter amendment*: "Education Bonds Pass; Overall Trend Is Rejection with AM—California Senate, BJT," AP, June 3, 1992; "Elections '92: LAPD Disciplinary System to Undergo Major Restructuring," *LAT*, June 4, 1992; Los Angeles Times, *Understanding the Riots*, 143.

PART TWO: SOMETHING BORROWED

Daryl Gates and Willie Williams, June 1992, Los Angeles

91 *Daryl Gates was forced to resign*: Anthony De Los Reyes interview; Michael Yamaki interview.

91 *Charter Amendment F*: Independent Commission on the Los Angeles Police Department, *Report of the Independent Commission on the Los Angeles Police Department*, 215; "Elections '92: LAPD Disciplinary System to Undergo Major Restructuring," *LAT*, June 4, 1992.

91 *Willie L. Williams, the first black commissioner of Philadelphia Police Department*: "1st Black to Head Police Department Willie Williams Replaces Tucker," *Philadelphia Inquirer*, June 3, 1988; "The Fast-Rising Williams Seems a Popular Choice," *Philadelphia Inquirer*, June 4, 1988; "Say Goodbye to Hollywood," *Philadelphia Weekly*, March 26, 1997.

91 *first black police chief of Los Angeles*: "Willie Williams Takes Oath as New Police Chief," *LAT*, June 27, 1992; "Give Willie Williams the Tools He Needs," *LAT*, July 1, 1992.

91 *not just as another cop, but as a hero*: "Officer Down, Willie Williams' Fall from Grace," *LA Weekly*, February 28–March 6, 1997.

91 *Campanile . . . standing ovation*: Ibid.; "Say Goodbye to Hollywood."

92 *Velvet Turtle*: "Williams' Open Door Sends Signal," *LAT*, August 16, 1992; "Officer Down, Willie Williams' Fall from Grace"; "Say Goodbye to Hollywood."

92 *sexual harassment and discrimination*: Connie Rice interview.

92 *Juggling over two hundred requests for meetings*: "Tale of 2 Chiefs: Gates Takes Swipes as Williams Builds Bridges," *LAT*, April 26, 1992.

92 *two standing ovations at the Black Women's Forum*: Ibid.

92 *First Methodist Episcopal Church*: "Williams, in Tour of L.A., Promises Reforms, Healing," *LAT*, April 17, 1992; "Officer Down, Willie Williams' Fall from Grace."

92 *"servant and son"*: "Williams, in Tour of L.A., Promises Reforms, Healing."

92 *Hollenbeck Youth Center*: AP, April 17, 1992; "Williams, in Tour of L.A., Promises Reforms, Healing"; "Officer Down, Willie Williams' Fall from Grace"; "Say Goodbye to Hollywood."

92 *The media coverage reflected their enthusiasm*: "Philadelphia Chief to Head LAPD," *LAT*, April 16, 1992; "Williams, in Tour of L.A., Promises Reforms, Healing."

92 *"citizens, to hold me accountable"*: "Officer Down, Willie Williams' Fall from Grace"; "Say Goodbye to Hollywood."

92 *"So who's gonna be the first female police chief in this city?"*: "Williams, in Tour of L.A., Promises Reforms, Healing"; "Officer Down, Willie Williams' Fall from Grace"; "Say Goodbye to Hollywood."

93 *World War II heroes*: "Why Chief Willie Williams Deserves Five More Years,"
    LAT, December 22, 1996.

93 *double-breasted business suits and power ties*: "Officer Down, Willie Williams'
    Fall from Grace"; Reese, "The Rise and Fall of a Public Leader"; "Willie Wil-
    liams Takes Oath as New Police Chief," *LAT*, June 27, 1992.

93 *the public as his "customer base"*: "Officer Down, Willie Williams' Fall from
    Grace."

93 *Gates, who loved to lash out at his critics*: "Willie Williams Takes Oath as New
    Police Chief."

93 *"no future . . . hasn't got a chance in the world"*: Ibid.

93 *A weak "disciplinarian" without a college degree*: "Tale of 2 Chiefs: Gates Takes
    Swipes As Williams Builds Bridges."

93 *"bunch of knucklehead liberals"*: "Willie Williams Takes Oath as New Police
    Chief."

93 *"one thing that sold [the] Los Angeles [Police Commission] on Williams"*: "Man in
    the News: Willie Lawrence Williams; An Astute Manager," *NYT*, April 16,
    1992.

93 *"shocked" and "embarrassed as a police officer"*: "Police View L.A. Video and
    Note Problems Here," *Philadelphia Inquirer*, March 24, 1991.

93 *"seen pictures of Vietnam or Korea"*: Ibid.

93 *"Our whole existence is to make sure"*: "Williams, in Tour of L.A., Promises
    Reforms, Healing."

94 *"Too many members of [this] Police Department"*: Willie Williams, "First Major
    Public Address"; "The New Chief: What's Going to Change at the LAPD,"
    KCRW, *Which Way, L.A.?* June 16, 1992, accessed on April 3, 2015, http://
    www.kcrw.com/news-culture/shows/which-way-la/the-new-chief-whats
    -going-to-change-at-the-lapd-1/#.

94 *"to apply the salve of cooperation"*: Ibid.

94 *Two decades earlier, a black-Jewish coalition*: Gary Greenebaum interview;
    Domanick, *To Protect and To Serve*, 211–12.

95 *"There was a whole sense, a kind of lament"*: Gary Greenebaum interview.

95 *"There was not another person in the country"*: Ibid.

95 *"In the midst of all that excitement"*: Ibid.

95 *"Or you want the Dalai Lama? We wanted Willie Williams!"*: Ibid.

96 *"We needed somebody from the outside"*: Ann Reiss Lane interview; "Officer
    Down, Willie Williams' Fall from Grace"; "Say Goodbye to Hollywood."

96 *"There was definitely a preference for going outside"*: Anthony De Los Reyes in-
    terview.

96 *all Democratic stalwarts*: "The Man Who Would Be Kingmaker: Stanley Shein-
    baum, High-Level Kibbitzer, Mentor and Fund-Raiser for American Liber-
    als," *LAT*, June 28, 1987; "Commission Agonized over Choice of Outsider
    for Chief," *LAT*, April 17, 1992; "Father of the Leftist Guard," *Jewish Journal*,
    September 9, 2004.

97 *Bill Parker was named chief in 1950*: "Leave Chief Parker Behind," *LAT*, April 11, 2009.

97 *"The police commission doesn't run this police department"*: "LAPD—How Good Is It?," *LAT*, December 18, 1977.

97 *"already had more power than the mayor"*: "Why Chief Willie Williams Deserves Five More Years"; "Ed Davis Calls It Quits: 'I Have Served Long Enough,'" *LAT*, January 29, 1992; "Chief Parker Molded LAPD Image—Then Came the '60s," *LAT*, May 25, 1992.

97 *Democratic presidential hopefuls would fly three thousand miles*: "The Man Who Would Be Kingmaker: Stanley Sheinbaum, High-Level Kibbitzer, Mentor and Fund-Raiser for American Liberals."

98 *New York City Jewish boy turned dirt poor*: Ibid.

98 *married a Hollywood rich girl*: Ibid.; "Father of the Leftist Guard."

98 *a would-be painter*: "The Man Who Would Be Kingmaker: Stanley Sheinbaum, High-Level Kibbitzer, Mentor and Fund-Raiser for American Liberals."

98 *political salons*: Ibid.

98 *American Civil Liberties Foundation*: "Stanley Sheinbaum: Applying His ACLU Past to New Role on Police Commission," *LAT*, March 22, 1992.

98 *Daniel Ellsberg's legal defense*: "The Man Who Would Be Kingmaker: Stanley Sheinbaum, High-Level Kibbitzer, Mentor and Fund-Raiser for American Liberals."

98 *divestment from apartheid South Africa*: "Father of the Leftist Guard."

98 *Yasser Arafat*: "Stanley Sheinbaum: Applying his ACLU Past to New Role on Police Commission"; "Commission Agonized over Choice of Outsider for Chief."

98 *phone call to Bradley*: "Commission Agonized over Choice of Outsider for Chief."

98 *Sheinbaum being named president of the commission*: "Stanley Sheinbaum: Applying his ACLU Past to New Role on Police Commission"; "Commission Agonized over Choice of Outsider for Chief."

99 *A wounded combat infantry captain*: Anthony De Los Reyes interview; Domanick, *To Protect and To Serve*, 217.

99 *the department's first black motorcycle officer*: Ibid.

99 *the department's first African-American assistant chief*: "Black Officer Named Assistant Chief of LAPD," *LAT*, November 20, 1987; "Jesse A. Brewer, Ex-Assistant Police Chief, Dies: LAPD: The Highest-Ranking African American When He Retired, He Was Force for Reform While on Police Commission," *LAT*, November 20, 1995.

99 *one of those men everybody liked*: "Naming Jesse Brewer to Commission Is Seen as a Deft Stroke by the Mayor," *LAT*, July 18, 1991; "Jesse A. Brewer, Ex-Assistant Police Chief, Dies: LAPD: The Highest-Ranking African American When He Retired, He Was Force for Reform While on Police Commission";

"Central Los Angeles: Station Named for Brewer," *LAT*, January 10, 1996; Domanick, *To Protect and To Serve*, 217.

99 *Educated at Tuskegee*: "Jesse A. Brewer, Ex-Assistant Police Chief, Dies: LAPD: The Highest-Ranking African American When He Retired, He Was Force for Reform While on Police Commission"; Domanick, *To Protect and To Serve*, 217.

99 *master's degree in public administration from USC*: "Jesse A. Brewer, Ex-Assistant Police Chief, Dies: LAPD: The Highest-Ranking African American When He Retired, He Was Force for Reform While on Police Commission."

99 *left the Chicago PD*: Domanick, *To Protect and To Serve*, 217; Honorable Julian C. Dixon of California, "Tribute to Jesse A. Brewer," U.S. House of Representatives, *Congressional Record* 141, no. 186 (November 20, 1995).

99 *after taking and passing the written exam*: Domanick, *To Protect and To Serve*, 217.

99 *doctor notorious for regularly flunking black applicants*: Ibid.

99 *Bradley too had been flunked . . . by the same doctor*: Ibid.

99 *he too appealed, got reexamined*: Ibid.

100 *written exam for lieutenant*: Ibid.

100 *rejected by white oral boards*: Ibid.

100 *made it on his fourth attempt, 1967*: Ibid.

100 *But he left with a copy of a report he'd commissioned*: Ibid., 337–39.

100 *Disrespect among officers was "out of control"*: Independent Commission on the Los Angeles Police Department, *Report of the Independent Commission on the Los Angeles Police Department*, 99.

100 *"We know who the bad guys are"*: Ibid., 31–32; "Civilian Control of LAPD Is Elusive Despite Reforms," *LAT*, November 14, 1999.

101 *De Los Reyes came to regard him as "a saint"*: Anthony De Los Reyes interview.

101 *Lane was "scrupulously honest"*: Ann Reiss Lane interview.

101 *Mike Yamaki compared Brewer to . . . John Wooden*: Michael Yamaki interview.

101 *"I could see the conflict in him"*: Ibid.

101 *Jewish resident . . . Hancock Park*: "Last Panelist Selected for Seat on Police Commission," *LAT*, July 20, 1991; "Lane Nominated to Panel," *LADN*, July 20, 1991; "For Women, Gun Control Adds Up to Child Safety," *LAT*, November 3, 1993.

101 *graduated from Beverly Hills High School*: Beverly Hills High School, "Beverly Hills High School Thrives in Its 86th Year," *Alumni: Beverly Hills Highlights* 32 (2012): 2.

101 *After also graduating from UCLA*: "Challenge Ahead for LA Police Board Member," *Santa Cruz Sentinel*, August 1, 1991.

101 *joined the League of Women Voters*: Ibid.

101 *Tom Bradley . . . first campaign for mayor*: Ann Reiss Lane interview.

101 *Leonard Nimoy*: Ibid.

101 *burst into tears*: Ibid.

101 *Los Angeles Fire Commission:* "Last Panelist Selected for Seat on Police Commission"; "Lane Nominated to Panel"; "New Police Commission Member Interested in Valley Stations, Women," *LADN,* August 3, 1991.

101 *Bradley appointed her to the Police Commission:* "Lane Nominated to Panel"; "New Police Commission Member Interested in Valley Stations, Women."

102 *Daryl Gates would pass her in the hallway:* Ann Reiss Lane interview.

102 *"I have read [the Christopher Commission Report]":* Ibid.

102 *Gates . . . opposed to the feminist and gay rights movements:* Anthony De Los Reyes interview.

102 *"he'd gotten complaints from female officers":* Ibid.

102 *His father was a Mexican musician of the Latin big-band sound:* Ibid.

102 *come of age in East L.A.'s Lincoln Heights:* Ibid.

102 *personal injury plaintiff's lawyer:* Ibid.

102 *supported Tom Bradley's failed run for governor:* Ibid.

102 *appointed to the city's Civil Service Commission:* Ibid.

103 *Bradley personally asked him to join the Police Commission:* Ibid.

103 *"I had cops and others' records":* Ibid.

103 *"masters of the half-truth":* "Perspectives on the LAPD: Are We Doomed to Repeat the Past?" *LAT,* July 6, 1995.

103 *"I had to ask very specific, precise questions":* Anthony De Los Reyes interview.

103 *Daryl Gates . . . "adamantly opposed" . . . gay festival:* Ibid.

103 *when one officer publicly came out:* "A Gay Officer's Lonely Patrol: Former Policeman Mitchell Grobeson's Suit Against LAPD Raises Questions About What Makes a Good Cop," *LAT,* April 28, 1989; "Gay Police Officer Who Sued LAPD over Bias Is Reinstated," *LAT,* July 20, 1993; "Gay Cop's 25-Year Battle with LAPD Rages On," *Advocate,* February 22, 2013.

103 *Gates's stated objection:* Anthony De Los Reyes interview.

104 *"He was very upset":* Ibid.

104 *took the commission sixteen hours . . . devoted to Willie Williams:* Ibid.

104 *highest grade among the initial civil service selection committees:* "Philadelphia Chief to Head LAPD."

104 *"confrontations with every single LAPD person":* Michael Yamaki interview.

104 *flown to Philadelphia:* "Officer Down, Willie Williams' Fall from Grace"; "Say Goodbye to Hollywood."

104 *"Please don't take my police chief away":* Ibid.

104 *"If I was looking for a job":* Ibid.

104 *The commission's first vote:* Michael Yamaki interview.

105 *Bernard Parks . . . disliked by both Lane and Brewer:* Ann Reiss Lane interview.

105 *"Remember, Bernie Parks":* Ibid.

105 *Willie Williams had "the right temperament":* "With Initiative, Williams Rides Out a Tough First Year," *Philadelphia Inquirer,* June 25, 1989.

106 *reputation* worse *than the LAPD's:* David Dotson interview.

106 *"how the Philadelphia police operated in those days":* Ibid.

106 *"had died for our sins"*: Charlie Beck interview.

106 *disapproval rating of 81 percent*: "Los Angeles Has Chance to Show Anger at Gates," *LAT*, May 31, 1992.

106 *distrust score at 85 percent*: Reese, "The Rise and Fall of a Public Leader."

106 *"Okay, fine, let's celebrate him"*: Michael Yamaki interview.

107 Sunday-*morning emergency meeting*: Anthony De Los Reyes interview.

107 *"That's when he finally caved"*: Ibid.

107 *"We love you, Chief"*: "Williams Takes Oath as New Police Chief."

107 *"phalanx of police motorcyclists"*: Ibid.

107 *host of a talk-radio show*: "What's Behind KFI's Firing of Tom Leykis?: Radio: Dropping of Host—and Daryl Gates in—Stuns Audience," *LAT*, October 1, 1992; "Daryl Gates Helps Make KFI Top Talk Gun: Radio: The Former Los Angeles Police Chief's Hiring in September Leads Station to Victory over Rival KABC," *LAT*, January 9, 1993; "Daryl Gates on Show's End: 'I Have Real Mixed Emotions': Radio: The Former L.A. Police Chief's 15-Month Stint as KFI Talk-Show Host Is over on Friday," *LAT*, December 30, 1993.

Willie Williams, Late Eighties to Early Nineties, Philadelphia, Pennsylvania

108 *The oldest of seven children*: "Willie Williams Feeling at Home: Commissioner Puts Family 1st," *LADN*, June 6, 1988; "Man in the News: Willie Lawrence Williams, an Astute Manager"; "Officer Down, Willie Williams' Fall from Grace."

108 *spindly, asthmatic child*: "Willie Williams Feeling at Home: Commissioner Puts Family 1st"; "Officer Down, Willie Williams' Fall from Grace"; "Say Goodbye to Hollywood."

108 *administered last rites*: "Officer Down, Willie Williams' Fall from Grace"; "Say Goodbye to Hollywood."

108 *His father labored in a meatpacking plant*: "Profile: Willie L. Williams," *LAT*, April 17, 1992; "Officer Down, Willie Williams' Fall from Grace"; "Say Goodbye to Hollywood."

108 *delivering newspapers*: "Willie Williams Feeling at Home: Commissioner Puts Family 1st"; "Say Goodbye to Hollywood."

108 *By fifteen he too was packing meat part-time*: "Officer Down, Willie Williams' Fall from Grace"; "Say Goodbye to Hollywood."

108 *almost losing his arm*: Ibid.

108 *1961 high school graduation*: "Fonder of Phila., Thanks to L.A. Willie L. Williams Returned to Speak About Unity. His Home Town, He Said, Is Ahead of His New One on That Point," *Philadelphia Inquirer*, October 18, 1993; "The Top Cop Talks: Commissioner Willie Williams Speaks His Mind About His Family, Future, Successes and Frustrations," *Philadelphia Inquirer*, October 25, 1989.

108 *city messenger for $2,600 a year*: "Officer Down, Willie Williams' Fall from Grace"; "Say Goodbye to Hollywood."

108 *double his annual salary overnight to $5,000*: "Willie Williams Feeling at Home: Commissioner Puts Family 1st"; "Officer Down, Willie Williams' Fall from Grace"; "Say Goodbye to Hollywood."

108 *wife, Evelina—a clerk-typist*: "Willie Williams Feeling at Home: Commissioner Puts Family 1st"; "The Top Cop Talks: Commissioner Willie Williams Speaks His Mind About His Family, Future, Successes and Frustrations."

108 *raised three children*: "Willie Williams Feeling at Home: Commissioner Puts Family 1st"; "Profile: Willie L. Williams"; "Officer Down, Willie Williams' Fall from Grace"; "Say Goodbye to Hollywood."

108 *three-bedroom row house*: "Willie Williams Feeling at Home: Commissioner Puts Family 1st"; "Philadelphia's Top Cop Offers a Reformist Style: Outsider: Willie Williams Expects Resistance if Chosen as L.A. Police Chief. But He Is Accustomed to Tough Battles," *LAT*, March 22, 1992.

108 *dog named Frisky*: "Willie Williams Feeling at Home: Commissioner Puts Family 1st."

108 *live together in the city for twenty-three years*: Ibid.

108 *took both the sergeants' test and the detectives' test three times*: Ibid.

108 *Philadelphia College of Textiles and Science*: "Profile: Willie L. Williams"; "Officer Down, Willie Williams' Fall from Grace"; "Say Goodbye to Hollywood."

108 *never fire his weapon*: "Willie Williams Feeling at Home: Commissioner Puts Family 1st."

109 *promoted to captain*: "With Initiative, Williams Rides Out a Tough First Year"; "Officer Down, Willie Williams' Fall from Grace"; "Say Goodbye to Hollywood."

109 *1985 dropping of a bomb*: "Police Drop Bomb on Radicals' Home in Philadelphia," *NYT*, May 14, 1985; "Philadelphia Bombing: Clash Is Recalled," *NYT*, May 14, 1986; "The MOVE Disaster: May 13, 1985, Day That Forever Changed the City," *Philadelphia Inquirer*, May 8, 2005; "Officer Down, Willie Williams' Fall from Grace"; "Say Goodbye to Hollywood."

109 *"single most stupid police action"*: "Timoney Isn't First Outsider Hired to Shake Up Police: 10 Years Ago, Kevin Tucker Had Similar Goals in Tougher Situation," *Philadelphia Inquirer*, April 6, 1998.

109 *federal convictions . . . thirty commanders and officers*: "Official Who Restored Respect to Philadelphia Police Resigns," *NYT*, May 28, 1988.

109 *The son of Irish immigrants*: "Former Police Commissioner Kevin M. Tucker," *Philadelphia Inquirer*, June 21, 2012; "Kevin Tucker Is Dead at 71; Led Philadelphia Police," *NYT*, June 22, 2012.

109 *working-class Brooklyn*: Ibid.

109 *joined the army after high school*: Ibid.

109 *single-handedly arrested three men*: Ibid.

109 *U.S. Secret Service . . . offered Tucker a job*: Ibid.

109 *guarding Jacqueline Kennedy Onassis*: Ibid.

109 *Goode named him police commissioner*: Ibid.

109 *fourth-largest police department in the nation*: "With Initiative, Williams Rides Out a Tough First Year"; "The Top Cop Talks: Commissioner Willie Williams Speaks His Mind About His Family, Future, Successes and Frustrations."

109 *"favoritism, corruption, and brutality"*: "The Nation: Philadelphia Police Hit," LAT, March 12, 1987.

110 *"unfocused, unmanaged"*: Ibid.

110 *South Philly high school dropout*: "Frank Rizzo of Philadelphia Dies at 70; A 'Hero' and 'Villain,'" NYT, July 17, 1991.

110 *his love of the blackjack*: Ibid.

110 *black population . . . 1980s . . . 40 percent of the city's residents*: "Minorities Accounted for Area Population Gain," Philadelphia Inquirer, February 20, 1991.

110 *as late as 1980 had no shooting policy*: "Guns Being Fired More Often by Police in Phila.," Philadelphia Inquirer, November 18, 1990.

110 *Saturday night raids, personally led by Rizzo, on gay bars*: "Frank Rizzo of Philadelphia Dies at 70; A 'Hero' and 'Villian.'"

110 *stripped Black Panthers naked*: Ibid.

110 *spy on his political opponents*: The Learning Company, Inc., "Frank Rizzo," 1998.

110 *acts of police brutality were so "widespread and severe"*: "'Stop and Frisk' or Sloppy Risk?" Philadelphia, June 27, 2011.

110 *first department ever sued by the U.S. Justice Department*: Ibid.

111 *sending fifty commanders . . . John F. Kennedy School of Government*: "Former Police Commissioner Kevin M. Tucker."

111 *diversifying the department*: "Saying Goodbye to Kevin Tucker," Philadelphia Inquirer, June 10, 1988; "Former Police Commissioner Kevin M. Tucker."

111 *three ranks to deputy commissioner*: "Tucker Deputy Named to Head Youth Center," Philadelphia Inquirer, March 23, 1988; "With Initiative, Williams Rides Out a Tough First Year."

111 *195-page blueprint*: "The Nation: Philadelphia Police Hit."

111 *a "Mutt and Jeff" comedy act*: "Williams Criticized at Hearing, Police Readiness Is Questioned," Philadelphia Inquirer, January 25, 1990.

111 *"living in a climate of fear"*: "Philadelphia Justice System Overwhelmed," NYT, August 15, 1990.

112 *"on the verge of collapse"*: Ibid.

112 *1988 jail-overcrowding federal lawsuit*: "Agreement May Delay Jail Cap," Philadelphia Inquirer, February 4, 1988; "City Jails Receiving Once Again," Philadelphia Inquirer, June 11, 1988.

112 *5,900 officers in 1988, compared to 8,400 in 1977*: "Philadelphia Justice System Overwhelmed."

112 *response time . . . as long as two hours*: "Shortage of Policemen Cited in Park Beating," Philadelphia Inquirer, October 13, 1988; "Williams: City Is Short 600 Police Officers," Philadelphia Inquirer, October 27, 1988.

112 *police facilities . . . without heat in the winter:* "Williams Criticized at Hearing, Police Readiness Is Questioned."

112 *165 were out of service:* Ibid.

112 *Forty of the department's 400 unmarked cars had broken sirens:* Ibid.

112 *"bidding on [police] hats?":* Ibid.

113 *1989 . . . murders in Philadelphia rose . . . 1990:* "Number of Killings Soars in Big Cities Across U.S.," *NYT,* July 18, 1990.

113 *nonviolent demonstrators:* "Panel's Report Puts Spotlight on Police Conduct; Williams Has Made Strides in Rooting Misconduct, Some Say, but More Could Be Done," *Philadelphia Inquirer,* March 22, 1992.

113 *"I'm trying to change a mentality":* Ibid.

114 *"Williams has paid lip service":* Ibid.

114 *Officer-involved shootings also increased:* Ibid.

114 *"The crime rate is up":* "With Initiative, Williams Rides Out a Tough First Year."

114 *"Watching him [in Los Angeles]":* Stanley Sheinbaum, "Willie Williams' First Major Public Address"; "The New Chief: What's Going to Change at the LAPD."

114 *"sent two teams of people to Philadelphia":* Ibid.

115 *expanded . . . mini-stations:* "Here's Why Murders Are Down in the City: They're Going After the Worst Drug Dealers and the Violent Offenders, and They're Making a Federal Case out of Them," *Philadelphia Inquirer,* January 15, 1992; "Profile: Willie L. Williams"; "Officer Down, Willie Williams' Fall from Grace"; "Say Goodbye to Hollywood."

115 *gender and racial diversity:* "Williams' Open Door Sends Signal"; "Williams Helped Show How Badge Can Be a Bridge; The Commissioner Is Leaving a Legacy of Community," *Philadelphia Inquirer,* May 17, 1992; "Officer Down, Willie Williams' Fall from Grace"; "Say Goodbye to Hollywood."

115 *officers fired:* "Panel's Report Puts Spotlight on Police Conduct; Williams Has Made Strides in Rooting Misconduct, Some Say, but More Could Be Done"; "Profile: Willie L. Williams."

115 *three hundred new officers:* "Phila. Police to Reassign 6 Inspectors, 20 Captains," *Philadelphia Inquirer,* April 19, 1990.

115 *Philadelphia newspapers:* "With Initiative, Williams Rides Out a Tough First Year"; "Williams Criticized at Hearing, Police Readiness Is Questioned"; "Judge Warns Top Cop of Jail: Willie Williams, City Held in Contempt over Order on Officers," *Philadelphia Inquirer,* May 10, 1991; "Promoted Cops Removed," *Philadelphia Inquirer,* May 11, 1991; "Panel's Report Puts Spotlight on Police Conduct; Williams Has Made Strides in Rooting Out Misconduct, Some Say, but More Could Be Done."

115 *took the lieutenant's test:* Charlie Beck interview.

115 *watch commander in Watts:* Ibid.

116 *the parties were simply a sham:* Ibid.

116 *"gathering of Bloods and Crips in huge numbers"*: Ibid.
116 *"driving around in circles in large convoys"*: Ibid.

Charlie Beck and Andre Christian, 1993, South Los Angeles

116 *1993 . . . homicides . . . 1,100*: "Bad Rap?: Despite Crime Image, L.A. Fails to
     Make List of Worst 15 Cities, but San Bernardino Does," *LAT*, May 25, 1994.
117 *"cowed organization"*: Charlie Beck interview.
117 *"We tried to stop illegal behavior"*: Ibid.
117 *"It's like your family"*: Ibid.
117 *shot thirteen times*: Andre Christian interview.
117 *"glad that [he'd] got shot"*: Ibid.
117 *"sighs of relief"*: Ibid.
117 *"it was a relaxed situation"*: Ibid.
118 *"There just wasn't enough nurturing"*: Ibid.

Willie Williams, June 1992, Parker Center

118 *"My first impression of Willie Williams"*: Reese, "The Rise and Fall of a Public
     Leader."
119 *"because he is fat"*: Gary Greenebaum interview.
119 *missing his fuckin' gun*: Reese, "The Rise and Fall of a Public Leader."
119 *"bunch of basic police-academy information"*: David Dotson interview; "Say
     Goodbye to Hollywood."
119 *failed the waiver three different times*: Reese, "The Rise and Fall of a Public
     Leader."
119 *The state legislature later changed the test requirement*: "Say Goodbye to Holly-
     wood"; Reese, "The Rise and Fall of a Public Leader."
120 *Daryl Gates . . . always had a gun*: David Dotson interview; "Say Goodbye to
     Hollywood."
120 *USC's School of Public Administration . . . denied entrance*: Reese, "The Rise and
     Fall of a Public Leader."
120 *gossip to the L.A. Times*: Tim Rutten interview.
120 *"Willie made a big mistake"*: Charlie Beck interview.

Willie Williams, September 1992,
Police Administration Building

121 *Willie Williams . . . asked if he could take a vacation*: Michael Yamaki inter-
     view.
121 *Williams's schedule had been grueling*: "Say Goodbye to Hollywood."
121 *"Jesse Brewer tried—desperately—to tell him to go out to roll calls"*: Ann Reiss
     Lane interview; "Say Goodbye to Hollywood."

Bernard Parks, Fall 1992, Parker Center

122 *Parks . . . would later be named by* People *magazine*: "The 50 Most Beautiful People 1998," *People*, May 11, 1998, 89.

122 *son of a thirty-eight-year veteran*: "Father of Councilman Parks dies," *LAT*, October 28, 2008.

123 *"It's easy to point"*: Domanick, *Covering Police in Times of Crisis*, 23.

123 *Parks was asked about a series of LAPD crises*: Ibid.

123 *"I think we've evolved"*: Ibid.

123 *"Parks always thought Jim was a good guy"*: Tim Rutten interview.

124 *Parks . . . in charge of about 85 percent of the force*: "Say Goodbye to Hollywood."

124 *"Parks didn't talk to Jess"*: Anthony De Los Reyes interview.

124 *"Parks was livid with Jesse"*: David Dotson interview.

124 *"Bernard knew everything about the Los Angeles Police Department"*: Charlie Beck interview.

124 *"undermine the chief"*: Curtis Woodle interview.

124 *bodyguard to the mayor*: Ibid.

124 *"talking bad about the top dog"*: Ibid.

124 *Williams . . . would later demote Parks*: Anthony De Los Reyes interview; "Chief Gives Parks 10 Days to Resign or Accept Demotion," *LAT*, September 15, 1994; "Say Goodbye to Hollywood."

125 *a $15,000 raise*: "City OKs Demotion, Raise for Police Aide," *LAT*, October 8, 1994; Reese, "The Rise and Fall of a Public Leader."

Alfred Lomas, Early to Mid-Eighties, Scotland, the Philippines, and L.A.

125 *Alfred Lomas decided to join the United States Marine Corps*: Alfred Lomas interview.

125 *fifth of whiskey*: Ibid.

125 *"other than honorable"*: Ibid.

125 *Assigned to Scotland*: Ibid.

125 *Reassigned to the Philippines*: Ibid.

125 *high-security . . . brig in North Carolina*: Ibid.

126 *Tami Amis*: Ibid.

126 *pretty Latina*: Ibid.

126 *Toles Motel*: Ibid.

126 *"an orgasm magnified—one hundred times"*: Ibid.

126 *chasing that crack high*: Ibid.

127 *"Hey, what's up, dawg"*: Ibid.

128 *"one of the best crack dealers I had ever seen"*: Ibid.

128 *"F13"*: Ibid.

129 *Lomas always made sure to be clean shaven*: Ibid.
129 *to make runs with women*: Ibid.
129 *freelancing his services to three or four other dealers*: Ibid.
129 *"I liked the action on the streets"*: Ibid.
129 *a house in Palos Verdes*: Ibid.
129 *sentenced to eighteen months*: Ibid.
129 *The Golden Rule in prison*: Ibid.
130 *you stay with your own kind*: Ibid.
130 *blacks, whites, and Latinos are all housed separately*: Ibid.
130 *Florencia 13 . . . kept him protected*: Ibid.
130 *After serving sixteen months*: Ibid.
130 *Lomas became a father*: Ibid.
130 *His new son's mother . . . a crack addict*: Ibid.
130 *His son was startlingly thin*: Ibid.
130 *"threw a Rambo"*: Ibid.
130 *landed a salesman's job with Safety Clean*: Ibid.

David Mack and Rafael "Ray" Perez, Tuesday, October 26, 1993, Hollywood, California

131 *Jesse Vicencio was leaning*: "Witnesses Say Officer Killed Unarmed Suspect," *LAT*, September 23, 1999.
131 *Datsun B210 parked on a dark Hollywood side street*: "Perez's Bitter Saga of Lies, Regrets and Harm," *LAT*, December 31, 2000.
131 *West Bureau [drug] Buy Team*: Ibid.
131 *"Just by its nature"*: Ibid.
131 *driving L.A.'s homicide rate to a record of 1,100 in 1993*: "Bad Rap?: Despite Crime Image, L.A. Fails to Make List of Worst 15 Cities, but San Bernardino Does."
132 *Jesse Vicencio, who'd lost his life over that potential sale*: "Witnesses Say Officer Killed Unarmed Suspect."
132 *David Mack . . . the department's second-highest medal for heroism*: "Who Killed B.I.G.?" *Rolling Stone*, June 7, 2001; "Perez's Bitter Saga of Lies, Regrets and Harm."
132 *two eyewitnesses . . . that Vicencio never pulled a gun*: "Witnesses Say Officer Killed Unarmed Suspect."
132 *first wife divorced him*: "Perez's Bitter Saga of Lies, Regrets and Harm."
132 *second wife, Denise, an LAPD dispatcher*: Ibid.
132 *Born in Puerto Rico in 1967*: Ibid.
132 *One of three children*: Ibid.
132 *Brooklyn . . . Paterson*: Ibid.
133 *northern Philadelphia*: Ibid.
133 *uncle . . . drug ring*: Ibid.

133 *U.S. Marine Corps infantryman:* Ibid.

133 *joined the LAPD in June of 1989:* Ibid.

133 *Assigned first to the . . . Harbor Division:* Ibid.

133 *then worked patrol in Wilshire Division:* Ibid.

133 *David Mack . . . raised on the cruel streets of Compton:* "Ex-LAPD Officer Sentenced in Bank of America Robbery," *LAT*, September 14, 1999; "The Dirtiest Cop Alive," *Maxim*, November 2000; "Bad Cops," *New Yorker*, May 21, 2001.

133 *attended the University of Oregon on a track scholarship:* "Officer Charged in Bank Heist That Netted $722,000," *LAT*, December 18, 1997; "The Dirtiest Cop Alive"; "Bad Cops."

133 *NCAA 800-meter champion:* Ibid.

133 *qualified for the Olympics:* "Ex-LAPD Officer Sentenced in Bank of America Robbery"; "Who Killed B.I.G.?"

133 *rumored to have dated . . . Florence Griffith Joyner:* "Dream Chaser," ESPN.com, August 26, 2009; "The Dirtiest Cop Alive."

133 *two children:* "Ex-LAPD Officer Sentenced in Bank of America Robbery"; "Bad Cops"; "Who Killed B.I.G.?"

Bill Bratton and Rudolph Giuliani, November 1993, New York City

134 *Rudolph Giuliani . . . grown up in Brooklyn and Long Island:* "Growing Up Giuliani," *Newsweek*, November 24, 2007.

134 *four uncles who were cops:* Kirtzman, *Rudy Giuliani: Emperor of the City*, 93.

135 *"We're Taking the Subways Back—for You":* Bratton and Knobler, *Turnaround*, 177.

135 *Bratton had been "pleased and flattered":* Ibid., 179.

136 *Maple began to scribble on a cocktail napkin:* "Jack Maple, 48, a Designer of City Crime Control Strategies," *NYT*, August 6, 2001.

136 *Miller . . . "best Rolodex in America":* William Bratton interview; "Journalism Scoops or Shortcuts?" *LAT*, December 14, 2002.

136 *sparring with . . . John Gotti:* Bratton and Knobler, *Turnaround*, xii; Kirtzman, *Rudy Giuliani: Emperor of the City*, 93.

137 *"Rudy hasn't taken credit for":* "Rudy to City, Pay Up and Shut Up!" *New York*, October 25, 1999.

137 *Jack Maple . . . homburg hat– and bow tie–wearing:* "Jack Maple, 48, a Designer of City Crime Control Strategies"; Kirtzman, *Rudy Giuliani: Emperor of the City*, 90.

137 *no accident that the three were sitting at Elaine's:* Bratton and Knobler, *Turnaround*, xii; Kirtzman, *Rudy Giuliani: Emperor of the City*, 93.

137 *Bratton, whose third wife had returned to Boston:* "Bratton, Wife Seen on Rocks," *NYDN*, January 13, 1998.

137 *"a very good time":* Bratton and Knobler, *Turnaround*, 259.

137 *"Broadway Bill"*: "Bratton Is Sworn In for Second Term," *LAT*, October 26, 2007.

138 *Maple called it COMPSTAT*: "Jack Maple, 48, a Designer of City Crime Control Strategies."

138 *NYPD . . . now thirty-eight thousand officers strong*: "NYPD Leader Finds Fame in Crime's Demise," AP, February 10, 1996; "Brass from Past; Fewer Finest Can Still Hack It: Ex-Top Cop," *New York Post*, April 27, 2003.

139 *special thirty-five-officer unit*: "Bratton: The Making of a Police Visionary."

139 *new public housing units commissioned by Mayor Ed Koch*: "Ed Koch Dead: Mayor Who Became a Symbol of New York Passes Away at 88," *NYDN*, February 1, 2013; "Ed Koch, Former Mayor of New York, Dies," *Boston Globe*, February 1, 2013.

139 *murders in New York City . . . dropped by almost 385 from 1994*: "Bratton: The Making of a Police Visionary"; *NYDN*, December 30, 2013.

139 *would fall by almost 590*: "Bratton: The Making of a Police Visionary."

139 *Total felonies in 1995 . . . decrease by 27 percent*: Ibid.

139 *robberies by over 30 percent*: Ibid.

139 *burglaries by 25 percent*: Ibid.

139 *his image, dressed in a 1940s tan raincoat*: "One Good Apple," *Time*, January 15, 1996.

Willie Williams, 1992–1993, Los Angeles

139 *Willie Williams . . . job approval rating was 67 percent*: Reese, "The Rise and Fall of a Public Leader."

140 *jumped to 72 percent*: Ibid.

140 *Los Angeles Times poll*: "The Times Poll: Riordan Rates Favorably with 45% of Citizens," *LAT*, November 7, 1993.

140 *and he would ignore them*: "L.A. Police Commission Moves to Oust Chief Willie Williams," *Chicago Tribune*, March 10, 1997.

140 *"in Philadelphia he had only one boss—the mayor"*: Gary Greenebaum interview.

140 *but in Los Angeles "he had 21 bosses"*: "LAPD Reform: Too Many Cooks in the Kitchen," *LAT*, June 4, 1996; "The Chief Looks Back," *LAT*, May 16, 1997; Gary Greenebaum interview.

140 *stopped attending L.A.'s Criminal Justice Group*: Reese, "The Rise and Fall of a Public Leader."

141 *"He never talked to the commission"*: Anthony De Los Reyes interview.

141 *"he said he'd get back to me"*: Ibid.

141 *"But he didn't want to know anything"*: David Dotson interview.

Richard Riordan and Willie Williams,
June 1993, Los Angeles City Hall

142 *"10,500 officers"*: "LAPD Cannot Meet Riordan's Goal, Chief Says," *LAT*, July 14, 1993; "Riordan Steadfast on LAPD Expansion," *LAT*, July 15, 1993; "Williams Finishes Plan to Bolster LAPD," *LAT*, September 3, 1993.

142 *Riordan . . . Williams and his wife for dinner at his home*: "Help Wanted," *LAT*, July 27, 1997.

142 *best police chief in America*: Ibid.

142 *"Sorry Mr. Mayor"*: "LAPD Cannot Meet Riordan's Goal, Chief Says"; "Riordan Steadfast on LAPD Expansion"; "Williams Finishes Plan to Bolster LAPD"; "Say Goodbye to Hollywood"; Gary Greenebaum interview.

142 *Richard Riordan . . . ex–New Yorker raised in Queens*: "New Mayor Faces Hard Part: Running Los Angeles," *NYT*, July 2, 1993.

142 *junk-bond industry*: "Riordan Puts His Millions Behind Bid to 'Rescue' L.A.," *LAT*, March 23, 1993; *Businessweek*, May 9, 1993; "L.A. Mayoral Contest: Voters Look for 'Neither,'" *Christian Science Monitor*, June 8, 1993; "Top Gun, Richard Riordan's Plans for Our Next Police Chief," *LA Weekly*, July 11–17, 1997.

142 *lavishly supporting L.A.'s Roman Catholic archdiocese*: "Riordan Is a Catholic, but He'll Be Judged on His Acts as Mayor," *LAT*, July 17, 1993.

142 *"Tough Enough to Turn L.A. Around"*: "Riordan Puts His Millions Behind Bid to 'Rescue' L.A."; Gary Greenebaum interview.

142 *hundreds of thousands of dollars into his own campaign*: "Riordan Puts His Millions Behind Bid to 'Rescue' L.A."

143 *add three thousand cops*: "Riordan Steadfast on LAPD Expansion."

143 *As a corporate CEO*: "Riordan Puts His Millions Behind Bid to 'Rescue' L.A."; "Perspectives on the Mayor's Race: Candidates Cut Through Campaign Distortions," *LAT*, June 6, 1993; "Say Goodbye to Hollywood."

143 *headed two law firms*: "Riordan Puts His Millions Behind Bid to 'Rescue' L.A."; "Mayor Should Round Out His Inner Circle," *LAT*, May 10, 1996.

143 *"a terrible position"*: David Dotson interview.

143 *LAPD chief's tenure*: Independent Commission on the Los Angeles Police Department, *Report of the Independent Commission on the Los Angeles Police Department*, 210.

Richard Riordan, 1993

144 *"business friendly"*: "GOP Maverick to Make Run for Governor/Ex–L.A. Mayor Riordan Shows Strength in Polls," *San Francisco Chronicle*, November 6, 2001.

144 *Protestant emigrants from the Midwest*: Domanick, *To Protect and To Serve*, 32.

144 *Bill Parker was Catholic*: Ibid., 91.

145 *hundreds of thousands of Latino immigrants:* "A Painful Choice Between a Parish and a Church," *LAT*, March 7, 1994.

145 *$3 billion in assets:* "Pope John Paul II Has Appointed Two Bishops," *Orlando Sentinel*, March 21, 1990.

145 *budget of nearly $300 million:* Ibid.

145 *284 parishes:* "A Painful Choice Between a Parish and a Church."

145 *Riordan would raise over $84 million:* "They've Gone on Offensive for Education," *LAT*, September 23, 1990.

145 *Cardinal Mahony . . . helicopter:* "Riordan Puts His Millions Behind Bid to 'Rescue' L.A."; "Riordan Is a Catholic, but He'll Be Judged on His Acts as Mayor."

145 *John F. Kennedy's presidential campaign . . . Wardlaw:* "Reign Maker," *Los Angeles Magazine*, January 2005; "Mayor Should Round Out His Inner Circle."

145 *Bill Clinton's crisis-filled first presidential campaign:* "Reign Maker."

146 *Riordan and McKenzie:* "Reign Maker"; "Mayor Should Round Out His Inner Circle."

146 *had been his protégé:* Ibid.

146 *$35 million cathedral:* *LAT*, September 3, 1999; "Reign Maker."

146 *Mount St. Mary's College:* *The Mount*, Winter/Spring 2005.

146 *gay officials:* "Riordan Asks Commission Appointees to Work for Free," *LAT*, July 31, 1993; "Mayor to Name 2 Attorneys to Police Panel," *LAT*, June 25, 1997; "Top Gun, Richard Riordan's Plans for Our Next Police Chief"; "2 Lawyers Backed for Police Commission," *LAT*, August 5, 1997.

146 *He liked Bernie Parks:* "Reign Maker."

146 *Tom Bradley and Daryl Gates . . . couldn't bear to speak with one another:* Gates, *Chief*, 329; "After the Riots; Los Angeles Mayor Comes under More Attacks in Police Chief's New Book," *NYT*, May 6, 1992; "LAPD's Response to the Riot," *LAT*, May 11, 1992.

Gary Greenebaum, Summer 1993, Parker Center

147 *"put on the commission partly because I was Jewish":* Gary Greenebaum interview.

147 *Brewer . . . was privately growing increasingly disappointed:* Michael Yamaki interview.

148 *"Not only was it a self-evaluation":* Gary Greenebaum interview; "Help Wanted."

148 *"I believe that I have met all expectations":* "Help Wanted."

148 *"Williams just didn't have the capacity to do the job":* Gary Greenebaum interview.

148 *"this city and this department have a long history of racism":* Ibid.

149 *"he would . . . say anything that popped into his head":* Ibid.

149 *"he never did anything":* Ibid.

149 *"you seem to lack focus"*: "Police Panel Rebuked Chief, Sources Disclose," *LAT*, May 24, 1995; "Say Goodbye to Hollywood."

O. J. Simpson, June 1994, Brentwood, California

150 *one in three black men*: Mauer, *The Crisis of the Young African American Male and the Criminal Justice System*, 3.

151 *Simpson had been introduced to about forty police officers*: "Details Emerge of Close LAPD Ties to Simpson," *LAT*, February 2. 1995; "O. J. Team Steps Up Attack on Witness," *San Francisco Chronicle*, February 2, 1995.

151 *he would appear at a Christmas party*: "Details Emerge of Close LAPD Ties to Simpson."

151 *Even the gun . . . registered to an LAPD lieutenant*: Ibid.

151 *frantic calls from Nicole Brown Simpson to the LAPD*: "The Simpson Case: The Victim; Nicole Brown Simpson: Slain at the Dawn of a Better Life," *NYT*, June 23, 1994; "Details Emerge of Close LAPD Ties to Simpson."

151 ninth *response in 1989*: Ibid.

151 *after horribly beating Nicole*: Ibid.

O. J. Simpson and Johnnie Cochran, Superior Court, Downtown Los Angeles

151 *F. Lee Bailey . . . "Boston Strangler" . . . Patty Hearst*: "Bailey Delivers Stock but Remains Jailed," *NYT*, April 17, 1996; "Boston Strangler Case: Officials Announce 'Major Development' in 1964 Killing," *Huffington Post*, July 11, 2013; "A Hearst Trial Hangover? Patty Thinks F. Lee Bailey Had One and Blew Her Case; Now He's Blown His Stack," *People*, September 4, 1978.

152 *Barry Scheck . . . Cardozo Law School*: "Simpson's Lawyers Attack Handling of Blood Samples," *NYT*, April 13, 1995; "Scheck Moves from Sidelines to Center Stage," *LAT*, September 29, 1995; "Where Are They Now?" *LAT*, February 11, 1997.

152 *Innocence Project*: "Scheck Moves from Sidelines to Center Stage"; "Where Are They Now?"

152 *Give me one black juror*: Dunne, *Another City, Not My Own*, 147.

152 *the trial would take place* not *in the white, affluent Westside*: "Location of Trial Can Be Crucial to Outcome, Experts Say," *LAT*, November 27, 1995.

Rafael "Ray" Perez, August 1995, Rampart Division

153 *Ray Perez . . . transferred to Rampart CRASH*: "Perez's Bitter Saga of Lies, Regrets and Harm."

153 *an elongated, wickedly grinning white skull*: "Insignia of Rampart Anti-Gang Unit Raises Concerns," *LAT*, February 8, 2000.

153 *the dead man's hand of aces and eights*: Frontline, PBS, May 15, 2001.

153 *most of whom . . . were "in the loop"*: Perez, BA109900, "Statement of Rafael Antonio Perez," September 22, 1999.

154 *Sammy Martin . . . "had a girl to go visit"*: Ibid.

154 *7.8 square miles of Pico-Union*: Blue Ribbon Review Panel, *Report of the Rampart Independent Review Panel*, 1; "One Bad Cop," *New York Times Magazine*, October 1, 2000.

154 *the most densely inhabited area west of the Mississippi*: "One Bad Cop."

154 *Pico-Union's slum housing . . . 267,000 . . . Central American immigrants*: Blue Ribbon Review Panel, *Report of the Rampart Independent Review Panel*, 1.

154 *Rampart Division . . . 150 homicides a year*: Frontline, PBS, May 15, 2001.

154 *thirty-six thousand people per square mile*: "One Bad Cop."

155 *Raquel Argomaniz . . . Rampart CRASH cops . . . made life so unpleasant*: Perez, BA109900, "Statement of Rafael Antonio Perez," September 17, 1999.

155 *"Throw-down" guns*: Ibid.; "The Dirtiest Cop Alive."

155 *planted evidence . . . in 40 percent*: Perez, BA109900, "Statement of Rafael Perez," December 14, 1999, 41.

155 *ten-sheet loose-leaf binder*: Ibid., 36.

156 *"plain and simple"*: Ibid., 26.

156 *"If you were in a bad position"*: Ibid.

156 *"Whatever the way they did it"*: Gerald Chaleff interview.

157 *77th's had crossed bones*: "Web Site Cashes In on Rampart Scandal," *LAT*, March 9, 2000.

157 *"77th Street eats their dead"*: Ibid.

157 *one-pound bag of cocaine and a beeper*: "One Bad Cop"; "The Dirtiest Cop Alive."

157 *steal the quarter pound of cocaine*: "One Bad Cop."

158 *three midlevel dope dealers*: Interview with confidential source.

158 *bunch of rock . . . flush it down the toilet*: Interview with confidential source.

158 *dropped the baggie*: Interview with confidential source.

158 *booked some of his dope*: Interview with confidential source.

158 *kept for themselves*: Interview with confidential source.

Willie Williams, October to December 1994, Las Vegas

158 *Willie Williams liked Las Vegas*: "Report of 'Rogue' Probe of Chief Termed False," *LAT*, May 31, 1995; "Willie Williams Still Seeks Turf: L.A. Is Not Philadelphia; That Makes the Police Chief an Outsider," *Philadelphia Inquirer*, July 4, 1995.

158 *not arriving until sometime Sunday*: Ibid.; "Say Goodbye to Hollywood."

159 *"Daryl's speeches always promoted the thin blue line"*: David Dotson interview.

159 *"the organization never gave Willie a fair chance to succeed"*: Charlie Beck interview.

159 *Stephen Downing letter:* "Chief's Critic Voices Fears of Reprisal," *LAT*, February 18, 1995; "Commission Goes Outside LAPD to Investigate Chief," *LAT*, February 28, 1995.

160 *"I have never accepted":* "New Charges Targeting Chief Concern Council," *LAT*, May 15, 1996; "Willie Officially Asks for New Term as Chief," *LAT*, January 3, 1997.

160 *comped rooms at Caesars Palace* five *different times:* Ibid.

160 *reprimand Willie Williams for lying to the commission:* Ibid.; Katherine Mader interview.

160 *City Council . . . overturned the reprimand:* "New Charges Targeting Chief Concern Council"; "Willie Officially Asks for New Term as Chief"; "Say Goodbye to Hollywood."

O. J. Simpson, January 1995, Los Angeles Superior Court

161 *"a lying, perjuring, genocidal racist":* "The Crime Does Not Fit: Defense Cochran Puts on Knit Cap and a Pair of Gloves," *NYDN*, September 28, 1995; "Simpson's Lawyer Tells Jury Evidence 'Doesn't Fit,'" *NYT*, September 28, 1995.

161 *Vannatter . . . not only notified the coroner very late:* "Delay in Notifying Coroner Hurt Simpson Case Probe," *LAT*, September 17, 1994.

162 *Furhman jumped over a wall:* "The O. J. Simpson Murder Trial: High-Stakes Testimony by Fuhrman Concludes," *LAT*, March 17, 1995; "Simpson Trial Focuses on Fuhrman Tapes," *Chicago Tribune*, August 21, 1995.

162 *"reckless disregard for the truth":* "Saber Rattling," *NYT*, October 19, 1994; "Vannatter Offers Explanations for Glove Questions," *LAT*, March 22, 1995.

162 *"Contaminated, compromised, and corrupted":* "Ito Sanctions 'Unfair' Defense Tactics; Cochran Resumes Opening Statement," *AP*, January 30, 1995; "The O. J. Simpson Murder Trial: Excerpts of Opening Remarks by Defense Counsel Cochran," *LAT*, January 31, 1995.

162 *Bill Pavelic:* "Into the Spotlight/Bill Pavelic: Simpson Case Throws LAPD Critic into Media Broiler," *LAT*, March 2, 1995; Bill Pavelic interview, 1995.

162 *Detective Vannater . . . put the evidence vial in his pocket:* "20-Year-Old O. J. Simpson Case Taught Police What Not to Do," *AP*, June 10, 2014.

162 *"a cesspool of contamination":* "The Simpson Case: The Fallout; Tough Job for Police to Regain Credibility," *NYT*, October 5, 1995; "20-Year-Old O. J. Simpson Case Taught Police What Not to Do."

162 *Dennis Fung . . . refrigerator in his van:* "The O. J. Simpson Murder Trial: The Reality Behind Assault on Fung," *LAT*, April 19, 1995.

162 *He got "Schecked":* "Where Are They Now?"; "Bar Takes Steps Against 2 Lawyers in Simpson Trial, Warns Third," *LAT*, June 13, 1997.

163 *"by far" the worst:* "DNA Expert Taints Juice Prosecution," *NYDN*, August 3, 1995; "Contamination Chronic at LAPD Lab, Expert Testifies," *LAT*, August 3, 1995.

163 *impound yard*: "Evidence," AP, October 3, 1995; "List of the Evidence in the O. J. Simpson Double-Murder Trial," *USA Today*, October 18, 1996.

163 *"genocidal racist"*: "Cochran Calls Fuhrman 'Lying, Genocidal Racist,'" *Philadelphia Inquirer*, September 28, 1995; "Families' Anger Erupts Outside the Courtroom," *LAT*, September 29, 1995.

163 *hadn't used the "N" word*: "Trial Gets Boost, Society Gets Blemish from Fuhrman Tapes," *Baltimore Sun*, September 1, 1995; "F. Lee Bailey: 'I Had No Idea There Were Any Tapes,'" *Chicago Tribune*, October 18, 1995.

163 *Howard University*: NBC News, October 4, 1995; "Think Simpson Was Guilty? You Must Be Multiculturally Skewed," *Deseret News*, October 15, 1995.

164 *"John and Ken"*: Author heard on radio, 1995; "The Simpson Murder Case: Twists and Turns Keep Radio Fans Talking About Simpson," *LAT*, June 18, 1994; "The Simpson Verdicts: Callers to Talk Radio Span the Dial with Debate," *LAT*, October 4, 1995; "They're Driven to Entertain," *LAT*, August 4, 1996.

164 *Brien Chapman . . . ordering a Bloody Mary*: "Cop Talk," *LA Weekly*, October 6–12, 1995.

164 *"Everybody here is so pissed"*: Ibid.

Katherine Mader and Willie Williams, May 1996, Parker Center

165 *Appointed IG*: "First Inspector General Chosen to Police LAPD," *LAT*, May 29, 1996; "The Inspector General," *Buzz*, March 1998, 50.

165 *UCLA and UC Davis Law*: "First Inspector General Chosen to Police LAPD"; "The Inspector General," 52.

165 *co–defense counsel for . . . Hillside Strangler*: Ibid.

165 *Los Angeles District Attorney's Office*: "First Inspector General Chosen to Police LAPD."

165 *"Williams is a reform chief"*: Katherine Mader interview.

166 *string of complaints*: Ibid.

166 *"you can pick out [positive] qualities"*: Ibid.

166 *"declined by 43 percent"*: "Say Goodbye to Hollywood"; "The Inspector General," 52.

166 *Mader very publicly disputed Williams's claim*: "Say Goodbye to Hollywood."

167 *"Glacial"*: "Panel Takes Over Monitoring LAPD Reforms," *LAT*, December 21, 1994; "The LAPD: Is Williams' Mission an Impossible One?" *LAT*, February 26, 1995.

167 *"Inexcusably slow"*: "Panel Takes Over Monitoring LAPD Reforms."

Bill Bratton and Rudolph Giuliani, Monday, April 15, 1996, New York City

167 *Bratton . . . celebrated by Time magazine*: "One Good Apple."

167 *"it's the mayor's department"*: Bratton and Knobler, *Turnaround*, 285.

167 *Giuliani's enforcer, Deputy Mayor Peter Powers:* "For Giuliani and Green, It Might as Well Be 1997," *NYT,* June 11, 1994; Bratton and Knobler, *Turnaround,* xxxi–xxxiii.

168 *Bill Bratton . . . forming his own security firm:* Bratton and Knobler, *Turnaround,* 308; "Bratton: The Making of a Police Visionary."

168 *When the 9/11 planes hit:* William Bratton interview; Rikki Klieman interview.

168 *James Lardner . . . "as leader and archetype of a generation":* "The Commish," *NYT,* February 1, 1998.

168 *by July of 1995, for example, crime had decreased nationally by 1 percent:* Bratton and Knobler, *Turnaround,* 290.

168 *but by 16 percent in New York City:* Ibid.

168 *over the next twenty years, crime . . . by over 75 percent:* "America's Real Criminal Element: Lead," *Mother Jones,* January/February 2013; "Prison Population Can Shrink When Police Crowd Streets," *NYT,* January 26, 2013.

168 *In 1994 . . . 1,561 homicides in New York City:* "Reported Crimes Continue to Show Decline," *NYT,* October 2, 1996.

168 *931 in Chicago:* Chicago Police Department, *2008 Murder Analysis in Chicago,* 2.

168 *and 850 in Los Angeles:* "LAPD Chief Beck: City Safer Than It's Been in Decades," *LADN,* January 13, 2014.

168 *By 2002 . . . Chicago recorded the highest number of murders:* Chicago Police Department, *2008 Murder Analysis in Chicago,* 2.

168 *Los Angeles had 647:* "Crime in L.A. Drops for 3rd Year in a Row," *LAT,* December 21, 2005.

168 *New York had just 587:* "Fewer New York Murders, and Even Fewer by Strangers," *NYT,* November 22, 2007.

168 *New York City had 75 percent fewer homicides, robberies, and auto thefts in 2012:* Zimring, *The Great American Crime Decline,* 106.

169 *"In New York . . . we changed the culture of permissiveness":* "The Reformer, on Honeymoon," *LAT,* January 19, 2003.

Rafael "Ray" Perez and Nino Durden, Sunday, October 13, 1996, 18th Street Territory, Rampart Division

170 *light-blue Taurus:* "One Bad Cop."

170 *large, low-hanging tree:* Ovando, BA139642, "District Attorney's Direct Examination of Rafael Perez," 58 and 61.

170 *9mm Berettas:* Ibid., 59 and 67.

170 *radios:* Ibid., 67.

170 *flashlights:* Ibid., 66.

170 *binoculars:* Ibid., 78.

170 *radio earpieces:* Perez, BA109900, "Statement of Rafael Antonio Perez," September 10, 1999.

170 *lifted a board*: Ibid.

170 *briefed at roll call*: Ibid.

170 *observation posts*: Ibid.

170 *corner window*: Ovando, BA139642, "District Attorney's Direct Examination of Rafael Perez," 65 and 68.

170 *found a guy called "Nene"*: Ibid.

170 *Javier Ovando, a member of the notorious 18th Street Gang*: Ovando B110980, 2; "One Bad Cop."

170 *They had thrown him out of the building the night before*: "One Bad Cop."

170 *Handcuffing the two men*: Ibid.

171 *Nene, who left immediately*: Ibid.

171 *a loud knock on the door*: Perez, BA109900, "Statement of Rafael Antonio Perez," September 10, 1999.

171 *"Police officer, drop the gun!"*: "Scandal Shows Why Innocent Plead Guilty," *LAT*, December 31, 1999.

171 *double-action Beretta*: Ovando BA139642, 59.

171 *firing off three rounds*: Ovando B110980, Ex. A, 2.

171 *Ovando . . . very different, very real story*: Ovando BA139642, 49; Ovando B110980, Ex. B, 2.

171 *shot him in the chest*: Ovando, B110980, "Declaration of Brian Tyndall," September 16, 1992, Ex. B, 2.; "D.A. Set to Charge Officer in Shooting."

171 *pulled Ovando off the floor by the front of his shirt*: "D.A. Set to Charge Officer in Shooting," *LAT*, July 28, 2000.

171 *Ray . . . fired a round into the side of his head*: Ovando B110980, Ex. B, 2.

171 *CRASH's secret radio code*: "Secret LAPD Testimony Implicated Nine Officers," *LAT*, February 27, 2003; "Police in Secret Group Broke Law Routinely," *LAT*, February 10, 2000.

171 *CRASH officers understood . . . everybody had a role to play*: Perez, BA109900, "Statement of Rafael Antonio Perez," September 10, 1999.

172 *Once the story was decided on*: Perez, BA109900, "Statement of Rafael Antonio Perez," September 17, 1999.

172 *The sergeant in charge that evening*: Ibid.; "One Bad Cop."

172 *The tale agreed upon . . . Javier Ovando . . . burst into the room*: Perez, BA109900, "Statement of Rafael Antonio Perez," September 10, 1999.

172 *"eliminate the police from [18th Street] territory"*: Ovando B110980, Ex. A, 3.

172 *Durden did all the explaining to the sergeant*: Perez, BA109900, "Statement of Rafael Antonio Perez," September 10, 1999.

172 *filthy red rag*: Ibid.; "One Bad Cop."

172 *Tech .22 . . . serial number Durden had previously scraped off*: Perez, BA109900, "Statement of Rafael Antonio Perez," September 10, 1999; "One Bad Cop."

172 *banana clip*: Ovando B110980, Ex. B, 1.

172 *Durden . . . placed the weapon next to Javier Ovando's fallen body*: Perez, BA109900, "Statement of Rafael Antonio Perez," September 10, 1999; "One Bad Cop."

172 *where Ray needed to be when he fired*: Perez, BA109900, "Statement of Rafael Antonio Perez," September 17, 1999.

172 *a stuffed chair lying on its back*: Perez, BA109900, "Statement of Rafael Antonio Perez," September 10, 1999.

172 *shooting position . . . consistent with the rest of it*: Perez, BA109900, "Statement of Rafael Antonio Perez," September 17, 1999.

173 *mug party*: Perez, BA109900, "Statement of Rafael Antonio Perez," December 14, 1999, 37.

173 *"the benches"*: Perez, BA109900, "Statement of Rafael Antonio Perez," December 14, 1999, 233; "Police in Secret Group Broke Law Routinely."

173 *Jack Daniel's and cold beer . . . steaks*: Perez, BA109900, "Statement of Rafael Antonio Perez," December 14, 1999, 37.

173 *award plaques from a sergeant*: Ibid.; "Police in Secret Group Broke Law Routinely."

173 *two framed playing cards with red hearts and red bullets*: Ibid.

174 *Javier Ovando . . . paralyzed and wheelchair-bound*: "One Bad Cop"; "Bad Cops"; "Los Angeles Paying Victims $70 Million for Police Graft," *NYT*, April 1, 2005.

174 *brought into L.A. County Superior Court on a gurney*: "Scandal Shows Why Innocent Plead Guilty"; "One Bad Cop."

174 *"The defendant . . . [had] equipped himself"*: Ovando BA139642, "Sentencing Memorandum," March 7, 1997, 6.

174 *"What would defense counsel have you believe?"*: "Scandal Shows Why Innocent Plead Guilty."

174 *as his pregnant girlfriend*: "One Bad Cop."

174 *Javier Ovando was found guilty of two counts of assaulting a police officer*: Ovando BA139642, "Sentencing Memorandum."

174 *Although Ovando had that number "18" tattooed on the back of his neck*: "One Bad Cop."

174 *he had no felony arrests*: Ibid.

174 *LAPD detectives had never even bothered to interview him*: Ovando B110980, Ex. B, 2.

175 *J. Stephen Czuleger . . . appointed during the 1980s by . . . George Deukmejian*: "Scandal Shows Why Innocent Plead Guilty."

175 *"What happened was dirty," Toister later told*: "One Bad Cop."

175 *Javier Ovando . . . twenty-three years, four months in state prison*: Ovando B110980, Ex. A, 2; "Scandal Shows Why Innocent Plead Guilty."

175 *"the defendant has no remorse"*: "Scandal Shows Why Innocent Plead Guilty"; "One Bad Cop"; "Bad Cops."

Richard Eide, Spring 1997, Los Angeles Police Academy

175   *Captain Richard Eide stood on a roadway*: Author's observations.

175   *"We don't have paramilitaristic [sic] training"*: Richard Eide interview; "Community-Based Skepticism," *LA Weekly*, February 28–March 6, 1997.

175   *"The Police Department . . . has a job to do"*: Ibid.

175   *"a catchall term"*: Ibid.

176   *"the report went up on some shelf"*: Ron Noblet interview.

176   *"The Police Commission Office started monitoring"*: Gary Greenebaum interview.

177   *"The people who think the LAPD had problems"*: Richard Eide interview; "Community-Based Skepticism."

177   *Sergeant Nicholas Titiriga . . . "compiled a total of eighteen misconduct complaints"*: "The Simpson Legacy: Just under the Skin: Pushed by Change, Pulled by the Past: As the LAPD Pursues Community-Friendly Policing, a Paramilitary Tradition Dies Hard," *LAT*, October 10, 1995.

177   *"What reformers reject in the old department"*: Ibid.

178   *Deirdre Hill . . . LAPD had "no in-service training"*: "LAPD to Issue Manual on Use of Force," *LAT*, September 1, 1995.

178   *"assassinating Williams behind his back"*: Allan Parachini interview; "Say Goodbye to Hollywood."

178   *"ultimate slam job"*: Ibid.

Willie Williams, March 1997, Parker Center

178   *"the department cannot continue"*: "Los Angeles Police Board Dumps City's First Black Chief," *Chicago Tribune*, March 11, 1997; "Williams Won't Get 2d Term as Los Angeles Police Chief; A Civilian Review Panel Pointed to Management Breakdowns; The Public Had Embraced Williams," *Philadelphia Inquirer*, March 11, 1997.

178   *"problem officers"*: Independent Commission on the Los Angeles Police Department, *Report of the Independent Commission on the Los Angeles Police Department*, x–xii; " 'They Hit Me, So I Hit Back': The Christopher Commission Spoke of 44 'Problem Officers' in the LAPD; Now Their Names Have Been Obtained, Allowing an Examination of Their Records; Some of Them Speak Out," *LAT*, October 4, 1992; "What Has Happened to the 'LAPD 44'?" *LAT*, October 15, 1995.

178   *Michael Falvo . . . shooting death*: "Officer Who Shot Boy Was 'Problem' Cop," *LAT*, August 3, 1995.

178   *Andrew Teague . . . falsifying evidence*: "LAPD Detective Won't Be Charged with Perjury," *LAT*, November 23, 1995.

179   *"business as usual"*: Gary Greenebaum interview.

179   *Willie Williams . . . an hourlong meeting*: "Frustrated Police Chief Chastises Top Staff at Meeting, Sources Say," *LAT*, October 31, 1995.

179 *The department needed to be "kick-started"*: Ibid.

179 *"Senior officers unwilling to back him"*: Ibid.

179 *"I'd like to get more help from you"*: Ibid.

PART THREE: SOMETHING BLUE

Bernard Parks, August 1997, Los Angeles City Hall

Note: Chief Parks refused to be interviewed for this book (Media Deputy Kimberly Briggs, e-mail message to Emily Maleki/Joe Domanick, August 1, 2014).

183 *"It was an absolute love-in"*: "Parks Sworn In as LAPD Chief After 12–0 Vote," *LAT*, August 13, 1997.

183 *standing ovation*: Ibid.

183 *not been asked a single question beforehand*: Ibid.

183 *a crowd estimated at three thousand*: "The LAPD: Chief Parks," Los Angeles Police Department, accessed January 25, 2015, http://www.lapdonline.org /history_of_the_lapd/content_basic_view/1118.

183 *the same belt*: "The 50 Most Beautiful People in the World 1998, Bernard C. Parks: Police Chief," *People*, May 11, 1998; Gary Greenebaum interview.

183 *"I'm a man of Los Angeles"*: Gary Greenebaum interview.

184 *"I don't view conflict as something bad"*: "Parks Sworn In as LAPD Chief After 12–0 Vote."

184 *"I'm so thrilled"*: Ibid.

184 *smart, knowledgeable, efficient technocrat*: Patrick Gannon interview; Charlie Beck interview.

David Mack, Thursday, November 6, 1997, South Central Bank of America

185 *three-piece suit, a tweed beret, and dark sunglasses*: "Bad Cops," New Yorker, May 21, 2001; "Who Killed B.I.G.?" *Rolling Stone*, June 7, 2001.

185 *$722,000*: "Officer Charged in Bank Heist That Netted $722,000," *LAT*, December 18, 1997; "Former Teller Pleads Guilty to Role in Bank Robbery," *LAT*, July 15, 1999; "Ex–LAPD Officer Sentenced in Bank of America Robbery," *LAT*, September 14, 1999.

186 *"I have a headache"*: "Officer Charged in Bank Heist That Netted $722,000."

186 *Mack knocked Romero to the floor*: "Who Killed B.I.G.?"

186 *he was joined by a black accomplice*: "Bad Cops."

186 *white getaway van driven by a third member*: "Former Teller Pleads Guilty to Role in Bank Robbery"; "Bad Cops."

186 *David Mack went to Las Vegas*: "Bad Cops"; "Who Killed B.I.G.?"

186 *a fellow cop named Sammy Martin*: Ibid.

186 *In addition to being Ray's lover*: "Fall of Partners Feeds LAPD Corruption Probe," *LAT*, September 13, 1999; "Bad Cops."

186 *Mack would also spend over $30,000*: "Ex–LAPD Officer Sentenced in Bank of America Robbery."

186 *Errolyn Romero . . . daughter of Belizean immigrants*: "Robbery Suspect Called LAPD Leader," *LAT*, December 19, 1997.

186 *she was working as a ticket-taker*: "Fall of Partners Feeds LAPD Corruption Probe"; "Who Killed B.I.G.?"

187 *polygraph test that declared her "deceptive"*: "Officer Charged in Bank Heist That Netted $722,000"; "Former Teller Pleads Guilty to Role in Bank Robbery."

187 *David Mack's LAPD business card*: "Officer Charged in Bank Heist That Netted $722,000"; *Frontline*, PBS, May 15, 2001; "Bad Cops"; "Who Killed B.I.G.?"

187 *Mack, in turn, didn't give them anybody*: "Fall of Partners Feeds LAPD Corruption Probe"; "Bad Cops."

187 *$1,500 cash in his wallet*: "Fall of Partners Feeds LAPD Corruption Probe"; "Ex–LAPD Officer Sentenced in Bank of America Robbery."

187 *owed the IRS $20,000*: "Ex–LAPD Officer Sentenced in Bank of America Robbery"; "The Dirtiest Cop Alive," *Maxim*, November 2000.

187 *$17,000 in credit card bills*: Ibid.

187 *sentenced him to fourteen years and three months*: "Ex–LAPD Officer Sentenced in Bank of America Robbery."

187 *Romero to two and a half years*: "One Bad Cop," *New York Times Magazine*, October 1, 2000.

187 *Biggie Smalls*: "L.A. Confidential," *Salon*, September 27, 2000; "Who Killed B.I.G.?"

Bernard Parks, Autumn 1997, Parker Center

187 *Dotson had always liked him*: David Dotson interview.

188 *"Bernie always got enmeshed in minutiae"*: Ibid.

188 *"his people didn't want to tell him anything"*: Ibid.

188 *"They just pulled their hair out"*: Ibid.

188 *"you can't get an organization moving in any direction"*: Ibid.

188 *"the kind of downward pressure"*: Ibid.

188 *"He didn't say, 'Hey, guys, let's get together' "*: Ibid.

189 *"yellow-sheeting"*: Independent Commission on the Los Angeles Police Department, *Report of the Independent Commission on the Los Angeles Police Department*, 159.

189 *can of Coke*: Charlie Beck interview.

Brian Hewitt, February 1998, Rampart Division

189 Brian Hewitt . . . blunt, hard-charging guy: "Good Cop, Bad Cop," LA Weekly, January 12, 2000.

190 Brian Hewitt/choking the handcuffed Jimenez: "Beatings Alleged to Be Routine at Rampart," LAT, February 14, 2000.

190 punched him . . . in the chest: "Good Cop, Bad Cop."

190 Jimenez threw up: Ibid.

190 Investigators would later find the outline of his blood-saturated vomit: Ibid.

190 doctor and security guard reported his injuries: Ibid.

Rafael "Ray" Perez, Monday, March 2, 1998, LAPD Property Division

190 On a rainy L.A. day: "Ray's World," New Times Los Angeles, August 17, 2000.

190 He'd disguised his face . . . Coke-bottle reading glasses: "Sloppy LAPD Evidence Rules Led to Coke Theft," LADN, February 27, 2000; "Ray's World."

190 "I need this": "Ray's World"; "The Dirtiest Cop Alive."

190 6.6 pounds of powder cocaine: "Bad Cops."

191 Joel Perez: Ibid.

191 Bisquick flour: "Sloppy LAPD Evidence Rules Led to Coke Theft"; "Bad Cops"; Frontline, PBS, May 15, 2001.

191 "rude" was the word: "Fall of Partners Feeds LAPD Corruption Probe"; "The Dirtiest Cop Alive."

191 Ray had "Negro" features: Frontline, PBS, May 15, 2001.

191 and spoke Spanish effortlessly: Ibid.

192 Kevin Gaines: "Bad Cops."

Matt Lait and Scott Glover, August 1998, San Fernando Valley

192 A briefing . . . suburban San Fernando Valley: Domanick, Covering Police in Times of Crisis, 44.

192 "LAPD only, check your guns at the door": Ibid.

193 a guy in a Hawaiian shirt and blue jeans: Ibid.

193 investigating seven shootings: Ibid.

193 Rampart CRASH "had a crash pad": Ibid.

193 "I had sex in this CRASH pad all the time": Ibid.

193 more secrets, which Lait and Glover memorized: Ibid.

193 "backgrounding" the officers: Ibid., 41.

193 "sounding weird": Ibid., 42.

194 The Times would hold off running the story: Tim Rutten interview; Domanick, Covering Police in Times of Crisis, 40.

194 a working-class Irish Catholic's sense of right and wrong: Tim Rutten interview.

194   married to the crusading firebrand defense attorney Leslie Abramson: "Thoughts on Tim Rutten," *L.A. Observed*, August 13, 2011.
194   *"Can we go with the story?"*: Tim Rutten interview.
194   *"We gave our word"*: Ibid.
194   *"they are going to fuck us"*: Ibid.
194   *"a little prissy, a little self-righteous"*: Ibid.
194   *"I'll be damned if that evening"*: Ibid.
195   *"glue yourself to this guy Perez"*: Ibid.
195   *"This story is your life"*: Ibid.

Curtis Woodle and Joel Perez, April and May 1998, Las Vegas and Los Angeles

195   *Woodle was in a Las Vegas casino with his ex-wife*: Curtis Woodle interview.
195   *"What the fuck?"*: Ibid.
195   *Hawaiian shirt*: Ibid.
195   *everybody in the Operations Central Bureau CRASH unit*: Ibid.
196   *"After the third memo"*: Ibid.
196   *"Sarge, I have never"*: Ibid.
196   *"This is crazy man, this is crazy!"*: Ibid.

Bernard Parks, Summer 1998, Parker Center

196   *if you were a reporter he didn't like*: Tim Rutten interview.
196   *"funny, cordial, and immensely personable"*: Charlie Beck interview.
196   *forty-page strategic plan*: Ibid.
196   *"clear to Parks. But it just wasn't clear to the rest of us"*: Ibid.
197   *"in a lot of ways . . . he was"*: Ibid.
197   *"Parks [would] demand a report and then grade it"*: Ibid.
197   *"his attitude was always 'I am teaching you and mentoring you'"*: Ibid.

Rafael "Ray" Perez, Summer 1998, Ladera Heights

197   *they discovered the Bisquick*: Frontline, PBS, May 15, 2001.
198   *Two of the phone calls . . . his girlfriend, Veronica Quesada*: Ibid.
198   *Ray dressed in a red running suit*: Ibid.
198   *new home . . . Ladera Heights*: Ibid.
198   *Eddie Bauer–model Ford Explorer*: Ibid.
198   *his wife a BMW*: Ibid.

Bernard Parks, August 1998, Parker Center

198 *Ray wasn't the only Perez*: "The Inspector General," *Buzz*, March 1998; "Police Panel Leader Admits to Anonymous Mailings," *LAT*, December 4, 1998; "Perez Won't Be Reappointed to Police Panel," *LAT*, June 16, 1999.

199 *85 percent of the Christopher Commission reforms*: "The Insiders," *LA Weekly*, March 8, 2000, accessed March 23, 2015, http://www.laweekly.com/news /the-insiders-2131735.

199 *"[bore] directly on the current [Rampart] scandal"*: Ibid.

200 *"There were comments made about Mader"*: "The Insiders."

200 *"Two directors of the Police Protective League"*: Ibid.

200 *anonymous brown envelopes*: "Police Panel Leader Admits to Anonymous Mailings."

200 *"unilaterally . . . putting restrictions on [him]"*: "LAPD Corruption Probe May Be Test for City Leaders," *LAT*, September 20, 1999.

Bernard Parks, Summer 1998, Parker Center

201 *"stealing her ovaries"*: "Cops on the Carpet," *LA Weekly*, July 3–9, 1998.

201 *25 percent increase in the number of civilian complaints against LAPD officers*: Ibid.

201 *400 percent rise in civilian complaints against officers overall*: Ibid.

201 *two hundred Board of Rights hearings*: Ibid.

201 *compared to eighty-one two years earlier*: Ibid.

201 *thirty-five officers had been fired*: Ibid.

201 *as opposed to seventeen in Willie Williams's last year*: Ibid.

201 *applications to join the LAPD had dropped*: "Parks Gets a Second Chance," *LAT*, July 15, 2001.

202 *LAPD officers had declined by eight hundred*: Ibid.

202 *"I was having the best . . . come into my office"*: Charlie Beck interview.

202 *"the ludicrous nature of the kind of prioritization"*: Ibid.

202 *"wedge between Parks and the rank and file"*: Ibid.

203 *"the smartest guy I have ever met"*: Patrick Gannon interview.

203 *"begging for leadership as an organization"*: Ibid.

203 *nine thousand strong-willed men and women*: William Bratton interview.

Rafael "Ray" Perez, Wednesday, September 8, 1999, Los Angeles District Attorney's Office

204 *the part of the probe . . . Parks had ordered shut down*: "L.A. Confidential"; "Who Killed Biggie Smalls?" *Salon*, October 16, 2000.

204 *Meeting over fifty times in two secret locations*: *Frontline*, PBS, May 15, 2001; "Ray's World"; "Bad Cops."

204 *more than four thousand pages of answers:* Frontline, PBS, May 15, 2001.

204 *"70 to 80 percent of Perez's allegations . . . corroborated":* "Perez's Credibility under New Attack," LAT, September 26, 2000.

204 *"Ray would say 'Oh, that's a bad one, that's a good one' ":* Patrick Gannon interview.

204 *"In some cases . . . Rafael was credible":* Ibid.

204 *"Rafael Perez was a liar":* Ibid.

205 *failed an LAPD polygraph test:* "One Bad Cop."

205 *had to move quickly:* Patrick Gannon interview.

205 *"limited only to Rampart CRASH":* Ibid.

Bill Boyarsky, December 1999, Downtown Los Angeles Minibus

205 *Bill Boyarsky loved public transportation:* Bill Boyarsky interview; Tim Rutten interview.

205 *"Are you a lawyer?":* Bill Boyarsky interview.

205 *working-class Jewish guy from the Bay Area:* "An Advocate for Jewish Interests in L.A.'s Diverse Public Schools," Jewish Journal, April 27, 2010; Tim Rutten interview.

206 *he had transcripts of the DA/LAPD Perez interviews:* Bill Boyarsky interview.

206 *unused city editor office:* Tim Rutten interview.

206 *sent for a messenger to start copying:* Ibid.

206 *"This guy has everything":* Ibid.

206 *check into a hotel:* Ibid.

207 *"One simply had to look at the L.A. Times":* Frontline, PBS, May 15, 2001.

207 *Richard Riordan became so angry:* Tim Rutten interview.

207 *Michael Parks, who essentially shrugged:* Ibid.

207 *Parks . . . had worked as a foreign correspondent in South Africa, China, and Moscow:* Ibid.

207 *Downing was never a journalist:* Ibid.

207 *"In the old days before Michael Parks":* Ibid.

Rafael "Ray" Perez, Friday, February 25, 2000, Downtown Los Angeles Superior Court

208 *"Whoever chases monsters":* "One Bad Cop."

208 *Nervously clutching her handbag . . . Denise Perez:* Author's observations.

208 *A former LAPD dispatcher:* "The Dirtiest Cop Alive"; "Perez's Bitter Saga of Lies, Regrets, and Harm," LAT, December 31, 2000.

208 *"I proudly wore a badge of honor":* "A Tearful Perez Gets 5 Years," LAT, February 26, 2000.

209 *Ray had "made a lot of eye contact with the female jurors":* Frontline, PBS, May 15, 2001.

209 Ray *"was too good-looking"*: Ibid.

209 *deadlocked 8–4*: Ibid.

209 *all the press corps' then national stars*: Author's observations.

209 "The atrocities committed by myself": *CBS*, February 24, 2000; *Frontline*, PBS, May 15, 2001.

209 "What I want most at this time": *Frontline*, PBS, May 15, 2001.

210 "living two unmistakable lives": "LAPD Whistleblower Apologizes," CBS, February 24, 2000; "A Tearful Perez Gets 5 Years."

210 *plea-bargained five-year sentence in prison*: Ibid.

Bernard Parks, March 2000, Parker Center

210 *"in the history of mankind"*: "Rampart Scandal Isolates Riordan," *LAT*, March 12, 2000.

210 *362-page inquiry*: "LAPD Condemned by Its Own Inquiry into Rampart Scandal," *LAT*, March 1, 2000; "Report on Rampart Scandal Has a Hollow, Disturbing Ring," *LAT*, March 3, 2000.

211 *After dismissing every pointed question . . . Parks then left the stage*: Author's observations.

Connie Rice, 2003,
NAACP's Advancement Project Offices, Los Angeles

211 *Connie Rice was still irate*: Connie Rice interview.

211 *seventy volumes of Rafael Perez's testimony transcripts*: Ibid.

211 *Kathleen Salvaty . . . "Connie, am I crazy or are there pages missing?"*: Ibid.; Rice, *Power Concedes Nothing*, 266.

211 *"Perez is answering willy-nilly"*: Connie Rice interview.

212 *"frustrated me very much about Rampart"*: Bill Boyarsky interview.

212 *"Absolutely. Absolutely"*: Patrick Gannon interview.

212 *Gerald Chaleff . . . was having deep concerns*: Gerald Chaleff interview.

213 *asked Bernard Parks to grant department immunity to officers*: Ibid.

213 *"Nope, can't do that"*: Ibid.

213 *"had nothing to do with officer discipline"*: Ibid.

213 *"They couldn't follow up"*: Connie Rice interview.

Bernard Parks, May 2000, Parker Center

214 *"The LAPD . . . is engaged in a pattern or practice"*: Bill Lann Lee to James K. Hahn, "LAPD Notice of Investigation Letter," *Esquire*, May 8, 2000.

214 *James Hahn . . . tens of millions . . . to settle police abuse lawsuits*: "City Attorney Targets Costs of LAPD-Involved Lawsuits," *LAT*, December 4, 1998; "Politics Trumps Justice," *LAT*, November 18, 2001.

215 *the City Council voted 10–2 to accept the consent decree*: "Outsiders to Oversee Reforms at LAPD," *Washington Post*, September 22, 2000; "Can the LAPD Reform Itself?" *LAT*, September 24, 2000.

Steve Cooley, Wednesday, November 7, 2001, Parker Center

215 *"With every book"*: "Politics Trumps Justice."
215 *"as high, wide, and deep as the facts indicated"*: Ibid.
217 *"Every time I talk with that guy"*: Tim Rutten interview.
217 *Police Commission voted 4–1 not to rehire Parks*: "The Bum Blockade, Zoot Suit Riot and Bloody Christmas," *LA Weekly*, September 4, 2002.

Summing Up

218 *150 stories on Rampart*: Domanick, *Covering Police in Times of Crisis*, 44.
218 *"counted on one hand"*: Ibid., 46.
218 *a new editor was brought in*: Bill Boyarsky interview.
218 *city paid over $75 million to the victims . . . of Rampart CRASH officers*: "Los Angeles to Pay $13 Million to Settle May Day Melee Lawsuits," *LAT*, February 5, 2009.
218 *Javier Ovando was awarded $15 million*: "The Bum Blockade, Zoot Suit Riot and Bloody Christmas"; "LAPD Has Shed Scandalous Image, City Leaders Say," AP, July 26, 2009.
218 *he was arrested near the Nevada state line*: "Alleged Rampart Victim Arrested on Drug Charges," *LAT*, March 21, 2001; "Rampart Victim Ovando in Court on Drug Charges," *LAT*, April 20, 2001.
218 *conspiracy to obstruct justice, perjury, and filing false reports*: "Ex-L.A. Cop Sentenced to 5 Years," CNN.com, August 13, 2002, http://www.cnn.com/2002/LAW/08/07/rampart.sentencing/index.html?_s=PM:LAW.
218 *Hewitt was banging Ishmael Jimenez around*: "Good Cop, Bad Cop."
218 *Ethan Cohan . . . fired . . . for failing to promptly report Hewitt*: Ibid.
219 *"spoken with Chief Parks six to twelve times about the Rampart investigation"*: *Harper v. City of Los Angeles*, 06-55519, 06-55715 (United States Court of Appeals, Ninth Circuit, 2008), 4.
219 *violating their civil rights*: Ibid.
219 *compensatory damages of $5 million each*: Ibid.
219 *"hounded" by the LAPD*: Ibid., 8.
219 *"Let's get the case behind us"*: Ibid., 4.

PART FOUR: SOMETHING NEW

William Bratton and Rikki Klieman,
Summer 2002, Los Angeles and New York

223 *Bratton had been flying from his home in New York to L.A.*: William Bratton interview; "NYPD's Ex-Head Eyes Job at LAPD," *LAT*, July 14, 2002.

223 *Kroll Associates*: Ibid.

223 Dragnet *and* Badge 714: Bratton and Knobler, *Turnaround*, 14.

223 *Police Commission wanted a black chief*: Gary Greenebaum interview.

223 *Los Angeles had almost 1,100 murders in 1992*: ABC News, November 22, 1992.

223 *had dropped to 419 in 1998*: Ibid.

223 *2002 . . . a troubling 647*: "Homicides Up 15% in Sheriff's Territory," *LAT*, January 12, 2006; "Top Cop in Los Angeles Says Cutting Crime Pays," *WSJ*, November 29, 2008.

224 *"start messing around within the department"*: William Bratton interview.

224 *"walking into a deep freeze"*: Ibid.

224 *"professional turnaround man"*: "NYPD's Ex-Head Eyes Job at LAPD"; "Partners in Crime," *Boston Globe*, August 29, 2002.

224 *"put down his prepared remarks"*: "Bratton: The Making of a Police Visionary," *Crime Report*, December 6, 2013; "They'll Take Manhattan," *Boston*, October 1999, 156.

224 *"the best of times and the worst of times"*: "Bratton: The Making of a Police Visionary"; "They'll Take Manhattan," 157.

225 *"The only losers in New York City"*: Ibid.

225 *"gains to the profession . . . undermined"*: William Bratton interview.

225 *On the July Fourth weekend of 2002*: Rikki Klieman interview.

225 *Rikki Klieman . . . "most outstanding women trial lawyers"*: "Law: The New Women in Court," *Time*, May 1983; "Partners in Crime."

225 *raised poor in a Chicago suburb*: Klieman and Knobler, *Fairy Tales Can Come True*, 3; "Partners in Crime"; "Rikki Klieman, the Play's the Thing," *Lifestyles*, Fall 2002, 17.

225 *garment-worker father and housewife mother*: Klieman and Knobler, *Fairy Tales Can Come True*, 1; "Partners in Crime"; "Rikki Klieman, the Play's the Thing," 17.

226 *"would buy dresses for her at the Salvation Army"*: "Partners in Crime."

226 *theater arts major from Northwestern University*: Klieman and Knobler, *Fairy Tales Can Come True*, 15; "Partners in Crime"; "Rikki Klieman, the Play's the Thing," 17.

226 *Waiting on restaurant tables*: Klieman and Knobler, *Fairy Tales Can Come True*, 30.

226 *Boston University Law School:* Ibid., 39; "Partners in Crime"; "Rikki Klieman, the Play's the Thing," 18.

226 *prosecutor . . . Middlesex County:* Klieman and Knobler, *Fairy Tales Can Come True,* 80–81 and 83.

226 *1981 . . . criminal defense attorney:* Ibid., 122–23; "Rikki Klieman, the Play's the Thing," 18.

226 *Valium:* Klieman and Knobler, *Fairy Tales Can Come True,* 103, 178, and 284; "They'll Take Manhattan," 156.

226 *losing fifteen pounds:* Klieman and Knobler, *Fairy Tales Can Come True,* 284.

226 *second marriage to a cop turned federal agent:* Ibid., 199–210; "Rikki Klieman, the Play's the Thing," 19.

226 *collapsed on the defense table:* Klieman and Knobler, *Fairy Tales Can Come True,* 198; "They'll Take Manhattan," 156.

226 *Court TV as a guest analyst during the O. J. Simpson trial:* Klieman and Knobler, *Fairy Tales Can Come True,* 288–89.

226 *hired as an anchor:* Ibid., 291–94.

226 *moving to New York:* Ibid., 294–97; Rikki Klieman interview.

226 *cohost with Johnnie Cochran:* Klieman and Knobler, *Fairy Tales Can Come True,* 307–8.

226 *Klieman had met Bratton . . . at a restaurant in Manhattan's Regency Hotel:* Ibid., 310–11; "Partners in Crime."

226 *"If you were single, I'd marry you":* Klieman and Knobler, *Fairy Tales Can Come True,* 311; Rikki Klieman interview.

226 *"You should call me for lunch":* Ibid.

226 *"By the time [she] got back to the office, he had called":* Ibid.

226 *Bratton-Klieman engagement/February 1999:* Ibid., 332.

226 *Central Park carousel:* Ibid., 333; "You Can Go Home Again," *Gotham,* Summer 2010; "Partners in Crime."

226 *"round and round with you":* Klieman and Knobler, *Fairy Tales Can Come True,* 333; "Public Lives, Round and Round Before a Proposal," *NYT,* February 10, 1999; "Partners in Crime"; Rikki Klieman interview.

227 *Klieman braced for bad news:* Rikki Klieman interview.

227 *"I want to go after the job of LAPD chief":* William Bratton interview; Rikki Klieman interview.

227 *survived and recovered from a heart attack:* William Bratton interview.

227 *"hip, chic, and glamorous":* "They'll Take Manhattan," 156.

227 *"Nine-eleven":* Rikki Klieman interview.

227 *"In your life as a police officer":* "Bratton: The Making of a Police Visionary."

228 *sprawled across the dining room table:* Rikki Klieman interview.

228 *fifty other candidates:* "Pick the Best Chief, Period," *LAT,* July 29, 2002; "Partners in Crime."

228 *long-standing practice of thoroughly researching the police department*: Rikki Klieman interview.

228 *"propaganda package"*: William Bratton interview.

229 *John Timoney . . . the only other candidate he regarded as serious competition*: Ibid.

229 *"showboating"*: Ibid.; Rikki Klieman interview.

229 *Rick Caruso . . . "made it quite clear through intermediaries"*: Ibid.

William Bratton, October 2002, Los Angeles

229 *Latino chief from the small city of Oxnard*: "NYPD's Ex-Head Eyes Job at LAPD"; "Pick the Best Chief, Period."

230 *"nearly killed my candidacy"*: William Bratton interview.

230 New York Post's *gossip column, "Page 6"*: Rikki Klieman interview.

230 *personal visit . . . to John Mack*: William Bratton interview.

230 *Black L.A. had turned out in large numbers to support Hahn*: "L.A. Mayoral Election: 'Voter Turnout Will Be Key,'" *Time*, June 4, 2001; "Black Voters Losing Clout but Still Crucial in L.A. Mayor's Race," *LAT*, April 9, 2013.

230 *"as a personal enemy"*: Connie Rice interview.

231 *"Bratton completely seduced Mack"*: Ibid.; "Saving Los Angeles," *Playboy*, February 2008, 134.

231 *"the mayor slid into my camp"*: William Bratton interview; "Saving Los Angeles," 133.

231 *one of Hahn's top aides . . . New York governor Mario Cuomo, with Judge Milton Mollen*: Ibid.

231 *"appreciating what I'd done there"*: Ibid.

231 *meeting of the Rite Aid Corporation*: William Bratton interview.

231 *the company's corporate jet*: Ibid.

William Bratton, Patrick Gannon, and Gerald Chaleff, Fall 2002, Parker Center

231 *Bratton hadn't a clue what Gannon's name was*: Patrick Gannon interview.

232 *"Hey, Pete"*: Ibid.

232 *Chaleff . . . "a card-carrying member of the ACLU"*: Ibid.

232 *how "strong" Chaleff was*: William Bratton interview.

232 *Bratton sent him a copy of his autobiography*: Ibid.

232 *Chaleff . . . also knew Rikki Klieman*: Ibid.; Rikki Klieman interview.

232 *A graduate of UCLA and Harvard Law School*: "Defense Attorney Chaleff to Lead Police Commission," *LAT*, July 28, 1999.

233 *Young Professionals for Kennedy*: Gerald Chaleff interview.

233 *night of the California Democratic primary*: Ibid.

233 *photo of Kennedy on his office wall*: Ibid.

233 *selected to go to New York*: Ibid.

233 *"Hillside Strangler"*: "Defense Attorney Chaleff to Lead Police Commission."

234 *office on the sixth floor of Parker Center*: Connie Rice interview.

235 *John Miller . . . Barbara Walters's partner . . . 20/20*: William Bratton interview.

235 *Miller also possessed exceptionally active eyes and ears*: Ibid.

235 *liked going to crime scenes*: Ibid.; Rikki Klieman interview.

235 *Mike Berkow . . . Orange County*: William Bratton interview.

235 *knew Berkow from back when he was a cop in Rochester, New York*: Ibid.

236 *flew into L.A. on their own dimes*: Ibid.

236 *Wasserman gave Bratton a copy of . . .* Policing a Free Society: Ibid.

236 *liaison to the gay community*: Ibid.

236 *John Linder . . . "cultural diagnostic"*: Ibid.

236 *Bratton considered Linder "a genius"*: Ibid.

236 *"how dysfunctional it was"*: Ibid.

236 *Bratton also flew in George Kelling*: Ibid.

237 *NYPD chief of department Louis Anemone*: "The Enforcer: Chief Bratton, 2004," *Los Angeles*, March 2004.

237 *Most . . . were eventually paid by the Los Angeles Police Foundation*: William Bratton interview.

237 *a strapping six-foot-three police officer named Manny Gonzalez*: Ibid.; Rikki Klieman interview.

237 *no police equipment of any kind*: William Bratton interview.

237 *"Hey, Manny"*: Ibid.

237 *It said a lot to Bratton*: Ibid.

237 *"I want a full police package"*: Ibid.

237 *"What Manny and the chief's office staff were trying to do"*: Ibid.

238 *"you had to let them know who was in control"*: Ibid.

William Bratton and Charlie Beck, Fall 2002, Los Angeles Police Academy, Elysian Park

238 *about 60 of whom were captains*: Charlie Beck interview.

238 *"He really chewed ass"*: Ibid.

238 *"I want you to get results"*: Ibid.

239 *Gannon . . . San Pedro*: Patrick Gannon interview.

239 *Gannon's family had a history*: Ibid.

239 *"I didn't know what to expect"*: Ibid.

240 *"Bratton wanted to take the shackles off"*: Ibid.

240 *"we're not just a suppression force"*: Ibid.

240 *"Conversely, if things are going bad"*: Ibid.

241 *submit a résumé*: Charlie Beck interview; William Bratton interview.

241 *a "face with a biography in a book"*: William Bratton interview.
241 *"who was good and who was bad"*: Ibid.
241 *applying for their own jobs again*: Charlie Beck interview; Patrick Gannon interview.
241 *"Hey, we understand force in the LAPD"*: Charlie Beck interview.
241 *"if you want to keep crows away"*: Ibid.
241 *"What's with this guy?"*: Ibid.
242 *"Well, read his book* [Turnaround], *man"*: Ibid.
242 *"We have nine thousand officers"*: William Bratton interview.
242 *"How does Bratton get credit for community policing?"*: Patrick Gannon interview.
242 *"As crime declined"*: Ibid.
242 *"Bratton didn't give us a blueprint"*: Ibid.

Charlie Beck, 2002, LAPD Central Division and Skid Row

243 *20,000 inmates*: "New Leader for Los Angeles County Sheriff's Department Must Overcome Scandals to Rebuild Public Trust," *LADN*, March 21, 2014.
243 *165,000 that flowed*: "How California Failed Kevin Evans," *Los Angeles Times Magazine*, August 26, 2001, story by author.
243 *2,300 mentally ill inmates*: Ibid.
243 *largest such mental-health facility in the nation*: "What Is the Role of Jails in Treating the Mentally Ill?" NPR, September 15, 2013; "Inside the Nation's Largest Mental Institution," NPR, August 13, 2008; "How California Failed Kevin Evans."
243 *largest skid row in the western United States*: "Reinventing Skid Row," *Politico*, March 5, 2014; "On Patrol with Skid Row's 'Angel Cop.'" CNN, January 3, 2015.
244 *About 40 percent of L.A. County's homeless were mentally ill*: "How California Failed Kevin Evans."
244 *"There are just no facilities for the mentally ill homeless"*: Ibid.
244 *By 2000 an estimated ninety-one thousand homeless*: "Homeless Need Help, Not ACLU," *LAT*, October 30, 2005; "Bratton's Plans for Homeless Debated," *LAT*, October 31, 2005; "Committee Formed to Fight Homelessness," *LADN*, December 21, 2005.
244 *eighteen thousand beds in shelters*: "Problem of Homelessness in Los Angeles and Its Environs Draws Renewed Calls for Attention," *NYT*, January 15, 2006.
244 *eighty-three single-room-occupancy hotels*: "Bratton's Plans for Homeless Debated"; "Single Room Occupancy Hotels (SRO)/Interim Control Ordinance (ICO)," Office of the City Clerk, City of Los Angeles, Los Angeles Housing Department, November 15, 2007.
245 *"a different standard of behavior"*: Charlie Beck interview.
245 *"It's not so much what the police let you do"*: Ibid.

245 *"How long you been in charge here?"*: Ibid.

245 *"Okay"*: Ibid.

245 *counting the tents and packing-box bedrooms*: Ibid.

246 *giving them a choice*: Ibid.

246 *At the rescue missions, Beck knew he'd have captive audiences*: Ibid.

246 *a series of talks to about four hundred of the homeless*: Ibid.

246 *"a slim grasp on reality"*: Ibid.

246 *"You're no longer going to be permitted"*: Ibid.

246 *"Folks that were lawless liked [L.A.'s] Skid Row"*: Ibid.

246 *" 'Where'd the homeless all go?' "*: Ibid.

246 *"that was way too many rules"*: Ibid.

247 *"At some point . . . Americans decided"*: "The Myth of Police Reform," *Atlantic*, April 15, 2015.

248 *Kevin Lamar Evans, a homeless thirty-three-year-old*: "How California Failed Kevin Evans."

248 *schizophrenic with cerebral palsy*: Ibid.

248 *died of cardiac arrest*: Ibid.

248 *strap-down room in the Twin Towers jail*: Ibid.

248 *baloney sandwich*: Ibid.

248 *"Don't be giving any food away"*: Ibid.

248 *convinced he was possessed by Satan*: Ibid.

248 *incarcerated there at least four times*: Ibid.

248 *cited or arrested on thirteen different occasions*: Ibid.

249 *Lancaster and Palmdale*: Ibid.

249 *six-deputy Los Angeles Sheriff's Department unit*: Ibid.

249 *"to deal with loitering, prostitution"*: Ibid.

249 *"over 100 volunteers"*: "Ibid.

249 *ticketed for loitering in a Lancaster shopping center*: Ibid.

249 *one of at least four . . . "incompetent to stand trial"*: Ibid.

249 *"how he died was just not that surprising"*: Ibid.

250 *judge Richard E. Spann . . . had "no idea" who Evans was*: Ibid.

250 *Spann had ruled in three thousand custody cases*: Ibid.

250 *"no independent recollection of him"*: Ibid.

250 *fifteen hundred chronically homeless people*: "L.A. Will Pay $725,000 to Lawyers Who Stopped Skid Row Police Sweeps," *LAT*, September 10, 2014.

250 *fifty-eight thousand homeless had drug and/or alcohol addictions*: "How to Prevent a Skid Row Death," *LAT*, March 5, 2015.

250 *"issue an anguished call for help"*: "On Skid Row, Sweeping Change Adds to Distrust."

250 *David O'Connell has been a Los Angeles priest for twenty-three years*: "The Reformer, on Honeymoon," *LAT*, January 19, 2003.

250 *pastor of two Catholic churches*: Ibid.

251 *"A week and a half ago, a member of our parish"*: Ibid.

251 *bridge by a school in East L.A.'s Lincoln Heights*: Ibid.

251 *"People live like cockroaches around here"*: Ibid.

251 *eighteen CRASH units had been disbanded by Bernard Parks in 2000*: "Chief Parks Orders Current Anti-Gang Units Disbanded," *LAT*, March 4, 2000; "Chief of Los Angeles Police Disbands Antigang Units," *NYT*, March 4, 2000.

251 *"there are so many wounds to heal"*: "The Reformer, on Honeymoon."

251 *"they don't trust the police"*: Ibid.

252 *"horrendous activities of the officers in Rampart CRASH"*: Ibid.

252 *"Senior Lead Officer" community policing program*: Ibid.

252 *"without getting his signature"*: Ibid.

252 *"You'll have access to me on a scheduled basis"*: Ibid.

252 *heading to a private home in Brentwood . . . speaking to the ACLU*: Ibid.

253 *"He's Code Green at the hospital"*: Ibid.

253 *"today's the wife's birthday"*: Ibid.

253 *"feel the pain of the family, of the city"*: Ibid.

253 *"Chief . . . We got another one"*: Ibid.

253 *"You need a scorecard"*: Ibid.

253 *"Looks like the ACLU's doing all right for itself"*: Ibid.

253 *"I'm being asked to try to reinvigorate"*: Ibid.

254 *"no shortage of people who want to get involved"*: Ibid.

254 *"a commonality of concern"*: Ibid.

254 *"That L.A. Metro group had a very realistic understanding"*: Ibid.

William Bratton, James Hahn, and Clive Jackson, December 2002, South Los Angeles

254 *"Stop the Killing. Choose Life, Not Death"*: "The Reformer, on Honeymoon," *LAT*, January 19, 2003.

254 *South Central community center*: Ibid.

255 *Clive Jackson, Jr. . . . shot dead*: Ibid.

255 *"The gangs of Los Angeles"*: Ibid.

255 *letter dated November 13, 2002*: Ibid.

255 *"Rosetta stone effect"*: Ibid.

256 *"gang-related" homicides in Los Angeles County from 1980 to 2000*: "Gang Homicides in Los Angeles County, 1980–2006," Los Angeles County Department of Public Health, Los Angeles Sheriff's Department, Los Angeles Police Department, Los Angeles Department of Coroner, California Department of Health Services—Center for Health Statistics, November 10, 2008.

256 *"an unchecked intra-tribal war"*: Hayden, *Street Wars*.

256 *"domestic terrorists"*: "Black Leaders Caution Chief," *LAT*, December 14, 2002; "Can William Bratton Turn Around the Big Apple Again?" *LAT*, December 6, 2013.

256 *"a disease"*: William Bratton interview; "The Reformer, on Honeymoon."

256 *"more of a national threat than [was] the Mafia"*: "The Reformer, on Honeymoon."

256 *"Al Capone is not what we're dealing with here"*: "For Los Angeles's New Police Chief, a New World," *NYT*, December 6, 2002.

256 *"shoot-from-the-hip" analysis*: Ibid.

George Gascon, 2002, Los Angeles Police Department Headquarters

257 *Nor, thought Bill Bratton, was he the kind of person "who would please you with a lie"*: William Bratton interview.

257 *"Go into Bill's office"*: Rikki Klieman interview.

257 *"Do it and you'll get what you want"*: Ibid.

257 *Gascon . . . met with Bratton*: Ibid.

257 *Gascon . . . new curriculum*: "He Said No to Naysayers," *LAT*, June 4, 2004.

258 *arrived in the U.S. with his parents in 1967*: Ibid.; George Gascon interview.

258 *political refugee from Cuba*: Ibid.

258 *father . . . had been supporter of Fidel Castro's revolution*: Ibid.

258 *"I got to see as a young person"*: George Gascon interview.

258 *his uncle . . . would spend twenty years in a Cuban prison*: "He Said No to Naysayers."

258 *Struggling to learn English*: Ibid.

258 *quit his Los Angeles high school*: Ibid.

258 *joined the army*: Ibid.

258 *became a military policeman*: Ibid.

258 *earned his GED*: Ibid.

258 *joined the LAPD in 1978*: Ibid.; George Gascon interview.

258 *selling cars*: "He Said No to Naysayers."

258 *rejoining the department in 1987*: Ibid.; George Gascon interview.

258 *degree in history from Cal State, Long Beach*: "He Said No to Naysayers."

258 *law degree from Western State University College of Law*: Ibid.; George Gascon interview.

259 Good to Great: William Bratton interview.

259 *"Risk taker"*: Ibid.

259 *In New York, Bratton had had thirty-eight thousand police officers*: Ibid.

260 *"District Policing"*: "He Said No to Naysayers"; George Gascon interview.

Charlie Beck, 2002, Parker Center

260 *to buy a deli sandwich*: Charlie Beck interview.

260 *"Make sure you clean up that fucking park"*: Ibid.

260 *"the entire extent of my instructions from him"*: Ibid.

261 *"Dope dealers would stand there"*: Ibid.

261 *"There was literally no grass in the park"*: Ibid.

261 *"Three hundred people were going to jail each month"*: Ibid.

262 National Forest Service: Ibid.

262 *"The criminals would just hunker down"*: Ibid.

262 *"You own it . . . I own it"*: Ibid.

262 The Department of Water and Power: Ibid.

262 *mounting of surveillance cameras*: Ibid.

263 *"we have cameras all over the park"*: Ibid.

263 *the city's new shopping cart ordinance*: Ibid.

263 *"Shopping carts were vehicles"*: Ibid.

263 They got the City Council to commit $2 million: Ibid.

263 *"If you remove crime from a location"*: Ibid.

263 *a take-back-the-park candlelight vigil*: Ibid.

263 Homies Unidos: Ibid.

263 *"They had some scary-looking guys"*: Ibid.

263 *"rallies around the park"*: Ibid.

264 *"the ones who shoot, pillage, rape"*: Ibid.

264 *continued to arrest "hundreds and hundreds of people for dealing"*: Ibid.

264 *"you can't come to MacArthur Park to buy narcotics"*: Ibid.

264 *"you don't see drug dealing in Mac Park anymore"*: Ibid.

264 *renovated band shell*: Ibid.

264 *"the answer's always outside of the [crime scene] tape"*: Ibid.

Connie Rice, December 2003,
Advancement Project Offices, Los Angeles

265 *"LAPD Chief Bill Bratton is on the other line"*: Rice, *Power Concedes Nothing*, 248; Connie Rice interview.

265 *"his greeting was breezy and familiar"*: Ibid.

265 *December 2003 symposium entitled "The Gangs of L.A."*: Rice, *Power Concedes Nothing*, 247; author observation.

265 *"to go where the evidence led"*: Rice, *Power Concedes Nothing*, 248.

265 *"after-action" report*: Ibid; Connie Rice interview.

265 *he wanted her to lead the effort*: Rice, *Power Concedes Nothing*, 249.

266 *"lessons learned" exercise*: Ibid.

266 Darren "Bo" Taylor: Ibid., 193–94; Connie Rice interview.

266 Blair Taylor: Connie Rice interview.

266 *white cops . . . "weren't fluent in the culture of black, underclass males"*: Ibid.

267 *change the definition of what an LAPD cop did*: Ibid.

267 *"battering ram"*: Ibid.

267 *$2 billion ... Los Angeles bus system*: "Both Sides of the Street," *Sun*, April 2008; "Right Makes Right," *Los Angeles Times Magazine*, January 2012.

268 *helped win $1 billion for the construction of schools in poor neighborhoods*: Rice, *Power Concedes Nothing*, 224.

Connie Rice, July 2003,
Advancement Project Offices, Los Angeles

268 *Connie Rice phoned Charlie Beck*: Connie Rice interview.

268 *blueprint of a veteran LAPD captain*: Ibid.

Martin Ludlow, Summer 2003, "The Jungle"

269 *given up for adoption*: "Councilman's Past Has Him Ready to Lead," *LAT*, June 20, 2005.

269 *Raised in Idaho*: Ibid.

269 *political director of a powerful local union*: Ibid.

269 *marry the daughter of one of L.A.'s most prominent black clergymen*: Ibid.

269 *conspiracy to divert union employee funds*: "Judge Sentences Ex-Councilman to 3 Years' Probation," *LAT*, April 22, 2006.

269 *"the Jungle"*: "Seeds of Change Are Sown," *LAT*, September 1, 2003; "He Makes a Difference, Finds Redemption," *LAT*, June 22, 2008.

269 *Black P. Stones ... twenty-eight murders ... fifteen hundred aggravated assaults*: "L.A. Fights Back," *LAT*, May 1, 2008.

269 *"the Summer of Success"*: "Seeds of Change Are Sown"; Connie Rice interview.

269 *violent crime had dropped 20 percent*: "Bratton, Baca Tout New Anti-Gang Program for LA," *LADN*, April 16, 2009.

Connie Rice, July 2006, Rampart Division

271 *"a few bad apples"*: Blue Ribbon Review Panel, *Rampart Reconsidered*, 8; "The Bum Blockade, Zoot Suit Riot and Bloody Christmas," *LA Weekly*, September 4, 2002.

272 *"There have been forty-plus years of debate"*: "Plan to Change LAPD Consent Decree Rejected," *LAT*, March 22, 2006.

Charlie Beck, 2006, South Bureau Headquarters

272 *sixteen hundred officers*: "Ex–LAPD Deputy Chief Named Burbank's Interim Chief," *LAT*, December 18, 2009; "Burbank Interim Police Chief," *Burbank Leader*, December 17, 2009.

272 *57.6-square-mile area of South Los Angeles*: "About South Bureau," Los Angeles

Police Department, accessed February 5, 2015, http://www.lapdonline.org /south_bureau/content_basic_view/1938.

272 *the kind of kid who had to grab the plate ten times:* Charlie Beck interview.

273 *Harvard's Kennedy School of Government:* William Bratton interview.

273 *"not . . . going to be the [South Bureau] chief that oversees the next riot":* Charlie Beck interview.

273 *640,000 residents of South Bureau:* "In City Numbed by Violence, the Death of a Young Boy Stirs Anguish," *NYT,* October 15, 2004; "About South Bureau."

273 *eliminated the name "South Central":* "Considering South-Central by Another Name," *LAT,* April 10, 2003; "In Los Angeles, South-Central No More," *NYT,* April 10, 2003.

273 *sixteen-square-mile area . . . "South Los Angeles":* "In Los Angeles, South-Central No More."

273 *Los Angeles's population . . . almost four million:* "California's Population Rises to 38.3 Million During 2013," *LAT,* April 30, 2014.

274 *0.5 percent jobs per worker:* Ong et al., *The State of South L.A.,* 12.

274 *versus 1.1 jobs in the rest of the county:* Ibid.

274 *30 percent poverty rate:* Ibid., 6.

274 *by 2006 its black population . . . 31 percent:* Ibid., 5.

274 *Mexican and Central American residents . . . 62 percent:* Ibid.

274 *"this amazing melting pot":* Charlie Beck interview.

274 *"All of Watts was black":* Ibid.

274 *515 murders in 2006:* "L.A. Home Turf for Hundreds of Neighborhood Criminal Groups," *LAT,* May 13, 2005.

274 *290 were gang-related:* Ibid.

274 *over eleven thousand gang-related homicides in Los Angeles County:* "Bratton: The Making of a Police Visionary."

275 *costing . . . L.A. County $2 billion a year:* The Advancement Project, *Citywide Gang Activity Reduction Strategy: Phase III Report,* 2007; "Gang Interventionists Distribute Food, Prayer—and a Sense of Change," *LAT,* June 28, 2009.

275 *gang-related killings countywide . . . 800 in 1995 to 464:* "Gang Homicides in Los Angeles County, 1980–2008."

Pat Gannon and Bo Taylor, Autumn 2005, 77th Street Division, South Los Angeles

275 *cruising down the freeway:* Patrick Gannon interview.

275 *wounded in the ankle:* Ibid.

276 *twenty—twenty—retaliatory shootings:* Ibid.

276 *if there's a problem, you own it:* Charlie Beck interview; Patrick Gannon interview.

276 *"stopping tons of people":* Patrick Gannon interview.

277 Bo Taylor . . . father of four: "Former Crip Became Gang Mediator, Peace-keeper," *LAT*, August 13, 2008.

277 *U.S. Navy veteran*: Ibid.

277 *"Dr. Phil–like"*: Ibid.

277 *Unity One*: Ibid.

277 *thirty mostly self-declared interventionists*: Patrick Gannon interview.

277 *"we were actual targets of law enforcement"*: Ron Noblet interview.

277 *Noblet . . . Eastern European studies*: Ibid.; Connie Rice interview.

279 *During the first two meetings*: Patrick Gannon interview.

279 *"I'm having serious trouble with the Rolling 60s"*: Ibid.

279 *"That worked"*: Ibid.

280 *at the end of a conveyer belt*: Charlie Beck interview.

280 *Bratton . . . graffiti*: "Bill Bratton Has a Deep Personal Hatred of Graffiti," *New York Post*, May 21, 2014; "The City's Top Cop Knows Why There's Crime—Criminals," *NYDN*, May 21, 2014.

281 *Malcolm Gladwell theorized . . . nineties crime drop under Bratton*: Gladwell, *The Tipping Point*, 140–46.

Charlie Beck, South Bureau, South Los Angeles, 2006

282 *"like creatures in the zoo"*: Charlie Beck interview.

283 *"people obey the law"*: "The Paradox of American Policing," *Cops Office*, July 2010.

284 *wearing a suit, rather than his uniform*: Charlie Beck interview.

284 *"talked to them like they were regular people"*: Ibid.

285 *"That there's nothing to be afraid of"*: Ibid.

285 *"building community cohesion"*: Ibid.

286 *Beck organized a barbecue*: Ibid.

286 *"We fed them and we talked"*: Ibid.

286 *"We were really inclusive in that way"*: Ibid.

286 *"we'd do the right thing"*: Ibid.

NYPD Commissioner Raymond Kelly, New York City; LAPD Chief Bill Bratton, Los Angeles; Stop-Question-Frisk

286 *pedestrian stops . . . Los Angeles . . . 275,000 to the NYPD's 660,000*: Peter Bibring interview; "Bratton: The Making of a Police Visionary."

287 *L.A.'s pedestrian stops . . . 35 to 40 percent*: Ibid.

287 *black population . . . 10 percent*: Ibid.

287 *New York—where 85 percent of the stops were of blacks and Latinos*: "Yes, Mayor Bloomberg, Stop-and-Frisk Is Really, Really Racist," *Slate*, July 1, 2013.

287 *LAPD . . . 700,000 vehicle stops a year*: Peter Bibring interview; "Bratton: The Making of a Police Visionary."

287 *blacks were ordered out of their vehicles 2.5 times more than were whites*: Peter Bibring interview.

287 *Latinos 2.3 times more*: Ibid.

287 *black motorists were twice as likely to get frisked as whites*: Ibid.

287 *frisked African-Americans . . . 40 percent less likely to have a weapon than whites*: Ibid.

287 *"over 40 percent less likely to happen"*: Ibid.

287 *late 2002, the LAPD . . . 585,000 . . . stops*: Stone et al., *Policing Los Angeles Under a Consent Decree*, 22; "Bill Bratton Expanded Stop and Frisk When He Ran Los Angeles Police Department: Study," *NYDN*, November 24, 2013.

287 *Six years later . . . 875,000 total stops*: Peter Bibring interview; Stone et al., *Policing Los Angeles Under a Consent Decree*, 22.

288 *Between 2004 and June 2012 the NYPD would engage in 4.4 million pedestrian stop-and-frisks*: "Stop-and-Frisk Campaign: About the Issue," New York Civil Liberties Union, accessed February 5, 2015, http://www.nyclu.org/issues /racial-justice/stop-and-frisk-practices; "NYPD Stop-and-Frisk Policy Yielded 4.4 Million Detentions but Few Results: Study," *NYDN*, April 3, 2012; "12 Years of Mayor Bloomberg," *NYT*, December 28, 2013.

288 *85 percent of which were black and Hispanic*: "Stop-and-Frisk Data," New York Civil Liberties Union, http://www.nyclu.org/content/stop-and-frisk-data, accessed February 5, 2015.

288 *guns were found in just 0.14 percent of the stops*: "Trial Weighs Importance of Arrests in Police Stops," *NYT*, May 17, 2013.

288 *marijuana . . . black New Yorkers were seven times more likely than whites to be arrested*: "Whites Smoke Pot, but Blacks Are Arrested," *NYT*, December 22, 2009.

290 *forty thousand gang members*: William Bratton interview; "L.A. Chooses Group to Run Anti-Gang Academy," *LAT*, January 8, 2010; "With Kids Dead, L.A. Vows Gang Crackdown," *AP*, January 21, 2007.

290 *"Twice a year . . . graduating fifteen hundred officers"*: William Bratton interview.

290 *"They were being surged into areas"*: Ibid.

290 *"we didn't use new recruits to stop people"*: Charlie Beck interview.

291 *"open-display" marijuana arrests*: "Dismal Tale of Arrests for Tiniest of Crimes," *NYT*, November 1, 2011.

291 *"It was abhorrent"*: William Bratton interview.

291 *gang injunction ran 276 pages, targeted six gangs*: "Promise and Peril in South L.A.," *LAT*, June 7, 2009.

291 *13.7 square miles of South Los Angeles*: Ibid.

291 *injunction made arrestable crimes*: Ibid.

291 *"What's lost in discussion about this method of enforcement"*: Peter Bibring interview.

292 *"not scaring the little old lady across the street"*: Charlie Beck interview.

292 *"African-American men between the ages of sixteen and thirty-seven"*: "Rights and Wrongs," *New Yorker*, May 27, 2013.

293 *13,212 murders in New York City*: "Ray Kelly; The NYPD: Guilty of Saving 7,383 Lives," *WSJ*, July 22, 2013.

293 *"You've got to have it"*: William Bratton interview.

Connie Rice, January 2007, Los Angeles City Council Meeting

294 *"I'm happy for Reggie"*: "Follow the Gang Money: Part One," *Witness LA*, August 16, 2010.

294 *At one thousand pages, it weighed in at twelve pounds*: "An LAPD Critic Comes in from the Cold," *Crime Report*, January 18, 2012; Connie Rice interview.

294 *"there's $1 billion in [city and county] programs for kids"*: "Both Sides of the Street."

295 *Wes McBride . . . His career . . . destroy three generations of one family*: Connie Rice interview.

295 *"Twenty-five years of containment-suppression"*: "Both Sides of the Street."

296 *"There were many things the report was not"*: Leap, "Los Angeles and Gang Violence," 22.

Bill Bratton, May Day 2007, MacArthur Park

296 *"so god damn stupid"*: David Dotson interview.

297 *immigrant protests . . . one in Chicago that numbered 400,000*: "Immigrants Take to U.S. Streets in Show of Strength," *NYT*, May 1, 2006.

297 *seven-hundred-mile border fence*: CNN, May 1, 2006.

298 *"a love fest"*: William Bratton interview; Domanick, *Anatomy of a Police Crisis*, 2.

298 *"managed to walk a tightrope"*: David Dotson interview.

298 *one million stops in one year*: Peter Bibring interview.

298 *"Bratton . . . provided visionary and progressive leadership"*: "Police Commission Reappoints Chief Bratton to Second Term," Los Angeles Police Department press release, June 19, 2007, accessed February 5, 2015, http://www.lapdon line.org/june_2007/news_view/35667; "Bratton's Coronation Affirms the Silence of Lambs," *Los Angeles Sentinel*, June 28, 2007.

299 *"Without minimizing the importance of [our] disagreements"*: Ramona Ripston, American Civil Liberties Union, to the Los Angeles Board of Police Commissioners, letter, April 27, 2007.

299 *In 1992 there had been over 1,000 homicides in Los Angeles*: "Homicides in 1992 Set Record for L.A. County," *LAT*, January 5, 1993; "L.A.'s Homicide Rate Lowest in Four Decades," NPR, January 6, 2011.

299 *By 1998 . . . fallen by nearly 60 percent to 419*: "13 Die in Four Days of Violence," *LAT*, November 19, 1992; "Violent Crime in L.A. Declines in Most Catego-

ries," *LAT*, December 14, 1999; "L.A. Homicide Rate on the Rise; Blamed on Gang Activities," *AP*, November 23, 2002.

299 *in late 2002 . . . risen again by over one-third to 647*: "Crime in L.A. Drops for 3rd Year in a Row," *LAT*, December 21, 2005; "Top Cop in Los Angeles Says Cutting Crime Pays," *WSJ*, November 29, 2008.

299 *dropping . . . under Bratton to 480*: "Save Money—Hire Police," *LAT*, November 22, 2011.

300 *to join Los Angeles mayor Antonio Villaraigosa*: William Bratton interview.

300 *Bratton . . . home . . . Los Feliz*: Ibid.

300 *rock- and bottle-throwing*: "Saving Los Angeles," 72.

300 *Antonio Villaraigosa . . . "surrounded by the Spanish-language press"*: William Bratton interview.

301 *"they're beating up people"*: Ibid.

301 *"there's nothing going on that I'm aware of"*: Ibid.

301 *"ordered the park cleared"*: Ibid.

301 *"the hair shot up the back of my neck"*: Ibid.

301 *150 Los Angeles police officers*: Hillman and Chaleff, *An Examination of May Day 2007*, 8–9.

301 *in English, not Spanish*: Domanick, *Anatomy of a Police Crisis*, 3.

301 *two-foot-long batons*: "Saving Los Angeles."

301 *fired off rubber bullets*: Ibid.

301 *women wheeling baby strollers and dozens of reporters*: Ibid.

302 *"the heart and soul of the LAPD culture"*: William Bratton interview; Domanick, *Anatomy of a Police Crisis*, 4.

303 *"we cleared the park"*: William Bratton interview; Domanick, *Anatomy of a Police Crisis*, 9.

303 *about thirty or forty*: William Bratton interview.

303 *Bratton called Mark Perez*: Ibid.

303 *Birotte . . . should come to the park as well*: Ibid.

304 *"I've never been part of that school"*: Ibid.

304 *Carter . . . had sent them home*: Ibid.

304 *The final tally was 166*: Hillman and Chaleff, *An Examination of May Day 2007*, 9–10; "LAPD Takes Blame for Park Melee," *LAT*, October 10, 2007.

305 *"a procedural mistake"*: William Bratton interview.

305 *"You don't use a fifteen-hundred-pound machine"*: Ibid.

305 *"legitimate, very rational group"*: Ibid.

305 *"change a flat tire while racing down a highway"*: Ibid; Domanick, *Anatomy of a Police Crisis*, 11.

305 *"calm the waters"*: William Bratton interview; Domanick, *Anatomy of a Police Crisis*, 12.

306 *"break the back"*: William Bratton interview; Domanick, *Anatomy of a Police Crisis*, 15.

306 *"insensitivity that the whole department was accused of"*: William Bratton interview.

306 *45 percent Latino, 15 percent black, over 20 percent female*: Domanick, *Anatomy of a Police Crisis*, 14.

306 *the city wound up paying nearly $13 million*: "Los Angeles to Pay $13 Million to Settle May Day Melee Lawsuits," *LAT*, February 5, 2009.

306 *Bratton . . . San Jose Marriott Hotel*: Author's observations; "Saving Los Angeles."

307 *"Go to a Home Depot"*: "Saving Los Angeles."

307 *"in my thirty-seven years of policing"*: William Bratton interview; "Saving Los Angeles," 131.

307 *he demoted and reassigned Lee Carter*: "Deputy Chief Demoted Over Melee Will Retire," *LAT*, May 17, 2007; Domanick, *Anatomy of a Police Crisis*, 15.

Laura Chick, February 2008, Office of Controller; Los Angeles Mayor Antonio Villaraigosa, City Hall

308 *Villaraigosa . . . who'd grown up . . . East L.A.*: "He's the Energizer Mayor," *LAT*, May 5, 2006; "Former Mayor Villaraigosa Portrait Complete, Bound for Los Angeles City Hall," *LADN*, January 29, 2014; "The Untold Story of the Mayor's Rise from Poverty to Power," *LADN*, November 19, 2006.

308 *caught having an extramarital affair*: "Mayor Reveals Romantic Link with TV Newscaster," *LAT*, July 4, 2007.

309 *"There was a lot of debate"*: Jeff Carr interview.

309 *"there was no guarantee"*: Ibid.

309 *"it was political suicide"*: Ibid.

309 *"You're the first Latino mayor in 137 years"*: Ibid.

309 *"we're gonna do it"*: Ibid.

310 *"Urban Peace Academy" . . . over one hundred hours of training*: "Gang Interventionists Distribute Food, Prayer—and a Sense of Change," *LAT*, June 28, 2009.

310 *interventionists . . . earn a minimum of $30,000 a year and health insurance*: Ibid.

310 *GRYD would receive $21 million in 2010*: "What Does It Take to Stop Crips and Bloods from Killing Each Other?" *NYT*, July 10, 2013; "Gang Interventionists Distribute Food, Prayer—and a Sense of Change."

310 *$700,000 for the first year of the gang academy's funding*: Connie Rice interview.

310 *then raise its budget to over $1 million*: Ibid.

Bill Bratton, August 2009, Parker Center

312 *"a slap in the face of the department"*: "Bratton Says LAPD Is Improved, Wants Consent Decree Lifted," KPCC 89.3, June 24, 2009.

312 *"never wanted to go and just maintain something"*: "Los Angeles Police Chief William J. Bratton to Step Down," *LAT*, August 5, 2009.

313 *"serious crime" had dropped by almost 35 percent*: Stone et al., *Policing Los Angeles Under a Consent Decree*, 6.

313 *30 percent drop in officer-involved shootings*: Ibid., 33.

313 *LAPD treated "all racial and ethnic groups fairly" . . . risen from 39 to 51 percent*: Ibid., 49.

313 *pedestrian and vehicle stops had risen by almost 50 percent*: Ibid., 22.

313 *"saw a lot of force displayed"*: Ibid., 37–38.

313 *"we're talking about a department"*: "LAPD Improves Its Image," *LAT*, May 19, 2009.

315 *Charlie Beck walked a beat in Jordan Downs*: Charlie Beck interview.

Pat Gannon, Ron Noblet, and Alfred Lomas, December 2010, Magnolia Place Community Center

316 *Ron Noblet . . . half-Mexican-American, half-Eastern-European*: Ron Noblet interview.

316 *ex-marine*: Ibid.

316 *native son of Los Angeles*: Ibid.

316 *Slavic studies major at USC*: Ibid.; Connie Rice interview.

316 *alcoholic father*: Ron Noblet interview.

316 *terrible beatings*: Ibid.

316 *"You don't know me, but you need me"*: Connie Rice interview.

317 *"Ron was very important"*: Ibid.

317 *"they help stop the next killing"*: Ron Noblet interview.

317 *Alfred Lomas . . . Looking like a lawyer late for court*: Author's observations.

317 *the Dream Center*: "Gang Interventionists Distribute Food, Prayer—and a Sense of Change."

318 *Olvera asked for a favor*: Alfred Lomas interview.

318 *"keep everybody calm and all the rumors from spreading"*: Ibid.

318 *"the kid had died of an aneurysm"*: Ibid.

318 *"Al was a generation behind in age"*: Ron Noblet interview.

319 *"They don't like hypocrisy"*: Ibid.

319 *Three times*: Alfred Lomas interview.

319 *Claiming to have suspicious surveillance pictures of Lomas*: Ibid.

320 *"who was real and who wasn't"*: Ibid.

320 *to do something other than being just a hard-nosed gang cop*: Curtis Woodle interview.

320 *Woodle had chosen a local middle school*: Ibid.

320 *"And Curtis . . . very good at figuring out how to do that"*: Charlie Beck interview.

320 *"He is the real deal"*: Connie Rice interview.

321 *"This year, right now"*: Patrick Gannon interview.

321 *"you begin to change the physics of the neighborhood"*: "Addicted to Guns," *Chicago Reader*, May 8, 2013.

322 *homicides by 2013 would drop to 250*: "Valley Sees Major Drop in Homicides,"
     LAT, December 31, 2013.
322 *2010 would end with under 300 homicides*: "Killing in L.A. Drops to 1967 Lev-
     els," *LAT*, December 26, 2010.
322 *marijuana became an infraction*: "Marijuana Possession in California Reduced
     to an Infraction," AP, December 1, 2010.
323 *"running a fatherhood project"*: Ron Noblet interview.
323 *"She's the first person in her family to go to college"*: Ibid.

Daryl Gates and Charlie Beck,
April 2010, San Clemente, California

323 *Daryl Gates . . . panoramic view*: Charlie Beck interview.
323 *hilltop condominium in San Clemente*: Ibid.
323 *cancer*: "Controversial LAPD Chief," *LAT*, April 17, 2010; "Former LAPD
     Chief Daryl Gates Battling Bladder Cancer," *LAT*, February 16, 2010.
323 *startled by how frail he looked*: Charlie Beck interview.
324 *open-at-the-collar LAPD blues*: Ibid.
325 *"I feel I can go now"*: Ibid.
325 *Beck . . . "top goal"*: "L.A. City Council Panel Confirms Charlie Beck as Police
     Chief," *LAT*, November 10, 2009.
325 *an LAPD helicopter appeared against the blue waters*: Charlie Beck interview.
325 *Daryl Francis Gates . . . snapped off his final salute*: Ibid.

EPILOGUE: 2014

328 *Eric Garner . . . "I can't breathe"*: "Relatives, Friends Say Goodbye to Eric Gar-
     ner, Who Died After NYPD Cop Put Him in Chokehold, at Brooklyn Fu-
     neral," *NYDN*, July 23, 2014; "Man's Death After Chokehold Raises Old Issue
     for the Police," *NYT*, July 18, 2014; "From 'Chokehold' Death to No Indict-
     ment: A Timeline of Events Since Eric Garner's Death," *NYDN*, December 3,
     2014.
328 *shooting death of an unarmed black teenager named Michael Brown*: "Grief and
     Protests Follow Shooting of a Teenager," *NYT*, August 10, 2014; "After Un-
     armed Teen Michael Brown Is Killed, the St. Louis-Dispatch Front Page Cap-
     tures Ferguson Burning," *Washington Post*, August 22, 2014; "Michael Brown's
     Shooting and Its Immediate Aftermath in Ferguson," *NYT*, August 25, 2014;
     "Official Autopsy Shows Michael Brown Had Close-Range Wound to His
     Hand, Marijuana in His System," *St. Louis Post-Dispatch*, October 28, 2014;
     "Timeline: Michael Brown Shooting in Ferguson, Mo.," *USA Today*, De-
     cember 2, 2014; "Federal Autopsy Released in Michael Brown Shooting—

Conclusions Seen Similar to Local, Private Examiner's," AP, December 9, 2014.

329 *protesters' popular rallying cry of "I Can't Breathe"*: " 'I Can't Breathe' Is Echoed in Voices of Fury and Despair," *NYT*, December 3, 2014; " 'I Can't Breathe': Why Eric Garner Protests Are Gaining Momentum," Reuters, December 5, 2014; " 'I Can't Breathe' Protests Hit Fifth Day," NBC News, December 7, 2014.

329 *"Hands Up, Don't Shoot"*: "Protestors Use Hands-Up Gesture Defiantly After Michael Brown Shooting," *LAT*, August 12, 2014; "The 'Hands Up, Don't Shoot' Gesture from Ferguson Moves to Hong Kong," PRI, September 30, 2014; " 'Hands Up, Don't Shoot' Could Start a Real Revolution," *Time*, December 4, 2014; "Pharrell's Grammy Performance Includes 'Hands Up Don't Shoot' Tribute," *Huffington Post*, September 2, 2015.

329 *"Black Lives Matter"*: " 'I Can't Breathe': Why Eric Garner Protests Are Gaining Momentum"; "Chanting 'Black Lives Matter,' Protestors Shut Down Part of Mall of America," AP, December 20, 2014.

330 *Beck . . . Community Safety Partnership Police*: "Op-Ed: Reappoint Charlie Beck as Police Chief," *LAT*, August 11, 2014; "What Police Departments Can Learn About Race Relations from the LAPD," Yahoo News, December 21, 2014.

330 *driver's licenses for undocumented immigrants*: "Beck Backs Driver's Licenses for Illegal Immigrants," *LAT*, February 23, 2012; "Driver's Licenses for Undocumented Immigrants? LAPD Chief Charlie Becks Says Yes," *Huffington Post*, February 23, 2012; "LAPD Chief Says Illegal Immigrants Should Get Driver's Licenses," NPR, January 23, 2012.

330 *Charlie Beck/stopped impounding cars/license-less immigrants*: "With Illegal Immigrants in Mind, LAPD to Change Impound Rules," *LAT*, December 14, 2011; "Newton: LAPD's Impound Dilemma," *LAT*, January 30, 2012; "LAPD's Vehicle Impound Reforms Put on Hold," *LAT*, February 15, 2012.

330 *"forty-six permanent gang injunctions in place in the city of Los Angeles"*: "Gang Injunctions," Los Angeles City Attorney's Office, accessed April 26, 2015, http://www.atty.lacity.org/CRIMINAL/GangInjunctions/index.htm.

331 *605 officer-involved homicides in all of L.A. County*: "The Homicide Report," *LAT*, accessed on April 26, 2015, http://homicide.latimes.com/cause/gun shot/officer_involved/true/year/all.

331 *228 deaths, were at the hands of LAPD officers*: "The Homicide Report."

331 *NYPD . . . had killed "at least 179 people"*: "Exclusive: In 179 Fatalities Involving On-Duty NYPD Cops in 15 Years, Only 3 Cases Led to Indictments—and Just 1 Conviction," *NYDN*, December 8, 2014.

331 *"at least 1,800 police killings in those 105 departments"*: "WSJ Analysis: Justifiable Homicides by U.S. Law Enforcement," *WSJ*, December 2, 2014; "Hundreds of Police Killings Are Uncounted in Federal Stats," *WSJ*, December 3, 2014.

332 *LAPD had misclassified nearly twelve hundred aggravated assaults*: "LAPD Misclassified Nearly 1,200 Violent Crimes as Minor Offenses," *LAT*, August 9,

2014; "Inaccurate LAPD Crime Statistics Prompt Larger Investigation," *LAT*, August 11, 2014.

332 *"hundreds of stabbings, beatings, and robberies"*: "LAPD Misclassified Nearly 1,200 Violent Crimes as Minor Offenses."

332 *"total aggravated assaults . . . 14 percent higher than the official figure"*: Ibid.

332 *"turned serious crime[s] into minor one[s]"*: Ibid.

333 *Los Angeles Police Commission voted 4–1 to rehire him*: "LAPD Chief Charlie Beck Appointed to Second Term in 4–1 Police Commission Vote," *LAT*, August 12, 2014; "LAPD Chief Beck Appointed to a Second Term on 4–1 Vote," *Whittier Daily News*, August 12, 2014; "LAPD Chief Charlie Beck Gets Another 5 Years," *LA Weekly*, August 12, 2014, accessed March 23, 2015, http://www.laweekly.com/news/lapd-chief-charlie-beck-gets-another-5-years-5002797.

333 *Beck released a major reform plan*: "LAPD Announces Reforms to Boost Accuracy of City Crime Statistics," *LAT*, December 16, 2014; "Violent Crime Rose 14.3% in L.A.; Officials Vow Action," *LAT*, January 12, 2015; "L.A. Violent Crime Rises for the First Time in 12 Years, LAPD Says," *LAT*, December 30, 2014.

333 *14 percent increase in violent crime*: "Violent Crime Rose 14.3% in L.A."

333 *rise of over 28 percent in every category of aggravated assaults*: Ibid.

333 *"identified 10 people . . . beaten, burned, suffocated, or shot"*: "The Truth About Chicago's Crime Rates," *Chicago*, April 7, 2014.

333 *"serious felonies"*: Ibid.

334 *"crimes are being downgraded"*: Eterno and Silverman, *The Crime Numbers Game*; "Policing by the Numbers," *NYT*, June 17, 2012; "The LAPD and the End of Charlie Beck's Honeymoon," Crime Report, November 14, 2014.

334 *Chicago police statistics . . . crimes dropped 56 percent*: "The Truth About Chicago's Crime Rates."

334 *"the miraculous"*: Ibid.

334 *de Blasio . . . 95 percent of the African-American vote*: "Activists: De Blasio Picks 'Not Diverse Enough,'" *New York Post*, April 18, 2014; "NYC Elections 2013: Exit Polls Show Bill de Blasio Swept Virtually Every Demographic over Joe Lhota," *NYDN*, November 5, 2013.

335 *NYPD . . . stopped-questioned-and/or-frisked over 97,000 New Yorkers*: "For New York Police, There's No End to the Stops," *NYT*, May, 14, 2012; "Stop-and-Frisk Data."

336 *By 2011, that number had exploded to over 685,000*: "For New York Police, There's No End to the Stops"; "Among Blacks and Latinos, Resentment Toward NYPD Lingers," *Washington Post*, December 24, 2014; "Too Many Innocents Harassed by NYPD's 'Stop and Frisk' Practices," *NYDN*, January 8, 2013; "Stop-and-Frisk Data."

336 *158,000 black males . . . stopped more than 168,000 times*: "New NYCLU Report Finds NYPD Stop-and-Frisk Practices Ineffective, Reveals Depth of Racial

Disparities," NYCLU, May 9, 2012; "Report Finds Stop-and-Frisk Focused on Black Youth," *WSJ*, May 9, 2012.

336 *"defining moment in [New York] history"*: "Mayor de Blasio Announces Agreement in Landmark Stop-and-Frisk Case," Office of the Mayor, City of New York, January 30, 2014; "De Blasio Announces Settlement to End Stop and Frisk Case Against City," *U.S. News & World Report*, January 30, 2014.

336 *"solemn promise to every New Yorker"*: Ibid.

336 *broken-windows policing*: "Broken Windows: The Police and Neighborhood Safety," *Atlantic*, March 1, 1982.

336 *choke hold banned by the NYPD since 1993*: "Kelly Bans Choke Holds by Officers," *NYT*, November 24, 1993.

337 *"It was evident"*: "Bill Bratton in New York, Take Two."

337 *less than twenty-five grams of marijuana . . . punishable by a $100 fine*: "Concerns in Criminal Justice System as New York City Eases Marijuana Policy," *NYT*, November 10, 2014; "Order for Summons, in Lieu of Arrest for Possession of Marijuana," *NYT*, November 10, 2014; "The War on Drugs Is Burning Out," *Rolling Stone*, January 8, 2015.

337 *homicides . . . new record low*: "Murders in New York Drop to a Record Low, but Officers Aren't Celebrating," *NYT*, December 31, 2014.

337 *homicides . . . had dropped yet again to . . . 328*: Ibid.

337 *robberies, meanwhile, had fallen by 14 percent*: Ibid.

337 *stop-and-frisks had plunged 79 percent*: "Contrary to Predictions, NYC Crime Down Despite Decline of Stop-and-Frisk," Crime Report, December 4, 2014; "NYC's Homicide Total Is Down 6.8% This Year, de Blasio Says," Bloomberg, December 2, 2014; "NYC 'Stop and Frisk' Almost Gone. Yet Crime Continues to Drop. Why?" *Christian Science Monitor*, December 3, 2014.

337 *By year's end . . . fewer than 50,000 stops*: William Bratton interview with Scott Pelley, *CBS Evening News with Scott Pelley*, December 4, 2014; "Bratton: Kelly's Stop-and-Frisk Caused Minorities to Fear Cops," *New York Post*, December 8, 2014.

338 *two-thirds of New Yorkers believed that Daniel Pantaleo . . . should have been indicted*: "Nearly Two-Thirds of New Yorkers Believe Officer Daniel Pantaleo Should Be Charged in the Death of Eric Garner: Poll," *NYDN*, December 13, 2014.

338 *"painful conversations"*: "De Blasio Draws upon His Family to Console NYC," *Salon*, December 3, 2014; "De Blasio Talks of Son Dante, Draws on Family Experiences After Garner Grand Jury Decision," NBC News, December 4, 2014; "Mayor De Blasio to New Yorkers: We Must Work to Build the Kind of City We Need to Be," *CBS New York*, December 4, 2014.

338 *an officer had his nose broken*: "NYPD Hunting for 6 Protestors After Melee Leaves Officer with a Broken Nose," *LAT*, December 15, 2014; "Amid Assaults on Officers, New York Police Rethink Their Response to Protests,"

NYT, December 14, 2014; "Man Sought in Assault on Officers During Brooklyn Bridge Protest Surrenders," *NYT*, December 18, 2014.

338 *Bratton had fake blood thrown on him*: "Bill Bratton Sprayed with Paint During Times Square Protest Following Ferguson Decision," *NYDN*, November 24, 2014; "Occupy Wall Street Protestor Busted in Fake Blood Attack on NYPD Commissioner Bratton During Ferguson Demonstration," *NYDN*, November 25, 2014; "Bratton Throws the Book at Fake Blood Splasher," *New York Post*, November 25, 2014.

339 *pepper-sprayed Occupy Wall Street protesters*: "3 Sue Over Pepper-Spraying by Police at Fall Occupy Wall St. Protest," *NYT*, July 31, 2012; "Police Use Pepper Spray on Demonstrators at 'Occupy Wall Street' Protest," *Time*, September 26, 2011; "Cops Caught Pepper-Spraying, Punching Occupy Wall Street Protestors Will Not Be Prosecuted: DA," *NYDN*, April 20, 2013.

339 *protests in Philadelphia, Chicago*: "Protests Flare After Ferguson Police Officer Is Not Indicted," *NYT*, November 24, 2014.

339 *Harvard and about forty other medical schools . . . protesting Brown and Garner's deaths*: "Medical Students Across U.S. Hold 'Die-Ins' to Protest Racism," UPI, December 10, 2014; "Harvard Students Stage 'Die-In' to Protest Ferguson, NYC Cases," *Boston Globe*, December 10, 2014; "After Protests, Harvard Law Students Request Exam Delay," *Boston Globe*, December 10, 2014; "Law Schools Delay Exams for Students Upset by Ferguson, Eric Garner Decisions," AP, December 10, 2014.

339 *LeBron James and Kobe Bryant wore "I Can't Breathe" T-shirts*: "President Obama Praises LeBron James's 'I Can't Breathe' Shirt," *Washington Post*, December 19, 2014: "At Nets Game, a Plan for a Simple Statement Is Carried Out to a T," *NYT*, December 9, 2014; "Kobe Bryant: 'I Can't Breathe' Protest Not About Race but Justice," *LAT*, December 10, 2014; "Kobe Bryant and Lakers Wear 'I Can't Breathe' Shirts in Show of Support for Eric Garner's Family," *NYDN*, December 10, 2014.

339 *Ismaaiyl Brinsley shot and killed NYPD officers*: "Two NYPD Officers 'Assassinated' While Sitting in Patrol Car in Brooklyn by Gunman Who Boasted on Instagram About 'Revenge' Killing Cops," *NYDN*, December 21, 2014; "Cop Shooter Ismaaiyl Brinsley Bragged to Brooklyn Bystanders Just Before Fatally Shooting NYPD Officers Wenjian Liu, Rafael Ramos," *NYDN*, December 21, 2014; "Gunman Executes 2 NYPD Cops in Garner 'Revenge,'" *New York Post*, December 20, 2014.

339 *"A predictable outcome"*: George Pataki's Twitter page, accessed February 9, 2015, https://twitter.com/governorpataki/status/546489605378551808.

339 *"an anti-police campaign"*: "Slain New York Officers 'Brought Back Horrible Memories,' Says Former NYPD Commissioner," *Good Morning America*, ABC, December 21, 2014.

339 *"set off this [post-murder] firestorm"*: Ibid.

340 *"starts on the steps of City Hall"*: "For Mayor de Blasio and New York Police, a

Rift Is Ripped Open," *NYT*, December 21, 2014; "NYPD Cops Furious with Bill de Blasio Turn Their Backs on the Mayor as He Enters Hospital Where Officers Died," *NYDN*, December 20, 2014; "NYC Police Deaths: Details on Suspect; Rift Between Mayor and Police," NPR, December 22, 2014.

340 *well over a dozen cops . . . turned their backs in unison:* "Police Turn Their Back on De Blasio," *New York Post*, December 20, 2014; "NYPD Cops Furious with Bill de Blasio Turn Their Backs on the Mayor as He Enters Hospital Where Officers Died"; "NYC Police Deaths: Details on Suspect; Rift Between Mayor and Police."

340 *funerals of Ramos and Liu:* "Cops Ignore Bratton, Turn Backs on de Blasio at Officer's Funeral," *New York Post*, January 4, 2015; "Police Turn Their Backs on Mayor During Second NYPD Officer Funeral," *Time*, January 4, 2015; "Police Officers Turn Their Backs on de Blasio During Eulogy for Officer Rafael Ramos," *NYDN*, December 27, 2014; "De Blasio Speaks at Funeral; Officers Turn Their Backs," *USA Today*, December 27, 2014.

341 *By the mid-1980s, two to three thousand drug raids:* "Ending the Era of the Warrior Cop?" Crime Report, November 5, 2013; "The Real Story of Ferguson," Crime Report, August 18, 2014; "Critics Knock No-Knock Police Raids," *USA Today*, February 13, 2011; "Rise of the Warrior Cop," *WSJ*, August 7, 2013.

341 *By 2010 . . . soared to seventy to eighty thousand per year:* "How 'Warrior Policing' Fails the Homeless Mentally Ill," Crime Report, April 15, 2014; "The Real Story of Ferguson"; "Critics Knock No-Knock Police Raids."

341 *"seriously injured, maimed, or killed by such flashbangs":* "Hotter Than Lava," *ProPublica*, January 12, 2015.

341 *$4 billion in surplus military equipment donated:* "Ferguson Shows the Risks of Militarized Policing," *NYT*, August 14, 2014.

341 *$34 billion in "terrorism grants":* Ibid.

342 *federal oversight . . . more than twenty cities:* "Police Reform's Best Tool: A Federal Consent Decree," Crime Report, July 15, 2014; "Can Anyone Fix the Ferguson Police Department?" *Slate*, August 18, 2014; "These 4 Cities Show What Federal Intervention Could Look Like in Ferguson," *Time*, August 15, 2014; "As Justice Department Scrutinizes Local Police, Cleveland Is Latest Focus," *NYT*, June 17, 2014.

342 *Obama also created a "Task Force on 21st Century Policing":* "Obama Plays Top Cop, Forms Task Force on Police Conduct Post-Ferguson," *Washington Times*, December 18, 2014; "Obama Appoints Task Force on Police Practices," *USA Today*, December 18, 2014; "White House to Launch Task Force on '21st Century Policing,'" NPR, December 1, 2014.

343 *"not a reform at all":* "The Myth of Police Reform," *Atlantic*, May 2015.

BIBLIOGRAPHY

Advancement Project. *Citywide Gang Activity Reduction Strategy: Phase III Report.* Los Angeles: Advancement Project, 2007.

Alexander, Michelle. *The New Jim Crow: Mass Incarceration in the Age of Colorblindness.* New York: The New Press, 2010.

Baldwin, James. *Nobody Knows My Name.* New York: Vintage Books, a division of Random House, Inc., 1961.

Blue Ribbon Review Panel, Rampart Community Police Station, Los Angeles Police Commission, Los Angeles Police Department. *Rampart Reconsidered: The Search for Real Reform Seven Years Later.* Los Angeles: Los Angeles Police Department, 2006.

Bratton, William, and Peter Knobler. *Turnaround: How America's Top Cop Reversed the Crime Epidemic.* New York: Random House, 1998.

Chemerinsky, Erwin. *An Independent Analysis of the Los Angeles Police Department's Board of Inquiry Report on the Rampart Scandal.* Los Angeles: Police Protective League, 2000.

Chicago Police Department, Research and Development Division. *2008 Murder Analysis in Chicago.* Chicago: Chicago Police Department, 2008.

Cook, Peter. "Robbery in the United States: Analysis of Recent Trends and Patterns." In *Violence: Patterns, Causes, Public Policy,* edited by Neil Alan Weiner, Margaret A. Zahn, and Rita J. Sagi. New York: Harcourt Brace Jovanovich, 1990.

"Declaration of Brian Tyndall," *People of the State of California v. Javier Francisco Ovando,* B110980 (Cal. Super. Ct., App. Div. September 16, 1999).

"Declaration of Richard Rosenthal," *People of the State of California v. Javier Francisco Ovando,* B110980 (Cal. Super. Ct., App. Div., September 16, 1999).

Diaz, Tom. *No Boundaries: Transnational Latino Gangs and American Law Enforcement.* Ann Arbor: The University of Michigan Press, 2009.

Domanick, Joe, *Anatomy of a Police Crisis: A Case Study in the Actions Taken by LAPD Chief William J. Bratton Following the May Day, 2007, Confrontation Between Police, Demonstrators, and the Media,* New York: Center on Media, Crime and Justice, John Jay College, 2012.

Domanick, Joe, *Covering Police in Times of Crisis,* Los Angeles: USC Annenberg Institute for Justice and Journalism, 2003.

Domanick, Joe. *To Protect and To Serve: The LAPD's Century of War in the City of Dreams*. New York: Pocket Books, a division of Simon & Schuster Inc., 1994.

Dunne, Dominick. *Another City, Not My Own*. New York: Ballantine Books, a division of Random House, Inc., 1997.

Eterno, John A., and Eli B. Silverman. *The Crime Numbers Game: Management by Manipulation (Advances in Police Theory and Practice)*. Boca Raton: CRC Press, Taylor & Francis Group, LLC, 2012.

Fix, Michael E., and Jeffrey S. Passel. *Immigration and Immigrants: Setting the Record Straight*. Washington D.C.: The Urban Institute, 2012.

Gates, Daryl F. *Chief: My Life in the L.A.P.D.* New York: Bantam Books, 1992.

Gladwell, Malcom. *The Tipping Point*. New York: Little, Brown and Company, Hachette Book Group, 2000.

Glazer, Nathan, and Daniel Patrick Moynihan. *Beyond the Melting Pot*. Cambridge: The MIT Press, 1970.

Hayden, Tom. *Street Wars: Gangs and the Future of Violence*. New York: New Press, 2006.

Hazen, Don, ed. *Inside the L.A. Riots: What Really Happened and Why It Will Happen Again*. New York: Institute for Alternative Journalism, 1992.

Hillman, Michael, and Gerald L. Chaleff. *Los Angeles Police Department Report to the Board of Commissioners: An Examination of May Day 2007*. Los Angeles: Los Angeles Police Department, 2007.

"The Impossible Dream: Thomas Bradley," interview by Bernard Galm, Department of Special Collections, University of California, Los Angeles Oral History Program; Los Angeles: The Regents of the University of California, 1984.

Independent Commission on the Los Angeles Police Department, *Report of the Independent Commission on the Los Angeles Police Department*. Darby: Diane Publishing, Co., 1991.

Kirtzman, Andrew. *Rudy Giuliani: Emperor of the City*. New York: HarperCollins Publishers Inc., 2000.

Klieman, Rikki, and Peter Knobler. *Fairy Tales Can Come True: How a Driven Woman Changed Her Destiny*. New York: HarperCollins Publishers Inc., 2003.

Leap, Jorja. "Los Angeles and Gang Violence." In *Los Angeles 2007: State of the City Report*, edited by Jaime Regalado and Ali Modarres. Los Angeles: Edmund G. "Pat" Brown Institute of Public Affairs, California State University, Los Angeles, 2007.

The Learning Company, Inc. "Frank Rizzo." In *Compton Encyclopedia Online* v.3. Boston: The Learning Company, Inc., 1998.

Los Angeles Board of Police Commissioners. *The Report of the Board of Police Commissioners Concerning the Shooting of Eulia Love and the Use of Deadly Force*. Los Angeles: Los Angeles Board of Police Commissioners, 1979.

Los Angeles Times. *Understanding the Riots: Los Angeles Before and After the Rodney King Case*. Los Angeles: Los Angeles Times Syndicate Books, 1996.

Los Angeles Urban League, American Jewish Committee, and the National Conference of Christians and Jews. "Joint Task Force on South Central Los Angeles—Fifteen Years Later." Los Angeles: Los Angeles Urban League, 1981.

Mauer, Marc. "The Crisis of the Young African American Male and the Criminal Justice System." In *The Sentencing Project*, prepared for U.S. Commission on Civil Rights, Washington, D.C., April 15–16, 1999.

Nadel, Mark V. *The Crack Cocaine Epidemic: Health Consequences and Treatment*. Gaithersburg: U.S. General Accounting Office, 1991.

National Drug Intelligence Center. *Attorney General's Report to Congress on the Growth of Violent Street Gangs in Suburban Areas*. Washington D.C.: U.S. Attorney General's Office, 2008.

Niggaz Wit Attitudes (N.W.A). "Fuck Tha Police." Ruthless Records SL-57102, 1988, vinyl LP, recorded 1987–1988.

Ong, Paul, Theresa Firestine, Deirdre Pfeiffer, Oiyan Poon, and Linda Tran. *The State of South L.A.* Los Angeles: UCLA School of Public Affairs, 2008.

People of the State of California v. Javier Francisco Ovando, BA139642 (Cal. Super. Ct., 1997).

Reaves, Brian A. *Using NIBRS Data to Analyze Violent Crime*. Washington, D.C.: U.S. Department of Justice, 1993.

Reese, Renford. "The Rise and Fall of a Public Leader: The Case of Willie Williams and the LAPD." *Journal of Public Management & Social Policy* (Cal Poly Pomona) 6, no. 1 (2000).

Rice, Condoleezza. *Extraordinary, Ordinary People: A Memoir of Family*. New York: Crown Archetype, an imprint of the Crown Publishing Group, a division of Random House, Inc., 2010.

Rice, Connie. *Power Concedes Nothing: One Woman's Quest for Social Justice in America, from the Courtroom to the Kill Zones*. New York: Scribner, a division of Simon & Schuster Inc., 2008.

Rothmiller, Mike, and Ivan G. Goldman. *L.A. Secret Police: Inside the LAPD Elite Spy Network*. New York: Pocket Books, 1992.

"Statement of Rafael Antonio Perez," *People of the State of California v. Rafael Antonio Perez*, BA109900 (Cal. Super. Ct., September 22, 1999, December 14, 1999).

Stone, Christopher, Todd Foglesong, and Christine M. Cole. *Policing Los Angeles Under a Consent Decree: The Dynamics of Change at the LAPD*. Cambridge: President and Fellows of Harvard College, Program in Criminal Justice Policy and Management at the Harvard Kennedy School, 2009.

Webb, Jack. *The Badge: True and Terrifying Crime Stories That Could Not Be Presented on TV, from the Creator and Star of* Dragnet. New York: Thunder's Mouth Press, an imprint of Avalon Publishing Group, 2005.

Webster, William H., and Hubert Williams. *The City in Crisis: A Report by the Special Advisor to the Board of Police Commissioners on the Civil Disorder in Los Angeles*. Washington, D.C.: The Police Foundation Inc., 1992.

Williams, Willie. "Willie Williams' First Major Public Address," American Jewish Committee annual dinner meeting, Regent Beverly Wilshire, Beverly Hills, California, June 16, 1992. Radio broadcast, "The New Chief: What's Going to Change at the LAPD," KCRW *Which Way, L.A.?* RealAudio and Windows Media formats, http://www.kcrw.com/news-culture/shows/which-way-la/the-new-chief-whats-going-to-change-at-the-lapd-1/#.

Zimring, Franklin. *The Great American Crime Decline.* New York: Oxford University Press Inc., 2007.

INDEX

Abramson, Leslie, 194
Advancement Project, 211, 267, 269–70, 294, 296, 308–10, 316
Altegrity, Inc., 311
American Civil Liberties Union (ACLU)
  Bilbring, Peter and, 287, 291
  Bratton, Bill and, 252–54, 298–99, 305
  Chaleff, Gerald and, 232–33
  gang arrests and, 291
  Gates, Daryl and, 34
  LAPD and, 287, 303
  Los Angeles and, 88, 144
  NAACP and, 83
  Parachini, Alan and, 167, 178
  Police Misconduct Guild and, 83
  Presser, Stefan and, 114
  Sheinbaum, Stanley and, 98
  war on drugs and, 341
  Wardlaw, Bill and, 146
  Williams, Willie and, 167
American Jewish Committee (AJC), 62, 94–95, 114
Amnesty International, 93
Anemone, Louis, 237
Annenberg School of Journalism (USC), 265
Arroyo Maravilla (gang), 74
Asian-American community
  hiring of Mike Yamaki and, 46–47, 361
  L.A. riots and, 5
  racial makeup of L.A. and, xviii, 350
  Williams, Willie and, 94
  Woodle, Curtis and, 78
  Yorty, "Mayor Sam" and, 12

Baca, Lee, 265, 310
Bailey, F. Lee, 151
Baldwin Hills neighborhood, 57, 269
Baldwin, James, 61

Beck, Charlie
  Bratton, William and, 238–39, 241–42, 286–87, 290–91, 293, 311, 314, 322, 327
  career, 16–17, 329–30, 331–33
  Central Division and, 243–47
  Christian, Andre and, 116–18
  community partnerships and, 282–86, 289
  drug war and, 17, 53, 131
  gangs and, 115–18, 291–92, 309–10, 315
  Gannon, Pat and, 239, 241, 275, 280, 315
  Gates, Daryl and, 33, 106, 323–25
  Jordan Downs housing project and, 315
  King, Rodney and, 16
  L.A. riots and, 15–16, 18–20, 23, 45–47, 75–76
  LAPD tactics and, 62, 65, 202
  Los Angeles Coliseum and, 75–76, 79
  MacArthur Park and, 262–64, 268
  Parker Center and, 260–62
  Parks, Bernard and, 124, 196–97
  Police Commission and, 159
  Rice, Connie and, 265–68, 270, 309, 321
  South Bureau HQ and, 272–75, 289
  Taylor, Bo and, 284
  Watts neighborhood and, 68–69
  Williams, Willie and, 120, 159
  Woodle, Curtis and, 320
  Yamaki, Mike and, 45–47
Bernstein, David, 333–34
Beyond the Melting Pot (Moynihan and Glazer), 96
Bibring, Peter, 287, 291
Biden, Joe, 25, 98
"Black Lives Matter," 329
Black P. Stones (gang), 269
Black Women's Forum, 92
Bloods (gang), 13, 26, 77, 81, 116, 198, 204, 276, 278, 318, 322
Bloomberg, Michael, 135, 289, 292, 336

Bobb, Merrick, 199
Boston Globe, 225
Boston magazine, 224, 227
Boston Police Department, 40–43, 235–36, 335
Boston Senior Management Institute for Police, 273
Boston University, 226
Boyarsky, Bill, 205–7, 212, 218
Boyle, Gregory, 256, 277
Bradley, Tom
  background, 9–10, 120
  Bratton, Bill and, 223
  Brewer, Jesse and, 99–100
  Christopher Commission and, 14–15, 24
  De Los Reyes, Anthony and, 102–3
  Gates, Daryl and, 14, 21, 24–25, 31, 98, 146, 180, 314
  Parker, Bill and, 10–11
  L.A. riots and, 10, 24, 54, 76–77
  Lane, Ann Reiss and, 101
  Parks, Bernard and, 122
  Police Commission and, 96, 98–103
  political career, 12–14, 25
  Rodney King verdict and, 12
  support for, 34, 147
  Williams, Willie and, 92–95
Braga, Anthony A., 283
Bratton, William
  ACLU and, 252–54, 298–99, 305
  background, 40–42
  Beck, Charlie and, 238–39, 241–42, 246–47, 260–61, 264, 273, 282, 324–25
  Boston PD and, 42–43
  "broken windows" theory and, 45, 246, 336
  Chaleff, Gerald and, 232, 234–35
  community policing and, 342
  consultants as LAPD chief, 235–38
  crime rate under, 113, 168–69, 276, 299, 338
  gangs and, 256, 281, 319
  Garner, Eric and, 339
  Gannon, Patrick and, 239–40, 242–43
  Gascon, George and, 257, 259–60
  Gates, Daryl and, 68
  Giuliani, Rudolph and, 134–39, 167–70, 225
  intervention organizations, 310–11
  Jackson, Clive and, 254–55
  Kelly, Raymond and, 286, 338
  Klieman, Rikki and, 223–27

  LAPD job and, 223–24, 227–32, 330, 332–33
  Linder, John and, 236
  May Day 2007 and, 296, 300–307
  NYTPD and, 36, 43–45
  public and, 251–52
  public perception of, 139
  reform of LAPD, 240–41, 245, 252–54, 322
  resignation from LAPD, 311–15
  return as NYPD commissioner, 329, 334–37, 342
  Rice, Connie and, 265–68, 271–72, 284, 289, 299, 321
  selection as chief, 36
  selection to second term, 298–99
  stop-and-frisk policy and, 286–91, 293–94, 337, 340
  Wasserman, Bob and, 236
  Watkins, Brian and, 39–40
Brewer, Jesse, 32, 97, 99–101, 104–5, 121–22, 124, 147, 149, 179, 254, 258
Brinsley, Ismaaiyl, 339–40
"broken windows" theory, 45, 138, 169, 236, 246, 329, 335–37
Brown, Michael, 328–29, 339–40, 342
Brown, Willie, 25
Buono, Angelo, 165, 233
Bush, George H. W., 76, 79, 113
Bush, George W., 297
Buy Team (LAPD), 131, 133, 153

Caesars Palace casino, 159–60
Call to Action (report), 294, 296, 308–10, 315
Cardozo Law School, 152
Carr, Jeff, 309
Carter, Lee, 301, 303–5, 307
Castro, Fidel, 258
Central Park Jogger case, 39
Chaleff, Gerald, 156, 212–13, 231–35, 313
Chandler, Otis, 13
Chapman, Brien, 164
Cherkasky, Michael G., 311, 313
Chicago, 28, 72, 79, 99, 116, 144, 168, 225, 273, 280, 297, 302, 321, 332–34, 339
Chick, Laura, 183, 308, 310
Christian, Andre, 48–55, 60, 62, 77, 116–18, 167, 315, 323
Christopher Commission, 14–15, 20, 24–25, 32, 62, 67, 91, 100, 102, 141, 143, 147–48, 165, 167, 177–78, 199, 201, 228, 234–35, 305

Christopher, Warren, 14
Civil Service Commission, 31, 102–3
Clinton, Bill, 14, 138–39, 145–46
Cochran, Johnnie, 151–52, 161, 163, 226
Collins, Jim, 259
Colombo, Joseph A., 38–39
Comey, James B., 341
community partnerships, 282
COMPSTAT, 138, 169, 237, 281, 333–34
Costello, Richard B., 105
Court TV, 225–27
crack cocaine
    black community and, 60, 95
    crack wars, 5, 13, 26, 113, 116, 275, 278
    gangs and, 3, 5–7, 51–53, 74–75, 126–31,
        278, 280
    Gates, Daryl and, 30
    LAPD and, 17, 131, 244, 322
    New York City and, 37, 138
Crime Numbers Game, The (Eterno and
    Silverman), 334
Crips (gang), xix, 13, 26, 48–50, 58, 75,
    77–78, 81, 116, 118, 255, 266, 276–77,
    322
Crips and Bloods: Made in America, 278–79
Cuomo, Mario, 98, 139, 231, 255
Czuleger, J. Stephen, 175

Dalton Avenue raid, 18–19, 63
Dateline, 209
Davis, Edward, 13–14, 25, 33, 35, 86, 97, 201
Davis, Gray, 255
de Blasio, Bill, 334–40
De Los Reyes, Anthony, 19, 24, 85, 96,
    101–4, 107, 124, 141
Death Row Records, 133
DeSalvo, Albert, 151
Denny, Reginald, 3, 5–6, 8, 12, 15, 36
Deukmejian, George, 175
Dinkins, David, 40, 134–35, 138–39
District Policing, 260
Don't Ask, Don't Tell, 146
Dorsey High School, 276
Dotson, David
    Bratton, William and, 296, 298, 300
    Christopher Commission and, 32, 62
    Gates, Daryl and, 32, 159, 302
    on King beating, 8
    on L.A. riots, 19–20
    on LAPD tactics, 61–62, 71, 106
    Parks, Bernard and, 124, 187–88
    on Williams, Willie, 106, 119, 141, 143

Dragnet (TV series), 28, 223
Durden, Nino, 157–58, 170–74, 210, 218

Eglash, Jeff, 200
Eide, Richard, 175–77, 188
8 Treys (gang), 77–78
El Sereno (gang), 317
Ellsberg, Daniel, 98
Esquire, 209
Eterno, John A., 334
Evans, Kevin, 248–50
Eynon, Bryan, 118

Fairy Tales Can Come True (Klieman), 226
FBI, xx, 76, 139, 186–87, 224, 332, 341
Feess, Gary, 234, 271, 298, 311–13, 324
Feinstein, Diane, 25
"five percenters," 127
Florencia 13 (gang), xix, 3, 5, 75, 128, 130,
    291, 319
Foothill Division (LAPD), 6, 8
Franklin, Barbara, 251
Frontline, 198, 207, 209
Fuhrman, Mark, 161–63
Fyfe, James, 109, 219

Gang Reduction and Youth Development
    Program (GRYD), 310
"Gangs of L.A." symposium, 265
Gannon, Patrick, 203–5, 212, 231–32,
    239–42, 260, 275–80, 283–84, 314–16,
    318, 320–22
Garcetti, Gil, 207, 215–16, 219
Garner, Eric, 328–29, 337, 339–40, 342
Gascon, George, 257–60, 314
Gates, Daryl
    "aggressive enforcement" policy, 67–68
    Beck, Charlie and, 323–25
    black community and, 60–63, 67–68, 70,
        96
    Bradley, Tom and, 14, 21, 24–25, 31, 98,
        146, 180, 314
    Bratton, William and, 254, 256
    Brewer, Jesse and, 32, 99–100, 147
    career as chief, 25–32
    Chief (autobiography), 31, 228
    Christopher Commission and, 14, 24–25,
        32, 141
    De Los Reyes, Anthony and, 85, 102–4
    discrimination and, 92, 102
    Dotson, David and, 141
    drug war and, 30–31, 131

Gates, Daryl (*cont.*)
  forced resignation, 87, 91, 96, 106–7
  investigations of, 35–36
  K-9 units and, 82, 84
  L.A. riots and, 21–22, 36, 45, 54, 85–87
  Lane, Ann Reiss and, 102
  Metro Division, 302
  Operation Hammer, 64–65, 282
  operational template for LAPD, 18–19
  Parker, Bill and, 13, 22
  Parks, Bernard and, 122, 184–85, 201–2
  public view of, 33–34, 327
  Rodney King verdict and, 19–21
  sexual harassment and, 92
  Sheinbaum, Stanley and, 98, 106–7
  sidearms, 119
  Williams, Willie and, 93, 96, 106, 159, 161,
    163, 166
gay community, 26, 30, 34, 102–4, 110, 144,
  146, 236
General Electric, 263
Gerdes, John, 163
Giuliani, Rudolph, 134–37, 167, 225, 227,
  229, 288, 290, 307, 314, 335
Glazer, Nathan, 96
Glover, Scott, 192–95, 206–7, 218
Gold, Scott, 291
Goldman, Ron, 149
Goldstein, Herman, 236
Goldstein, Richard, 38
Goode, W. Wilson, 109
Gotti, John, 136
Grady, Mary, 304
Grape Street Crips (gang), xv, xix, 48–51, 58,
  75, 77, 117–18
Great Recession, 296, 310
Greenebaum, Gary, 95, 119, 146–49, 164,
  176, 179–80, 183

Hahn, James, 214, 216–17, 223, 228–31, 254,
  285, 308, 314
Hahn, Janice, 285
Harlins, Latasha, 58
Harvard University, 43, 68, 111, 232, 273,
  313, 339
Hewitt, Brian, 189–90, 192, 218–19
Hicks, Joe, 167
Hill, Deirdre, 178
Hillman, Michael, 54
Hillside Strangler, 165, 233
Hohan, Mike, 198
Holder, Eric, 340

Hollenbeck Youth Center, 92–93
Holliday, George, 7
Homicide Report blog, 331
Homies Unidos, 263
homophobia, 27, 146
Hoover, J. Edgar, 139
housing projects
  Charlestown, 41
  crime and, 322–23, 330
  Maravilla, 74
  Pueblo del Rio, 318
  see also Jordan Downs; Nickerson Gardens

"I Can't Breathe," 329, 339
Imus, Don, 135, 227
Innocence Project, 152
intervention programs, 176, 263, 273,
  276–79, 284, 294–95, 309–10, 315–17,
  319–21
Isackson, Noah, 333–34

Jackson, Clive Jr., 255
Jackson, Jesse, 25
Jennings, Peter, 321
Jewish community, 12, 25, 62, 94–95, 97, 110,
  114, 147
Jim Crow, 9, 61, 99, 341
Jimenez, Ishmael, 189–90, 192, 219
John Jay College, 109, 280
Johnston, David Cay, 35
Jordan Downs (housing project), 48–51, 54,
  68, 74–75, 77–78, 80, 116–17, 284–85,
  315, 323, 330
Joyner, Florence Griffith, 133
Justice for Janitors, 297

K-9 units, 68, 82–84, 266
Keith, Damon J., 81
Kelling, George, 45, 236
Kelly, Raymond, 135, 281, 286–89, 292–93,
  336–38, 340
Kennedy, David, 280
Kennedy, Jacqueline, 109
Kennedy, John F., 12, 145
Kennedy, Robert, 12, 232–33
Kennedy, Ted, 98
Kerik, Bernard, 225, 227
King, Larry, 19
King, Martin Luther, 12–13
King, Rodney
  acquittal of officers and, 6, 153
  beating of, 3–5

Beck, Charlie and, 16, 19
black community and, 134, 150–51
Bradley, Tom and, 14, 96, 98, 103
Brewer, Jesse and, 100
Christopher Commission and, 24–25, 100
civil suit against city, 67
Denny, Reginald and, 5
Gates, Daryl and, 25, 31, 33, 98, 147, 180
Internal Affairs (IA) and, 16
L.A. riots and, 5–6, 76, 177
LAPD and, 22, 72, 150, 177, 201, 289, 296
Parks, Bernard and, 123
Police Commission and, 96
public reaction to beating of, 7–8, 48, 304,
    328
reforms and, 93, 96, 234, 289, 296
USJD and, 86, 214
Williams, Willie and, 122
Klieman, Rikki, 223, 225–30, 232, 257
Knight, Marion "Suge," 133
Koch, Ed, 139
Koon, Stacey, 7
Krajewski, Joan L., 114
Kroll Associates, 223, 311
Kumasi, 278

L.A. riots
Asian-American community and, 5
Beck, Charlie and, 15–16, 18–20, 23,
    45–47, 75–76
Bradley, Tom and, 10, 24, 54, 76–77
Dotson, David and, 19–20
Gates, Daryl and, 21–22, 36, 45, 54,
    85–87
Lomas, Alfred and, 55
Los Angeles Times and, 46, 54–55, 57,
    59, 76
Rice, Connie and, 80–85
Watts neighborhood and, 54, 58–59, 75
Yamaki, Mike and, 58–59
Lait, Matt, 184, 192–95, 206–7, 218
Lane, Ann Reiss, 20, 24, 96, 101–2, 104–5,
    121
Lardner, James, 168
Latin Kings (gang), 317
Latino community
Beck, Charlie and, 286, 289, 330
Bratton, William and, 259, 282, 298,
    306–7
Catholic Church and, 145
drugs and, 157
gangs and, 292

growth of, 26, 34
L.A. riots and, 56
LAPD and, 11, 26–27, 94, 229–30, 292
May Day and, 296
Police Commission and, 102
poverty and, 7–8, 322–23
prisons and, 130
stop-and-frisk and, 287
UPA and, 316, 320
Villaraigosa, Antonio and, 309
Williams, Willie and, 94
League of Women Voters, 101
Leap, Jorja, 296
Lennox, Ian H., 93
Leovy, Jill, 331
Lewis, David, 206
Lewis, Marlon, 249
Linder, John, 236
Lomas, Alfred
arrest and incarceration, 129–30
background, 73–75, 125–27
Denny, Reginald and, 3, 5–8
drugs and, 51–52, 127–29
gang ties, 291
King, Rodney and, 8
L.A. riots and, 55
police brutality and, 8, 15, 48
UPA and, 317–20
Lopez Maravilla (gang), 74
Los Angeles Herald-Examiner, 35
Los Angeles Times
Beck, Charlie and, 17, 291, 325, 332–33
Bradley, Tom and, 13
Bratton, William and, 228–29, 247, 291,
    312
Christopher Commission and, 167
Gates, Daryl and, 22, 24, 34–36, 65
history with LAPD, 297
investigations of LAPD, 35–36, 65, 67,
    192, 194, 200, 250
L.A. riots and, 46, 54–55, 57, 59, 76
Lomas, Alfred and, 320
Parks, Bernard and, 123, 184
Rampart CRASH and, 131–32, 192, 194,
    205–7, 214–16, 218, 266
reports on LAPD K-9 unit, 82
Williams, Willie and, 92, 120, 140, 142,
    160, 177–79
Los Angeles Urban League, 230, 266
Lota Maravilla (gang), 74
Lutz, Bobby, 131
Lynch, Pat, 340

MacArthur Park, 261–62, 264, 268, 271, 296, 300–304, 306–7, 315
Mack, David, 131–33, 185–87, 190, 192–93, 198, 204, 209, 230–31, 266, 289, 298–99
Mader, Katherine, 164–66, 199–200, 233
Mahony, Roger, 145–46
Maple, Jack, 136–38, 315, 333
Maravilla (housing project), 74
marijuana, 52, 288–90, 322, 337
Martin, Sammy, 154, 186
Martínez, Rubén, 55
May Day 2007 protest, 296–98, 300, 305, 308
McBride, Tim, 178
McBride, Wes, 295
McCarthy, Gary, 334
McDonnell, Jim, 257
McGovern, George, 98
McKesson, Kevin, 209
Meares, Tracey, 283
Metropolitan Division (LAPD), 302, 306
Metropolitan Transit Authority, 46, 267
Miller, John, 136–37, 167, 235
Mollen, Milton, 231
Mooring, Mark, 83
Morgan, Joe, 67
Morrison, Patt, 312
MOVE, 106, 109
Moynihan, Daniel Patrick, 96

NAACP, 25, 80, 83, 211, 267
National Association of Hispanic Journalists, 306
National Guard, 47, 54, 59, 76, 86
New Centurion policy, 60, 66
New York City Transit Police Department (NYTPD), 36, 41
New York magazine, 39, 137
New York Post, 40, 136, 230
New York Times, 38, 93, 98, 136, 209, 256
Newton, Jim, 123, 179
Newton neighborhood, 128, 212, 318
Nickerson Gardens (housing project), 50, 54, 68, 116, 118, 285
Noblet, Ron, 176, 277, 316–18, 323
N.W.A, 17, 133
NYPD
    Bratton, William and, 41, 138–39, 167–68, 224–25, 235, 334–37
    COMPSTAT and, 334
    corruption and, 38, 231
    crime rate and, 37, 139

Garner, Eric and, 328–29, 336, 339–40
Giuliani, Rudolph and, 167, 227–28
Kelly, Ray and, 135, 293
LAPD and, 119
officer-involved killings, 332
"open-display" marijuana arrests, 290
stop-and-frisk policy, 287–88, 336

O'Connell, David, 250–51
O'Connor, Rory, 224
O'Melveny & Meyers law firm, 14
Occupy Wall Street, 339
Olvera, Mark, 318, 320
"open-display" arrests, 290
Operation Hammer, 64, 240, 280, 282
Ovando, Javier, 170–71, 172, 174–75, 193, 207, 210, 217, 218

Pantaleo, Daniel, 339
Parachini, Allan, 167, 178
Parker, William H.
    background, 10–11, 120, 144
    Brewer, Jesse and, 100
    LAPD tactics and, 32–34, 60, 86
    legacy, 13, 21–22, 25, 28–29, 97, 239
    Parks, Bernard and, 201
    Police Commission and, 31
    reform and, 28
    Watts Riots and, 9, 11
Parker Center, 15–16, 18–19, 23–24, 45, 47, 92, 103, 107, 120, 148, 162, 164, 179, 195–96, 234, 243, 252, 254, 300–301, 305
Parks and Recreation Department, 261–62
Parks, Bernard
    Beck, Charlie and, 196–97, 238
    black community and, 287
    Bratton, Bill and, 237, 254
    Brewer, Jesse and, 105, 124
    career, 122–23
    Chaleff, Gerald and, 233–34
    crime rates under, 299, 313
    Dotson, David and, 187–88
    gang crime and, 299
    Gannon, Patrick and, 239
    Gates, Daryl and, 122
    Hahn, James and, 229–30, 314
    Inspector General's Office and, 199–201, 303
    Mack, David and, 187
    Mader, Katherine and, 199–200

minutiae flaw, 188–89
Newton, Jim and, 123
ouster as chief, 217–18
Perez, Edith and, 198–99
Perez, Rafael and, 197–98, 201–4
Rampart investigation and, 187, 194,
    210–16, 218–19, 230, 251–52, 265
reform and, 185, 327
rigidity, 239
selection as chief, 183–85
stop-and-frisk policies under, 259
Wardlaw, William and, 146
Williams, Willie and, 105, 124–25
Parks, Michael, 207
Pataki, George, 340
Patton, George S., 93
Paysinger, Earl, 301
Peralta, Stacy, 278
Perez, Edith, 198–200, 233
Perez, Mark, 303
Perez, Rafael "Ray"
    arrest, 194–95
    drugs and, 190–93, 202
    Durden, Nino and, 170–71
    fallout from testimony of, 217–19
    investigation of, 193–97
    Mack, David and, 185–87, 193
    Ovando, Javier and, 170–71, 174
    Parks, Bernard and, 197–98, 201–4, 210
    parole, 217
    Rampart CRASH and, 133, 153–58, 171,
        203–5, 251, 289
    transcripts of questioning, 206, 211–12,
        216
    trial, 203–5, 208–14
    Vicencio, Jesse and, 131–32
Perry, Robert, 208, 210
Philadelphia, 28, 30, 79, 82, 91, 93, 104–6,
    108–15, 120, 133, 140, 144–45, 158, 176,
    280, 332, 339
police brutality, 14, 31–32, 35, 81, 100, 105,
    107, 109–10, 113, 115, 302
Police Commission
    Beck, Charlie and, 159
    Bradley, Tom and, 96, 98–103
    Latino community and, 102
    Parker, William H. and, 31
    Rodney King incident and, 96
Police Executive Research Forum, 43
Police Protective League, 92, 142, 197,
    200–201, 203, 266, 314
Pomeroy, Martin, 224

Poston, Ben, 332
Public Safety Committee, 111–12, 114
Pueblo Bishops (gang), 318–19
Pueblo del Rio (housing project), 318

Quesada, Veronica, 186, 198

racial profiling, 283, 298–99, 336
Ramos, Rafael, 339–40
Rampart CRASH
    Christopher Commission and, 199
    Cooley, Steve and, 215–16
    Gannon, Patrick and, 239
    Gascon, George and, 257
    Hewitt, Brian and, 189–90
    investigations into, 192–93, 204–8, 218
    Parks, Bernard and, 187, 194, 210–16,
        218–19, 230, 251–52, 265
    Perez, Ray and, 133, 153–58, 171, 289
    Rice, Connie and, 211–13, 265–66,
        270–71, 284, 294
    USJD and, 214, 234
Rampart Reconsidered (report), 268
retention rate, 202
Rice, Condoleezza, 81
Rice, Connie
    Advancement Project and, 211–12, 270,
        309
    background, 80–81
    Beck, Charlie and, 265–68, 270, 309–11,
        321
    Bratton, William and, 265–68, 271–72,
        284, 289, 299, 321
    Call to Action (report), 308–11, 315
    gangs and, 81, 116, 284, 294–96
    Gannon, Patrick and, 320
    K-9 units and, 82–85
    L.A. riots and, 80–85
    on Mack, John, 230
    Noblet, Ron and, 316–17
    Rampart and, 211–13, 270–71, 284
    Taylor, Bo and, 277
    UPA and, 316, 321
    Villaraigosa, Antonio and, 308–9
Riordan, Richard, 142–47, 160, 180, 184,
    199–200, 202, 207, 210, 215–17, 314
Ripston, Ramona, 299
Rivera, Geraldo, 209
Rizzo, Francis "Black Jack," 30, 110
Rollin' 40s (gang), 255
Rolling 60s (gang), 77, 276, 279
Romero, Errolyn, 185–87

Rubin, Joel, 332
Rutten, Tim, 123, 194–95, 205–7, 216, 218

Safer Cities Initiative, 246–47, 260
Safir, Howard, 225
Sambor, Gregore J., 109
Satz, Wayne, 35
Scheck, Barry, 152, 162
Seedman, Albert, 38
Serpico scandal, 288
Sharpton, Al, 134
Sheinbaum, Stanley, 22, 95, 97–99, 101–2,
    106–7, 114, 179
Shipp, Ronald, 151
Shriver, Maria, 209
Simon, David, 280
Simpson, Nicole Brown, 149, 151
Simpson, O. J., 150–52, 160–63, 166, 226,
    232
Sinatra, Frank, 134
60 Minutes, 209
Skolnick, Jerome, 168
Smith, Corina, 22
Smith, David, 200
Southern Christian Leadership Conference,
    167
Spann, Richard E., 250
Special Investigation Section (SIS), 66–67
Stahl, Lesley, 30, 209
Stone, Christopher, 313
stop-and-frisk, 71, 138, 169, 259, 280–81,
    288–90, 292–93, 298, 307, 315, 328,
    334–38
Summer of Success program, 269–70, 294,
    310
Sunset Junction Festival, 103
surveillance, 63, 66, 170, 194, 198, 263, 319

Tami Amis bar, 126
Taylor, Blair, 266
Taylor, Darren "Bo," 266, 277–79, 283–84,
    310, 318, 321
Teague, Andrew, 178
Timoney, John, 228–30
Titiriga, Nicholas, 177
Toles Motel, 126–27
Toshima, Karen, 63–64
Truce Parties, 116–18
Tucker, Kevin M., 109–12, 115
Turnaround (Bratton), 42, 44, 228, 238, 242
Tyler, Tom, 283
Tyndall, Brian, 209

Urban League, 25, 62, 230, 266
Urban Peace Academy (UPA), 310, 316–17,
    320–21, 330
US Justice Department (USJD), 214

Vannatter, Philip, 161–63
Vernon, Robert, 18, 20–21
Vicencio, Jesse, 131–32
Villaraigosa, Antonio, 300, 308–10, 314, 321

Wall Street Journal, 292, 332
Walters, Barbara, 235
Wambaugh, Joseph, 60–62
Wardlaw, William, 145–46, 216–17
Wasserman, Bob, 236
watchdog groups, 165, 303, 305
Watkins, Brian, 39–40, 255
Watts neighborhood
    Beck, Charlie and, 69, 116, 202
    drugs and, 48–49, 51
    Gannon, Patrick and, 275
    gangs and, 50, 77, 116–17, 285
    L.A. riots and, 54, 58–59, 75
    Parks, Bernard and, 122–23
    South Bureau and, 274–75
    Watts Community Action Committee, 59
    Watts Gang Task Force, 285
    Watts Riots, 10–11, 13, 21, 26, 49, 54, 62,
        100
    Yamaki, Mike and, 58–59
    see also Jordan Downs; Nickerson Gardens
Webb, Jack, 28, 65
Weisberg, Stanley, 4
Weisburd, David L., 283
White, Jack, 62
Will, George, 25
Williams, Willie
    background, 108–9
    Bratton, Bill and, 223, 235, 237–38, 241,
        254
    Brewer, Jesse and, 147
    crime rates under, 313
    Dotson, David and, 141–42
    Eide, Richard and, 175–77
    failures of, 178–80, 234, 327
    first impression of, 118–20
    gangs and, 299
    Gates, Daryl and, 91–96, 161
    Greenebaum, Gary and, 147–49
    Las Vegas and, 158–60
    Mack, David and, 133
    Mader, Katherine and, 164–66, 199–200

McBride, Tim and, 178
Parks, Bernard and, 123–25, 183–85, 197, 201–2
Philadephia PD and, 111–15
public approval, 139–40
resentment toward, 120–22
Riordan, Richard and, 142–43, 314
selection as commissioner, 104–6
Sheinbaum, Stanley and, 114
Simpson, O. J. and, 161–63, 166
Tucker, Kevin and, 114–15
Wardlaw, William and, 146
Wilson, James Q., 45
Wilson, Pete, 54, 76
Windham, Thomas, 22
Wire, The (TV series), 280

Wooden, John, 101
Woodle, Curtis, 70–73, 78–79, 124, 195–97, 320, 346

Yamaki, Mike
 Brewer, Jesse and, 101
 De Los Reyes, Anthony and, 85
 Gates, Daryl and, 106–7
 L.A. riots and, 58–59
 as police commissioner, 46–47
 Williams, Willie and, 104, 121
Yorty, "Mayor Sam," 12
Young Professionals for Kennedy, 232

Zimring, Frank, 168
Zoot Suit riots, 123

ABOUT THE AUTHOR

Joe Domanick is an award-winning investigative journalist and author and an associate director of John Jay College's Center on Media, Crime, and Justice, City University of New York. His first book, *Faking It in America*, was optioned for film by New Line Cinema; his second book, *To Protect and To Serve*, won the 1995 Edgar Award for Best Fact Crime book; his third book, *Cruel Justice*, was selected as one of the Best Books of 2004 by the *San Francisco Chronicle*. He lives in Los Angeles.